Life and Letters of Toru Dutt

Life and Letters of Toru Dutt

Harihar Das and Toru Dutt

MINT EDITIONS

Life and Letters of Toru Dutt was first published in 1921.

This edition published by Mint Editions 2021.

ISBN 9781513283357 | E-ISBN 9781513288376

Published by Mint Editions®

MINT
EDITIONS

minteditionbooks.com

Publishing Director: Jennifer Newens
Design & Production: Rachel Lopez Metzger
Project Manager: Micaela Clark
Typesetting: Westchester Publishing Services

This Memoir
of her Beloved Indian Friend
Toru Dutt

is Affectionately Dedicated to
Mary E. R. Martin

in Grateful Recognition of
her Tender Sympathy

Mais elle étoit du monde, où les plus belles choses
Ont le pire destin;
Et, rose, elle a vécu ce que vivent les roses,
L'espace d'un matin.

—Malherbe

Mourn rather for that holy Spirit,
Sweet as the spring, as ocean deep;
For Her who, ere her summer faded,
Has sunk into a breathless sleep.

—Wordsworth

Nor blame I Death, because he bare
The use of virtue out of earth:
I know transplanted human worth
Will bloom to profit, otherwhere.

—Tennyson

Contents

FOREWORD

The subject of this volume is an Indian girl who, dying at the age of twenty-one, has left behind her a legacy in verse and prose which, quite apart from its true and delicate poetic quality, constitutes an amazing feat of precocious literary craftmanship. Toru Dutt was a poet with a rare genius for the acquisition of languages not her own. In her all too brief life she mastered Sanskrit and wrote in French and English with a grace, a facility, and an individual distinction which have given her rank among the authentic voices of Western literature. Her ear, indeed, sometimes betrayed her. On points of diction she was not always beyond reproach. Here and there in the *Ancient Ballads and Legends of Hindustan* or in her amazing renderings from the French poets, we come across a word, a phrase, a discord, which remind us that the poet was not of our race or speech, and much the same has been said of her French prose romance by those best qualified to judge of it. Yet when every deduction has been made for unessential blemishes, this child of the green valley of the Ganges has by sheer force of native genius earned for herself the right to be enrolled in the great fellowship of English poets.

I do not think that there was ever a mystery about the character of this frail and sensitive Indian lady. Even were nothing known of the external facts of her life, we should have been able to infer from her published writings the essential qualities of a nature, pure, innocent, religious, alive to beauty in all its forms, and capable of a wide range of appreciation in the field of poetic literature. The pious labours of Mr. Das have now added some welcome and altogether attractive touches. They show us how devoid was Toru of the foibles often attaching to the literary character, how exempt from ostentation, vanity, self-consciousness, how childlike and eager, with how warm a glow of affection she embraced her friends, how free was her composition from all bitter and combustible elements. They enable us also to realize how much she was helped by the fact of her Christian training to an appreciation of certain aspects of Western literature (her love of *Paradise Lost* and Lamartine are illustrations) not usually congenial to the Indian mind, and how personal friendships formed during a girlhood spent partly in France and partly in England united to strengthen her hold upon the essential soul of the two languages in which she wrought. It is pleasant too to learn more of that garden home in Calcutta which is described in "Our Casuarina Tree", one of the loveliest of the lyrics contained in the *Ancient Ballads and Legends of Hindustan*. Here is a *vignette* taken from one of her letters:

"The night was clear, the moon resplendent, one or two stars glimmering here and there; before us stretched the long avenue bordered with high casuarinas, very like the poplars of England, dim in the distance the gateway; around us the thick mango groves; the tall betel-nut trees, straight 'like arrows shot from heaven'; the cocoanut palms with their proud waving plumes of green foliage, and all wrapped in a sweet and calm silence."

Yet it is characteristic that all this tropical loveliness never completely contents or confines her. Home, after all, is in part exile. She cannot forget the beloved West, the enchantments of frost and snow, the delicate landscapes of France, the vivid, eager College life at Cambridge. In comparison with the stir and bustle of the West, the days in India seemed monotonous and without event. So in the midst of the profuse splendours of the East her thoughts continually reach out to that other home beyond the Ocean, which travel and study had made so dear to her, as, for example, to the world (known only through books) of the Brontë sisters, living "among the lonely wild moors of Yorkshire, all three so full of talent, yet living so solitary amid those Yorkshire wolds," or to the days which stood out with such cameo-like distinctness in her memory, when she enjoyed the free life of a student by the banks of the Cam, passing "nice cosy evenings" with her friend, and on Sundays drinking deep draughts of music from the College organ. In the long history of the contact and interfusion of East and West, I doubt whether there is a figure more encouraging or significant.

H. A. L. Fisher

April 3, 1920

Author's Preface

B iography is a subject which until recently Indian writers have somewhat neglected. The whole trend of India's history and philosophy has been against it. This is of itself sufficient to account for the fact that, although it is now forty-three years since Toru Dutt's death, no biography of her has yet been written. But now that India is beginning to realize her own solidarity as an Empire, along with the birth of this consciousness she has begun to cherish the memory of those who have added to the literary wealth, not only of India, but also of the world.

I feel, then, that no further apology is needed from me for this attempt to do honour to an Indian maiden, in truth an "inheritor of unfulfilled renown", in view not only of what was lost to the world through her early death, but also of the comparative oblivion into which her name has sunk.

It was during boyhood, in my native village at Sidhipasa, that I first heard the name of Toru Dutt from a student in whose examination text-book her poem "Buttoo" was included. After reading these verses a desire to know something of its author was immediately born in me—a desire that was for several years to remain unsatisfied. Then, on glancing through a Bengali book, which contained sketches of famous Indian women, I found one of Toru Dutt. It was, however, so incomplete that it merely served to whet my appetite for still further knowledge.

A few years later, on scanning the titles of the books in my father's library, I found a beautiful volume entitled *A Sheaf gleaned in French Fields* by Toru Dutt. Seizing it eagerly, I found in it a prefatory memoir written by her father. Even this was not full enough to allay my thirst for a thorough acquaintance with the biography of my heroine, and at this juncture the idea of writing myself what I could not find elsewhere began to take shape in my mind.

In December 1911, I began the task of collecting materials for the biography, and was fortunate in obtaining an introduction to some of Toru Dutt's relatives in Calcutta. Through them I was placed in touch with Miss Martin, who had known Toru intimately in Cambridge. In reply to my request for reminiscences, she wrote, "I am much interested in hearing that you are wishing to bring out a memoir of my dear friend, Toru Dutt; I have already begun my notes for it. It is very wonderful after these many years of silence, that people should be beginning to think of her again."

Miss Martin's visit to India in the winter of 1913 gave me an invaluable opportunity of gaining the information I sought. Through her kindness I am able to publish Toru's letters, which had been treasured with zealous care for so many years. My indebtedness to Miss Martin for her unvarying kindness in giving me access to all the available material in her possession, in addition to her constant and stimulating encouragement, cannot be over-estimated. Suffice it to say, that without this help the biography would never have been written. The correspondence between Toru and Mlle Bader concerning her *La Femme dans l'Inde Antique* has been translated and added to the appendix.

I should like to thank my friends, Mr. and Mrs. Barun Chunder Dutt, and other members of the Dutt family who have supplied me with useful information. Grateful acknowledgements too are due to another friend, Principal E. J. Thompson, B.A., M.C., of the Wesleyan College, Bankura, Bengal, who has revised the MS. and written the supplementary review which appears in this book. Mr. P. C. Lyon, C.S.I., sometime Member for Education on the Bengal Executive Council, the late Bishop Lefroy of Calcutta, and my friend Mr. G. C. Ghose, President, Christian Convention League, Bengal, have also laid me under a debt by their kindness in giving advice, encouragement, and many valuable suggestions.

I have also to thank Mr. Edmund Gosse for permission to quote from the Introductory Memoir to the *Ancient Ballads of Hindustan*, and the following publishers for permission to quote from the books mentioned after their names: Messrs. Longmans, Green & Co. (*The Dutt Family Album*); Messrs. Kegan Paul & Co. (*Ancient Ballads of Hindustan*); and Messrs. T. Fisher Unwin, Ltd. (Mr. R. W. Frazer's *Literary History of India*).

"Read no history: nothing but biography, for that is life without theory," said Disraeli, and I venture to commend this Memoir to my readers, in the hope that they may find in it an illustration of the truth of that maxim.

H. Das

London
January 20, 1920

I

The Dutt Family

Among the poets whom the gods have loved there are, surely, few more remarkable than Toru Dutt. Writing in a foreign language, seeking her models in a foreign literature, interpreting a foreign religion, she built up in three years an eternity of fame. In an Introductory Memoir prefixed to Toru's *Ancient Ballads and Legends of Hindustan*, Mr. Edmund Gosse wrote in 1881: "If Toru Dutt were alive, she would still be younger than any recognized European writer, and yet her fame, which is already considerable, has been entirely posthumous." The great French critic James Darmesteter says of her: "This daughter of Bengal, so admirably and so strangely gifted, Hindu by race and tradition, an Englishwoman by education, a Frenchwoman at heart, poet in English, prose-writer in French; who at the age of eighteen made India acquainted with the poets of France in the rhyme of England, who blended in herself three souls and three traditions, and died at the age of twenty (*sic*), in the full bloom of her talent and on the eve of the awakening of her genius, presents in the history of literature a phenomenon without parallel."

It will interest the reader to learn something about the family from which the poet descended, more especially as genius must derive much of its form, if not its force, from the environment in which it has been nurtured. The following summary will show that Toru Dutt owed something to her ancestry, and that the gift of poesy may have been inherited from her father Govin Chunder Dutt, who with his brothers had embraced Christianity under circumstances that will be described in their due place. Govin Chunder was a man of large views, great sympathy, and freedom from prejudice, and possessed a remarkable command of the English tongue. He contributed a great number of his own verses to the *Dutt Family Album*, and of him it might almost be said that "he lisped in numbers for the numbers came". Toru Dutt thus breathed in her infancy an atmosphere in which lofty thoughts naturally found rhythmical expression.

The Dutts of Rambagan are an old and well-known *Kayastha* Hindu family of Calcutta.[1] The early home of the family was at Ajapur in the district of Burdwan, where Nilmoni Dutt, one of the patriarchs of the family, was born on the 3rd January, 1757. We do not possess any reliable information as to the time when the Dutts left Ajapur for Calcutta, but we know that while one branch of the family went to Burdwan, Nilmoni Dutt's father migrated to Calcutta and finally settled there. Nilmoni Dutt was a distinguished resident of Calcutta during the latter part of the eighteenth century, that is, shortly after the foundation of the British power in Bengal. It is said that Nilmoni threw his house open to all sorts of guests and was famous far and wide for his hospitality. Pious Brahmins and others who went every day to perform their ablutions in the sacred stream of the Ganges gathered at Nilmoni's house on their return and received a warm welcome. The foremost citizens of Calcutta regarded him as one of their chief friends. Maharaja Navakissen of Sobhabazar and Maharaja Nandkumar were constant visitors at his house. His opinions were so liberal and he himself was so sympathetic that many prominent Englishmen even among the Christian missionaries were his friends. When the missionary[2] William Carey was destitute and without a home, harassed by his wife's insanity and his children's illness, Nilmoni gave him a home in his garden-house at Manicktollah. Carey never forgot the deed, and long afterwards, when his benefactor was in poverty, returned the kindness. A well-known, honest, hospitable, and kind-hearted man, he lived the blameless life of a Hindu of the highest class in the eighteenth century. Orthodox in his principles, he never omitted to perform the usual *Pujas* and ceremonies enjoined by the Hindu *Shastras*, and spent money lavishly in alms and charities. He died in the early part of the nineteenth century.

In tracing the various influences which help to form people's characters in this world, it is sometimes necessary to go far back in order to estimate the value of the forces acting on future generations. In the days of the East India Company and afterwards, when the knowledge of English was in its infancy, it would have required a prophet's foresight to predict the extraordinary revolution in Indian thought and literature which was to result from the general dissemination of the

---

1. For this and other facts about the Dutt family see *The Life and Work of Romesh Chunder Dutt*, by J. N. Gupta, M.A., I.C.S. (Dent, 1911.)

2. See p. 83 of the *Life of William Carey*, by George Smith, LL.D., John Murray, London, 1885.

English language. It was the failure to estimate the influences of the future which caused the controversy between the Orientalists and the Anglicists, resulting as every one knows, in the triumph of the latter in 1833. The latter party were clearly of opinion that, in order to ensure progress in the Arts and Sciences, to build up national greatness and to keep abreast of the enlightened peoples of the West, it was necessary that English should be made the vehicle of instruction in the East; and teaching on the lines laid down by the master-minds of England would assuredly tend to bring about the much-desired result in India. A study of the writings of the great Sanskrit and Arabic authors was looked upon as merely subsidiary to the real end of education. It was in connexion with this controversy, that Lord Macaulay wrote his famous minute of 1835 in which he said: "What Greek and Latin were to the contemporaries of More and Ascham, our tongue is to the people of India." Sir John Seeley referring to Macaulay's minute says, "Never was there a more momentous question discussed." But even before the publication of Macaulay's Minute advising the use of the English language for purposes of higher education, other influences tending in the same direction were already at work. David Hare founded the Hindu College in January 1817, and so gave an impetus to the study of English literature in Bengal. Carey founded the Serampore College in 1818 mainly with a view to Christian enlightenment. But it was reserved for a European missionary, in the person of Dr. Duff, when establishing his scheme for the education of the youth of Calcutta in 1830, to set forth the effect that the English tongue would have on the religious atmosphere of India. Dr. George Smith[3] remarks that Dr. Duff had argued years before that "what the Christian Reformation did for Europe through the Greek tongue, the Roman Law, and the Bible in the vernaculars, it would similarly do for India and Further Asia through the English language and the British administration. It is difficult to say whether he showed more genius in instinctively seizing the position in 1830, in working out the parallel down to 1835, or in influencing the Indian Government and the British public by his heaven-born enthusiasm and fiery eloquence."

Moreover, apart from the ideals of higher education as conceived by Dr. Duff and others, the growing trade of Calcutta was causing the

3. *The Life of Alexander Duff, D.D., LL.D.,* by George Smith, LL.D., Hodder and Stoughton, London, 1879.

practical importance of the English language to be felt in commercial and Government circles. "Interpreters, clerks, copyists, and agents of a respectable class were in demand, alike by the Government and the great mercantile houses."

Among the leading Bengali gentlemen in Calcutta at that time were Raja Ram Mohun Roy, founder of the Brahmo Somaj, one of the earliest fruits of the new educational movement, who had gained a first-hand knowledge of the Bible by the study of Greek and Hebrew; Dwarkanath Tagore[4] and his cousin, Prosunno Kumar Tagore;[5] Ram Komul Sen;[6] Ram Gopal Ghose;[7] and Rasamoy Dutt, at that time "Banian" to Messrs. Cruttenden, Mackillop and Co. The last mentioned was the most distinguished of the three sons of Nilmoni Dutt, great-grandfather of Toru Dutt. All these personages were great friends, and, being conversant with English culture, were amongst the most active in spreading English education among their countrymen. The British Government welcomed the participation of such influential Bengalis as these in spreading English education and in the adoption of other measures calculated to promote it, and soon came to appreciate the brilliant abilities of Rasamoy Dutt. He was appointed Honorary Secretary to the Hindu College Committee and afterwards Judge of the Small Cause Court, then a position of the highest trust and responsibility. Later, he was made a Commissioner to the Court of Requests. He led the way in all public movements during the first part of the nineteenth century, and was a staunch advocate of the cause of education at a time when few people in Bengal recognized that in that direction lay the line of most useful service to the motherland. He had a rare and choice

4. Dwarkanath Tagore was the father of Maharshi Debendranath Tagore and grandfather of our poet, Dr. Rabindranath Tagore. He was among the most enlightened Indians of his time and a friend of the great Raja Ram Mohun Roy. He was well known for his princely and charitable disposition. He died in London in 1846, and was buried in Kensal Green Cemetery.

5. Prosunno Kumar Tagore was a big landholder and lawyer. It was he who founded the Tagore Law Lectureship in the University of Calcutta. His statue now adorns the portico of the Senate House of the University.

6. Ram Komul Sen was "Dewan" of the Bank of Bengal. He distinguished himself as the author of the *English and Bengali Dictionary* which was published by the Serampore Press in 1834, and dedicated to Lord William Bentinck.

7. Ram Gopal Ghose was a partner of the firm of Messrs. Kelsall, Ghose and Co. He became famous rather as a public speaker than as a literary man. He obtained a seat in the Council of Education through the influence of Mr. Bethune, and was an influential member of the British Indian Association.

HARIHAR DAS AND TORU DUTT

collection of English books, and created in his children that remarkable devotion to English literature which distinguishes the family to this day. He was catholic in his views, and opposed the extravagance in connexion with Hindu *Pujas* and ceremonials which had involved his father in pecuniary difficulties. He was consequently in bad odour with the Brahmins and other orthodox people. The life of Rasamoy Dutt constitutes a landmark in the history of the transformation of Hindu society under the influence of the English. He died on the 14th May, 1854.

Rasamoy Dutt had five sons—Kishen Chunder, Koilash Chunder, Govin Chunder, Hur Chunder, and Girish Chunder, of whom Govin Chunder became the best known. In describing the early life and times of Govin Chunder we should say something about the English professors who moulded in a large measure the character and aspirations of the rising generation and who made India the land of their adoption. Govin was a pupil of the celebrated Professor Richardson of the Hindu College.

David Lester Richardson, better known as Captain Richardson, came out to India in the service of the East India Company in 1819. Although he was a soldier by profession, his natural inclinations were towards literature. He soon severed his connexion with the army and devoted himself to the cause of education. In 1836 through the influence of Lord William Bentinck, at that time Governor-General of India, he joined the staff of the Hindu College, Calcutta. He had already made some mark as a man of letters by publishing poems and contributing to the literary periodicals of the day. Richardson's works, particularly his *Literary Leaves*, exerted a more profound influence on the immediately subsequent generation in Bengal than those of any other contemporary writer. His poetry and the polish of his style elicited admiration from all interested in literature and were largely responsible for the efforts of the Bengalis of his day in the direction of English scholarship. He excelled as a teacher. All the leading artists connected with the theatres of Calcutta made a point of taking lessons from him in the recitation of Shakespeare, and even Lord Macaulay is reported to have said to him, "I can forget everything of India, but not your reading of Shakespeare." Like Mr. Henry Vivian Derozio, one of his predecessors at the Hindu College, he aimed at developing the minds of his pupils. But there was an essential difference between the methods of these two great teachers; Derozio sought to stimulate the thinking powers of the students committed to his charge by discussing social, moral, political, and religious questions, whereas Richardson confined himself to the literary aspects of education and attempted to awaken the dormant energies of the mind by creating in his students a true literary taste, which would enable them to appreciate graces of style. Both, being poets and thinkers, were well calculated to inspire their young pupils with noble and lofty thoughts.

The teaching of Professor Richardson exercised a wholesome influence on the future life of Govin Chunder. Among his contemporaries signally distinguished in the field of literature and other callings, were Michael Madhusudan Dutt,[8] Peary Charan Sircar,[9] Ganendra Mohun Tagore,[10] Bhudeb Mookerjee,[11] Bholanath Chunder.[12] Govin Chunder was a proficient linguist, and he added to this a talent for poetry. A small volume of English verses composed by him at an early age received an appreciative review from *Blackwood's Magazine*. The *Calcutta Review for* December 1849, in a critical notice of his poems and those of his brothers and his cousin Shosee Chunder, singled him out for special commendation. These early productions of his, with additions, and others by his two brothers and a nephew, were published in England in 1870 in a handsome little volume under the title of *The Dutt Family Album*. He married Kshetramoni Mitter, daughter of Babu Brindaban Mitter, a son-in-law of the well-known Dutt family of *Hatkhola*. She knew the vernacular well and was well versed in Hindu Mythology, and although at the time of her marriage her knowledge of English was very limited, in later years she translated from English into Bengali a book, *The Blood of Jesus*, which was published by the Tract and Book Society of Calcutta. Her philanthropy was well known, and after her

---

8. Michael Madhusudan Dutt, born at Sagardari in the district of Jessore. He was educated at the Hindu College and afterwards at Bishop's College, where he was baptized. He became early known to the world of letters by an English poem "The Captive Ladie", and later on by that marvellous creation of fancy *The Megnadh Badh*, the first successful attempt at Bengali blank verse. He is sometimes called the Milton of Bengal.

9. Peary Charan was a Senior scholar of the Hindu College. He was Editor of the *Education Gazette*, and was for some time a Professor of the Presidency College, where he distinguished himself as a teacher.

10. Ganendra Mohun Tagore was the first Bengali barrister, and also Professor of Bengali language and Hindu Law in the University College, London, from 1860–6.

11. Inspector of Schools in Behar and North Central Divisions, Bengal.

12. Well-known as the author of *Travels of a Hindu*.

death in 1900 she left a handsome contribution towards the building of the Oxford Mission Church at Barisal, one of the finest in Bengal.

Govin Chunder held a high post under the Government of India and was afterwards promoted to the position of Assistant Comptroller-General of Accounts, which he soon resigned, owing to his claims not finding recognition at the hands of the superior authorities, for at that time they hardly did justice to the merits of their Bengali subordinates, being obsessed by the notion that the latter were unwilling to transplant themselves far from their place of birth. But Govin Chunder was a man of independent spirit, and offered to serve the Government anywhere they pleased to appoint him. He was accordingly transferred to Bombay; but this not bringing him the promotion he had been led to expect, he threw up his post the very same year. Being now free to follow his own inclinations, he devoted himself to the cultivation of letters and to the prosecution of religious studies. Later in life he was an Honorary Magistrate and a Justice of the Peace in Calcutta, and was also made a Fellow of the University. His disposition was gentle, and his erudition and literary attainments place him in the front rank of Indian writers of English in those days. He became a Christian, together with all his family. As a fuller account of these conversions to Christianity may be of interest, we quote the following extract from a letter sent home by Dr. W. S. Mackay dated Calcutta, 29th June, 1854:[13]

"Strange events are passing around us; and though our fears exceed our hopes, no man can say what the issue may be. You may have heard that Rasamoy Dutt is dead; and you know that the family had always a leaning towards the Gospel.

"While attending his father's burning, the eldest son, Kishen, was taken ill of fever, and died also after a few days" illness. The next day, Girish (the youngest son) wrote to Ogilvy Temple, asking me to go and visit him. I was very ill at the time, and confined to bed; so I got Mr. Ewart to accompany Ogilvy; and they saw nearly all the brothers together. They conversed with Ewart long and seriously, and begged him to pray with them, all joining in the Amen. It gradually came out that their dying brother had a dream or vision of the other world; that

13. See pp. 248–50 Vol. II. of the *Life of Alexander Duff, D.D., LL.D.,* by George Smith, LL.D.

he professed, not only his belief in Christianity, but his desire to be immediately baptized, and desired me to be sent for. Objections were made to this, and then he asked them to send for Mr. Wylie. This also was evaded; and at last, Girish offered to read the baptismal service, to put the questions, and to baptize him; and thus the youngest brother (himself not yet a Christian) actually baptized the other in the name of the Father, the Son, and the Holy Spirit of God! The dying man then called all his family around him, and, in the presence of Mr. Naylor, bore dying testimony to Christ, and besought his family to embrace the Gospel. It appeared that old Rasamoy himself had been a careful reader of the Bible, and that he had made all the ladies of the family write out the whole of the Psalms in Bengalee.

"We found that all the brothers and most of their sons were so far believers in Christianity that they were making preparations in their families, getting their affairs in order, and conversing with their wives, with a view of coming over to the Lord in a body—their cousin, Shosee Chunder Dutt, with them. The wives were willing to remain with their husbands, but are still firm idolaters. We have had several interviews with them since of a very interesting nature, and Lal Behari[14] has been particularly useful. . . If the whole family are baptized together, you may suppose what an excitement it will produce; for, take them all in all, they are the most distinguished Hindoo family under British rule. Their ideas of Christian doctrine are vague, but sound on the whole. Their guide in reading the Bible has been Scott's *Commentary*; and they seem to acquiesce in his views of the Trinity and Atonement. But alas, our dear friend Wylie hangs between life and death, and I fear the worst. He went to see the Dutts at my request on Wednesday week—was eagerly interested—and as soon as he got home, began a letter to one of them. While he was writing the fever struck him, and he had to lay down his pen. The half-finished letter, with a few words added by Milne, and a note from me, describing the circumstances in which it was written and Mr. Wylie's desire that it should be sent as it was, have all been sent to Girish."

---

14. Dr. Mackay here alludes to the late Rev. Lal Behari Dey, author of *Bengal Peasant Life* and *Folk Tales of Bengal*.

Dr. Duff writing in October 1854, speaks of the case as

"one of the very rarest, if not the rarest that has yet occurred in India. The old man,[15] the father, was the very first of my native acquaintances. Many a long and earnest talk have I had with him. From the first he was singularly enlightened in a general way, and superior to native prejudices. His sons were wont to come constantly to my house, to discuss the subject of Christianity and borrow books. I need not say how, in my sore affliction, the tidings of God's work among them has tended to let in some reviving beams on the gloom of my distressed spirit. Intelligence of this sort operates like a real cordial to the soul, more especially now as I am slowly emerging from the valley of the shadow of a virtual death. Praise the Lord, O my Soul!"

After further instruction all the families were baptized in Christ Church, Cornwallis Square in 1862.

From private sources we learn that the German missionary, the Rev. C. Bomwetsch, C.M.S., was also of great spiritual assistance to the Dutts. In a letter from Professor E. B. Cowell[16] to his mother, dated Calcutta, June 26, 1863, we read:

"Dr. Kay is coming to dine with us next Monday, and in the evening those Hindu converts, the Dutts, are coming to meet him. You will remember the Dutts and our being sponsors for two of their children.[17] We met them at the Bishop's[18] at tea not long since. They are a wealthy family in high position."

Mrs. Barton, widow of the well-known C.M.S. Missionary, the Rev. J. Barton, who knew the family intimately in Calcutta from 1865 to 1870, writes:

---

15. Rasamoy Dutt.
16. Professor Cowell was for some time Principal of the Sanskrit College, Calcutta, and afterwards Professor of Sanskrit in the University of Cambridge and well known as an Orientalist. He was a friend of the Dutts for many years.
17. The children of Hur Chunder Dutt.
18. Dr. Cotton. See p. 187 of the *Life and Letters of E. B. Cowell*, by George Cowell: Macmillan and Co., London, 1904.

"They were all Christians and highly respected by their townspeople. All spoke English well and were educated in European literature far above the average of other Bengalis of their generation. These Dutt families were the backbone and mainstay of the Christian Church and congregation which was in Cornwallis Square. I am told by Mr. Joseph Welland that he learned from these educated Dutts, that they always, even among themselves, made use of all the theological terms needed, in the English language, even when conversing in Bengali. Govin Chunder was a delightful man and most highly educated; he spoke excellent English, and was an earnest-minded and religious Christian in faith."

The wives of the Dutt brothers, though they were baptized at the same time as their husbands, were still idolaters at heart. Govin Chunder refers to this fact in his touching poem in which he appeals to his wife to follow him in his admiration and worship of Jesus Christ. We give an extract from this poem which is entitled "The Hindu Convert to his Wife":

Nay, part not so—one moment stay,
Repel me not with scorn.
Like others, wilt thou turn away,
And leave me quite forlorn?
Wilt thou too join the scoffing crowd,
The cold, the heartless, and the proud,
Who curse the hallowed morn
When, daring idols to disown,
I knelt before the Saviour's throne?

It was not thus, in former hours,
We parted or we met;
It was not thus, when Love's young flowers
With hope and joy were wet.
That kindling cheek, averted eye,
That heaving breast and stifled sigh,
Attest thy feelings yet.
It was not thus, reserved and cold,
Like strangers, that we met of old.

In a sonnet Govin Chunder fondly describes his family as follows:

> *Most loving is my eldest[19] and I love him most;*
> *Almost a man in seeming, yet a child;*
> *And may it long be thus! I would not boast;*
> *But of his age who taller? less defiled?*
> *My next, the beauty of our home, is meek;[20]*
> *Not so deep-loving haply, but less wild*
> *Than her dear brother;—brow and blushing cheek*
> *Her nature show serene, and pure, and mild*
> *As evening's early star. And last of all,[21]*
> *Puny and elf-like, with dishevelled tresses,*
> *Self-willed and shy, ne'er heeding that I call,*
> *Intent to pay her tenderest addresses*
> *To bird or cat,—but most intelligent,*
> *This is the family which to me is lent.*

The companion sonnet which refers to his son Abju shows his firm trust in a future life. To those who are familiar with Indian thought and aspirations, a father's anguish on the death of a son is not surprising; but such anguish, touched with a Christian's hope, is indeed an object lesson to all Indians:

> *To me is "lent"—was rather—one is gone,*
> *Gone where the "many mansions" glorious rise;*
> *The one most loving, in whose innocent eyes,*
> *As in a mirror, his pure nature shone;*
> *And I am left heart-broken and alone*
> *With weary mind to count the weary days.*
> *Oh happy hours! when dwelt with me mine own;*
> *Your very memory half my grief allays,*
> *Whispering, what matters if we part awhile?*
> *Love never dies, and there no parting's known;—*
> *The hour approaches, soon the morn must smile,*
> *And I shall stand before the awful throne*

---

19. Abju, who died July 9, 1865.
20. Aru.
21. The reference is to Toru.

> *With him my loved one, when the ransomed raise*
> *The never-ending hymn of prayer and praise.*

We give here a few other quotations from Govin Chunder's poems. Of nearly two hundred poems in the *Dutt Family Album* many are written by him. They are mostly didactic in character. Amongst those more purely descriptive are some containing beautiful poetic imagery and lessons of morality. His intense love of nature, imbibed from the inspired writings of Wordsworth, distinguished him as a fitting disciple of the great English poet. The reflective poems and sonnets deal with the mysteries of birth, death, and the after-life, written from the Christian point of view, and abound in sentiments both truly poetical and prophetic. His vindication of Lord Canning is dictated by his love of justice and fair-play. We need hardly dwell on the intrinsic beauty of the "Lines" which mirror the troubles of his heart and his pious resignation to the Will of God in bereavement. These poems speak for themselves and do not require any commendatory notes.

> *. . . We have on earth*
> *No city for continuous stay;*
> *As children of the second birth*
> *We seek another far away;*
> *Nor, with our hands upon the plough,*
> *Dare we look back and break our vow.*

The following is quoted from a poem addressed to Lord Canning during the Mutiny of 1857:

> And the next life? is there not one when God shall judge us all,
> The peasant from his cottage and the ruler from his hall?
> Then who shall justified appear, and who shall win the crown?
> The man that strove for duty, or the man that sought renown?

The following two stanzas are extracted from *Lines in a Bible*:

> *I sought for Fame—by day and night*
> *I struggled, that my name might be*
> *Emblazoned forth in types of light,*
> *And wafted o'er the pathless sea.*

But sunken cheek and vision dim
Were all I had from that vain whim.

I sought for Wealth—the lust of gold
Sucked my best feelings, seared my heart,
Destroyed those aspirations bold
That formed my nature's "better part";
And at the last, though seeming fair,
The prize I clutched was empty air.

Mr. and Mrs. Dutt during their latter years became associated with the Oxford Mission to Calcutta, which more than any other Mission carries on Dr. Duff's ideal, though on different lines. In concluding our account of Govin Chunder, we refer the reader to a letter written by the late Mlle Bader to Toru's English friend, Miss Mary E. R. Martin, who corresponded with Mr. Dutt after his daughter's death, till his own death on Good Friday, 1884. Both these friends shared in the great privilege of comforting a heart bruised by sorrow.

The following is the letter translated from the French:

Paris, rue de Babylone, 62,
May 30, 1884

DEAR MADEMOISELLE,

There are strange coincidences in life. The day before yesterday, when you were writing to me, I was reading over again the letters which you did me the honour of addressing to me in 1880. I found them in the great heap of letters received from our poor Calcutta friends, letters which I was reading over again with deep emotion since receiving the Indian mail which brought me the dreadful news. Without ever having seen Babu Govin Chunder Dutt, I regarded him as one of my dearest friends. The father of our dear Toru Dutt had a deep affection for me, and this, he used to say, made him always associate my name with his daughter's memory. His great soul, warm heart, and high mind, revealed themselves strongly in his letters, and above all, his firm and valiant faith, which on his death-bed was the support of his last moments as it had been during his life.

The Attorney-at-Law,[22] who in Mrs. Dutt's name wrote to announce our friend's death, described with eloquent brevity the religious beauty of that supreme moment: "A word or two, indicative of firm trust in God, an assurance, twice repeated, that he departed in charity with all, and everything was over." You are right, dear Mademoiselle, he is happy, happy in having at last rejoined the dear and well-beloved children whom he was longing with such courageous patience to see again. In endeavouring to console his widow, I could only quote from himself the beautiful words of resignation found in his letters. It seemed that thus she might hear again the beloved voice, for ever silenced on earth. . . May the memory of our dear Calcutta friends now passed away form a link between us, dear Mademoiselle. With my best sympathy,

CLARISSE BADER

The life of Govin Chunder Dutt and the history of the Dutt family would be incomplete without a brief reference to the careers of the other members of his family. Hur Chunder his fourth brother and Girish Chunder his youngest brother shared his inheritance of literary taste and his poetic gifts. Hur Chunder was a regular contributor to the pages of the *Bengal Magazine* and the author of two beautiful works entitled *Writings, Spiritual, Moral and Poetic* and *Heart Experience or Thoughts for Each Day of the Month*. Girish Chunder's best work is his *Cherry Blossoms*. Having been the chief instrument in bringing the whole Dutt family within the fold of Christianity, the name of Abraham was bestowed on him by his niece, Toru. Mrs. Barton has written a few lines from her recollections, for the present memoir, which bear testimony to the literary and spiritual attainments of both Mr. and Mrs. Girish Chunder Dutt. "Girish Babu was such a cultivated man, and taught his wife both French and German. One day Mr. Barton called and found them both reading Schiller. Girish Babu said 'God has denied us children, so these are our children'. And, turning to his wife he said, 'Show Mr. Barton how many of these classics we have read.' She got up shyly and ran her fingers along a shelf containing twelve or twenty volumes."

---

22. Mr. N. C. Bose, a second cousin of Toru—the well-known attorney-at-law of the Calcutta High Court.

The cousin of Govin Chunder, the "estimable" Rai Shosee Chunder Dutt Bahadur, was a voluminous writer in English. He continued to be a voracious reader almost to the last moment of his life. His *Historical Studies* are his best-known work. Of his minor works, *The Reminiscences of a Kerani's Life* are the most interesting. Shosee Chunder's work bears the impress of an original and independent mind. His "Vision of Sumeru" and "My Native Land" are two of his best poems. Mr. J. N. Gupta tells us in his *Life and Work of Romesh Chunder Dutt* that "the success of Shosee Chunder as a writer lay, said the *Indian Echo*, in the extreme ease and felicity of his style, directness of narrative, brilliant anecdote, quiet humour, and chaste sentiment". His services for thirty-four years as Head Assistant in the Bengal Secretariat were recognized by successive Lieutenant-Governors. On his retirement the title of *Rai Bahadur* was conferred on him, a mark of distinction bestowed in those days only on the most distinguished men.

Omesh Chunder Dutt, also well known as a French and German scholar, was a nephew of Govin Chunder. He wrote original verses in English and made metrical translations from some of the French and German poets. The major portion of the poems in the *Dutt Family Album* is his work.

The literary mantle of the Dutt family latterly fell on the shoulders of Mr. Romesh Chunder Dutt, C.I.E., one of the ablest members of the Indian Civil Service, and also one of the greatest administrators that Bengal has ever produced. His literary abilities were unquestionably of a very high order. Romesh Chunder's first Bengali novel *Banga-Bijeta*, a tale of the times of Akbar; *Madhavi-Kankan*, which he afterwards translated into English under the title of *The Slave Girl of Agra; Rajput Jivan-Sandhya*; and two social novels *Sonsar* and *Somaj*, the first of which he translated into English as *The Lake of Palms*:—all these works have passed through several editions in Bengali, and all combine to place him in the front rank of Indian novelists. In consequence of the love he bore to his mother tongue, he was reluctant to accede to entreaties to translate his works into English, although he was as facile with his pen in English as in Sanskrit and Bengali. His translation of the *Rig Veda* into Bengali, and those invaluable works, *The History of Civilization in Ancient India, The Literature of Bengal* (in English), besides his translations from the *Ramayana* and the *Mahabharata* into English verse forming part of the published collection of the Temple

Classics, afford evidence of the spirit of research into ancient literature which pervades his later writings.

Enough has been said to show that the Dutts of Rambagan far excelled the other aristocratic families of Bengal in their intelligence and literary culture. They did not share in the general belief that English education served only to undermine the deep-rooted ancient faiths and the ideals of life cherished by the Indian people; they saw in it the hope of a new intellectual life and a means of gradually uplifting the whole nation. Poetry seemed to be as natural to them as song to birds. Indeed, it was a happy expression of Professor Richardson's when he styled them "The Rambagan nest of singing-birds".

THE FOLLOWING IS NOT A complete genealogy of the Dutt family, but it shows the connexion between Toru and Romesh Chunder Dutt, the two members of the family best known to the English reading public:

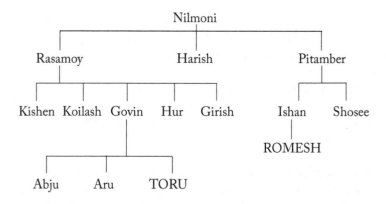

II

EARLY LIFE, VISIT TO EUROPE, AND PREPARATION FOR A CAREER

Toru, the youngest of the three children of Mr. and Mrs. Govin Chunder Dutt, was born in her father's house in Rambagan, 12, Manicktollah Street, in the very heart of Calcutta, on the 4th of March, 1856. "The childhood shows the man, as morning shows the day" is peculiarly true in her case. The intelligence shown in her early years, while going through the alphabet and the rudimentary parts of education under the eyes of her loving father, foreshadowed her astonishing literary achievement. Her mother exercised great influence over the formation of her children's characters, and the old songs and stories of the country recited by her had an irresistible attraction for Toru and fired her youthful imagination. At the same time Mrs. Dutt inspired in her heart a deep reverence for Christ. The glimpses we get of Toru in those early years gave promise of those Christian graces with which she became so richly endowed in after life. The intense reality of religion to children is not always appreciated. The following anecdote brings us face to face with one of the difficult problems of Christian ethics: When Toru was five years old, one day as they were playing together, her elder sister Aru said to her, "You are a Christian, are you not? It is written in the Bible that, if any one smites you on one cheek, you must turn the other also. Now, supposing any one struck you on one cheek, would you be able to turn the other to him?" Toru replied, "Yes, I should," Aru immediately gave Toru a hard smack on her cheek. Toru burst out crying, but did not retaliate.

As the young Dutts grew older, the seeds of education bore an abundant harvest, and later on, their studies were continued under the care of Babu Shib Chunder Bannerjea, an elderly man of exemplary Christian piety and character, who enjoyed the love and confidence of his pupils. Toru, in describing her recollections of these early days, says:

"He used to teach us English when we were quite young. As children, we were very fond of him; and older, that affection grew, mixed with esteem. He was gentle, yet so firm, during lessons. He is such a truly Christian man and sympathizes in all our joys and sorrows. How we used to try and wile away lesson time, by chatting, talking about trifles! But he never allowed us to chat long. We used, I remember, to ask one by one about the health of every one engaged in the Financial Department. How interested and anxious we used to get all at once, about Mr. So-and-so's doings, health, and affairs. We used to read Milton with him latterly; we read *Paradise Lost* over and over so many times that we had the first book and part of the second book by heart."

Here were two Bengali sisters deep in the beauties of *Paradise Lost*, and appreciating its wealth of imagery "far more completely than do most English girls of seventeen".[1] Toru learnt the art of singing under the care of a European singing mistress, Mrs. Sinaes, and soon grew proficient in it.

Toru's early years were spent in Calcutta and in the country house at Baugmaree—an extensive garden in the suburbs of Calcutta, covering many acres of land and shaded by fruit-trees and having in the centre a comfortable and spacious house, a perfect place for repose and a fitting place for poets. In after life Toru Dutt described the country house and its surrounding garden in a beautiful sonnet. It was the delight of Toru's childhood to spend her holidays there and to share rural sports with her brother and sister.

The photograph facing this page represents Abju standing between the two sisters. Toru, somewhat short for her age, hardly coming up to Aru's shoulders, is gazing with all her might at the camera.

In 1863, the family went by sea to Bombay, in one of the Peninsular and Oriental Company's steamers, there being no railway in those days between the two cities. They returned to Calcutta in 1864.

On July 9, 1865, Toru's brother Abju died at the age of fourteen years, and the two sisters were then left the only hope and solace of the bereaved parents. Mr. Dutt never left his daughters, taking them always with him, either to the city house in Rambagan or to the country residence at Baugmaree. This continued till 1869, when he decided on taking his wife and daughters to Europe. They were, in fact, the first Bengali ladies to visit Europe. Mr. Dutt and his family landed at Marseilles and spent a few months in the south of France, at Nice,

---

1. *The Englishwoman in India*, by Maud Diver.

where Toru and her sister went to school, at a French *pensionnat*. This was the only school to which they ever went, and there was laid the foundation of that proficiency in the French language which afterwards distinguished the younger sister. At Nice they stayed at the Hotel Helvétique. Toru at this time wrote a letter to a young cousin, Arun Chunder Dutt,[2] in Calcutta, describing her experiences during their stay at Nice.

Hotel Helvétique,
Rue de France, Nice.
March 7, 1870

MY DEAR ARUN,

I received with gladness your letter of the 8th February yesterday evening as we were dining. I knew it was your letter before I opened it, for in one corner of the envelope I saw your initials.

When the letter arrived we were dining at the "table d'hôte", as I said before, and two musicians were playing on a harp and a violin in the room, to give us a *bon appetit*. This is the French way. We went to see the "Carnival" here; that is, the people wear masks, and colour themselves, and throw bonbons at people, and are very merry just before Lent, for in Lent they are kept very strict, being Catholics, and they want to be very jolly just before Lent. Mr. Elliott said to Papa, that he must take us to see the Carnival, and Mr. Elliott said he would wait on the Terrace to take care of us.

The roads were very muddy, and Mamma, Aru, Papa and myself walked a little, which made our clothes a little dirty. Papa hired a carriage; it was a very bad and broken one, I think the worst that can be had in Nice (for almost all the hired carriages here are as good as the best in Calcutta). We went in the carriage and it rolled on; Mamma said the cover of it was going to fall off (horrible idea), for then we will be very much pelted with bonbons. Papa said, "Just wait a few minutes and you will see the cover and the windows and

---

2. He afterwards graduated from Corpus Christi College, Cambridge, and spent the remainder of his life in England, where he married, dying in January, 1912, at Hull, where he was a well-known and respected member of the medical profession.

doors come off and lie in the street." At last we went on the Terrace without such mishaps as were predicted by Papa. Mamma and Papa waited in the carriage, and we went with Mr. Elliott to see the Carnival on the Terrace. There were crowds of people on the Terrace, and we stood upon chairs to see the Carnival pass. They threw lots of bonbons, and the spectators threw at them too. There were crowds of people and soldiers below the Terrace too. The soldiers to keep order, and there were other soldiers who played on the trumpet and drum and other musical instruments. We came back to our hotel and saw that many people, who lived in our hotel, had also dressed themselves in character at the Carnival; some of them tried to throw bonbons at our window, but did not succeed, we were very high on the third storey. Madame Lahuppe, the doctor's wife, is very fond of us; she does not know English, only French, and she makes me talk to her in French, and be it ever so bad, encourages me, saying "Très bien".

We have found many friends here, among whom are many Englishmen. We went today to a shop of curiosities in mosaic woodwork, and bought some fine books and other things.

We do not go to the school now, we have left it, and we read French with Madame Schwayer, Papa's French teacher.

We go to take long walks on the "Promenade des Anglais". Aru had recovered, but is ill again. We are all well except Aru. And now, my dear cousin, I have come to the end of my paper, so I must close it. Please kindly show this letter to Omesh Baboo. I hope all of you are in good health,

Yours very affectionately,
Toru Dutt

Mrs. Barton furnishes us with the following information about the education of the two sisters and their days in France:

"They (the parents) were determined to give their two clever girls the best possible education. They took advantage of our escort to come to Europe that winter, as we were returning home. By my husband's advice, they came with us to Nice, where my parents were then living, and the Dutts spent three or four months there, if I remember aright. We introduced them to several residents at Nice, and they all soon learnt French."

The anecdote that follows is also obtained from the same source:

"Their knowledge of history and of art was extraordinary, all taught them by their father. I remember one day we took them all four to Canon Childer's house at Nice, to introduce them there, before we left ourselves. On the table stood a good-sized bronze reproduction of the 'Dying Gladiator'. Mr. Barton (or their father) touched it and looking at the two girls said, 'Do you know who that is?' Without a moment's hesitation both said, 'It must be the "Dying Gladiator"!' We were astounded, for they could only know it from books and had never been to Rome. I never saw such a bronze or marble in India, and I am sure they had not."

England at that date had little to offer to young travellers from foreign countries, and the Higher Education of Women had hardly begun. It was perhaps a period in which the insularity of Britain was most marked. We are not surprised to read that France, the France of the Second Empire, had much more to teach the Dutt sisters and left deeper and more fruitful impressions on their minds. "One would like to have fuller details", says M. James Darmesteter, "of their brief sojourn in France, which had a wonderful influence on the ideas and imagination of Toru. French became her favourite language and France the country of her election."[3]

After several months Mr. Dutt went to Paris with his family. Twenty-five hours of continous railway travel had so completely exhausted his companions that he resolved to make some stay in what he has called "the capital of the World—for Paris is indeed, gainsay it who will, the greatest of all cities in point of beauty, comfort, climate, and cleanliness, taken all in all". After a prolonged stay in Paris, they started for England, via Boulogne, in the spring of 1870. Mr. Dutt determined this time to travel in a more leisurely way. Boulogne, too, was a place worth stopping at for a while; a quaint old place, of which Thackeray wrote so often.

---

3. *Essais de Littérature Anglaise*, p. 271.

When they arrived at Boulogne—in Mr. Dutt's words—"on the one hand it appeared such a wretched little maritime town with houses apparently built for sailors only, and on the other hand, the sky seemed so cloudless, the sun so bright, and the sea so calm, that it was unanimously resolved not to delay there a moment, but to cross over at once to England, and take the train at Folkestone for London." On arriving in London they stayed at the Charing Cross Hotel, and afterwards took a furnished house at Brompton. It was here that Toru began to develop a taste for translating poetry and later wrote poetry herself. Mr. R. C. Dutt, who was then in England preparing for the Competitive Civil Service Examination, describes the times spent with his relatives: "It is needless to say that I often visited them there, and spent many pleasant hours with my young cousins. Literary work and religious studies were still the sole occupation of Govin Chunder and his family, and they made the acquaintance of many pious Christians."

In London they knew Sir (then Mr.) George Macfarren, and his wife was their singing mistress. Sir Bartle Frere[4] and his family they also knew very well, and "many a merry day did Aru and I pass with them at Wimbledon". Another friend the Dutts knew very well by correspondence was the Chevalier de Châtelain, a friend of Victor Hugo, and a well-known translator of several of Shakespeare's plays and Chaucer's *Canterbury Tales*.

In 1870, *The Dutt Family Album* was published by Messrs. Longmans, Green and Co., with the following preface:

> "The writers of the following pages are aware that bad poetry is intolerable, and that mediocre poetry deserves perhaps even a harsher epithet. There is a glut of both in the market. But they venture on publication, not because they think their verses good, but in the hope that their book will be regarded, in some respects, as a curiosity. They are foreigners, natives of India, of different ages, and in different walks of life, yet of one family, in whom the ties of blood-relationship have been drawn closer by the holy bond of Christian brotherhood. As foreigners educated out of England, they solicit the indulgence of British critics to poems which on these grounds alone may, it is hoped, have some title to their attention."

4. Sir Henry Bartle Edward Frere, Governor of Bombay from April 1862 to March 1867.

Mr. R. C. Dutt wrote: "When the *Dutt Family Album* came out, Govin Chunder presented me with a copy, marked out the poems which were his own, and read, almost with tears in his eyes, the verses he had written on his deceased son."

The sisters passed their days happily in London in reading books and in intercourse with earnest-minded Christians. Of Toru her father wrote: "She had read more, probably also thought more, and the elder sister generally appeared to follow the lead of the younger; so that I have often been asked by strangers, which of the two is Miss Dutt? . . . It seemed perfectly natural to Aru to fall in the background in the presence of her sister. The love between them was always perfect."

In another place he says[5]:

"Let me recount two scraps of conversation out of a hundred that come crowding into my memory. The scene is in London, and not very long after our arrival there.

"*G. C. Dutt.* 'I say, Aru, you wanted much to see Lord L.[6] when in Calcutta. Here is Lord L. as our visitor.' *Lord L.* 'Did you want to see me—well! and what do you see? (rather pathetically)—an old, broken, weary man. What book is that you have in hand?' *Aru.* 'One of Miss Mulock's novels, *John Halifax.*' *Lord L.* 'Ah! you should not read novels too much, you should read histories.' No answer from Aru, Toru answering for her sister. 'We like to read novels.' *Lord L.* 'Why!' *Toru* (smiling). 'Because novels are true, and histories are false.'"

With regard to the latter part of this conversation, Mlle Bader observes in the memoir prefixed to Toru's *Le Journal de Mlle d'Arvers*: "Toru Dutt, in replying with such a paradox, proved a true daughter of this poetical Hindu race who prefer Legend to History."

Another conversation is quoted as having taken place between Sir Edward Ryan[7] and the sisters:

---

5. See *The Sheaf gleaned in French Fields*, Calcutta edition.
6. According to surviving members of the Dutt family this refers to Lord Lawrence, Viceroy of India 1864–9.
7. Sir Edward Ryan was Chief Justice of the Supreme Court, Calcutta, from 1833 to 1843, when he retired. He became a Member of the Judicial Committee of the Privy Council, 1843, and Vice-chancellor of the University of London, June 1871 to June 1872.

"*Aru.* 'I often wish, Sir Edward, we had made your acquaintance some years ago.' *Sir Edward.* 'Why?' *Aru* (hesitating). 'Well!' *Toru* (taking up the word). 'Because then you could have introduced us—that is Aru's thought, I am sure—to Mr. Justice Talfourd, the author of *Ion.*' *Sir Edward.* 'Ah yes! I should have been so happy; *Ion* was played at his house, and there was such a literary company. Everybody of any note in London. But how do you know I was a friend of Talfourd?' *Toru.* 'He mentions you in *Ion*, in the preface, and speaks of your walks together, when life was young, between Ross and Monmouth, or in the deep winding valleys indenting the tableland above Church Stretton, "or haply by moonlight"—those are his words, I think—"in the churchyard of Ross".' *Sir Edward.* 'Ah, yes, yes.' *Toru.* 'And he mentions you again in his *Vacation Rambles*, when he met you on the continent quite by chance.' *Sir Edward.* 'Ah, yes (looking pleased), yes, you seem to have read a great deal.'"

Both sisters had been assiduous novel-readers.

"It was ever thus", wrote Mr. Dutt, "that Aru walked under Toru's protection and guidance. The fostering wing of the younger was stretched forth from earliest childhood to protect the more gentle elder sister." With touching pride in her achievements, Mr. Dutt delights to acknowledge her superiority, laying aside the authority of a father, and deferring to her judgement as one scholar to another. He writes:

"Not the least remarkable trait of Toru's mind was her wonderful memory. She could repeat almost every piece she translated by heart, and whenever there was a hitch, it was only necessary to repeat a line of the translation, to put an end to it, and draw out of her lips the whole original poem in its entireness. I have already said, she read much: she read rapidly too, but she never slurred over a difficulty when she was reading. Dictionaries, lexicons, and encyclopaedias of all kinds were consulted until it was solved, and a note taken afterwards; the consequence was that explanations of hard words and phrases imprinted themselves, as it were, in her brain, and whenever we had a dispute about the signification of any expression or sentence in Sanskrit, or French, or German, in seven or eight cases out of ten, she would prove to be right. Sometimes I was so sure of my ground, that I would say, 'Well, let us lay a wager'. The wager was ordinarily a rupee. But when the authorities were consulted, she was almost always the winner. It was curious and very pleasant for me to watch her when she lost. First a bright smile, then thin fingers patting my grizzled cheek, then perhaps some quotation from Mrs. Barrett Browning, her favourite poetess, like this: 'Ah, my gossip, you are older, and more learned, and a man', or some similar pleasantry."

Here are some more personal recollections by Mr. Dutt in the *Bengal Magazine*, July 1878, of the time when he and his daughters were all on their way to Sir Edward Ryan's.

"Very pleasant is the journey from Onslow Square. Past Holland House with its glorious reminiscences of Lord and Lady Holland, and Sydney Smith, Macaulay, and Rogers. One beloved child says she had seen the very snuffbox which Napoleon gave Lady Holland—at the British Museum, a few days ago—and repeats, in her sweet soft voice, the verses which Byron ridiculed, and which Archdeacon Wrangham translated into Latin so beautifully:

> *Lady! reject the gift, 'tis tinged with gore,*
> *These crimson spots a dreadful tale relate.*
> *It has been grasped by an infernal power*
> *And by that hand which sealed young Enghien's fate.*
>
> *Lady! reject the gift—beneath its lid*
> *Discord and slaughter and relentless War,*
> *With every plague for wretched man—lie hid,*
> *Let not these loose to range the world afar.*
>
> *Think on that pile, to Addison so dear,*
> *Where Sully feasted, and where Rogers' song*
> *Still flings its music on the festal air,*
> *And gently leads each Muse and Grace along.*

"And another beloved child pulls her father by the sleeve with 'Won't they let us see Holland House, if we stop a moment?'

Then on, along the road through fields of cabbages and turnips and mangel-wurzel until: 'Here we are—Addison Road—this must be it.' 'Not at home. Sir Edward Ryan has gone out.' 'Ah, what a pity! Let us leave our cards—we shall call again.'

"Next day, just as we had done our breakfast, rat-tat-tat goes the knocker. *Sir Edward*. 'I am so sorry I missed you yesterday. You must come again. Will you now come with me in my carriage and see my office, the place where the Civil Service candidates are examined? Would you like to see the Duke, the Secretary of State for India? Not today? Well, never mind; but I shall expect to see you at my house very soon.' Then long conversation about old times and Indian friends—and then Sir Edward takes his leave.

"A few days after we are in Addison Road again. Sir Edward Ryan is at home and we have a warm welcome. In the vestibule there is a beautiful marble bust of Dwarkanath Tagore. There is an exact copy of this bust in the Town Hall at Calcutta. In the dining-room there is an engraving of Rasamoy Dutt, from the painting by Charles Grant; an oil-painting of Lord Macaulay—the hair combed back, thick, bushy, Walter-Scott-like eyebrows—and a portrait of Lord Auckland. 'But you must come and see my library first.' So we moved onwards out of the dining-room.

"I think it is Sir John William Kaye, the historian of the Afghan War and the great champion of the late East India Company, who said in an essay in the *Cornhill Magazine* that he had never seen any place more suitably fitted up for the work of a literary man than the library of Lord Macaulay. Was Sir Edward Ryan's library fitted up in imitation of that of his friend, the great historian? I do not know, perhaps it was; certainly it looked a paradise for a literary man. A table near the window—large, clean, free from litter, with a few bundles tied in red tape upon it; another table opposite, with sundry articles thereon, which we did not notice at first, but which were afterwards shown to us by the owner. Book-cases all round the walls rising up to the ceiling, filled with books, and on the top of them, rolled up inside wooden frames, maps which when pulled out would cover and conceal the book-cases and form a sort of geographical tapestry. One or two globes and telescopes, I think. Not many pictures, one only I remember—an oil-painting of

Mr. Babbage (of the calculating machine), who was a relative of Sir Edward Ryan. Glancing over the books I thought the collection complete. Not a history, not a poem, not a novel of any celebrity, wanting; and the whole so beautifully arranged. Sir Edward Ryan let us look at his books for some time. There were many presentation copies from recent authors, living and dead. A copy of Henry Sumner Maine's *Village Communities* was open on a small table in a corner. Sir Edward Ryan, who had evidently been reading it very recently, spoke very highly of it. Then he took us to the table with the mysterious objects to which I have already made a reference. What do you think they were? Masks, a crown, daggers, a sword, false beards, periwigs, and all the small paraphernalia of the stage. There had been amateur theatricals in the house lately. Sir Edward was always stage-struck when in Calcutta, and was one of the warmest patrons of the Chowringhee and Sans Souci theatres, though I do not know that he ever acted himself. Perhaps the office of Chief Justice which he held was the obstacle in his way. Members of the Board of Revenue, like H. M. Parker, or Secretaries thereof, like Henry Torrens, might wear the buskin—but a Chief Justice! He put on one of the masks and donned the crown, to the great amusement of my young ladies. 'Had they been to any of the London theatres yet?' 'Yes.' 'Where had they been?' 'Drury Lane, the Queen's, the Gaiety, Covent Garden.' 'Well, and what had they seen?' 'Shakespeare's *Midsummer Night's Dream*.' 'Ah, that was very good; it had been got up magnificently. What else?' '*Amy Robsart*.' 'Ah, had they seen *Amy Robsart* at Drury Lane? I was just going to recommend you to take them there. Sir Walter Scott's plot has been altered—I cannot say for the better. It is Varney who falls through the trapdoor and not Amy. Did you enjoy it?' 'Yes, Sir Edward, we enjoyed it immensely.' Then there was talk of Talfourd and Dickens, and Thackeray, and what not besides. 'You at least know'—to the youngest lady in the room—'that Talfourd was a friend of my youth. Dickens I knew.' 'Yes, he dedicated *Pickwick* to Talfourd, and as Talfourd was so much your friend, we thought you must have known him also.' 'Oh yes, I knew him, but Thackeray was a very intimate friend.' 'Thackeray was born in Calcutta and was a relative of Mr. Ritchie, our Advocate-General in Calcutta.' 'Do you know Thackeray's daughters? they are living in your neighbourhood?' 'No.' (We did not then. But afterwards we made the acquaintance of Miss Thackeray at the house of the Master[8] of Trinity College in Cambridge.) 'Which of Thackeray's novels do you like best?' 'Oh, *Esmond*, of course.' 'Which do you like?' '*Pendennis.*' '*Pendennis* is the most popular novel. But surely *Esmond* is far superior as a work of art.' 'I think it is the best novel that ever was written— better than the best of Scott's—and that surely is high praise.' 'Ah, you are young, you will modify that opinion by-and-by—but Thackeray himself considered it his best work, and Trollope, no mean judge, thinks very, very highly of it. Have you read *The Small House at Allington*?' 'Oh yes, and I like it very much. There is nothing sensational in Trollope, that is what I like best in him. His novels are so like ordinary life.' 'Is that praise or censure?' 'Well, that is as you take it; ordinary life is dull and insipid often, so are the novels of Trollope; sensational stories can only please the young.' 'And what are you? are you not young? I consider your father quite a young man. I have seen him when he was younger than you are now. I have got the silver vase still, which you students of the Hindoo College gave me when I came away from India.' Some of the ladies in the house, Sir Edward Ryan's daughters, having taken entire possession of my womenkind, Sir Edward and I had some conversation on serious subjects— religion, social progress in India, Civil Service Examinations, and the like. He was surprised that myself and all my brothers had become Christians. 'Prosono Coomar Tagore's son too', he added thoughtfully; 'as to social progress', he continued, 'you have brought such evidence with you, that I can hardly believe my own senses. It is a very great credit.'"

Toru was very fond of children, and wrote a characteristic Bengali letter from Brompton, London, on September 26, 1870, to a little cousin in Calcutta. It also shows the poor knowledge she had of her mother tongue, even to the extent of mis-spelling her own name.

The following letters were sent from the same address to Arun Chunder and another cousin in Calcutta.

---

8. Dr. Thompson.

No. 9, Sydney Place,
Onslow Square,
Brompton, London.
October 7, 1870

My dear Arun,

I was very glad to receive your letter, but very sorry to answer it, for, really there is great dearth of news. I had not been able to go out for nearly two weeks, on account of having got a rather bad sprain in my foot. I am now quite well.

We have now hired a new house, and came to it on Tuesday night. It belongs to Mrs. Murray, who, now being married to the clergyman of our Church, is very glad to let it. It is a very nice little house, not as large as our other house was. We have no piano in this house, so Papa is going today to hire one.

The cat which we brought from the Square is still with us, and the kitten is very playful now.

Does Mrs. Sinaes come to teach Saccoon?[9] And if she does, what piece is she learning now? I suppose by this time she has finished Hamilton's *Instructions.*

You ask when we are coming back. When Plato's year comes round, eh? But really I know as much about that subject as you do. We will go back some day, or perhaps we shall not go back any more, for man proposes, but God disposes.

May God keep us all in His holy keeping, and bless us.

My love to you, and my respects to my uncles and aunts.

Yours very affectionately,
Toru Dutt

November 3, 1870

My dear Arun,

I have just come in from my walk, that is, from my six turns in the Square. It is densely foggy and cold today. We went to the Mildmay Park conference. We heard Saphir, who is the translator of Auberlen from the German, deliver

---

9. A sister of Arun.

a speech. He spoke English very well. When coming out of the Hall we saw a Highlander standing near the entrance. Mrs. Barton was here today with Arthur, and her brother, Mr. Elliott, a Punjab Civil Servant.

The trees are now quite bare, except a few. The square looks quite desolate with the naked trees. We see robins every day when we go to the square, hopping about the ground, or sitting on the bare trees. They are very pretty little birds, as you know.

We are now reading *Extraits Choisis* with Mrs. Lawless.[10]

How is Saccoon getting on with Signor Nicolini? We are getting on capitally with Mr. Pauer. I am now learning with him *Schmetterlinge* or *Butterflies*. It is a very pretty and easy piece. Aru is learning a Sonata by Mozart, edited and revised by Mr. Pauer.

Mrs. Macfarren, our singing governess, is coming tomorrow. She has a beautiful contralto voice. We are now learning to sing a duet "Hame never cam He", a very pretty and touching Scotch song. Aru is learning for a solo, "Sunbeams of Summer," and I am learning "My soul to God, my heart to thee", a very pretty French song. I have now exhausted my news-bag, so adieu.

Yours very affectionately,
Toru Dutt

November 22, 1870

My dear Cousin,

I have hardly time to write any letter, as our time is entirely given up to study. First we practise on the piano from seven to half-past seven, when we have our breakfast, then we have our Bible reading. It is generally over at half-past eight. Then we practise again on the piano till half-past nine. After that I read *The Times*, for I take a great interest in the War, and I am sure I know more about it than you do. At ten, Mrs. Lawless comes. She goes away at half-past three. Then we generally read with papa at four, and on Fridays, Mrs. Macfarren comes to teach singing, and on Mondays

---

10. Toru Dutt's governess, a lady of birth.

we go to have our music lessons from Mr. Pauer. We then practise again on the piano.

We are going to meet Dean Alford at dinner at Mr. Bullock's, who is his son-in-law.

We want to speak French more fluently than we do, and for this purpose we speak in French with our servant, who is an Italian, and knows French very well. I hope to speak it much better than I do, in a few months.

I am now learning with Mr. Pauer *Souvenir de Collonges* and *Schmetterlinge* No. I. I have learnt No. II, and am going to learn No. III.

I think my letter will be worse than yours. I have given all the news I could muster to *ma cousine*, and I cannot think of anything to write to you.

I hope that England may not embroil itself in a war. *The Times* of today says that Russia's intentions are very pacific.

There is something the matter with our bath again. Mamma went to see to it, but it was nothing.

We have taught Isabella to cook some Indian dishes, and on our table, with mutton cutlets and roly-poly, comes up hot *Kuchooree* or cabbage *Churchuree* or *ambole* of eels. Isn't this nice?

My love to all of you. Hoping you are all well,

Yours very affectionately,
Toru Dutt

To Omesh C. Dutt, Esq.

December 11, 1870

My dear Cousin,

I did not yawn while reading your letter as you predicted; on the contrary, like Dr. Johnson after reading *Robinson Crusoe*, I wished it were longer.

We had a great deal of snow on Monday and Thursday last. On Monday we went to Mr. Pauer's to take our music lessons. The streets and the front steps of our house were so slippery from the snow that at the outset I got a fall on the doorsteps in the snow. Was not this pleasant? In this cold weather too? On Thursday I got another fall in the snow. But, excluding the falls that I got, it was very pleasant (though I am sure Papa did not think so) walking on the snow. It was very funny to see the street boys snow-balling one another, first in play, and then in real earnest, many a foot-passenger getting his share of the snow-balls. We too made some snow-balls. Our balcony was quite white with the snow. We threw our snow-balls at Mamma's conservatory, or at the chimney—not having anything better to throw them at!

You ask why we do not go to any theatre. Well, we are going to the Drury Lane Theatre next Wednesday to see *Amy Robsart* acted. I am sure we shall enjoy it very much.

It is sure, as you say, that the Rev. Mr. —— has long passed the noon of life. His new wife has long passed hers too. You ask if she is pretty. Well, she is what English people call sweet-looking, and what I consider plain enough. We did not go to church today, for the newly-married Reverend gent holds forth so long, that he realizes what that hymn says:

> *Where congregations ne'er break up*
> *And sermons never end.*

We are now reading with papa Shakespeare's *Midsummer Night's Dream*. We have finished *Waverley*. I like Fergus MacIvor so very much. I like Evan Dhu too. *Waverley* is all very good for a hero, but he is rather too sentimental. Is not he?

You seem to be quite a Republican, and very much against the Emperor. I am not, though. The *Evening Standard* calls Gambetta, *Sham*betta, for generally all his news about French victories are fabulous. I will give you a pun of Shirley Brooks in lieu of the *bon-mot* of the Pope. What is the difference between a certain agile animal of the Alps and the present war? Do you give it up? Because the one is a Chamois (*Sham* war) and the other a real war.

I am learning with Mr. Pauer a piece called *Myrthenblüthen* No. III. It is very pretty, soft, and melancholy, We are learning to sing the duet "I know a Bank" with Mrs. Macfarren, I am very glad that you like the *Dutt Family Album's* exterior. . .

My dear cousin, I think I must stop here, for I have had my lunch just now, and it is not very pleasant to do anything after one has had a very good repast.

I must apologize if my letter is dull, but I hope you will not find it so. My love to all of you and my respects to my aunt. May God guard us from all kinds of danger and sin!

Yours very affectionately,
Toru Dutt

To Omesh C. Dutt, Esq.

Toru was a good singer. Aru also could sing, but she was greater as an artist. "In the performance of all domestic duties Aru and Toru were exemplary. No work was too mean for them. Excellent players on the piano were they both, and sweet singers with clear contralto voices."

Toru was an enthusiastic admirer of France, and had deep sympathy for her misfortunes of 1870.

"Toru Dutt loved not only our language and literature," says Mlle Clarisse Bader, "but also our country, and gave proof of her affection when France was dying." The following account will give us some idea how deeply Toru was stirred by the contrast between the magnificence of France as she first knew it in 1869 and the sufferings and ultimate defeat of 1870. The "child who was barely fifteen at the time, the Asiatic girl has drawn and written our patriotic sufferings", says Mlle Bader, "with an anguish worthy of the heart of a French woman." Toru was in London during the Franco-German War, and the unfortunate plight of the French made a deep impression upon her. She recorded in her diary at this time: "29th January, 1871, London, No. 9, Sydney Place, Onslow Square. What a long time since I last wrote in this diary! How things have changed in France since the last time I took this diary in hand. During the few days we remained in Paris, how beautiful it was! what houses! what streets! what a magnificent army! But now how fallen it is! It was the first amongst the cities, and now what misery it contains! When the war began, my whole heart was with the French, though I felt sure of their defeat. One evening, when the war was still going on, and the French had suffered many reverses, I heard papa mention something to mamma about the Emperor. I descended like lightning, and learnt that the French had capitulated. The Emperor and all his

Army had surrendered at Sedan. I remember perfectly how I ascended the stairs, and told the news to Aru, half choked and half crying."

Toru was an earnest Christian, and she thought that the misfortunes that befell France at this time were due to the depravity of the French people. She remained unshaken in her love for the French in spite of their defeat and of her Christian education, which caused her to consider the downfall of France a punishment for irreligion.

"Alas! thousands and thousands of men", says she in her diary, "have shed their hearts' blood for their country, and yet their country has fallen into the hands of their enemies. Is it because many were deeply immersed in sin and did not believe in God? There have been, however, and there are still, thousands among them who fear God. O France, France, how thou art brought low! Mayest thou, after this humiliation, serve and worship God better than thou hast done in those days—Poor, poor France, how my heart bleeds for thee!" She had hoped for a long time, and hoped till the end. Here is a posthumous poem, one of her early attempts, which refers to the disaster of 1870, and expresses a ray of hope for the future.

Not dead,—oh no,—she cannot die!
Only a swoon, from loss of blood!
Levite England passes her by,
Help, Samaritan! None is nigh;
Who shall stanch me the sanguine flood?

Range the brown hair, it blinds her eyne,
Dash cold water over her face!
Drowned in her blood, she makes no sign,
Give her a draught of generous wine.
None heed, none hear, to do this grace.[11]

The family went to Cambridge in 1871. Here Toru, with her sister, sedulously attended the Higher Lectures for Women, with great zeal and application. Toru knew that her knowledge of French was defective, but now in Cambridge it was ably directed by the late M. Boquel, in his French lectures, and also afterwards privately by M. Girard at St. Leonards, during the last part of

---

11. *Ancient Ballads and Legends of Hindustan*, amongst the *Miscellaneous Poems*.

their stay in England. Mr. J. C. Dutt tells us, in his article in the *Twentieth Century* on Toru Dutt, that she and her sister had had their first lessons in French from his father, Mr. O. C. Dutt. In a letter referring to this time at St. Leonards, Toru says: "Mr. Girard, the French teacher, used to come twice or thrice a week to give papa and me lessons in French. Aru, of course, did not read with us.[12] He is very fond of poetry and translated some two or three pieces from the *D.F.A.*[13] into French verse." Later on he spoke with warm admiration of the *Sheaf gleaned in French Fields*. When they were girls of sixteen and eighteen respectively Miss Arabella Shore[14] met them in Cambridge. She records the impression made upon her mind by their excellent command of English and especially by their wide knowledge of European life and thought. The photograph of Aru and Toru taken together at St. Leonards shows Aru sitting, still suffering from the effects of her recent illness, and Toru standing beside her, in an attitude of affectionate protection, beaming and vivacious, with abundant curly black hair falling over her shoulders, dark eyes full of fire, the picture of health and strength. In September, 1873, the Dutts returned to Calcutta in the P. & O. steamer *Peshawur*.

Toru wrote two letters to Miss Martin on their return voyage to India, dated respectively, September 29, 1878, Gibraltar, and October 3, Alexandria. Before the original letters were destroyed, the following *résumé* of their contents was taken. Both the sisters had suffered from sea-sickness during the somewhat rough weather, which had now passed away, and they were both enjoying the present beautiful weather and the sunsets. The pets, guinea-pigs, &c., were doing well so far, and Toru's father visited them every day and reported on their condition to Aru. In the second letter it was mentioned that one of the birds had died. The Dutts had made friends on board, but they were too shy to join in the singing and playing, and the time was passing pleasantly but idly. Toru had been reading some of Erckmann-Chatrian's stories from the *Contes et Romans populaires* and also some pieces of Shakespeare translated into French by the Chevalier de Châtelain. Mention was made of a very nice service held on deck one Sunday. Porpoises had been seen and birds had alighted on the deck.

---

12. This was because of her recent illness, when Toru tended her most affectionately.
13. *The Dutt Family Album.*
14. Author of "Fra Dolcino" and other poems and editor of the "Journal of Emily Shore".

We have referred already to Toru's English friend, to whom this volume is dedicated, and whose life and work are so inseparably connected with the name of Toru. Miss Martin is the only child of the late Reverend John Martin, M.A., of Sidney Sussex College, Cambridge, and vicar of Saint Andrew's the Great, in the same town, from 1859 to 1884. In 1856 he married Sophia Jane Rodd, youngest daughter of the Rev. Dr. Rodd of St. Just, in Roseland, and later of Trebartha Hall, Cornwall. After Miss Martin grew up, she shared with her mother the ordinary duties of a clergyman's family, and in consequence of her friendship with Toru she early grew to love the missionary work of the Anglican Church and became an ardent student of the problems connected with the spread of Christianity and education in India and elsewhere. Miss Martin left Cambridge after her mother's death in 1894 and has since resided in Bournemouth. She takes a keen interest in English social problems and in Indian affairs generally, for she loves the Bengali people, and sympathizes with their hopes and aspirations. Two visits have been paid by her to Calcutta in 1910 and 1913.

Miss Martin says of Toru:

"There is no note of our first meeting, but it must have been in the summer of 1872, before my fifteenth birthday. The Dutts lodged in my father's parish, at Regent House, in Regent Street, overlooking a large open space called Parker's Piece, the latter word being a corruption of an old Saxon name for 'open space', a term very familiar in Cambridge. The family did not attend St. Andrew's the Great, but St. Paul's Church, which was perhaps one reason that their acquaintance was not made as early as it might have been. Anyhow, it was not until some cousins who also attended St. Paul's said to us one day: 'Why have you not called on the Dutts?' that we went. They were naturally a familiar sight in Cambridge, and the two sisters were often seen walking on the Trumpington Road and elsewhere. After we became friends, no notes were kept of our conversations or meetings, but, fortunately, many years after, some entries were found in an old diary of my mother's. None of us at that time had any conception of the fame to be connected with the name of Toru Dutt. Many friends were made by them during their stay in Cambridge and elsewhere, and though, owing to my absence at school at Malvern Wells, others had more opportunity of intercourse, yet we, from the first, claimed friendship from each other. During the school terms we wrote weekly. Her letters were always received on Tuesday mornings, and the eagerness with which they were expected is still vividly remembered.

"My mother's diary from December 1872 to April 1873 contains references to almost daily intercourse between the Dutts and ourselves, to walks with Toru and teas at 11, Park Terrace. The last entry is dated April 29, 1878: 'The Dutts left for Hastings.' We never met again, and perhaps our correspondence became the more intimate in consequence."

Alluding to these happy meetings, Toru wrote as follows in one of her letters from India:

"I remember some of our walks so vividly. Do you remember the visit we paid with your mother to Addenbroke's Hospital and how on our way back your mother stumbled in Downing College, while we were coming through that building's grounds? And that long walk, when you showed me the Gog Magog Hills in the distance? It seems all so far off, dear, does it not? And those nice cosy evenings, when I took tea with you, dear, only you and I; once we had A. L. with us and papa used to come at nine or ten to take me back to our lodgings. Do you think we shall see each other again? I do not think we shall, but we shall meet in that happier world. I long to see our darlings again, and each day past but brings us nearer to the happy goal,

A day's march nearer Home.

And again: "How is Mrs. Babington's Orphanage getting on? I well remember the day when we visited it. You were with me and the J.'s, our fellow-lodgers. You said to me in a whisper that 'You would have better liked the walk alone with me'."

III

Return to India

The four remaining years of Toru's life after her return from Europe were spent partly in the city house at Rambagan and partly in the Garden House at Baugmaree, where

> *The light green graceful tamarinds abound*
> *Amid the mangoe clumps of green profound.*

Mr. Gosse has told us "she was born to write, and despairing of an audience in her own language, she began to adopt ours as a medium for her thought". The story of these later years is best told in her letters. Toru's letters written in England contained constant references to French and English literature. These letters were destroyed many years ago, a source of great regret, as they would have thrown additional light on a life of which the slightest detail is precious. We believe, however, that they were neither so well written nor so interesting as the later ones from India.

In July 23, 1874, her only sister, Aru, died of phthisis at the age of twenty, the seeds of which were sown in her constitution when in England, and Toru, now left alone, engrossed herself in her literary pursuits. Her proficiency in the French language was, as we have seen, acquired in Europe. Her departure from Europe interfered with her studies for a time, but she never lost sight of the object on which she had set her heart. Shortly after her return home, when she was barely eighteen, she published her first essay, on Leconte de Lisle, in the *Bengal Magazine*, December, 1874, containing some translations from his works into English verse. Of this essay, Mr. Gosse tells us that the subject was "a writer with whom she had a sympathy which is very easy to comprehend". In the same number of the *Bengal Magazine* appeared her essay on Henry Vivian Derozio. This was followed by occasional translations from French poetry. Her knowledge of French literature, especially of contemporary French poetry, as we shall presently see, was very unusual for a girl of her age. "To the end of her days," says Mr. Edmund Gosse, "Toru was a better French than English scholar.

She loved France best, she wrote its language with more perfect elegance." She was soon to complete also the translations contained in *The Sheaf gleaned in French Fields.*

Toru Dutt commenced the study of Sanskrit in conjunction with her father, who remained to the last her constant companion in all pursuits, literary or otherwise. To her rich store of Western learning there was now added a good acquaintance with Sanskrit literature. Unfortunately, her failing health prevented her from plunging into its depths, and her study of Sanskrit lasted not quite a year. During that period she made several translations.

Let us add that a few months before Toru's death, a book written by the late Mlle Clarisse Bader, a French authoress of repute, *La Femme dans l'Inde Antique*, fell into her hands. Toru was so charmed with it that she asked the writer to allow her to translate it into English for the benefit of Indian readers less informed than herself. The correspondence ensuing therefrom ripened into a warm friendship between minds which, though widely separated by race and language, were united by similarity of sentiments. Toru's letters to Mlle Bader, written in French, have a charming simplicity. It begins with Mlle Bader's response to Toru's request.

Paris, ce 16 Février 1877. Rue de Babylone 62

CHÈRE MADEMOISELLE,

Eh quoi! C'est une descendante de mes chères héroïnes indiennes qui désire traduire l'œuvre que j'ai consacrée aux antiques Aryennes de la presqu'île gangétique! Un semblable vœu, émanant d'une telle source, me touche trop profondément pour que je ne l'exauce pas. Traduisez donc *La Femme dans l'Inde Antique*, mademoiselle; je vous y autorise de tout mon cœur; et j'appelle de tous mes vœux le succès de votre entreprise.

Je montrai hier soir votre lettre et votre charmant recueil à un illustre indianiste, dont la réputation doit vous être connue, M. Garcin de Tassy, Membre de l'Institut. C'est un ami de votre savant voisin, Rajendralala Mitra. M. Garcin de Tassy fut si émerveillé de votre généreux courage qu'il prit votre adresse pour vous envoyer aujourd'hui même l'un de ses ouvrages.

Vous êtes Chrétienne, mademoiselle: votre livre me le dit. Et, en vérité, votre rôle nous permet de bénir une fois de plus la divine religion qui a permis à une Indienne de développer et de manifester cette valeur individuelle que le brahmanisme enchaîna trop souvent chez la femme.

Si, comme historienne de la femme, je suis charmée de féliciter en vous une émule, je ne suis pas moins touchée comme Française d'avoir à remercier en vous l'élégante traductrice des poètes, mes compatriotes. Votre beau livre m'apprend que vous aviez une sœur qui, elle aussi, partageait vos goûts poétiques. Le Seigneur a rappelé auprès de Lui l'âme qui avait si fidèlement interprété le chant de "La Jeune Captive", et qui cependant, parvenue à l'heure suprême, n'a plus redit:

> The world has delights, the Muses have songs:
> I wish not to perish too soon.

Lorsque vous aurez publié dans l'Inde votre traduction de *La Femme dans l'Inde Antique*, je vous serai reconnaissante de vouloir bien m'envoyer deux exemplaires imprimés de votre version. Je serais aussi très-heureuse de recevoir votre photographie si toutefois vous la possédez déjà.

Laissez-moi vous redire, en terminant, combien la sympathie d'une enfant de l'Inde m'est précieuse. Depuis les heures délicieuses que m'avaient fait passer vos ancêtres, j'ai suivi la femme, chez les Hébreux, chez les Grecs, chez les Romains. Quatre volumes ont ainsi succédé à *La Femme dans l'Inde*. . . et cependant il y a peu de jours encore, comme mon second père, le grand Evêque d'Orléans, me demandait chez quelles femmes j'avais trouvé le plus de beauté morale, je répondais: "Si j'en excepte les femmes bibliques, c'est chez les Indiennes que j'ai trouvé le plus de pureté et de dévouement."

Croyez, mademoiselle, à mes cordiales sympathies.

CLARISSE BADER

Chez son père, officier supérieur en retraite, officier de la Légion d'Honneur, attaché au Ministère de la Guerre, rue de Babylone 62, à Paris.

P.S. Ainsi que vous me l'écrivez, mademoiselle, c'est dans l'Inde que sera publiée votre traduction anglaise. Ce ne serait que dans le cas où cette version serait publiée en Angleterre que l'intervention de mon éditeur serait nécessaire. Mais, comme il me l'a dit lui-même, il ne voit aucun inconvénient à ce que votre traduction paraisse dans une région aussi lointaine que l'Inde.

Miss Toru Dutt to Mlle Clarisse Bader.

Calcutta, ce 18 Mars 1877

CHÈRE MADEMOISELLE,

Je vous remercie bien sincèrement de votre bienveillante autorisation de traduire *La Femme dans l'Inde Antique*, et aussi de votre bonne et sympathique lettre, qui m'a causé le plus vif plaisir.

Je suis désolée de n'avoir pu commencer la traduction encore; mais ma constitution n'est pas très forte; j'ai contracté une toux opiniâtre il y a plus de deux ans, qui ne me quitte point. Cependant j'espère mettre la main à l'œuvre bientôt.

Je ne peux dire, mademoiselle, combien votre affection— car vous les aimez; votre livre et votre lettre en témoignent assez—pour mes compatriotes et mon pays me touche; et je suis fière de pouvoir le dire que les héroïnes de nos grandes épopées sont dignes de tout honneur et de tout amour. Y a-t-il d'héroïne plus touchante, plus aimable que Sîta? Je ne le crois pas. Quand j'entends ma mère chanter, le soir, les vieux chants de notre pays, je pleure presque toujours. La plainte de Sîta quand, bannie pour la seconde fois, elle erre dans la vaste forêt, seule, le désespoir et l'effroi dans l'âme, est si pathétique qu'il n'y a personne, je crois, qui puisse l'entendre sans verser des larmes. Je vous envoie sous ce pli deux petites traductions du Sanscrit, cette belle langue antique. Malheureusement j'ai été obligée de faire cesser mes traductions de Sanscrit il y a six mois. Ma santé ne me permet pas de les continuer. Je vous envoie aussi mon portrait et celui de ma sœur. Dans la photographie elle est représentée assise. Elle était si douce et si bonne. La photographie date de quatre ans, quand j'avais dix-sept ans et elle dix-neuf ans à peine. Moi aussi, mademoiselle, je vous serai reconnaissante de vouloir bien m'envoyer votre photographie. Je la garderai comme un de mes plus grands trésors.

Il faut que je m'arrête ici, je ne veux plus empiéter sur votre temps. Comme M. Lefèvre-Deumier il faut que je dise

Adieu dono, mon amie, que je n'ai pas connue,

car, mademoiselle, je vous compte parmi mes amies, et parmi les meilleures, quoique je ne vous aie pas vue.

Croyez, mademoiselle, à la nouvelle assurance de mon amitié.

TORU DUTT

Chez son père, M. Govin C. Dutt, Honorary Magistrate and Justice of the Peace, Calcutta.

P.S. J'ai retardé jusqu'ici de faire remettre ma lettre à la poste; j'espérais recevoir le livre que M. Garcin de Tassy voulait bien m'envoyer. Mais je ne l'ai pas encore reçu, et la poste part demain. Je crois que peut-être j'aurai bientôt le bonheur de vous serrer la main. Nous espérons quitter l'Inde le prochain mois. Mon père veut absolument partir pour l'Europe. Il dit qu'il y a en France et en Angleterre des médecins plus savants que ceux de Calcutta; et de plus, nos médecins nous conseillent de changer de climat; cela, disent-ils, me fera plus de bien que toutes les drogues d'une pharmacie. Ce changement de nos projets m'oblige de vous prier de ne m'écrire qu'après avoir reçu encore de mes nouvelles.

Miss Toru Dutt to the same.

Calcutta, ce 13 Avril 1877

MA CHÈRE MADEMOISELLE,

Ecrivez-moi, je vous prie, à l'adresse que je vous ai donnée dans ma lettre précédente. Je suis très malade au lit depuis une quinzaine; votre lettre et votre portrait me feront du bien. Tous nos plans sont changés; nous ne pourrons pas aller en Europe en Avril. L'homme propose et Dieu dispose.

Voulez-vous bien avoir la bonté, mademoiselle, de remercier M. Garcin de Tassy de ma part pour sa Revue? Elle est très-intéressante. Je lui écrirai quand je serai plus forte.

Croyez, mademoiselle, à la nouvelle assurance de mon dévouement et de mon amitié très-sincères.

TORU DUTT

Mlle Clarisse Bader to Miss Toru Dutt.

Paris, ce 11 Mai 1877

CHÈRE MADEMOISELLE ET GRACIEUSE AMIE,

Quelle déception m'apporte votre dernière lettre! Je m'étais fait une véritable fête de vous voir, et de vous offrir verbalement l'expression de la vive sympathie que m'inspirent non-seulement vos œuvres si remarquables, mais vos lettres, qui révèlent une âme délicate et charmante, et aussi votre portrait si vivant et si expressif! Je prie Dieu qu'il vous guérisse bien vite, et croyez que dans ce vœu il y a aussi une part d'égoïsme, puisque c'est de votre rétablissement que dépendent vos projets de voyage. Vous êtes jeune, et la jeunesse est si puissante en ressources, surtout quand elle est doublée de la belle constitution que révèle votre charmant portrait! Savez-vous, chère mademoiselle, que ce portrait et vos lettres font des conquêtes dans mon entourage, à commencer par mon père et par ma mère? Ma famille et mes amis partageaient mon vif désir de vous voir, et aujourd'hui, hélas! ils prennent grandement part à ma déception!

S'il m'avait été possible de me faire photographier en ce moment, j'eusse recommencé à votre intention de tenter une épreuve qui ne m'a jamais réussi. Il paraît que la mobilité de mes traits fait le désespoir des photographes. Mes portraits sont tous plus laids les uns que les autres, et si j'étais coquette je ne les donnerais jamais, surtout à ceux qui ne me connaissent pas. Mais je ne suis pas coquette. Je vous envoie donc sous ce pli deux photographies qui remontent à 1872. C'était peu de mois après les terribles épreuves patriotiques que nous avions subies pendant les deux sièges de Paris, et j'avais encore les traits fatigués par de cruelles émotions. Ces portraits ont été faits à la campagne par un amateur, un officier supérieur de nos amis. Mon père est auprès de moi dans l'une de ces photographies. Lui aussi a été singulièrement vieilli par cette épreuve.

Quand je poserai de nouveau je vous enverrai le résultat de cette tentation si celle-ci est couronnée de succès. Je ferai mon possible pour seconder le photographe par ma tranquillité.

Je suis bien touchée d'avoir la douce image de votre regrettée sœur, qui partageait vos savantes et poétiques occupations. Je vous remercie de tout cœur de m'avoir envoyé ce pieux souvenir de famille.

Quand je verrai M. Garcin de Tassy je m'acquitterai de la mission que vous me confiez auprès de lui.

Je vous écris dans le petit oratoire qui est aussi mon cabinet de travail, et où je prie le bon Dieu de vous rendre force et santé. Je confie cette prière à la sainte Vierge.

Croyez, chère mademoiselle, que vous avez en France une amie qui serait heureuse de presser votre main.

Toute à vous,
Clarisse Bader

The next letter to Mlle Bader, written on the 30th of July, 1877, is pathetic in its simplicity, and shows that almost to the very last she was curiously unconscious of the approaching end.

Miss Toru Dutt to Mlle Clarisse Bader.

Ce 30 Juillet 1877

Chère et très-aimable Amie,

Voilà bien quatre mois que je souffre de la fièvre; cela m'a empêchée de vous écrire et de vous exprimer plus tôt le grand plaisir que votre lettre et les portraits m'ont causé.

Cette bonne et sympathique lettre, arrivée dans un temps où je souffrais beaucoup, m'a fait plus de bien que tous les remèdes du médecin.

Je vous prie, chère mademoiselle, de vouloir bien m'excuser la brièveté de cette lettre; je ne suis pas tout à fait rétablie encore; et je ne puis aller de ma chambre à la chambre voisine sans sentir de la fatigue.

J'ai été bien malade, chère mademoiselle, mais le bon
Dieu a exaucé les prières de mes parents; et je me rétablis peu
à peu.

J'espère vous écrire plus longuement avant peu.

Toute à vous,
Toru Dutt

Mlle Clarisse Bader to Miss Toru Dutt.

Ce 11 Septembre 1877

Chère et charmante Amie de l'Inde,

J'ai manqué le dernier courrier de Brindisi, et je regrette
d'autant plus ce retard involontaire que votre bonne et
affectueuse lettre m'apprend que vous avez été malade et
que vous étiez encore convalescente au moment où vous
m'avez écrit. Eh quoi! la maladie a pu atteindre cette
vive organisation que révèle votre portrait? Ces beaux
yeux pleins de feu ont pu s'alanguir? Oh! mais alors, cela
n'a pu être qu'un choc accidentel? Vous êtes tout à fait
rétablie, n'est-ce pas, à l'heure actuelle? Et, à l'époque
de l'Exposition, vous viendrez dans notre doux pays de
France, dont les tièdes brises vous feront du bien, vous
qui avez souffert de votre ardent climat. Des cœurs amis
vous attendent avec une joyeuse espérance. Mes parents et
moi nous vous aimons beaucoup—sans vous avoir jamais
vue; mais vos lettres et vos œuvres nous ont révélé la bonté
de votre cœur, la candeur de votre âme. Venez donc, mon
aimable amie, sceller de votre présence une affection qui
vous est déjà acquise.

Un véritable torrent d'occupations ne me permet pas
de prolonger cette lettre, écrite d'ailleurs sous l'impression
d'une extrême fatigue nerveuse. Je me ressens encore
d'une indisposition qui n'a assurément rien de grave, mais
qui vient d'ébranler ma forte santé. Cette indisposition
m'a été amenée par un surcroît de travail que je me suis
récemment imposé pour continuer à défendre la grande
cause religieuse, qui malheureusement est toujours
attaquée dans mon cher pays, mais qui, grâces en soient
rendues à Dieu, trouvera toujours des défenseurs parmi

nous. Qu'importe si, dans ces luttes où nos seules armes sont la foi et la charité, nous ressentons quelquefois l'atteinte de la fatigue et de la souffrance physiques! Ce sont là les blessures du combat, et ces blessures nous sont chéries.

Dites à vos dignes parents combien nous les félicitons de votre retour à la santé. Mon père et ma mère ont été particulièrement émus de cette phrase si simple et si touchante qui termine votre lettre: "J'ai été bien malade, mais le bon Dieu a exaucé les prières de mes parents, et je me rétablis peu à peu."

Et moi aussi, chère et intéressante amie, je demande au Seigneur de vous conserver la bonne santé qu'Il vous a sans doute déjà rendue, et, en faisant ce vœu, je vous embrasse avec effusion.

CLARISSE BADER

P.S. Je dépose sous ce pli une fleurette de mon pays. C'est ma plante favorite. On l'appelle rhodanthe. Cette jolie fleur rit toujours, même desséchée. Je trouve que par cela même c'est un vrai emblème de l'affection. La fleur que je vous envoie provient de ma petite chapelle domestique. Puisse-t-elle vous apporter une douce bénédiction du Seigneur en même temps que mon fidèle souvenir![15]

It Toru's life had been spared, the acquaintance thus begun would have ripened into a deep and lasting friendship. But no sooner had it begun than it ended, and Mlle Bader had only the melancholy satisfaction of seeing Toru's French novel through the press. "Without ever having seen Toru, I loved her," says Mlle Bader, in her preface to this novel, *Le Journal de Mlle d'Arvers*, to be noticed hereafter. "Her letters revealed a frankness, sensibility, and charming goodness and simplicity, which endeared her to me, and showed me the native qualities of the Hindu Woman developed and transformed by the Christian civilization of Europe. And how could I rest insensible to such spontaneous and ardent affection evinced for me, across the distant seas, by a descendant

---

15. This correspondence first appeared in a memoir of his daughter, written by Mr. Dutt, in the edition of *A Sheaf gleaned in French Fields*, published by Kegan Paul & Co., in 1880.

of those Indian women who had inspired the work of the twenty-second year of my life?" The late Dr. A. C. Dutt of Hull, whilst on a visit to Paris, called on Mlle Bader. This was the only opportunity afforded her of personal intercourse with any member of the Dutt family.

IV

LETTERS TO MISS MARTIN

DECEMBER 1873–DECEMBER 1875

The letters of any well-known character are of twofold interest: the one biographical, the other literary. In many cases, the literary interest is but secondary, for the main purpose of a letter is never to produce a literary creation, but it may be an equivalent to talking with a. friend. They should be, in fact, more or less "Table Talk". "Letters must not be on a subject", says Mackintosh; "conversation is relaxation, not business, and must never appear to be occupation; nor must letters." There is, then, as much difference between the author's "works" and his "letters" as between the truthful snapshot and the pose of the professional portrait; and the severely critical point of view is as out of place in the one as it is right and necessary in the other.

Letters, therefore, very rarely can (from the nature of the case) rank as classics (although where the writer is an author, literary style becomes more or less of a habit). The letters of Chesterfield, Cowper, Charles Lamb, Coleridge, Shelley, and Robert Louis Stevenson, for instance, may fairly rank among their authors' "works". In the case of Toru Dutt, too, we have reason to believe that, if her genius had been allowed to reach maturity, her letters might have ranked as English classics.

The beautiful colouring of a dish of Indian fruit, the strong, sweet-scented flowering shrubs of the garden, the personalities by whom she is surrounded, all are visualized by her graphic pen before the eyes of her English friend. The artist's soul reveals itself even in the sick chamber, as the invalid watches the wonderful effect of the patterns woven on the floor by the sunshine falling through the window bars.

Apart from the keen artistic sense, which the letters of Toru reveal, their prevailing characteristics are naturalness and sincerity, and in these they remind one of the letters of Cowper. Like his, too, is the quiet vein of humour running through them, which is touched, sometimes, into a pathos caused by physical weakness—like his, too, is the deep religious feeling, a piety natural as breathing.

From a biographical point of view, the letters of any literary character are invaluable. The main purpose of any biography is to throw light on the personality of the individual concerned. Without actual letters, however, this light is apt to become artificial, the unnatural, steady glare of the limelight, rather than the natural play of sunlight and shade. "Biographers", says Cardinal Newman, "varnish; they assign motives, they conjecture feelings, they interpret Lord Burleigh's nod—but contemporary letters are facts." In letters written to intimate friends, if anywhere, we may expect to find a man at his best, because most at his ease. In reading them, we become unseen visitors in his home, and watch him at his relaxations. We gain some idea of him in his most intimate relationships, and also see his attitude towards the world at large. Sometimes, it may be, we are privileged to read his very soul. In short, we have before us the living, breathing man. So it is with Toru's letters. Their chief value for us lies in the revelation of her character, and before attempting to sketch that character, we would first of all leave the reader to study them and then form his own judgement.

The first letter from India is dated December 19, 1873, and was "most eagerly looked for". This was written from the loved Garden House, "the scene of many family reunions and the favourite playground of all the younger generation". The letter gives a charming description of the young people she had last seen as little ones, four years ago, and who were now fast growing up.

Baugmaree Garden House,
Calcutta
December 19, 1873

My dear Mary,

I got your welcome and very interesting letter some days ago. I could not answer it before; the reason is, we were very busy settling ourselves for the first several days. I hope you will excuse this delay in writing on my part.

All at home were so glad to see us back. Old Maja, our favourite cat, is as pretty and well mannered as ever! Everyone, especially the children, were so changed. We hardly recognized the little toddlings we had left four years ago, in the big boys and girls who stood to welcome us at the gateway. The children were at first rather shy and silent, but now they are fast friends with us; at any mention of our return to England, they immediately cry out that they will never let "Aunts Aru and Toru" return to England!

Our voyage all through was very pleasant; only after we had passed Madras, we had two or three days of rather rough weather and some rain. We all landed at Ceylon and spent a very pleasant day there. Unfortunately, our steamer was detained at Galle, for four days—that was very tiresome; while we were in harbour there, our steamer bumped three or four times pretty strongly against the sunken rocks, which are rather dangerous around Ceylon. The captain took our steamer out of harbour every night, for he was afraid she might sustain some injury from these rocks. Many of the passengers, about two hundred, left us at Galle and went in another steamer, *The Bangalore*, bound for Australia. Among these, there were some very nice and agreeable people, and we were sorry that they left us so soon. There was one very interesting little girl—one of the Australian passengers—who was both deaf and dumb; but she had such high animal spirits, never quiet, always laughing and playing. We used to speak with her in signs; she, her elder sister, and her father were all very agreeable acquaintances. There were also Mr. Layard, the brother of the celebrated Nineveh explorer, who was going out as Governor of the Fiji Islands; his wife and son were with him, the latter as the Consul of the Fiji Islands. They too were very nice people. Mr. Layard and his son were very fond of shooting, and used to land at almost every place where the vessel stopped, with their guns and accompanied by Lieutenant Brewer of the Royal Navy; they used to bring on board lots of seagulls and other birds, which Mr. Layard used to stuff. He would sit stuffing them a whole day without being tired. Lieutenant Brewer was a very nice fellow too, not given to much reading, but knowing his own business thoroughly. He would insist on talking French with us, which he knew very imperfectly, and he went away with the idea that he had improved himself thereby highly in that language; he had a high opinion of our French; he a thorough sailor and seemed "to have come out of a book". He left us at Ceylon to join his vessel, *The Pearl*, in Australia.

We stuck two or three times in the Suez Canal, but only for a few minutes. We went at a very small rate through the canal, and at night we had to anchor at Ismailia. The canal is very narrow, and you see land all the way on both sides; the salt lakes are very pretty. The land on both sides is very arid and sandy; we hardly saw any trees or houses near, only at Ismailia there is verdure and houses, the French engineers having settled here.

Aru is progressing pretty well, her general health is much better, but she has still got a very bad cough. I hope by next summer she will have got rid of it. Her birds, those that are left of the thirteen she brought, are thriving well; but five of them died, three linnets in the canal because of the heat, and one goldfinch and canary here. She bought some very pretty birds at Ceylon; they were not love-birds, but they were very like them; three of them are dead already and only one is left.

Last Saturday one of my cousins caught a very large fish from the "jheel", or the little lake, that is in our garden. That was the only fish we ate of our own garden since our return, and didn't we relish it! Aru and I angle or play croquet in the afternoon. It soon becomes dark here after six o'clock; there is hardly any twilight.

I am now reading *Histoire d'un Paysan*, by Erckmann-Chatrian. It is very interesting, and relates the Revolution of 1792. I have been reading lately some of De Vigny's works. Have you read any of them? *Grandeur et servitude militaires* is very good.

We are very comfortable here in our own garden-house. The Calcutta residence is so hedged in, as it were, by other buildings, that there is hardly room enough to walk about. The Garden is all that can be wished in that respect. Though it is December now, there are roses, hibiscus, marigold, asters, &c., blowing plentifully. While you are in deep winter, with snow on the ground, and the roads hard with frost, we are enjoying a cool summer! For here the coldest winter is like an English summer. Mamma has planted many English flower plants in our Garden. She brought a packing case, full of bulbs, roots, and seeds from England. The hyacinths are just beginning to grow. I hope Mamma will succeed in her attempt to introduce English plants in India. Our tanks look very pretty with white water-lilies and blood-red lotus!

Aru's guinea-pigs are thriving. Mamma has bought one pair of geese, very large and white, which she means to give to Aru; I am going to have a pair too in a few days; as we have got three or four tanks, it is very convenient for keeping ducks and geese, &c.

We get plenty of fresh fruits now; guavas which are something like the English pears, plantains, oranges, of which you can never get the like in England, Batavian limes (you may have seen the latter in Covent Garden), and other kinds of Indian fruit. In summer we shall get mangoes, jumrools, &c. Aru and I long to taste a mango of our own garden. Our garden is famed for its mangoes.

We have got a piano, a rather old and cracked one, but Papa says he will get us a new one as soon as possible; the present one answers pretty well now, but I am afraid that in a year or two it will become quite useless. We have also got a harmonium; it has now gone to be tuned.

All our books have been removed from the town house to the Garden, and I read to my heart's content. What with our own library and the Calcutta library, of which Papa is a shareholder, I have no lack of books.

The other day we killed a snake in our garden; it was a pretty large one, about four feet, but it was not very poisonous. We see plenty of wild monkeys; it is very pretty to see the young ones play with each other; their mothers are very fond of them, and embrace them as affectionately as any human mother! Some of the males are very big, almost as tall as papa, my papa I mean, not the young monkey's papa; these large ones are rather dangerous; but they will all run away at the very sight of a gun. We never shoot them, for they stanch their wounds with their hands and act like a human being, and it seems as if you had shot a man. They are very destructive to young plants, and sometimes eat up all the young leaves off the rose plants.

I have been some time writing this letter. I began it on the 19th and I am finishing it on Christmas Day. A merry Christmas and a happy New Year to you, dear Mary, and yours. We hope (D. V.) to return to England and settle there for good; wouldn't that be jolly? Please give my love to A. L. and remind her of her promise to give us her photograph. Tomorrow the mail goes off early, so I must send off my letter today, if I wish to post it this week. Your letters you may be sure will be always welcome, and I answer them with the greatest pleasure.

My best love to you and your mamma, in which Aru joins, and with kindest regards from us all to your father,

Believe me, yours very affectionately,
Toru Dutt

Baugmaree Garden House
March 10, 1874

I was so glad to receive your two letters dated respectively the 30th December 1873 and 3rd February 1874. You must forgive me for not answering them sooner, for I have been ill with a bad fever and cough. I was laid up in bed and could not go a step beyond my bedroom for more than a month; for the last four or five days I am feeling much better and am allowed to stir about a little. The hot weather has set in, and I hope to be quite well in a few days. Aru is getting on very well, her cough is much better, and she is, I hope, gaining ground.

You will, I am sure, sympathize with me and Aru in the loss of Maja, our favourite cat, which died on the 23rd February, 1874. When I received your first letter, she was quite well, a few days after she got a kitten, and eleven days after she left her poor babe an orphan. Fortunately another cat of ours (Maja's grown-up daughter) had also just then presented us with four kits! We placed the poor orphan under her care; she loves it as any of her own little ones. Maja was buried under the shadow of some South Sea pines in our Garden near our little lake. Papa and Mamma attended the funeral; I was unable to go, being laid up in bed then. Aru *could* not go, she was so sorry. You must be told that Maja had lived with us for more than eleven years, so no wonder everybody is sorry she is dead; her illness was acute asthma; for the last seven or eight days of her illness she refused all food and drink, she got so thin, poor thing! she used to search out the quietest corner and would sit there for hours, her mouth open, gasping for breath; death was a relief to her, she suffered very much.

I am obliged to drink milk (the doctors being very peremptory on that head), though I dislike it very much. A week ago our cow calved, and in a day or two I shall be able to drink fresh *home* milk every morning. Aru wants to try once to milk the cow herself; unfortunately that is not very feasible, for our cow is very obstinate, and kicks everybody who tries to milk her, except the man we keep especially for her. The calf is not very pretty. Aru and I hoped it would be a white one, but it is a light brownish colour.

We have caught a very large porcupine near our garden; I have not seen it yet (for I am not allowed to go out yet), but Aru and Papa say it is a splendid animal. Unhappily in the struggles which it had made to get out of the trap when caught a great many of its quills had fallen off, and it has got some rather deep scratches here and there. It takes every kind of fruit greedily; plantains and potatoes it is very fond of.

We caught yesterday a very large fish from our small lake; it is called the *Rohit* in Bengali and is the Indian salmon. We have caught another today, which Papa weighed and found to be fourteen pounds; we caught besides many small fishes of the stickleback and whitebait species.

I wish you could see the basket of beautiful flowers, roses especially, which Papa gathers for me from our Garden every morning: they are so lovely and fragrant. There is very little fragrance in English flowers compared with ours. Mamma's English flower plants have grown and budded, hyacinths, nasturtiums, crocuses, &c.

We have got a big poultry yard; just now Mamma sent up a bevy of chickens newly hatched for me to see; aren't they pretty little creatures? We get fresh eggs every morning for breakfast.

12th.

I could not write any more of my letter yesterday, firstly because grandfather and grandmother came to spend the day with us, secondly, I had a slight return of the fever. Tomorrow the mail leaves for England, so I must try and finish my letter today. Yesterday also we caught another large fish from our jheel (that is the Bengali name for the small lake in our Garden). It is generally one of our servants who catches these fishes. He has been long in our service and is a good hand at angling. Aru has not yet tried to catch any fish of size; she says she will wait till she is a little stronger, as she is afraid that the fish when hooked, might, in its attempts to get off, drag her into the water! I abstain from angling for big fishes, for these same excellent reasons also! The fever has rendered me rather weak.

I was glad to learn that Mr. Bose[1] took such a good place in the Mathematical Tripos; I hope his success will induce many of my countrymen to enter the Engish Universities and try to win University Honours.

The doctor who attended me in my illness, Mr. Day, has a son at St. John's; he is going up for the Classical Tripos, I hope he will succeed. It is indeed surprising that the Senior Wrangler should be of Caius this year; I am glad of it, though, for after Trinity and St. John's, Caius is the one I like best.

The monkeys in our Garden are very mischievous; they destroy so many young plants; they are very fond of the tamarind fruit, and there are always many of them to be seen on the tamarind tree opposite our window; they are very bold, and sometimes even come into the dining and bed rooms!

---

1. The late Mr. A. M. Bose, barrister-at-law, first Bengali Wrangler.

I was so glad to receive Miss A. L.'s photograph; I will try and write a note to her this mail.

The other day we killed another large serpent. Now that the summer has come, I am afraid they will be getting out from their winter quarters to bask in the sun. The kittens have become very playful now; and it is very interesting to see them at their gambols. Maja's kitten is the most active one among them all, and runs about the whole room.

I have not been downstairs for a long time, and so have been unable to touch the piano for weeks.

I have been lately reading Carlyle's *History of the French Revolution*. It is very interesting, and I am sure you will like it when you come to read it.

I am so very, very glad you have done so well in the Examination.

I have not read the book you mention, *Voyage sous la terre*. Is it by Jules Verne? I am now reading *Valentine*, by George Sand. It is very interesting.

Many thanks for the Christmas cards. I need not assure you how prized they will be.

Have you read M. Hue's *Souvenirs d'un voyage*? It is very interesting. I have not read it myself, but Papa has and likes it very much.

Aru's guinea-pigs are doing well; lately they added three more young ones to their number; the little ones are very pretty and active; there are altogether six of them now. Aru wants to get rid of some of the big ones, for they quarrel with each other very much. The birds are flourishing. How are your doves and canary? You do not speak a word of them in your letters!

Many thanks for your kind wishes for my birthday.

We hope to go to England, I do not know if we shall be able to go; this time Papa says he will sell all we have here and go to England and settle there for good.

I hope to be able to write to you again soon. Papa and Mamma send their kindest regards to your father and mother, in which we join.

Best love from me and every one to yourself. The Lord be with us all wherever we are.

Baugmaree Garden House,
May 9, 1874

Your welcome and long-looked-for letter came to hand this evening. I was rather anxious about you at not getting any news from you for some time. I am glad to learn from your letter that you are all quite well, and that you are enjoying your holidays to your heart's content. Your letter is very interesting and I read it aloud to Papa, Mamma, and Aru.

You will be glad to hear that I am quite well now; my cough is almost gone, so is Aru's—but I am afraid that Aru does not make the progress she ought to; she is suffering now from a slight attack of fever and her stomach is out of order, which makes her weak and thin. I hope she will soon be better.

It is dreadfully hot now here; the heat is quite unbearable during the middle part of the day. No noontide walks here as in England! If you walk even a mile or two, you are sure to have cholera! We do so miss our country walks in England. In the evening it gets cooler and pleasanter, and then it is very refreshing to sit out on the verandah. The rainy season will be soon upon us and then we shall have to move to our town residence, for the Garden gets unhealthy at that time. It is very jolly, though, during the rains, when the tanks overflow in our garden, and the fish come out on the grass. It is such fun catching them with a piece of rag or even with your handkerchief; one is sure to get numberless shrimps and Indian sticklebacks and whitebaits. We had a hailstorm some weeks ago; the hailstones here are fifty times larger than the biggest I ever saw in England.

The leechies, mangoes, water-melons, dates, and other kinds of fruits are now in season. The two former are the best fruits in the world. They are so refreshing, cool and juicy. We have let out our fruit trees to husbandmen, and we buy from them daily what we want. It is difficult to keep the fruit trees ourselves, for then the fruits are sure to be stolen, so the best way is to let them out—and it saves trouble and expense. I wish I could send you a basket of our fruits of the season. It would gladden your eyes! Yellow or vermilion mangoes, red leechies, white jumrools and deep violet *jams*; this last resembles the plum. How I wish you were here or that we were all in England! But that is impossible.

I am now reading *Histoire de la Révolution Française*, by Mignet. It is very interesting, as you may well conceive, but I find the subject rather stale, for I have read three or four histories of the Revolution, including Carlyle's. I have been lately reading another of Erckmann-Chatrian's stories, *Les Deux Frères*. It is very interesting. I like Erckmann-Chatrian's tales very much, for they are always healthy and amusing. I have also been reading some of Corneille's and Molière's plays. I like the latter's comedies very much, but I have not read his *Le Bourgeois Gentilhomme*; I mean to read it whenever I get hold of his works. I like Shakespeare immensely—I have read all his plays except five. I read in some French book that Lord Collingwood, the great English Admiral, wrote to his daughters to read Shakespeare "tant qu'il leur plaira". Papa often says that when he sees me with a copy of the Bard of Avon in my hand. I must stop here for tonight.

11th May

Maja's (our late beloved cat) kitten is doing well; her elder sister ("Missus" is her name) has now only one of the four kittens she had; we disposed of the three others to some of our friends. The remaining one Aru kindly gave to me on my last birthday. It is a great favourite of mine and has no rival in my affections, as I have no other pets! It is very playful, and I call it "Baguette". I often address to it the lines of the French song:

> *"Baguette,*
> *Si bien faite,*
> *Donne-moi ton cœur,*
> *Ou je vais mourir!"*

It is "Rojette" in the song, but that is all the same.

We have got a number of ducks now, seventeen, and all except three are home-reared—is it not satisfying? We have also got a turkey chicken: some turkey's eggs were given to us by our grandfather, our hens sat upon those eggs, and hatched five young turkeys. One has been, unhappily, carried off by a kite, and three others have died. The one that is living has grown big and strong and is likely to live. Aru's guinea-pigs have had young ones again, five this time; one of the little ones is very pretty, all white like snow with ruby eyes. Her birds are flourishing; they seem to have got accustomed to the Indian climate. We have got two squirrels, which we caught in our Garden some time ago. They are not of the reddish-brown colour of the English squirrels, but are striped on the back. They are very frisky and amusing. We keep them in a large cage.

I have not heard from the Miss Halls since our return. Mary (the eldest) was inclined to be very tall always. I suppose Reginald, their brother, is gone to school, as there was talk of his going during our last visit to Cambridge.[2] Please give our best remembrances to old Mr. and Mrs. Baker,[3] if you see them. Are the Joneses still lodging there?

We all want so much to return to England. We miss the free life we led there; here we can hardly go out of the limits of our own Garden, but Baugmaree happily is a pretty big place, and we walk round our own park as much as we like. If we can fulfil our wishes and return to England, I think we shall most probably settle in some quiet country place. The English villages are so pretty. But before we go, we have to get *quite well*, and then sell our property here, for it is very expensive keeping up two houses here, we being in England in another.

I practise pretty often on the piano now; the instrument we have got is rather an old and cracked one, but it answers our purposes for the present; no use buying a splendid piano, if we do not mean to stay here. We have also got a small harmonium; we used to play it in our Church before we went to England.

Please give Aru's and my love to A. Is she going to leave school soon? It is a pity that you are not in the same class with her, for it would have been so much nicer. When are you going to leave Cambridge House?[4] I do so want to see your dear old face again! "Oh, to be in England now that April's there!" sing I with Robert Browning.

12th May

I was rather too hasty in saying that I was quite well—for the last two days I have had a very bad cough, with spitting of blood; Aru has still got some fever. At nights the fever generally comes on very strongly, but during the day she feels better. I hope she will soon get well. My cousin, Charoo Chunder Dutt, who went to be a barrister, to England, has come back. He came only a few weeks before the end of April. His wife and children are very glad to have him back again. He also wants to go back to England. My uncles and other cousins are quite at a loss to find out what there can be so attractive in England, as to make us all long to go back there! We assure them that if they went once to England, they would very soon be of our opinion. The other day, Uncle Girish (Papa's youngest brother, his sonnets are very good in the *D. F. A.*), invited us to lunch at his house. He had a freezing-machine, and he made a delicious

---

2. The son and eldest daughter of the late Rev. H. Hall of St. Paul's Church, Cambridge.

3. The proprietors of Regent House, where the Dutts lodged in Cambridge.

4. The school at Malvern Wells where her friend Miss Martin was.

ice-cream in our presence. We enjoyed the day immensely. Uncle is so hearty and aunt is so kind. They are talking of accompanying us to Europe on our return to England, but we have no more faith in Uncle's ever going to England: he has been so long talking about it, for the last four years! It would be nice though, if he could go. Our grandfather and grandmother never can hear of our return to Europe; the latter weeps at even the mention of it. I wish you knew her: she is, I am sad to say, still a Hindu, but she is so gentle and loves us so much. She had many children, but now only Mamma and Mamma's brother are living.

The other day one of our geese was killed by a snake: it had been bitten on the beak and near the eyes; the beak had become quite blue. It had been bitten during the night. All the poultry are shut up in a room at night. There were some holes in the floor of the room, and the serpent, no doubt, came out from one of them; the goose very likely pecked at the reptile and so was bitten. This morning, one of our servants saw a very big snake in the room where we keep our fire-wood; it was very likely the same serpent which bit the goose. All the holes have been filled up, and I hope there will be no more deaths by snake-bites among our poultry. A large cobra was killed the other day at our town house. If the small piece of ground there is to be infested with cobras, I do not know what we shall do. This is the third cobra that has been killed there.

I shall write to you again as soon as I can. I often think of you, dear, and long to see you again. If we ever go to England, we shall be sure to find you out the first thing. Your letters give me great pleasure, and I look out for them every mail.

We think of going on the banks of the Ganges for a change—it would be very pleasant, especially at this time of the year.

How gay Cambridge would be during the whole of this month. I should like to be there now. I hope you will enjoy all the gaieties of the May term. Our kindest regards to your father and mother and love to you, especially mine. God bless you and be with us all.

12, Manicktollah Street,
Calcutta
September 19, 1874

I could not write before to you. The Lord has taken dear Aru from us. It is a sore trial for us, but His will be done. We know He doeth all things for our good. She left us on the 23rd July last, at eleven in the morning. She was very peaceful and happy to the last, though she suffered intensely from fever, dyspepsia, and great debility during her last illness. She lies beside my brother in our little cemetery beyond the bridge. We feel lonely without her, who was the life of our small family. She was so cheerful and happy always. Think of us sometimes, dear.

I have received your letters. One, I received during Aru's illness, so I was unable to reply to it, the other I have got this morning by the early post. I thank you sincerely for it. Please write to me as often as you can, for your letters are a source of great pleasure and enjoyment to me. I have to thank you also for the photograph of Cambridge House, which you enclosed in your last letter but one. I penned a letter to you some time ago, but could not send it on account of Aru's illness. I will try and write oftener and more interesting letters.

I am glad to hear you are well and enjoying yourself. Westmoreland is a place where Papa longs to live, for it was by the Windermere Lakes that Wordsworth lived, and you know he is Papa's favourite poet. Southey used to live at Keswick, and Coleridge and Professor Wilson of *Blackwood's Magazine* had their homes there too. The latter (Professor Wilson) had a small sailing boat of his own on the lake, and he used to be on the lake whenever he pleased in his own little boat; was not that jolly?

I hope you will have better weather by and by. I believe it rains a good deal up in Westmoreland. The items in your letter are very interesting. I remember Miss Pullen very well; she used to attend the French lectures. Mr. Jebb[5] too, you say, is to wed an American widow—he is such a shy man, he dared hardly deliver his lectures to us with his face towards the class; he used *almost* to have his back towards us while he was at his desk delivering lectures on English Literature. I do not remember to have seen the lady he is going to be united to.

Today is Sunday, but we were unable to attend service in the Old Church as it is undergoing repairs. The services are held at St. John's, but at such an unreasonable hour, 7 A.M., that we can hardly get ready to be in time; it is also a great distance from our place. Mr. Goldsmith, curate of the Old Church, is a Cantab, and we like him very much. Mr. Welland, the pastor, is an old friend of ours; he went to England with us in the same steamer four years ago; he returned here sometime before we did. He is a very pleasant man, an Irishman; his sister has

---

5. Afterwards Sir Richard Claverhouse Jebb, Public Orator; Fellow of Trinity; Professor of Greek, Cambridge.

just been married here. The poem in the Appendix of the *Dutt Family Album* is from his pen; it was written in answer to one of Papa's poems. I should so like to go back to Cambridge and have a look at you all.

20th.

In May last a dreadful thing happened in our Garden. One of our gardeners, while going round the jheel (lake) found a man hanging on a tree, stark dead, just between our garden and a neighbouring field. Papa immediately sent notice to the police station and soon two policemen arrived and they were quickly followed by the police sergeant. Nobody could identify the body. Papa was asked by the police officer to come and see the body. Papa went, though he did not like it very much. He said the man must have been about fifty, and was of course a native. The police officer ordered the body to be taken to the station that same night—all this happened about four in the afternoon. The case was investigated and the body examined but no clue was found to the mystery, as to whether the man had been murdered or had committed suicide. Our Garden becomes very lonely at nights, for there are very few houses round it and our grounds are very extensive. We heard of a dacoity having been committed very near it when we were in England. The servants said that the robbery was committed by night, and in the morning they gathered up some weapons which the dacoits had thrown in our Garden after they had done their work. This makes it rather unpleasant, and Papa bought a good revolver a few months ago in case of need. I was so frightened after that affair about the dead man, found hanging from the tree, that I could not sleep the whole blessed night!

Aru's was such a lively and merry disposition, that she seemed to fill all the large Garden House with life and animation.—Now, without her, the place seems so lifeless and deserted that Mamma can hardly bear going there. We are thinking of disposing of it, if we go to England; for if we do go, as we all wish to, again, we shall settle there. The free air of Europe, and the free life there, are things not to be had here. We cannot stir out from our own garden without being stared at, or having a sun-stroke. And the streets are so dirty and narrow, that one feels quite suffocated in them. Of course not *all* the streets, for there *are* a few broad and clean streets newly opened.

Aru's pets are getting on very well: her guinea-pigs have increased wonderfully their number; they are now eighteen, although we have given some away—dear Aru would have liked to see them come and take their breakfast of bread and milk. It makes one sad looking at her pets though, she is so far away; God have mercy upon us. Her pet kitten, *Peenoo*, is now become pretty big, so is *Baguette*, the kitten she gave me on my last birthday. *Baguette* has now got three kittens of her own. I am in a great perplexity how to dispose of them. *Baguette* and *Peenoo* are very fond of each other; *Peenoo* is the sharper of the two, she catches butterflies and brings them to *Baguette* to play with; is not that friendly of *Peenoo?*

I am now brushing up my arithmetic with Papa. I am rather backward in it, so I am now going into it heartily. We are looking out for a German master: it is hard getting a good one here; I wish we were in Cambridge under the teaching of Herr Steinhelper.

Papa has disposed of our piano, as it was a very old and jingling instrument: he means getting a new one soon.

21

Tomorrow is mail-day, so I must try and post this letter today.

I am now reading from the volumes of the *Revue des Deux Mondes*. The magazine is conducted very ably, and its contents are always very interesting and instructive, we get the volumes from the Calcutta Public Library, of which Papa is a shareholder—we can get as many books as we like at a time and keep them as long as it pleases us—unfortunately there are not many French works, I mean readable French works, in the Library, but the volumes of the *Revue des Deux Mondes* make ample compensation for this defect. The library possesses all the volumes of the *Revue* from the beginning. I had also been lately reading a tale recently published from the pen of Victor Hugo—*Quatre-vingt-treize* is its title. It is a *very* interesting work and treats of the French Revolution of '93. I liked the book exceedingly; some parts of it are highly poetical; it is a very big book, three large volumes: but I never got tired in getting through it. I was also reading a criticism of his poem "Les Châtiments" from the *Revue.* I should like to see the poem itself very much; the extracts I read of it are sublime.

I am so glad of your success at school—I knew you would be first in French, for you are a great scholar in French. I congratulate you heartily. . .

We see very few people here, except our own relations and friends—

indeed we seldom go out of our own house and garden. Oh, for the walks in Cambridge with you!

Baguette is here interrupting me, coaxing me for a caress and a loving pat—breakfast is also ready, so I must stop here for the present; I shall finish this letter after breakfast. I shall post it to your address in Cambridge.

There has not been much rain this year, and the famine is beginning to be felt in Lower Bengal; already famine-stricken people are coming down from the up-country. I hope that this time it will be not so great as it was some years ago, while we were at Calcutta. I remember then, there used to come to our garden, women, men, and children, thin as skeletons, all their bones sticking out: when food used to be given them, it was painful to see how they fell greedily to it. Mothers would snatch out of their children's hands. They used sometimes to stay in the garden for a few days for the sake of the simple rice and dal they got every morning.

The weather is very hot now, especially at nights—Papa does not allow me to sleep with my window open on account of my cough; this makes me very uncomfortable in bed. I am quite well at present, though I have still got some cough. Mamma has had very few attacks of her pains since she has been in India; Papa thinks it is from the change of diet, that she has necessarily undergone, from meat to rice. She is now suffering from a persistent rheumatic pain in her left foot. I hope as soon as this damp weather is over she will be quite well. Papa has had two or three attacks of fever lately, but he is pretty well now.

I am sorry to hear of your father's indisposition, I hope he is now quite well. I suppose you will leave Cambridge House soon. Did you not write sometime before that you will leave it by next May?

We have got a large turkey now; it was hatched by a hen from a turkey's egg that my grandfather gave us—he gave us several, and seven young turkeys were hatched, but they all died when young (two were stolen), except this one. It has grown a fine-looking bird now. The ducklings I wrote to you about some time ago have grown into very beautiful ducks now, of varied and sleek plumage.

I must close here. Papa and Mamma send their kindest regards to you all, in which I join. With best love to you from me.

P.S. I enclose a small flower and some leaves from the *Toru-Lota* plant. They have not been pressed and dried very well, but I know you will like to have them.

12, Manicktollah Street,
Calcutta
November 17, 1874

This letter will reach you just about Christmas time, so I wish you a Merry Christmas and a Happy New Year, with many many happy returns of both.

We are keeping pretty good health here. Papa had an attack of fever a few days ago, but he has got over it at present. I have still got a slight cough, but there is no blood-spitting with it now. Mamma seldom gets her old attacks of pain here; we think that the climate and the diet of this country have done this benefit to her health.

It is beginning to be pleasantly cold here; the mornings are often rather chilly like those of an English summer. The cold season is very pleasant in India; it reminds us of English springs or early summer weather.

We all long to go to Europe again. We hope, if we go, to settle in England and not return to India any more. I expect my youngest uncle and aunt will accompany us to Europe this time; it will be very nice if they do so. My uncle is a thorough *casanier*, as the French have it, and it will be a miracle if he goes with us; (he says he will;) he has never been a whole day from home I believe! The pets are all doing well, there are now twenty-four guinea-pigs! We hope to dispose of some of them soon; the birds are thriving, especially the canaries, the bullfinch died some months ago; our cats had a litter of kittens; we gave them away as soon as they were old enough; they are all sought after, on account of old Maja, who was famed, all the country round, for her hunting powers! We caught a wild parrot some time ago; it must have been very hungry, for it came on the table to pick some dried peas that we had strewn there to entice it. We have got two turkeys now; unfortunately the male one has lost one eye, through fighting with a cock of the neighbourhood,

I have been reading a good deal lately, French especially. I finished a translation of Sir Bulwer Lytton's *Last of the Barons*, a few days ago. I have not read the original, but the translation is excellently done, and the book has high merits. It treats of the time of Edward the fourth of England, and the *Last of the Barons* is the great Warwick, the "Kingmaker" as he was called. I have also read lately Lamartine's *Lectures pour tous*. It is a very interesting collection from all his works and is very readable. I like the *Revue des Deux Mondes* very much; as the Calcutta Public Library has got all the volumes of the *Revue* there is no limit to my reading. The articles in the *Revue* are so interesting, and give me so much information on various subjects. I have lately been reading in the *Revue* a description of the inhabitants of the Jura mountains, their occupations and their ways and manners of living. The perusal of the article gave me great pleasure. The articles are written by able writers and the Magazine is conducted excellently well.

Papa has hired a piano for me; it is a very good one. It is unfortunate that we cannot get here the small-sized *cabinet* pianos which we got in Europe; all the instruments dispatched here are very big and cumbrous and occupy a great deal of room.

A friend of mine wants to send his daughter to England and have her educated there. He wants to know the terms of Cambridge House, and if a child of nine, who hardly knows any English, will be admitted in your school. He is adverse to putting his girl in one of the schools of Calcutta, as the instruction here is far inferior to what one gets in England. Please kindly let me know all about Cambridge House.

20th.

We went to the Garden yesterday. It has become very *junglified*; we are going to have it cleared in a few days, as soon as the rainy season is *quite* over. It is very pleasant now in the suburbs of Calcutta. Perhaps we shall spend the winter in the Garden, but we have not made up our minds about it yet.

Papa wants to buy a carriage and pair of horses; but I am set against it. I tell him if he allows himself to be entramelled in Calcutta by equipages and gardens, we shall never be able to go to Europe again. I go usually of an evening to my uncle's garden. He and my aunt are never tired of listening to the accounts of Europe which we give them. We attend the "Old Church", of which Mr. Welland is the pastor. The Church has been lately renewed and looks very grand and magnificent.

Several weeks ago, a large cobra was killed in my uncle's garden by one of his servants. My grandfather, who was here about a fortnight ago, related how they had killed a big alligator in his tank, inside his garden. He lives at Connaghur, near Serampore, on the banks of the Ganges; the alligator must have come from the river, during the night, in search of prey. It was killed after a great deal of trouble.

Papa has got a bad cold; the winter here is the most dry and pleasant season of the year, still it is very damp and almost everybody has coughs or colds.

The Hooghly Bridge (a floating bridge across the Ganges) has created a great sensation here. Street ballads are sung and written in its honour and that of the builder. Hindu ladies go to see it, in closed carriages, by thousands. We have not seen it yet; my uncles and aunts and numerous cousins have been to see it, and wonder that we do not follow their example. What is a floating bridge to people who have seen the Suez Canal, and have been through the underground railway in England?

The famine is happily at an end, and Government is selling off the remaining supplies at a very low rate; the poor people are very glad at this; the Government is also disposing of all the horses and mules, which had been required for the transmission of supplies to the parts of India where famine had made its appearance. The cheapness of rice will make everything cheap.

Calcutta has been very noisy and gay during the past fortnight in consequence of the *Poojahs.* The streets were blocked up by crowds of devotees going to throw their idols in the river Ganges; our ears were deafened by the continual din of drums, fifes, flutes, violins, &c., all imaginable instruments of music, playing altogether in exquisite discordance! The holidays are now over, and Calcutta has re-entered into its lethargic state. Papa is going out today, in the city, for some little affairs.

Pinoo, one of our cats, is a great bird-catcher; she is out all day seeking for prey, and is sure to catch either a wagtail, or sparrow, or some larger bird. She brings her prey into our sitting-room, and then I take it from her; she is very docile, so she lets me do what I like. Often I find the bird alive, then I let it off, and reward Pinoo with a good bit of fish!

I must now close. Dear Mary, think of us sometimes. Forgive this dull scrawl.

12, Manicktollah Street,
Calcutta
December 15, 1874

I received your very welcome letter two weeks ago, as also the kind note from Miss A. L.: please thank her from me very much; Papa has also received the kind letter from your dear mother, which you enclosed in yours.

We are all well at present, only my cough troubles me; I hope I shall soon get rid of it, for it's a long time that I have had it.

We purpose going to the Garden in the mornings for walking and exercise; would you believe it? I have hardly walked *one* mile at a stretch since we left England! Mother gets up at five in the morning and walks about my uncle's miniature garden till sunrise. I am too lazy to get up as early as that; I find it more comfortable to lie under the blankets at five A.M. than take exercise in the "trim kept lawns" of 13 Manicktollah Street (vide *Dutt Family Album*). I go on reading from *les Revues des Deux Mondes*: they afford to me a vast field of amusement and instruction, and the subjects in each number are so varied: political questions, social questions, geological, literary, theatrical, and all subjects of interest are discussed and set forth clearly before the reader. I was lately reading an article on Voltaire and Shakespeare, and another very interesting one about Sergeant Hoff who figured in the last war. Papa says he will publish our translations from the French poets as soon as there are two hundred pieces. At present, I send them to the *Bengal Magazine*, edited by Mr. Dey, a native minister; Papa means to publish them in a collected form, as soon as the required number is ready.

Our cat Pinoo caught a bulbul the other day. The bird was quite alive and had not even a scratch; I snatched it away and we have still got it with our other birds. Pinoo was rewarded with a good bit of fried fish. Isn't he a "fameux chasseur"?

My uncle went some days ago to shoot; he brought home only two water-fowls. He is very fond of shooting, and was in high spirits when he came back, though he had only shot two birds.

A gentleman of Cambridge, whom we met there several times, is now officiating in place of Mr. Welland (who has gone to the North West), at the Old Church. Mr. Clifford has hardly been yet a month here. He called to see us the other day. It is so pleasant to us to meet people whom we used to know in Cambridge.

December 26

It is now more than a week since I began this letter; I had an attack of fever which kept me in bed all that time. I am well now of the fever, but the cough has not left me. The doctor advised Papa to travel a little and take me to the North-West Provinces, as it might do my chest some good. Ah! we do not mean to go such a little way from Calcutta as that; when *we* travel it will be for a trip to Nice and St. Leonards!

Christmas passed very quietly with us; I was ill, so we did not go to Church. My uncles and cousins decked their houses with garlands of marigolds; there were no hot Christmas puddings as in England, but there were Christmas cakes full of plums.

Papa is going on the 1st January, 1875, to a College Reunion, to be held at the country residence of a rich native gentleman whom he knows. He is going there because he is very likely to meet some of his old college companions. My uncle too is going with him.

December 31

Tomorrow is mail-day, so I must try and finish this letter today.

We went yesterday to the Garden. I walked as much as I could. The sun had not then gone down, so we walked under the shadow of the mango trees; we climbed the small mound, which is called a *hill* by everybody, and walked up to the gate; the afternoon was very pleasant. Oranges are in full season now; they are beautiful, we cannot get the like of them anywhere in England; they are as large as any of the English or Maltese oranges and the skin peels off like that of the Mandarin ones, and they are sweet as honey. Then we have now in season the Batavian oranges; our Garden is full of them; they are quite yellow outside and red inside, they are as big as a large water melon, and look very pretty amongst the dark-green leaves. The jungle in the Garden has been thoroughly cleared off, and the place looks clean and neat.

Our cow, at least one of them, for we have got two, has got a calf, The milk which we get is therefore very fresh and good; we make our own butter and cream, for it is a very good cow and gives plenty of milk.

1st January, 1875

A happy new year to you, dear, and many many glad returns of the same!

We see from the papers that the winter is very severe in England this time; the last telegram said that there has been heavy snow-storms and severe frosts during the last fortnight in England. Oh, how I should now like to be there! though Papa tells me to thank my stars that I am out of all this severe weather with my cough!

I saw in the *Indian Daily News* last night the death of Sir Ronald Martin, an old physician in India. He was in St. Leonards when we were staying there, and Papa took dear Aru to him for consultation, and he advised us to leave England before the winter. The paper says he was seventy-five years old when he died and that he succumbed to the severity of the winter.

I was sorry to hear of the death of the father[6] of the Misses Fisher; are they going to leave Cambridge?

One of our parrots is beginning to learn to speak; Mamma has a kitten called Judy, and Polly calls it so prettily—"Poor Judy, poor Judy," and then Polly says—"Sweet—Polly!" Mamma is now teaching it a long sentence—"Toru dear, don't cough, take a little milk." Polly just stutters out my name so funnily.

We went to my uncle's yesterday; he is never tired of listening to us when we speak about England, and he questions us on the most minute details; he will talk about England by the day till my cousin vows that he, my uncle, knows more about England, though he has never been there, than we do.

The guinea-pigs are increasing as rapidly as we are getting rid of them!

Papa promises to post my letter on his way to the College Reunion. I wonder how many of his schoolfellows he will meet there.

I have not done any arithmetic lately. It is optional to me to do it or not, as I have finished it; Papa means to go on to geometry and algebra, but I am afraid I am too thickheaded for that.

Dear Mary, I must now close. Please give my kindest regards to A. L. and also to your father and mother. With best love to yourself.

12, Manicktollah Street,
Calcutta
January 11, 1875

I have as yet not got any letter from you, but as I expect one soon, I have sat down to pen a reply.

I have had another attack of fever last week, but I am much better now; I am happy to say that both Papa and Mamma are keeping well. Last Monday we took a long drive all round the Maidan; we went along the river for a long time; such a number of vessels were anchored there; two or three steamers were just having their steam up, ready to start for

---

6. William Webster Fisher, Downing Professor of Medicine.

merry England; I had a great mind to tell the coachman to stop, and get up in one of these "homeward bound steamers"!

We met the carriage and six of Sir Salar Jung, a great up-country dignitary. We saw the magnificent statue in bronze of Sir James Outram on horseback; it is the work of Mr. Foley, the celebrated sculptor, and had been expressly made to be sent out to India. We passed the Eden Gardens, which are the admiration of all Calcutta, and the promenade of the fashionable; and then the Calcutta Newgate or jail; it is very large and surrounded by a high wall;—sentries were pacing up and down, all round the building, armed with bayonets. The streets in the native quarter of Calcutta are so dirty, narrow, and blocked up that it is a wonder to me how we get through them without some accident.

The European part of the town is far better; though far inferior to some of the fashionable parts of London. We had a drive of about twelve miles that day. Our turkey has hatched seven of the nine eggs she was sitting upon; the young turkeys are so nimble, and it is so funny looking at them, when they pick up their rice or grain with their tiny beaks. Two of the bulbuls died, so we let go the third one for fear it should die too.

I have not been reading anything for the last few days, but I am a regular contributor to the *Bengal Magazine*. They are so slow in Calcutta (by *they*, I mean the printers). Would you believe it? the December number of the Magazine has not come out yet!

A few days ago one of my cousins, who is a Hindu, came here with his wife and two daughters and his son; the latter is a very fine, handsome boy, "like a prince," as the Bengalis say, of about ten. His two sisters are younger than me, but they look much bigger and older—the eldest has a boy of four, she has just lost her two younger children; the younger sister has a girl of about two, so plump and pretty; I took her on my lap, and she sat there very quiet for some time, but catching sight of Papa's beard, she burst into tears; and her mother had to take her and send her out for a walk in the garden to calm her.

I hope you will excuse, dear Mary, my dull letters; they are a poor return for your interesting ones.

I hope you have not suffered from the severe weather this winter. The papers are full of the cold that is felt all over England; all the country covered under a sheet of snow. Here the weather is delightful, only in the mornings there is sometimes an unhealthy fog—but by nine o'clock, the sun shines warm and dispels all dampness and fog.

It is a long time since I began this letter; I have been very ill, and it is only yesterday that I went downstairs. I have been ill with a very bad cough, accompanied with a good deal of blood-spitting and fever. I am glad to say I am better now, though still rather weak. Dr. Cayley of the new Mayo Hospital was called in, besides the native doctor. I have had such a number of blisters put on my chest and back, that they are quite sore—luckily they heal up in a day or two. Papa wishes to call in Dr. Cayley again—but I tell him, that one doctor is enough, for—

> *Faut des docteurs; pas trop n'en faut;*
> *L'excès en tout est un défaut.*
> *J'ai mis en parallèle*
> *Les coursiers et le médecin:*
> *A son char plus on en attèle,*
> *Plus on abrège son chemin.*

Dr. Cayley says that we shall be able to go to Europe in April or May—he advises us to go to Italy or to the sea-coast in the South of England.

Papa has purchased a very nice and comfortable barouche and a splendid pair of bay mares, belonging to the Government stud; the pair are an excellent match—I have named them "Jeunette" and "Gentille". They have to go every morning to Dunnett's to be broken in; they are very quiet, and the coachman thinks they will be ready for us in three weeks.

By last mail we sent for some French books from London, through Messrs. Hachette & Co. We hope to receive them by April. My uncle has had a lot of books out from England, both French and German. It is a long time since we attended Church; I have been too ill to go anywhere; I hope next Sunday we shall be able to go to the Old Church.

One of my cousins has bought a mare very lately—the mare he had ran off from the carriage somehow or other, and in its mad course knocked down a woman who was passing, and hurt her so dreadfully that she was immediately taken to the Hospital and is not likely to live; the animal hurt another person, but not so seriously; it has itself got three or four very deep flesh wounds which had to be sewed up. We have sold off a lot of the guinea-pigs; there are only six pairs left now; we are going to keep two pairs; one, the old pair which dear Aru brought from England, and another quite white. I have not been able to read much lately. I have neither practised much.

The weather is getting very warm here now; last night it was very hot. I must rest a little now.

February 8th.

I am not quite sure about the affair of the little girl I wrote about—whether she will be sent to England, and if so, when she is to go. When I shall hear definitely about it, I shall let you know. It will be indeed very sad for her, if she does go, for she has never been from home, even for a day. Many thanks for the trouble you have taken for me. I shall write to Miss Fletcher either by this mail or the next; it is very kind of her to write to me herself. I am very glad to hear that it is very likely that Mademoiselle[7] will come to stay in Cambridge.

The Rev. Mr. Dey, editor of the *Bengal Magazine*, to which I contribute, has very lately published a novel in two volumes, in English. He got a prize for it offered by a rich Zemindar for the best novel on humble rural life in India. I have not seen the book yet; I hope it will be successful.

We have not been able to go to Church for some time on account of my illness; I hope we shall be able to attend the Old Church next Sunday.

They have just brought into the compound Jeunette and Gentille. I regaled the pair with some sugar-cane, of which they are extremely fond. I like to look at them so much—they are my prime favourites now. They are kept in the Garden just for the present, till our stable in town is quite ready.

How are your pets getting on, doves and canaries? How nice it is for you to be at home again in Cambridge. Parker's Piece must be full of football players now of an afternoon. And the lectures *vont leur train*, I suppose; and is M. Boquel still in Cambridge? and Dr. Garrett as crusty as ever? I shall write to Mrs. Baker at the earliest opportunity.

February 9th.

I began yesterday a very interesting book, *Papiers posthumes de Rossel*. You know Rossel was shot because he held some position among the Communes. He was formerly an officer in Bazaine's army, but

---

7. Mademoiselle Verry, Miss Martin's French governess, who resided for many years at Park Terrace till her pupil went to school at Cambridge House, Malvern-Wells, in 1872.

he deserted when Metz capitulated. The last part of his diary is so pathetic. I remember all the English papers were of opinion that he was condemned unjustly—I think so too; his mistake lay in that he, an *officier de génie* of the French army, became one of the leaders of the Commune; but if he had lived, he would have been one of the best soldiers of the day. He was a Protestant; he loved his country "not wisely but too well". He has written a book, *L'Art de la guerre*; I saw some reviews of it in the English papers.

February 10th.

Yesterday, I went out for the first time since my illness; my uncle and aunt were so very glad to see me out.

I have not yet gone for a drive: as soon as Jeunette and Gentille are throughly broken in, I shall be able to drive about comfortably in our own carriage. The cabs here are so bad and uncomfortable that it is a feat of power and dexterity to get in or out of them!

The December number of the *Bengal Magazine* has at last come out! The January number has not come out yet, but it will soon, for they sent me the proof sheets of my translations some time ago. Papa sometimes gives an article to the Magazine, but not always.

One of our cats has now got three kittens; we shall dispose of them as soon as they are big enough, by giving them to friends.

I hope you will excuse my dull letters, they are but a poor return for your interesting ones, but

> *Croyez qu'avec vous de moitié*
> *Mon cœur tout autrement raisonne,*
> *Et qu'il ne redoute personne*
> *Au grand concours de l'amitié.*

I have handed the prospectus to the little girl's father; as soon as I know his decision, I shall write to you.

I must now close my letter. Give my kindest regards to your father and mother.

P.S.—Reading over my letter, I find I have written twice over about our going to Church, but never mind, you will excuse all such *bêtises*.

T. D.

12, Manicktollah Street,
Calcutta
March 14, 1875

I was glad indeed to receive your letter, dated the 3rd February, this morning. I enjoyed reading it so much. I am very sorry to hear that you have got a bad cold. I hope you are quite well by this time. I, myself, am much better now; the warm weather has set in and we are obliged to have the punkah going all through the day.

I asked the little girl's father about her; she is not going to England just now; I do not know if she will ever be able to go. Thank you very much for the information about Cambridge House. Please give my very best thanks to Miss Fletcher, when you see her, for her kind letter.

Yesterday, Dunnet, the horse-breaker, came here; and we had the first ride in our own carriage and pair. Jeunette and Gentille go splendidly and are very quiet. We had a pretty long drive.

My cousin's new mare was tried in his brougham; she went very well too. Dunnet is coming again tomorrow, to accustom our coachman to the horses.

April 3rd.

It is some time since I began this letter; for the last fortnight Papa has been suffering from strong fever; he has now got rid of the fever, but is still rather weak.

I go out for a drive almost every day. Papa is not able to accompany me every time, because of his weakness. We are going to spend the day in the Garden and have our luncheon there.

Last night we had a thunderstorm, accompanied with hail. It is very fresh and cool this morning in consequence.

My birthday was the 4th of March. Mamma gave me Dickens's *Barnaby Budge*, and Papa a beautiful volume of Mrs. Barrett Browning's poems. I have already read both of them, and I like them very much.

We expect our books from England on Thursday next; I am looking forward for it.

April 5th.

We went to the Garden on Saturday last, and spent the day there. My uncle and aunt joined us there in the afternoon, and we took a walk when the sun had set. Papa and I are going out shopping today. I am now reading Dickens's *Bleak House*. I have only just begun it, but as far as I have read, it is very interesting. We are going to live in the Garden during the hot season; I think we shall be able to remove by the end of this week.

April 6th.

We had a great deal of rain last night, which has made the morning very pleasant and cool.

The delicious mangoes will be soon in season; unripe ones are already to be got; they are very nice boiled with a little sugar. Pineapples are to be got, but they are very dear, almost as dear as in England. Then we have now the *Rose-berry*, with its beautiful odour of fresh roses, and the *Lokut*, with its bright orange colour; and the water-melon, and the sugar-cane, and the *Bael*, which is very good, strained and made into a drink with ice and sugar.

I continue to contribute translations from the French poets to the *Bengal Magazine*; some of the Indian papers review them favourably, which makes me very happy and proud!

I get up early now, at five in the morning, because I have Jeunette and Gentille fed before me, and they come at six, so I am dressed and ready by the time they come. In the Garden, they will have plenty of pasture and free air. Here, of course, they are kept almost the whole day in their stable.

April 8th.

I got your letter dated the 10th March this morning; oh, the long interesting letter! I was so glad to receive it, but I feel quite ashamed of my own remissness in my correspondence.

I have not got Voltaire's *Charles XII*. I returned all the books you kindly lent me. I am very sorry to hear about the Fishers; will they stay on in Cambridge? I see from your letter that your father sees Mr. Hall very often. Do you meet Mary and Lizzie sometimes? If so, give my best love to them. All the Cambridge news you give in your letter is very interesting. Mr. George Macfarren (who is one of the candidates for the Cambridge professorship) we knew in London; his wife, Natalia Macfarren, was our singing mistress during our long sojourn in that city. I hope Mr. Macfarren all success with my whole heart. Many thanks for the little pin-cushion; I shall treasure it up for your dear sake. I was so sorry to learn of your illness and am so glad you are quite well now. I am pretty well now, but the cough has not quite left me yet. There is very little chance of our going to England just now, but still we hope to go soon. My uncle seriously declares that he will very soon start for England; but we have heard this so often that we do not think he will be able. What a severe winter you have had! Papa says we are well out of it! Here the weather is intolerably hot. We went yesterday for a drive. Jeunette and Gentille are so quiet, strong, and fleet that Papa was quite pleased with them. I have such merry tiffs with my uncle and aunt about the merits of their horse (a grey and rather small-sized stud-bred) and Jeunette and Gentille's. My aunt calls her horse Peerless Roland, but I call him Rosinante, in remembrance of Don Quixote's famous steed!

I am afraid my letter will be very short and dull this time. Are you going to leave Cambridge House next May? If so, you have left school by the time this reaches you. We have not been to Church for a long time, on account of sickness amongst us. Tomorrow is mail-day, so I must post this today if I wish it to go by this mail. I am quite ashamed of this scrawl. Please give my love to your dear Mother, and best love to yourself.

Baugmaree Garden House
April 23, 1875

I begin this letter now, so as to be able to make it long if not interesting. Papa has been suffering very much for the last week from an abscess in his right leg. The doctor wanted to make a slight incision, but Mamma is very much afraid of operations of any kind. I am glad to say that the sore is now in a fair way of getting well. You will see by the address that we have settled down at old Baugmaree for the hot season; it is so much cooler and pleasanter here than in town. We came here on the 15th instant.

The books we sent for from England have at last come to hand; there are only two more to come, Those that we have already received are: *Les Châtiments*, by Victor Hugo, a book which I have been longing to see; the poems therein are very beautiful; if I have time and space, I shall copy and send one of the smallest pieces with a translation by your humble servant! Then there are *Voyage aux Pyrénées* by Taine, *Seul!*, by Saintine. The latter is the well-known history of Alexander Selkirk, from which Defoe made out his *Robinson Crusoe*. Then we have received also: *Napoléon le Petit*, by Victor Hugo; *Les Fiancés du Spitzberg*, by Marmier, "ouvrage couronné par l'Académie Française"; *La roche aux mouettes*, by Sandeau; *Histoire d'une bouchée de pain*, by Macé. This is a scientific book treating of the organs of the human body and also of the animals, but the whole is so simply told, and so well explained, that it is most interesting reading. Then there are two volumes of Charles Nodier's charming *Contes*. I have only read two or three of the whole lot as yet; I was so glad to receive them that a whole fortnight was passed in looking at them and hugging them! Yesterday our coachman, who is a good angler, caught a small *Roheet* from one of our tanks; he is going to try again today. Two or three nights ago, one of our servants saw two wild boars in our Garden. We had seen one before we went to England. My uncle is anxious to have a shot at them, if they make their appearance again. I saw a weasel this morning, while I was taking my "constitutional". There are many weasels in our Garden; I am going to try and catch one if possible. There has been quite a murrain among our pets: almost all the kittens have died, only two are left, and Mamma's pet cat, Judy, is dead too, and three of our rabbits also have had the same fate. Isn't it distressing?

The *leechies* will be in soon now, the mangoes will come in later about the beginning of May. I am pretty well at present, only the cough has not left me yet. Mamma is quite well.

I went this morning to see Jeunette and Gentille bathed. They are so gentle, and are very fond of me! I go out driving almost every day in the evening. Papa is unable to accompany me just now, and Mamma stays at home for him. My uncle and aunt came to see us yesterday.

25th, Monday

Last evening we received a letter of receipt from Messrs. Hachette & Co., accompanied by the last book of those we sent for. It is the *Scènes historiques*, by Mme de Witt, *née* Guizot; it is a beautifully and richly bound volume, with illustrations. Last night, we had what the English papers would call a thunderstorm, and which we would denominate a refreshing shower! Yesterday, our coachman caught two large fishes; he is a lucky angler, indeed he supplies our daily consumption of fish; it is so pleasant having fresh fish from our own tanks.

The mornings are so pleasant in the Garden. Very early, at about three in the morning, the *Bheem-raj*, a little bird, begins his song; half an hour afterwards, all the bushes and trees burst into melody, the *Kokila*, the *Bow-kotha-kow*—which means, "Speak, O bride"—the *Papia*, &c. And the gay little hummingbirds, with their brilliant colours, dive into the flowers for honey with busy twitters. Oh, it is so cool and pleasant in the morning till ten o'clock, when the warmth increases; from noon to about four in the afternoon, all is quite still, except some lone woodpecker tapping at some far-off tree. Then in the evening, all the birds are astir again, till it gets dark, when, like wise little creatures that they are, they go to bed!

Jeunette and Gentille are thriving. I sometimes lead them to grass in our compound; they follow me as meek as lambs. I must stop here, for breakfast is ready.

April 27th.

Yesterday my grandfather came here with one of his grandsons; he wished to consult Dr. Cayley about the health of the boy, who is rather weakly. Yesterday, in the afternoon, we had a good deal of rain and wind, which continued almost the whole night.

Of all the English birds that Aru brought from England, only six are living, two pairs of canaries, one goldfinch, and one chaffinch. The guinea-pigs increase their number weekly, and I continue to "drive a roaring trade" as Papa says, by selling them by lots of eighteen or twenty at a time! I hope you are all quite well. By the time this letter reaches you, you would have left Cambridge House for good, I suppose. Where are you going this summer during the vacation? What do you think of coming out here for a summer-trip? We should be charmed to see you and should be happy to bring about this joyous event in any way, if you will just give a hint that it will suit you!

The weather looks cloudy, and as the Garden gets unhealthy during the rainy season, we shall soon have to decamp. Write to me at our Calcutta house, for I am afraid of the letters being lost if you were to address them here. Papa is pretty well, but as I said before, it will be some time before he is able to move about. He and Mamma join in sending kind regards to your father and mother and with best love to yourself.

CHANSON

FROM VICTOR HUGO's LES CHÂTIMENTS

(*Original*)

La femelle? elle est morte.
Le mâle? un chat l'emporte
Et dévore ses os.
Au doux nid qui frissonne

Qui reviendra? personne.
Pauvres petits oiseaux!

Le pâtre absent par fraude!
Le chien mort! le loup rôde
Et tend ses noirs panneaux
Au bercail qui frissonne.
Qui veillera? personne.
Pauvres petits agneaux!

L'homme au bagne! la mère
A l'hospice! ô misère!
Le logis tremble aux vents;
L'humble berceau frissonne.
Que reste-t-il? personne.
Pauvres petits enfants!

CHANSON
(Translation)
The female? She is dead.
The male? The cat has fed
On his flesh and his bone.
To the nest which will come?
Oh, poor birdlings, be dumb;
But they moan, the weak things, and they moan.

The shepherd? Gone or fled.
The dog? Killed, and instead
The wolf prowling alone.
He peers in.—Ho, I come!
He may pity, hope some,
Oh poor lambs, the wolf's heart is of stone.

The man? To prison led.
The mother? sick-a-bed
In a workhouse is thrown.
It is cold—will she come?
They cry—cry for a crumb,
Poor children, look to God on his throne.

From *Les Châtiments* of Victor Hugo
(*Original*)

—Sentiers où l'herbe se balance,
Vallons, coteaux, bois chevelus,
Pourquoi ce deuil et ce silence?
—Celui qui venait ne vient plus.

—Pourquoi personne à la fenêtre,
Et pourquoi ton jardin sans fleurs?
O maison! où donc est ton maître?
—Je ne sais pas, il est ailleurs.

—Chien, veille au logis.—Pour quoi faire?
La maison est vide à présent.
—Enfant, qui pleures-tu?—Mon père.
—Femme, qui pleures-tu?—L'absent.

—Où s'en est-il allé?—Dans l'ombre.
—Flots qui gémissez sur l'écueil,
D'où venez-vous?—Du bagne sombre.
—Et qu'apportez-vous?—Un cercueil.

The Political Prisoner
(*Translation*)

—Paths that from trees dark shadows borrow!
Green vale and wood and pebbled shore!
Wherefore this silence and this sorrow?
—A step that came here, comes no more.

—Closed window, sign of some disaster!
Garden, where never flowers are seen!
And grey old house—where is the master?
—Long in his home he has not been.

—Mastiff keep watch.—O stranger rather
On Desolation look thou here.
—Child why weepest thou?—For my Father.
—And thou O woman?—For my dear.

HARIHAR DAS AND TORU DUTT

—Where is he gone?—He left no traces.
—Whence come ye, Waves, that thunder loud?
—We come from earth's dark cruel places.
—And what bear ye?—A hammock shroud.

—T. D.

12, Manicktollah Street,
Calcutta
June 6, 1875

I got your long-expected and welcome letter yesterday. So you have been to London! Is this your first visit to it? I am glad you enjoyed yourself; did you go to the Royal Academy? Aru and I were charmed when we saw the Zoological Gardens, and went there several times. I have never had the luck to see the elephant processions you mention; they very often take place, but I never had the curiosity to go and see them.

I have read all the books we have had brought from England, except one, *Scènes historiques*, by Mme de Witt, which I am now reading. Our next batch of books will come to hand about the middle of July; among them is M. Littré's Dictionary, in four volumes. *Les Fiancés du Spitzberg*, by X. Marmier, is a very interesting and nice book. It is well worth reading, and I should recommend you to read it, if it comes in your way.

We are all well now. Mamma lately had a very bad carbuncle on the neck. We were afraid that it would have been necessary to cut it, but happily it got well through applying warm poultices and touching it up with caustic lotion.

I am very sorry to hear what you tell me about Mrs. Baker. Does she understand all one says to her? I will write to her and enclose the letter in yours. Please kindly send it over to her.

I have still got the cough, but have nothing else to complain of. Papa is quite well, he had an acute attack of the gout lately, but is now very well. We have left the Garden House, as the rainy season has commenced. The mangoes are in their full season now, and we are enjoying them to our hearts' content.

I am not able to go out driving now, as Gentille is laid up with a strained shoulder. Jeunette is quite well and is in such excellent condition! My cousin, who is very fond of horses, never tires looking at her, and whenever he calls, he never fails to ask me to order Jeunette and Gentille to be brought in the compound of our house. I wanted very much to have a book about horses, and Mamma gave me one yesterday; it is written by an officer of the British army, and is intended for non-professional horse-owners in India. It is very interesting and gives so much information; I have been reading it all yesterday.

9th.

Papa has had two rooms built lately over our kitchen and store-room, because we were hard up for rooms. They are not quite finished yet, but they will be so in a few days.

Among the list of those who have passed the Civil Service Examination, there is not one Indian gentleman; this is very unfortunate. One of our relations went up for the Examination, and has failed; this is very sad for him. It is harder when a Bengali fails than when an Englishman has the same mishap; the Bengali leaves all his friends and relations and stakes all his fortune for a successful examination, the expenses of going and coming are so great. There were three or four natives who went up this year, but they have all failed, it seems.

My letter will be dull this time, as I have literally nothing to write about. I get up very early now, at four or half-past four at the latest, so as to be able to pat and caress Jeunette and Gentille when they come for their morning feed. Mamma says I am mad about horses, and gives me a scolding now and then for getting up so early. One day Jeunette got loose in the Garden, and oh! didn't she race! jumping clean over hedges and quite wild with joy! She was caught at last, when the grooms led Gentille to her. They are so very fond of each other. Now that Gentille is laid up with a bad shoulder Jeunette was made to go in a pair with my cousin's horse, and stayed out some time. Gentille neighed and was restless all the time she was absent! I am getting very tiresome, am I not? always horses, horses, horses! Ah! but if you could see my Jeunette and Gentille!

The papers say that the Duke of Buckingham is coming out from England to be the Governor of Madras. This is, I believe, the first *Duke* that has ever come out to India as Governor.

The papers say that he is very likely to succeed Lord Northbrook as Governor-General of India. The Prince of Wales intends to give us the honour of a visit in November: some papers are in the seventh heaven about this visit, others depreciate it, saying it will only be an occasion for the increase of taxes. The Princess of Wales will not accompany him out, it seems, as then she will have to leave her children in England. Dr. Fayrer and Sir Bartle Frere are likely to bear him company. The Flying Squadron will come with him out to India. It will be a grand affair.

The Indian maize is coming into season. Papa is not very fond of it, but I am, when it is young and *cuit sous les cendres*; oh, then it is delicious!

We want to sell off the Garden before we leave India, as then we shall be able to settle for good in England. Already we have had some very good offers for it, but not such as *we* would wish to have.

The front of our town house was full of huts and small shops. One of my cousins has now bought it, and cleared it thoroughly, which is a great improvement. I believe the ground will be turned into a nice garden.

Has Miss A. L. left Cambridge House? Give her my best regards when you see her. By the time this reaches you, you will have left the old dear school. Where do you mean to go this autumn? Are the Fishers still in Cambridge? I suppose the usual boat-races in Cambridge between the Colleges took place in May. Who came out first? I am afraid you were in school then and did not see the boat-procession.

Polly is just beginning to say: "Toru, dear, give me some bread." She is even now squeaking the sentence out in great triumph! I want to know the date and year of your birth, because I want to put it in my Birthday Scripture text book; I have a good many names in it already, chiefly of our own relations.

The rains have fully set in, and the sky looks as dismal as the London *summer* skies. The rainy season will continue about two months more; it is the most dull and unhealthy season of the year.

I enclose a letter for Mrs. Baker and a penny stamp, please kindly forward the note to her. Give my kindest regards and those of Papa and Mamma to your father and mother.

12, Manicktollah Street
Calcutta
July 22, 1875

I have not got a letter from you for such a long time that I am getting a little anxious about you all. Tomorrow we shall receive letters from Europe; I hope there will be also one from you among them.

We are all well here at present. I hope to be able to go out again soon, as Gentille has got well of her strain in the shoulder under my *own* treatment. The weather is not very fine now-a-days, as the rainy season is in its height now; the sun nevertheless shows his bright face now and then for a day or two. The weather has become in no wise cooler on account of the rains; indeed, it is hotter now than ever. The thermometer, now, 6.30 A.M. in this room, under a punkah, stands at eighty-two!

The wife of my cousin, Charoo, who went to England to be enrolled as a barrister, had a baby, but it died the seventh day after its birth, of tetanus. The poor young mother (she is only twenty-two) is sorely tried; this is the first child she has lost; she has four children now, three boys and one girl. My great-grandmother died also on the 7th instant. We could not go to see her, as I had an increase of my cough, which again necessitated applying a blister on my chest.

My grandfather and grandmother came here on Thursday last, to consult the doctor about my grandmother's eyes; she is suffering very much from them and can hardly see; the doctor says she will get well in a month.

We got a letter from Messrs. Hachette & Co.; we learn from it that our books will come to hand by the 1st of August. They write that they have still a balance of one pound and odd shillings in our favour, so we are going to send for some more books. Our old music-mistress, who used to teach us piano and singing before we went to England, came to see us the day before yesterday from Serampore, where she now resides. She brought her daughter Marie with her. I was so glad to see Mrs. Sinaes again! She is such a good motherly woman. She was quite shocked at my not having a piano!

We shall not be able to go to the Garden till November, when the rainy season will be over. The garden is very unhealthy now, and one is sure to get malaria if one stays there during the rains. The two rooms over our kitchen and store-rooms are quite done now, and we use them. We shall be able to bring some of our bookshelves from the Garden, as there is more room here now.

I suppose you have left Cambridge House for good now. Is Miss A. L. there still, or has she left?

I am not reading anything now, except articles from the *Revue des Deux Mondes*. I have just got hold of *L'année terrible*, by Victor Hugo; I had written several times for it from the Calcutta Public Library, but the invariable answer had always been, "Out, sorry to say!" But the librarian got tired of my perseverance, and I have received the book at last. It is much inferior to *Les Châtiments*. It has for subject the late war of 1870 and its *suites*. In one of the pieces, the poet addresses General Trochu thus:

"Participe passé du verbe Tropchoir," &c., &c.

Some verses entitled "A l'enfant malade pendant le siège" and addressed to his little grandchild, Jeanne, are exceedingly good. Have you read Mrs. Gaskell's *Life of Charlotte Brontë*? It is a very, very interesting book. I was lately reading a review of it, in the *Revue des Deux Mondes*, which interested me very much.

All the *bigwigs* are still up at Simla. I believe Lord Northbrook, our Governor-General, will go to Bombay in November, to receive the Prince of Wales there. Our new Chief-Justice, Sir Richard Garth, has been entertained at dinner by the barristers of Calcutta at the Town Hall. He seems to have pleased everybody by his warm and hearty manner.

Our second crop of mangoes is now come in, and we get some every day; but they are neither so plentiful nor so good as those which come to season first. Today, the durwan from our Garden reported that a large snake had been seen in the room where the poultry used to be kept; but they could not kill it, as it escaped through a hole. The fruits we now get are delicious: pineapples, custard-apples, of which I am very fond; pomegranates, large and fresh, and the native almonds, very like newly-come-in and green walnuts, plantains, guavas, and the large jack-fruits which we get from our Garden.

One of my cousins, Varûna, only four years old, is fond of us, very much. He sometimes comes and stays the whole day with us. He is very intelligent and has a wonderful ear for music. You would be delighted to hear him sing some of Moody's and Sankey's hymns:

"Hold the fort! for I am coming!"

He sings that standing, with his little hand raised in a most imposing attitude! He is very fond of firearms! Give him a gun or a pistol, and he will do anything for you. His love for watches and medicine-chests seems in no wise to have diminished.

July 23rd.

I received your letter, dated the 22nd of June last. I am glad to see you are well, as I was getting a little anxious about you. I am sorry to hear about the Fishers. Poor girls! it must be trying to them to live so far from home. Is Mary the one who is a little shorter than the other two, and is she the eldest of the three? Where shall you go in September? I shall continue to write to your address in Cambridge. I shall be so glad to get a likeness of yours, when you are taken in Cambridge. Please do not forget to send me one.

Yesterday, Jeunette was put to harness with a mare of my cousin's. As she had several days' rest on account of Gentille's lameness, she was very fresh, and went splendidly, plunging and so fiery that Papa was afraid of some accident. She came back quieter, but still full of spirit and fire. It reminded me of Browning's description of a horse in a poem entitled "How they brought the good news from Ghent":

"With his nostrils like pits, full of blood to the brim."

Gentille is quite well now, and I shall be able to use her in a few days. We sold off some guinea-pigs, keeping only four. As to the birds dear Aru brought from England, only two pairs of canaries and one goldfinch are alive.

I was reading some French translations of Henri Heine's poems in the *Revue des Deux Mondes*. I liked them very much. "Le Négrier," "Soucis Babyloniens," "Les fiancés prédestinés," are very good, and also some ballads of a lighter vein.

"Polly" has learned a big sentence now; she says "Toru, dear, give me some bread" quite plainly now; she says it to me whenever she sees me with any fruit in my hand.

I must bid you good-bye now, dear. With best love to yourself and kind regards to your father and mother.

Calcutta
September 10, 1875

Many, many thanks for your very interesting letter, dated the 9th August last, which I received this morning. So you have left school at last! How glad your dear mother must be to have you all to herself now! She used to miss you so much when you went back to school after the holidays. The small piece from your father's pen, I like very much; Papa also was pleased with it.

Your description of Sir Samuel Wagtail of Wagtail Hall, Berkshire, or Barkshire, is very funny. I laughed so much when I read it.[8]

---

8. This was an allusion to a dog belonging to a friend of Miss Martin.

Calcutta is now looking forward to the proposed visit of the Prince of Wales to India. Preparations are already being made for his reception. A committee has been appointed by the native community to consider the best way of showing the loyalty of his Indian subjects to the Prince. Papa was asked to be one of the committee; he is going tomorrow to a meeting, which is to be held at the British Indian Association Rooms, to consider how the Prince should be *fêted* and received by the Bengali community of Calcutta.

We have brought all our books here from the Garden, and I have been very busy arranging them. We shall go to the Garden and stay there as soon as the rains are over, which will be about the beginning of November. Our French books have arrived. Littré's Dictionary, in four large volumes, is splendid; it is very good and instructive reading too, and I have been reading it often. The quotations and the history of each word are very interesting. Besides Littré's Dictionary, we have received Alfred de Musset's works, Alfred de Vigny's poetical works, Mme Desbordes-Valmore's *Poésies de l'enfance* and Soulary's *Sonnets* and *Vert-Vert, ou, Les aventures d'un perroquet*, by Gresset. We have sent for some more books.

Gentille is now quite well, and I go out for an evening drive very often. I went yesterday to the Strand along the river, which is the fashionable "drive" of Calcutta.

You promised to send me a likeness of yours; I expected that I should find it in your letter; your father's poem made the letter feel hard to the touch, as if it enclosed a carte-de-visite. I suppose you have not had yourself taken yet; when you have, please do not forget to send me a copy. You know how I shall value it, dear.

Baguette has got two kittens, and Pinoo one. Baguette's kits are very pretty: one is white, with a small black mark on the forehead and the tail black; the other is dark grey and white, intermingled. They are so full of playful tricks, it is quite amusing to watch their funny antics.

My cousin has sold off that frisky mare of his, which ran away and killed a poor old woman some time ago; he has now only a beautiful black mare. Just now I saw his brougham pass in the street opposite our window.

A great epidemic lately broke out among our ducks and geese; from two to four died every day, and out of twenty only eight are now living. We kept only three guinea-pigs and sold off the others, but yesterday, on going into their room, I saw the number increased to six! Three little ones had been born overnight. The four canaries and the goldfinch are thriving. The young bulbul which I had in the Garden has grown into a very fine bird now. The fruits in season now are custard-apples (I am very fond of them), Batavian oranges, green almonds, Indian plums, and plantains of course.

We lead a very quiet life here, and so I have very little news to give you. I get up at half past four, prepare two cups of chocolate, one for myself and one for Papa, then I go to dress, and by the time I come out from the dressing-room, Papa and Mamma get up, and I find the former smoking his morning cigar. Then I go to the roof of the house; it is very cool, early in the morning, up there. After that I give Baguette and Pinoo their morning pittance of fried fish. I come down and install myself in the window of this room, below which Gentille and Jeunette take their feed of gram and bran, and a delicious drink of *suttoo* (flour of oats), and water, which is given to horses in India, to keep them cool during the very hot months. Then we go down to breakfast. After breakfast we have prayers, after which Mamma goes to her household duties, I either take up a book or play for a quarter of an hour with the kittens, and Papa reads or writes or pores over the *Indian Daily News*. At twelve, we have our lunch, after which I read or write till three, when I take either a custard-apple, or a slice of Batavian orange. At five, we dress, and go out, I generally for a drive, and Papa and Mamma to my uncle's garden. At seven, we have dinner, and at half-past eight, a cup of tea, and at ten to bed. I must stop here for the present, for breakfast is ready.

We had a sharp shock of earthquake five or six days ago. We were then at prayers, and we all felt it plainly; the punkah swung backwards and forwards; the water in the tank at the back of our house rose and fell, like waves of the sea; and all the clocks stopped. My uncle, who is rather nervous about earthquakes, was up in the third storey, when he felt the shock; he rushed downstairs and stationed himself at the front door, for fear the house should topple down! I laughed at him so much, but he declared that he felt the shock more plainly, being in the third storey, than we possibly could have felt it in the second.

September 14th.

My grandfather and grandmother came to see us yesterday and they brought Mamma's brother's eldest wife with them; for my uncle has *two* wives, as many Hindus here have the right to have three or four wives, which is not at all contrary to the Shastras! My eldest auntie is very good, she loves us very much, and was very glad to see us: it is more than a year since she had seen us.

We went to the Garden two or three days ago and met some of our cousins, who had gone there before, with Papa's permission, to angle. They insisted on our taking a middle-sized *roheet* that they had caught, so we had fresh *roheet* fried for dinner.

Mamma had an attack of her pain some weeks ago; it was a very sharp attack, and after that she had a little fever, but she was quite well in two or three days. Papa and I are both quite well now.

We go to the Old Church every Sunday; it is very far from our house, that is the only inconvenience.

There has been a great deal of cholera up at Simla, where the Governor-General goes usually with his staff and officers during the hot season. Of course he was obliged to *déguerpir* as soon as the cholera broke out.

I shall address my letters to you at Cambridge, though I suppose you will probably be somewhere near the Lakes for five or six weeks.

Mrs. Baker has not written to me yet, but I hope she will soon.

Why don't you go to the Continent for a tour? I am sure you would enjoy yourself immensely. I should like to go down the Rhine and also to the Pyrenees; there is such a nice piece in French, descriptive of the scenery round the Pyrenees, by Napol le Pyrénéen (Xavier Navarrot), a protestant *pasteur*; it is the only poem he wrote, but it is a beautiful one; his critic, M. Charles Asselineau, thus speaks of the piece: "Ce n'est pas un pays deviné, rêvé, recréé, pour ainsi dire, par l'imagination puissante d'un poète grand magicien, mais un pays vu, compris et admirablement rendu en quelques coups d'un savant pinceau: la *vermeille* Orléans, Limoges *aux trois sveltes clochers*, l'Aveyron *murmurant entre des pelouses pleines de parfums*, les *grèves pensives* du Tescoud, le Tarn *fauve et fuyant*, la Garonne *aux longs flots, aux eaux convulsives* où nagent des *navires bruns* et des *îlots verdoyants*, parleront à l'œil de quiconque a suivi le même itinéraire. Tout le reste de la pièce, écrit d'un mouvement rapide, comme la course du voyageur, ou comme le galop des chevaux de Muça-el-Kevir, étincelle de vives couleurs et de traits brillants qui sautent à l'œil. C'est: Toulouse, jetée comme une *perle* au milieu des fleurs; les blancs *chevaux* à la *crinière argentée,* dont le pied grêle a des poils noirs *comme des plumes* d'aigle, c'est encore Fénelon le *cygne aux chants divins,*

c'est enfin, à la dernière strophe, les armées, passant par Ronceveaux:—
soldats, canons, tambours, chevaux, chants tonnant dans l'espace, &c.—
Voilà bien l'art de 1833."

I'd better stóp here, I am afraid you are yawning!

12, Manicktollah Street,
Calcutta
October 12, 1875

I received your most welcome and interesting letter, dated 29th August, from Keswick, last Monday. I delayed answering it in hopes that something new might turn up, about which I could write to you and which would interest you, but as my hopes have been frustrated, you must content yourself with my usual long rigmaroles. Now that the modest preface has been written, I feel relieved, as you have fair warning of all the dull things that are to follow. How I should like to be with you now! What a pity you did not see the "four fraternal yews"! When Papa heard it, he was scandalized; he said he should not have thought *you* capable of such a thing!

Papa has been suffering from another small abscess, but he is now quite well. So are we all for the present.

I have bought a splendid book about horses, with beautiful large coloured illustrations. Papa has bought for me Mayhew's *Illustrated Horse-doctor*, which I have wanted long to have.

Papa has hired a piano and I am practising away all the morning. Varûna, my little cousin, has a great ear for music. He knows almost all Mr. Sankey's hymns and sings them in English, though he does not know the language. Play the first bar of any of Mr. Sankey's hymns, he immediately catches the tune, and sings it to the last line, in perfect measure, keeping time with his foot. He is more and more attached to me, and the reason is, I let him play two or three notes on my piano when he comes!

13th.

I have just come in from the small garden; I have been leading about Jeunette and Gentille there, while the grooms were busy at something or other. Jeunette is so very fond of bread; I have been giving her some every morning; she searches all my dress, pokes her nose into my pockets for a slice.

The last batch of French books arrived by last mail; they are *Fleurange* by Mme Augustus Craven; *Anthologie Française*, a collection of small poetical pieces from the oldest times to our days; and *Le nouveau seigneur*, and another book, I forget the name; the two latter we did not ask for, but they were sent in place of the *Critiques et caractères contemporains* of Jules Janin, which we asked for and which is unfortunately out of print. *Fleurange* is a very interesting and readable book; if you read it, I am sure you will be pleased. *Le gentilhomme pauvre*, by Henri Conscience, recommended by our French master, M. Girard of St. Leonards, is very sentimental, dull and worthless. *Au coin du feu*, by E. Souvestre, also recommended by M. Girard, is good in its way, but meant more for children than adults. *Gazida*, by Marmier, is very nice but inferior to his other work, which I liked very much, namely, *Les fiancés du Spitzberg. Germaine*, by M. About, is very readable but not very moral. M. About does not know how to be dull, for from the driest subject he can easily bring forth a generous supply of amusement and interest. Enough of books has been said, so I had better drop that subject.

Our winter is coming in rather early this year; the weather is already pleasanter and the mornings are fresh and cool. Of course the *punkah* is yet a source of comfort, but very soon it will be no longer so. I want to go to the Garden for the winter, but Papa is rather averse to moving again, when we have just settled down here with our books. I hope Mamma and I shall be able to persuade him to dislodge. We went to the Old Church last Sunday. Our pastor, Mr. Welland, was absent; I think he has gone to the North West for a change, and so Mr. Clifford conducted the service and gave the sermon.

The *Doorga-Poojah* holidays have come, and all business men have left town for a change. Last Sunday was the day that the Hindus throw the goddess Doorga into the river, after a three days' worship! The streets were crowded to excess, processions, with the goddess, I mean with her image, borne in a triumphal throne and with music, marched towards the river. We thought we should be able to escape all the noise and crowd by going to Baugmaree for a day or two, but somehow we were prevented.

I have nothing to write about, so I will copy out for you one of my latest translations of French poetry. It is taken from the *Anthologie* which we received a fortnight ago and the author is M. Eugène Manuel, a poet of our times.

The History of a Soul

In secret from among the throng
God sometimes takes a soul,
And leads her slow, through grief and wrong,
Unswerving to her goal.

He chooses her to be His bride,
And gives her from His store,
Meek tenderness and lofty pride,
That she may feel the more.

He makes her poor, without a stay,
Desiring all men's good,
Searching the True, pure, pure alway,
But still, misunderstood.

Beneath a weight of pains and fears
He makes her often fall,
He nourishes her with bitter tears,
Unseen, unknown of all.

He spreads the clouds her head above,
He tries her hour by hour,
From Hate she suffers and from Love,
And owns of Each the power.

God's rigour never, never sleeps:
She waits for peace? In vain.
She struggles or resignèd weeps,
He strikes and strikes again.

In beings that she loves the most,
He wounds her till, half mad,
She wanders like a restless ghost!
A problem strange and sad.

Thus stricken, reft of joy and light,
God makes her fair and clean,

Like an enamel hard and bright,
A sword of temper keen.

Subject to Adam's debt below
And every curse and pain,
The Judge inflexible would know
If she will staunch remain.

Will she fight on, 'gainst every ill?
Brave every storm? Stand fast,
Her lofty mission to fulfil
With courage to the last?

And when He sees her ever true,
Like needle to the pole,
Upon His work He smiles anew—
Thus forges God a soul.

Do you like it? I have not given the original because it is long. If you are not tired, I will put in a piece of Mme Desbordes-Valmore's, the original and the translation.

ROMANCE, "S'IL L'AVAIT SU"

S'il avait su quelle âme il a blessée,
Larmes du cœur, s'il avait pu vous voir,
Ah! si ce cœur, trop plein de sa pensée,
De l'exprimer n'eût gardé le pouvoir,
Changer ainsi n'eût pas été possible;
Fier de nourrir l'espoir qu'il a déçu,
A tant d'amour il eût été sensible,
S'il l'avait su.

S'il avait su tout ce qu'on peut attendre,
D'une âme simple, ardente et sans détour,
Il eût voulu la mienne pour l'entendre.
Comme il l'inspire, il eût connu l'amour.
Mes yeux baissés recélaient cette flamme;
Dans leur pudeur n'a-t-il rien aperçu?

Un tel secret valait toute son âme,
S'il l'avait su.

Si j'avais su, moi-même, à quel empire
On s'abandonne en regardant ses yeux,
Sans le chercher comme l'air qu'on respire,
J'aurais porté mes jours sous d'autres cieux.
Il est trop tard pour renouer ma vie;
Ma vie était un doux espoir déçu:
Diras-tu pas, toi qui me l'as ravie,
Si je l'avais su?

Translation

If he had known—known what a soul he has wounded!
O heart, if thy tears had been seen but to flow,
Or if thou at his step less wildly hadst bounded
And guarded the power thy deep feeling to show,
He could not, he could not so lightly have altered,
Proud to nourish a hope now hurled from its throne,
By a love so profound, he, touched, must have faltered
If he had known.

If he had known what might be hoped and awaited,
From a heart in its candour, deception above,
For mine he had longed, with a joy unabated,
And as he inspired, would have felt also love.
Mine eyes bent down ever, concealed my emotion,
Guessed he nothing from that? was't shyness alone?
A secret like mine was worth search—and devotion,
If he had known.

If I had known—I—of the empire he wielded!
Over hearts that lived in the light of his eyes,
As one breathes a pure air—unconscious, unshielded—
My steps would have sought other countries and skies,
It's too late to talk of love-sign or love-token!
My life was a hope, but the hope now has flown!

HARIHAR DAS AND TORU DUTT

Wilt thou say when thou knowest?—"Oh heart I have broken
If I had known!"

I must close my letter now. I am sure you are quite tired deciphering it, by this time. I shall cover the next page and then close.

October 15th.

All Aru's pets are doing well. My bulbul too is in a flourishing condition, but unfortunately it has lost the power to fly; I wanted to set it at liberty, but it only hopped about; the reason is, I think, its being so very young when I had it and reared it by hand; it had been so long shut up in a cage that it had lost the power to use its wings, poor thing!

The Prince of Wales has left England, but he will not be in Calcutta till about the middle of December, just before Christmas. His carriages, nine in number, have arrived already in Bombay. I must close here. Give our kindest regards to your father and mother, and Papa's and Mamma's love to yourself.

12, Manicktollah Street,
Calcutta
November 8, 1875

Many, many thanks for your nice long letter, which I have just received and read with the greatest pleasure. The mail goes tomorrow, so I have sat down at once to write an answer and send it if I can, by tomorrow's outgoing mail.

We are all doing well, including Jeunette and Gentille, cats and guinea-pigs, but sad is the news about the birds: two of the canaries have been killed by rats; how they got into the cage is a mystery, but there were the poor canaries, one half-devoured and the other with a broken wing. There now only remain two canaries and one goldfinch.

Several days ago, a snake-charmer came here to show off his serpents; there were three cobras, two pythons and three two-headed snakes and several smaller ones, also ten or twelve mountain scorpions. Of course all the serpents had their poison fangs broken; the men are obliged to break them at least twice a month; it must be dreadful work. One of the cobras bit the man's finger so as to bring forth a few drops of blood, but of course it did the man no harm, as the poison tooth was broken. There is a root called in Latin, *Aristolochia Indica*, which has a marked effect on the most poisonous snakes; the man held this to the serpents and it was marvellous how it cowed them at once: they tried to sidle away as soon as they smelt it. But I doubt very much whether it would have any effect when a cobra is wild and free and attacks one; it is then blind with rage and no earthly power will turn it from its victim.

Drainage works are going on near our house, just in front of our coach-house, so we have sent our carriage to the Garden. We went there yesterday; my grandfather is ill with intermittent fever and as Connaghur (where he lives) has become very unhealthy, he wants to stay in our Garden for a fortnight or so; we went therefore to the Garden to make things ready for him.

The Prince of Wales will arrive at Bombay today; as soon as the news is received of his landing, every fort in India is to fire a salute. He will be here about Christmas. Some of the papers say he will never return to England, that his grave will be in India: cholera, fever, tigers, poison, the poniard, all are to be feared. I hope the papers will turn out false prophets!

We know the Reverend Mr. Vaughan of Calcutta; he lately lost his wife and went to England some months ago.

I am glad you like *Mill on the Floss*; I like it very much too. Have you read any of Thackeray's? I like his books immensely. *Esmond* is the best, and *Newcomes* and *Pendennis* are excellent. His books make me laugh, cry, smile, look grave, by turns; after having finished one of his books, one remains thoughtful for an hour afterwards. *Vanity Fair* too is very good.

9th.

The Prince of Wales must have landed at Bombay yesterday in the afternoon, for the Calcutta Fort (Fort William) fired a grand salute. Lord Northbrook has gone over to Bombay to welcome him. Among the suite of the Prince is Sir Bartle Frere, who was formerly Governor of Bombay, and whom we know very well. His daughters are very nice and amiable; many a merry day did Aru and I pass with them at Wimbledon. One of his daughters, Mary Frere, is the authoress of a book of Indian Tales, called *Old Deccan Days*; it is a very readable volume, and is illustrated by one of her sisters, I believe.

I am sorry to hear that Mrs. Hall is ailing, I hope she will soon be better. I trust your father too is quite well. I am sure you will be first at the French Lectures, if you attend them. We liked them very much; I suppose M. Boquel is the lecturer still. Do the Misses Hall attend them or have they left off? Do you see much of Mary and Lizzie Hall? If so kindly remember me to them and give our best regards to Mr. and Mrs. Hall.

As to our going back to England, it is still very uncertain, dear, but I hope we shall be able to go sometime or other, if not very soon. Instead of going to the Continent, as you purpose, what do you think of taking a trip out to India? It would be so nice, wouldn't it, dear? Oh! I do long to see you again! How kind of you to think so often of me! "Eh bien! vous pensez donc à moi!" said I, when I read that part of your letter, like the old *Sergent Trubert*, in one of Erckmann-Chatrian's tales, when his host brought him a glass of *kirschenwasser* early on a cold December morning, while he was at his post on the watch for the enemy.

Papa says the mail-day has been changed and that the day is Friday now instead of Tuesday, so I shall have ample time to write my letter.

The cold weather has fairly commenced. The mornings now are exceedingly cool and pleasant. The dews are very heavy in Calcutta during the early mornings and the late evenings, and the mosquitoes become more troublesome as the cold season advances. Oranges are coming in season; I am very glad of it, for I am very fond of oranges.

I have not received any letters from Mrs. Baker yet, but I hope I soon shall. Please give my kindest wishes to her when you see her.

An exhibition of pictures is to be opened this afternoon by Sir Richard Temple, the Lieutenant-Governor, in Calcutta. All the pictures have been brought out by an enterprising man, I forget his name, from England, and are the works of the most celebrated artists, past and present; viz., Lely, Gainsborough, Landseer, Reynolds, Delaroche, &c. Our Lieutenant-Governor is a little bit of an artist in his way, and is very fond of paintings. Have you ever been to the Royal Academy in London? I remembered how we enjoyed the pictures all the three seasons that we went there during our stay in England. I am exceedingly fond of pictures, though I cannot draw the easiest cottage, if I tried. Aru used to draw beautifully though she never learned drawing; she did flowers and fruit exceedingly well.

My uncle Girish and my aunt are going for a day's trip on the river in a boat tomorrow. They wanted us to accompany them, but as my grandfather and his family will arrive tomorrow at the Garden, we thought it better to go there and see them settled comfortably.

A few days ago, Jeunette ran away from the groom, while he was giving her the usual hourly exercise in the morning. This is how it happened. Jeunette is exceedingly fond of Gentille, and the moment Gentille is taken away from her sight, she begins to grow restless, fret, and paw and neigh in a state of great impatience. Well, the other day, they were both at exercise, but Gentille was a little ahead, and a turn of the road hid her for some time from Jeunette, who at once grew restless and at last broke from the groom and came galloping through streets and by-lanes straight to our house. She would have been off again, but our porter caught hold of the halter and led her back to the stable. Fortunately no one was hurt.

How pleasant your trip has been! I see from your letters, that you enjoyed yourself immensely. I am glad to hear that the Fishers have also had their holidays, and enjoyed themselves. Please give my regards to them when next you write to them. How pleasant it must be to go down the Rhine! I remember one of the Reverend W. Lisle Bowle's sonnets,—

> —On the sparkling Rhine
> We bounded, and the white waves round the prow
> In murmurs parted;—varying as we go,
> Lo! the woods open, and the rocks retire,
> Some convent's ancient walls, or glistening spire,
> 'Mid the bright landscape's track unfolding slow.

I am glad you took some sketches, during your trip, of the scenery round you; it will be very nice doing them up when you are at leisure.

I have not been reading much lately, except Reviews and Monthlies. My book of French poetical translations is almost finished. I have only to translate three or four pieces more and then I shall be able to print the book if I like.

Some days ago my uncle Girish and my aunt had fireworks in their compound: we all went of course to see them, they were very pretty. There will be grand fireworks on the Maidan on the 24th December, when the Prince of Wales will be here. When the Duke of Edinburgh came here, in 1869, I think, they spent more than £9,000 in fireworks. Was it not literally converting money into smoke and ashes?

Papa says he will take me to see the races on the Maidan, which take place usually in December. I should like to go very much.

Baguette, my pet cat, has got two very nice kittens, just like two little Persian kits; they are very playful; Mamma has named them "Day" (abbreviation of Daisy) and "May" respectively.

I have no news that would interest you, so I copy below two of Heine's smaller poems, translated by himself into French, and by *my*self into English.

"Le Message"

Allons, mon écuyer, en selle!
Plus rapide que l'ouragan,
Cours au château du roi Duncan,
Pour me quérir une nouvelle!

Parmi les chevaux glisse-toi,
Et dis au valet d'écurie:
"Quelle est celle qui se marie,
Des deux filles de votre roi?"

Et s'il te répond: "C'est la brune,"
Viens vite, et me le fais savoir;
Si "La blonde," reviens ce soir,
Au pas, en regardant la lune.

Entre en passant chez le cordier,
Prends une corde et me l'apporte,
Ouvre bien doucement la porte,
Et ne dis rien, mon écuyer!

(*Translation*)

To horse, my squire! To horse and quick!
Be wingéd like the hurricane,
Fly to the château on the plain,
And bring me news, for I am sick.

Glide 'mid the steeds and ask a groom,
After some talk, this simple thing—
"Of the two daughters of our king,
Who is to wed, and when, and whom?"

And if he tell thee—"'tis the brown",
Come sharply back and let me know:
But if "the blonde", ride soft and slow:
The moon-light's pleasant on the down.

And as thou comest, faithful squire,
Get me a rope from shop or store,
And gently enter through this door,
And speak no word but swift retire.

"NI HAINE NI AMOUR"

J'ai connu plus d'une inhumaine
Parmi les filles d'alentour,
J'ai beaucoup souffert de leur haine
Et plus encore de leur amour.

Elles ont dans ma coupe pleine
Versé du poison chaque jour,
C'était tantôt poison de haine,
C'était tantôt poison d'amour.

Mais celle qui m'a fait la peine
La plus déchirante, à son tour,
N'a jamais eu pour moi de haine,
N'a jamais eu pour moi d'amour.

(Translation)

Of girls unkind, though fair and stately,
This neighbourhood may count a score;
From their hate I have suffered greatly,
But from their love, oh more, still more.

In my brimming cup they have lately
Their poison shed as oft before,
Hate-potions sometimes, and then straightly
Love-philters that distress me sore.

> *But she whose name I love innately,*
> *Who gave the wound that struck the core,*
> *Moves tranquil on her way sedately,*
> *Nor hate, nor love, she bears or bore.*

Which do you prefer? Heine, you know, is a Jew by birth; he wrote a great deal in German: a French critic says that "nul écrivain depuis Gœthe n'a façonné l'idiome germanique avec cette puissance magistrale; on dirait parfois de véritables tours de force".

The *Poojah* holidays are over; yesterday was a holiday; there will be no more holidays till, I think, about Christmas.

Is Mr. Steinhelper, the German Lecturer, still in Cambridge? I suppose you never see the Cowells?[9] How are the Misses Oakes and their mother?[10] Please remember me kindly to all of them, especially to "Aunt Emily" as Mr. Smith used to style her. We are akin, "Aunt Emily" and I, because here I am styled by everybody, "Sister Toru"; my grandfather calls me so, and all my uncles and aunts, as also my cousins, and Papa sometimes, too, calls me "Sister Toru".

My letter must appear very dull to you, I am afraid, but I have tried my best that it should turn out the contrary. I have made it long, you see; I hope you are not tired making out my scrawl, are you?

Our pastor, Mr. Welland, has been in the North West for a change; so Mr. Clifford had to do the whole service last Sunday.

It gets very dark soon, now that the winter is coming on; before six it gets pitch dark and the heavy dews begin to fall. In the morning all the grassy compound and all the green leaves are glistening with big drops of dew like pearls;

> *"Là, tous les diamants de la rosée en pleurs"*

as says a French poet, M. le comte de Gramont.

I must bid you good-bye now. Papa and Mamma send their love to your dear self and their kindest regards to your father and mother. Please give my love to your mother and my best regards to your father, and with the very best love to yourself.

---

9. Professor Cowell and his wife.
10. Cousins of the Martin family.

Calcutta
November 23, 1875

I did not receive any letter from you by last mail. But I am writing to you now that you may receive this by Christmas.

We are all well here, the weather is beautifully cool and pleasant, real Indian winter weather. I suppose it is now beginning to be very cold in England. I wish I were there! You are aware how fond I am of the snow; *you*, I remember, dislike it very much.

The Prince of Wales has been highly pleased with the reception he has met with at Bombay. He is now out shooting near Bombay, he will have fine sport and no end of it in India. He will not be in Calcutta till about the 23rd December.

My grandfather and his family have settled down comfortably in our Garden, we went to see them yesterday and passed the whole afternoon with them.

Papa and I are going to begin Sanskrit in December; Papa says as there is no good opportunity to learn German now, we had better take up Sanskrit instead of doing nothing. I am very glad of this. I should so like to read the glorious epics, the *Ramayana* and the *Mahabharata*, in the original. I shall be quite a Sanskrit Pundit, when I revisit old Cambridge! Ah! I so long to be there, and like the Poet Laureate hear

> ——*Once more in college fanes,*
> *The storm their high-built organs make,*
> *And thunder-music rolling shake*
> *The prophets blazoned on the panes.*

and catch

> ——*Once more the distant shout,*
> *The measured splash of beating oars*
> *Among the willows——.*

I was reading the "Siege of Corinth" of Lord Byron lately; it is very beautiful; my uncle says it is the most complete of his smaller poems. Byron's "Lines written on attaining my thirty-fifth year", are very pathetic: they were written only three months before his death.

A great many people have died from cholera and fever lately, in Calcutta and the suburbs. One of our cousin's daughters, a girl of nine, died from cholera about a week ago; her father is a Hindu; she was taken ill on a Saturday morning and she died during the following night.

I have finished my book of French poetry translated into English; it is to be entitled *A Sheaf gleaned in French Fields*. I hope you like the title, do you? It is to be printed if I like. The concluding sonnet I shall copy out for you; it is not from the French, but is original.

Sonnet

"A mon Père"

The flowers look loveliest in their native soil
Amid their kindred branches; plucked, they fade
And lose the colours Nature on them laid,
Though bound in garlands with assiduous toil.
Pleasant it was, afar from all turmoil
To wander through the valley, now in shade
And now in sunshine, where these blossoms made
A Paradise, and gather in my spoil.
But better than myself no man can know
How tarnished have become their tender hues
E'en in the gathering, and how dimmed their glow!
Wouldst thou again new life in them infuse,
Thou who hast seen them where they brightly blow?
Ask Memory. She shall help my stammering Muse.

Do you like the sonnet? Papa does very much. There are 165 pieces of poetry in the volume, besides the notes affixed to each and all of the pieces. I have now nothing to do, so Papa and I are going to take up Sanskrit. It is a very difficult language and it is hard to learn it perfectly in less than six or seven years; but I will try my best. My grandfather, Papa's father, used to know and understand Sanskrit like a pundit; and he only learnt it for two or three years when he was forty-two or forty-three years of age; so I hope my case will not be hopeless.

November 29th.

We went to Church yesterday; and on our way we were stopped by a great crowd, with shrieking musical instruments in a narrow lane. It was some Hindu Festival. Jeunette got a little frightened and excited, and threw up her head and shook her silky mane in a manner that filled Papa's heart with terror and mine with admiration: Jeunette looked so handsome. If the carriage had been stopped in the midst of all this babel of noise a few minutes longer, I doubt if Jeunette would have stood it; but the cries of "*Khupper-dah*" (or "*gare*" in French) cleared the way in a trice, and we arrived at Church in safety.

My grandmother is very ill with fever; we shall go to see her today; my grandfather is quite well now, I am happy to say. It is pretty cold here now, like English spring weather, and the mornings are almost sure to be ushered in by a slight mist which puts me in mind of Longfellow's lines:

> *And resembles sorrow only,*
> *As the mist resembles rain.*

December 4th.

I have been rather busy for the last few days. On Saturday, Miss Ada Smith, a friend of ours, arrived in Calcutta from England. She came to see us on Monday; she is very nice and amiable; she has come here to teach in the Zenanas. We know her cousin very well, Mr. Algernon H. Smith, who was curate to Mr. Hall of Cambridge; he is now Rector of a parish in Tunbridge Wells. Papa passed three or four days at Miss Smith's uncle's house in Kent; Mr. A. H. Smith took him there and he enjoyed his stay with them immensely, and speaks even now about it. I like Ada very much. We took her on Friday last to our Garden. She was very pleased to see my grandmother and aunts, and was lost in admiration when my youngest aunt showed her her "casket of gems". She was charmed with the Garden and said she wondered we long to return to Europe when we had such an earthly paradise to live in and enjoy. She took me to be twenty-nine years old and my uncle to be twenty-six only! She herself is twenty-nine years old. I showed her your likeness and told her what a dear good soul you are. I am going to take her for a drive on Monday evening. It is a great pity that she is not going to stay in Calcutta; the Secretary of the Society has chosen Amritsar for her destination; he says that there a great field is open for Zenana teachers and that there are not half so many teachers there as are wanted. Ada is to go there by the middle of next week. I feel rather sorry at this; I like her so very much; she is like a whiff of the free bracing air of dear old England.

We have begun Sanskrit: the pundit is very pleased with our eagerness to learn, and hopes great things from our assiduity. It is a very difficult language, as I said before, especially the grammar, which is dreadful. It is not so difficult to read and understand it, for one who knows Bengali.

December 6th.

My grandmother is now quite well, but she is quite worn out by watching by my uncle and grandfather during the night: my grandfather had a recurrence of fever for the last three days, and on Saturday he was seriously ill. He is better now, I am happy to say. My uncle Genoo (that is my mother's brother) was taken ill four days ago; he is also in a fair way of speedy recovery. I hope he will soon be well, for my poor grandmother is in a sad state of perplexity and trouble. We went to see them yesterday, and very glad they were to see us. We met three of Mamma's second cousins there: one of them praised Jeunette and Gentille highly, and of course won my esteem at once! He admired their action and speed (he had seen me on the Maidan, he said), and how they were always up to their bits and how beautifully they carried their heads. He came out on the verandah when we left, to see them go. I am sure if I wanted to sell off my Gentille and Jeunette he would be the first to come forward as a purchaser; in fact he almost made an offer to buy them! I am so happy, I like my horses to be praised and deservedly too.

A few days ago a small cobra was killed in my uncle's garden. My aunt is very much frightened; she wants to have a snake-catcher and have the reptiles caught, if there are any more in her garden; but uncle Girish says, it would be great folly to try such a thing, for if the snake-catcher was bitten by a cobra, sure death would follow, and that such things had better be left alone. But my grandfather says, that he is sure that no such things would happen. He has seen the most venomous snakes caught alive by these professional snake-catchers and not one of them has he seen killed or bitten by a snake. A few days ago a cow in our Garden was killed by snake-bite; it was well and hearty overnight, but early the next morning, when it was brought out, the cow-keeper found it quite dull and foaming at the mouth; the floor of the cow-house was half covered with froth: the poor animal made a few steps, then tottered and fell and had frightful convulsions before it died.

The Prince of Wales is in Ceylon now; he has been enjoying himself heartily; he has had good sport around Bombay; he has ordered all that he has killed to be stuffed—from a crow to a tiger—to be borne home as trophies when he goes back to England.

I have nothing else to write about, and as the mail goes tomorrow, I had better close my letter. Please give my kindest regards to your father and mother, and with best love to yourself.

P.S.—Do not forget to send your likeness when it is taken. Papa and Mamma send their best regards to your father and mother and best love to you. I hope you will be able to read this scrawl. The ink is execrably bad and pen ditto. A Merry Christmas and a Happy New Year to you and yours.

12, Manicktollah Street,
Calcutta
December 13, 1875

On our return from Church yesterday morning, I received your most welcome and interesting letter. I first felt it when I was holding it in my hand, with my fingers, to see if it enclosed your photograph, and I was disappointed at not finding your likeness within your letter. Please have your likeness taken, dear, as soon as possible; you do not know how anxious I am to see it. I will send you the three different views taken of our Garden House and Garden at Baugmaree; I hope you will like them; our Calcutta house has also been photographed, but the photograph has turned out such an ugly one that I do not care to send it to you. You need not pay for the postage, dear, I hope I am not so reduced in circumstances just yet!

We are very very sorry indeed to hear of poor Mrs. Hall's serious illness. We liked her very much, and dear Aru and I were very fond of her good motherly ways. It will be indeed a hard blow for her family, especially for Reginald, her only son: she is so fond of him and he of her. God help them all.

I do not know Mr. Haldar personally himself, but I know his father very well, for he is our family doctor; that is, it is Dr. Haldar whom we generally call in if anybody is ill in our house. He is now treating my grandfather, who is still very ill; indeed the doctors gave up all hope; there was no pulse and the limbs and feet were clammy; Papa went at midnight to see him. He got over it however, and we hope he is out of danger now. I shall tell Dr. Haldar that you met his son; I am sure he will be glad to hear it.

Your account of your drive with the C.'s and your horror on discovering who would drive, put me in mind of one of John Leech's sketches.— Scene, Greenwich: the last train has gone, and the senior party, under the impression that the vehicle was a brougham, has accepted the offer of a lift to town.—*Senior Party*. "Dog-cart! Good gracious! But *you* are never going to drive?"—*Junior Party*. "Not going——a——dwive? Why not going——a——dwive? Jus——ain't I, tho?"—You should see the picture, it is a masterpiece.

Great preparations are going on to welcome the Prince. Up-country Rajas and Maharajas are coming down in great numbers. Every day we see one or two of these Rajas with mounted retinues, all in gold and purple, pass along the broad streets of Calcutta. All the thoroughfares through which the Prince of Wales is likely to pass are almost blocked with building materials for arches, &c. The fort and the barracks have been newly painted. Even the lamp posts are re-painted a bright green. The Prince is only going to stay a week here. Some Raja or other has had an upper garment made, all studded with pearls and precious stones, which he means to wear when he meets the Prince, and which has cost him fifteen lakhs of rupees! Another will spend thirty lakhs during the three days the Prince will stay in his dominions.

During the Prince's sojourn in Bombay he visited Lady Sassoon, a Parsee lady: her husband is very rich, and they have bought a house and lands somewhere near London. On the landing of the Prince, Parsee maidens, daughters of rich and influential men in Bombay, went before him, scattering flowers and singing a welcome. One day when the Prince was out driving, a Parsee lady came out of the door of her mansion (I forget her name, she was the wife of a rich merchant and we used to know some of her kin, when we were in Bombay), and stopping the carriage, presented the Prince with a gold-embroidered smoking cap, made by her own fair hands. Of course the Prince accepted the present with many thanks and much grace, as befits a gallant gentleman! The Parsee ladies are far ahead of our Bengali ones.

I have not read anything lately, so busy am I with my Sanskrit. The grammar is awfully difficult, though in reading and understanding we get on pretty swimmingly. I have not read *Middlemarch*. I have read many reviews and critiques on the book, both in French and English, and of course that gives me a good idea of the work. You should read *Wives and Daughters* by Mrs. Gaskell; it is a highly interesting and well-written work; I am sure you would like it.

All my pets are doing well; Jeunette and Gentille are quite well and sprightly; they are both exceedingly fond of me and have come to know even my step when I come downstairs; they prick up their ears and Gentille neighs and Jeunette paws with pleasure at my approach. They are beautiful trotters, especially Gentille; they will trot their fifteen miles within the hour easily, without sweating. I am so fond of my horses!

Miss Ada Smith, of whom I wrote to you in my last letter, is going to stay here till the 20th instant, and then she will leave for Amritsar; I am very glad of this delay; I shall see more of her.

So you are not going to have any more "bald-headed darlings" just now! Papa laughed at that so, and declared what a dear little soul you were and what a good memory you had to remember all our little doings amongst you! O Mary, I do so wish to see you again! I hope we shall be able to sell off the Garden soon, and then set sail for England! So Miss A. L. is making quite a sensation, and is the "toast of a' the town". Please give her my love, when you next write to her.

I hope you like M. Boquel. He is rather rough with ladies, but he has a great sense of justice and wrong, and gives every one her due among his lady-pupils. We liked him very much indeed when we used to attend his lectures. Many funny incidents happen during the lectures; is it not so? I remember how everybody was amused when a certain young lady translated, "Quel beau barbe!" into "What a beautiful *beard*!" when it ought to have been, of course, "What a beautiful Barbary-horse!" What books do you read at the lectures? Are there many pupils? Do you have dictation? Do Mary and Lizzie Hall attend the French lectures still? I want specially to know what French books you read at the lectures and from what French books M. Boquel gives the dictations. I am sure they will be very nice and interesting books and very healthy in their tone too; I should therefore like to read them; we used to have *Le Philosophe sous les toits* by Emile Souvestre and *Le Roman d'un jeune homme pauvre* by Octave Feuillet. They are both very interesting and readable books. I suppose you do not take any music-lessons now, do you? Does Dr. Garrett give the lectures on Harmony still? Why do you not attend the German lectures too? I suppose you have hardly the time for them.

It is very cold here now, that is, very cold for Calcutta; in England this would be considered nice pleasant spring weather. The oranges are in full season now; I wish I could give you a taste of our oranges, they *are* so delicious! Even the celebrated Maltese oranges are nothing compared to ours. Then we now get the beautiful pomegranates from Afghanistan, and the grapes and the pears from Cabool. The grapes are not larger than the English ones, only they are of a different shape, being rather longer than the English ones, which are round and far better than our grapes. The English grapes have a luscious flavour, mixed up with their sweetness, which reminds me of very good wine; our grapes, or rather those that we get from Cabool, are only very sweet; they have no tempting flavour like the English ones. We get very good cauliflowers, cabbages, peas, carrots, &c. I mean to give a feed to Jeunette and Gentille daily of carrots, when they are cheaper. Horses are very fond of carrots.

The Christmas holidays will not begin till about the 18th. I do not think we shall have any Christmas tree here this time. We generally used to have one in our house every Christmas. We used to go all together on the morning of Christmas Eve to the Garden-House and choose out a goodly, immense, and leafy branch, which the gardeners used to hew down in our presence; we used to place it on the top of our carriage and bring it home amid triumphant and happy laughter. "Hélas! le bon temps que j'avais!"

December 15th.

We are just come in from a drive and from shopping. Mamma did not go with us. Only Papa and I went. Papa showed my book of French translations to a publisher here; but Calcutta publishers are a very timid class of people, not at all enterprising, and they are besides more given to the sale of books than publishing new ones. The publisher referred Papa to another one, who, he said, knew more about these things, and was a better judge in such matters. Of course he praised the translations very much, and was half willing to take them and publish the book.

Calcutta is extremely busy with the preparations for the welcome to the Prince. As we went to the European quarter of the town we saw the preparations going on.

I must close now; a merry Christmas and a happy new year to you and yours. I have written a letter to you by last mail, so I shall not make this one longer.

V

Letters to Miss Martin,
January 1876—December 1876

Calcutta
January 13, 1876

My dear Mary,

I received your welcome letter on Sunday last. I have not been able to answer it sooner, on account of being very busy copying out my book for the press and correcting the proofs. The book consists of about one hundred and sixty pieces of French poems translated into English. I shall send you a copy as soon as the book is out. It is to be printed only, not published, and it will be ready about the end of February.

Many many thanks for your kind wishes, and for the Christmas card; it will be all the more precious as being made by yourself. I should indeed very much like to have a sketch or two of your own drawings, if it is no trouble to you.

I have sent off a packet to your address, containing three photographs of our garden at Baugmaree. I hope you will receive it safely.

The Prince left Calcutta on Monday last. We had capital opportunities of seeing him, though we did not go out with the fixed purpose of seeing His Royal Highness. Once we were out driving in the forenoon, on the Strand, and we saw him driving down to the *Serapis*, to lunch. We were going rather slowly, and his carriage was also going at a slow rate, so we had a good look at him. Our carriages passed each other, and I had a good view of his pleasant and rather handsome face and his merry blue eyes. I suppose you have seen him, have you not? He has very beautiful auburn hair, though he is a little bald near the forehead. Russell described him, when he was going to be married to the Princess, in the well-known lines of Scott, only varying one or two words for the occasion.

Blue *was his eagle eye,*
And auburn of the richest dye
His short moustache *and hair.*

We saw him again on the morning when he was going to open the Chapter for conferring the honour of knighthood on several of the big-wigs here. Papa saw him very well at the Belgachia entertainment given to him by the native community of Calcutta. We have also seen some of the Rajas and the Maharajas who came down to Calcutta during the Prince's sojourn there. The Maharaja of Cashmere had a *pugree* (headdress) on his head, which was at least worth forty lakhs of rupees, so bejewelled it was. He has given a great many very valuable presents to the Prince, amongst which are hundred and one Cashmere shawls of the best material and the most "cunning" workmanship, a *hookah* of gold set with diamonds and precious stones, a gold tea service, a gold dinner service, a silver bedstead, a tent of Cashmere workmanship with silver posts, and I do not remember the others: besides presents for the Princess. The Prince is now in Lucknow; at Benares a rich zemindar presented to him a crown worth six lakhs of rupees.

There is a good deal of talk at present about a Bengali gentleman and a pleader, Babu Juggodanundo Mukherjee, because he permitted the Prince to see his Zenana. All the papers conducted by natives are loudly crying out against this "Outrage on Hindu Society". The Prince did not visit any private gentleman at his own house, and only went to Babu Mukherjee's because he was promised that he would there be shown a real Zenana of native ladies of high position. This "Scandalous behaviour", as the papers say, of the above-named Babu, is unpardonable in the eyes of the greater number of Hindus. The *Daily News* of Calcutta had a very sensible article on the subject. It said that if the Babu means to bring out his family, as in English society every European does, and let his friends visit and mingle with his family, as behoves civilized men and manners, he is a very well-meaning man, and his aims are very laudable; but if he has only made an exception for the Prince and his suite, and means to "lock up" his wife and family, as all Hindus do, his allowing the Prince to visit his family is a bit of flunkeyism, quite unpardonable, and worthy of the highest disapprobation. Is not this sensibly and fairly put?

Lord Carrington, who is with the Prince, is very unlucky on horseback; he had a fall from his horse at Bombay, but fortunately escaped; he lost some of his teeth, while out on a shooting-party near here, by the handle of a spear, with which he had speared a boar, striking his mouth, and now he has had another fall, during the last shooting-expedition, which has dislocated his collar-bone. He will be all right in a fortnight or so, the papers say. Lord Hastings, who also accompanied the Prince, died of jungle fever at Madras. He was very young, being only twenty-one years of age. It must be sad for his family, who sent him away on this pleasure trip, full of youth and hope; it makes me sad to think of it.

Our Governor-General, Lord Northbrook, has resigned. He will be a great loss to India; he is greatly liked both by the native and European community. He will leave in the spring. Lord Lytton, son of the famous author of that name, is to succeed him. Lord Lytton is a poet himself; his *nom de plume* is Owen Meredith. Lord Northbrook's horses are to be sold by auction on Saturday next, which is a piece of rather interesting news to me!

The *Serapis* and the *Osborne* are open to the public, but we do not care much to go and see them.

I am very sorry to hear that your father has been so ill; I am very glad that he is better now. Is the winter very severe and trying this year? Our winter is now very pleasant: imagine the warmest day of spring with cloudless blue sky!

One of my aunts, who was a Hindu and a widow, and who used to live next door to us, died very suddenly, about a fortnight ago, of heart disease. She was subject to sudden and severe attacks of pain near the heart, but she did not think them anything serious. On the night of the 27th December (the night of the Belgachia entertainment) she returned at about eight o'clock from witnessing the street illuminations; at four in the morning she was taken ill with one of her attacks of pain, and in half an hour she died. Her death was so sudden and unexpected that her daughter (who was staying with her at the time) had not the time to send for a doctor. She sent word to her two brothers soon after her mother was taken ill, but when they arrived they found her dead. She was taken to the *Ghaut*, and burned the same day, according to the Hindu rites.

A rather amusing story is told about the Prince. While at Bombay he visited some school (I forget the name). On seeing a prismatic compass lying on the table, he asked the school boy nearest him what it was; the boy (somewhat agitated I suppose at being questioned by Royalty itself) answered, stammering: "A royal com—com—pass, your prismatic Highness!" At this the whole company could not help smiling, and the Prince himself burst into a hearty laugh.

There is another amusing story about the Duke of Sutherland. He did not come to Calcutta from Madras with the Prince, but came a day later and by rail. His train, though, was three hours later than the appointed time, and the carriages sent from Government House to receive him at the station, tired of waiting, as they well might be, returned. When the train arrived, the Duke, finding nobody waiting for him, told the station master to get him a "cab". The hackney coachman refused to take a *sahib* he did not know; he had fears about his hire. He was told that the *sahib* was the *burra-sahib's* (Governor-General's) brother, but he held out till a policeman got up on the coachbox and obliged him to carry his lordship to Government House.

We went to see the horses at Chitpore, a place three miles from here, where annually, in the cold season, horses are brought down from the upper provinces and from the Government studs for sale. There are a great number of them this season. Beautiful cows and sheep are also brought down from the upper provinces for sale at Chitpore. The cows and calves are extremely handsome; some have ears quite drooping, and hiding their pretty faces: they also give more milk than the Calcutta cows. My own Jeunette and Gentille are doing well. I often apply to them (when speaking of them to any one) the words which M. Scaufflaire, in Hugo's *Les Misérables*, applied to his horse, when recommending him to a purchaser: "Elle est douce comme une fille, elle va comme le vent." My uncle used to pride himself on the swiftness of his horse, but my Jeunette and Gentille beat his horse twice; and since then my uncle does not mention the speed of his galloway!

I am very very sorry to hear all what you say about dear Mrs. Hall. I am afraid that in your next letter you will announce her death. Poor lady! We all used to like her very very much.

I am glad to hear that you met Mrs. Cowell. Please give her my love and Mamma's when you next meet her. I daresay the book she has promised to lend you is *Govinda Samanta*, for Professor Cowell had, I know, very kindly undertaken to correct the proofs and to do the needful.

How is Mrs. Baker? I have not yet got any answer from her to my note. I hope she is quite well.

All the drainage works in and near our house are finished. I cannot describe the relief we find at this! When are you going to have your likeness taken? I hope very soon, and please to send me one as soon as you can.

I have not been reading anything lately; indeed I have entirely been taken up with my book for the last week. The printer makes such dreadful mistakes sometimes. In one of Victor Hugo's *chansons*, where the lines should have run,

> *If there be a loving heart*
> *Where* Honour's *throne is drest,*

they printed as follows:

> *If there be a loving heart*
> *Where* Horror's *throne is drest.*

And again in another piece: "The Mother's Birthday," the children, addressing their mother, say:

> *Then to please thee in our duties,*
> *We shall try to do our best,*
> *Never lift our heads while* praying,
> *Just before we go to bed.*

The printer has it thus:

> *Then to please thee in our duties,*
> *We shall try to do our best,*
> *Never lift our heads while* prying *(!)*
> *Just before we go to bed.*

Mamma had one of her attacks of pain a week ago; but she is quite well now, I am happy to say. I am pretty well at present; the cough is there still, a little more troublesome than it was in the summer, with blood-spitting off and on; but, on the whole, I am better now than I was in January last, a year ago.

We are going on with our Sanskrit lessons. When we have finished the book we are reading now, we shall take up Valmiki's *Ramayana*. My uncle has followed our example, and has commenced reading Sanskrit also, with another pundit.

I hope you will be able to decipher this scrawl. Please give our kindest regards to your father and mother. Mamma sends you her love, and with best love from myself,—Believe me, yours very affectionately,

Toru Dutt

Calcutta

February 28, 1876

I am so very very happy to receive your dear likeness. I am never tired of looking at it, and I have placed it already in my album. So kind of you, dear, to wear my hair always in a locket round your neck. Mamma says she will be highly pleased to get a copy of your likeness; she says she must have one as soon as possible.

I have received two letters from you during the last fortnight, one containing the Sanskrit grammar marker[11] (for which many thanks to you and your mother), and the other enclosing your long expected photograph. I have been unable to answer them sooner, on account of my having been taken ill with fever and dysentery, with an increase of the cough. It is a fortnight or more that I have been obliged to keep my bed. Now I am able to get up and move about a little and take a drive in the afternoon, according to the doctor's orders. The dysentery is gone, and though the fever comes on now and then, it is always slight. The cough is still troublesome, but I hope it will soon get better. Now that my health-bulletin is written, I shall go on to other things. I hope you will be able to read this scrawl, for I am writing in bed. I do not know how long it will take me to finish this letter, perhaps a week; but, dear, I feel such an irresistible desire to write to you, and above all, to thank you again and again for your photograph. O, I do wish to go and see you once again so much!

Des ailes, des ailes, des ailes,
Comme dans les chants de Rückert!

My book is almost ready now; I hope to be able to send you a copy before the end of March.

I must stop here for the present, for I feel a little tired.

It is beginning to get hotter now here. The evenings are cool enough, but the days are a little too warm, though there is almost always a nice refreshing south wind in the afternoon.

I had Gentille and Jeunette taken by a native photographer. I wanted to send you two copies, but the photographs turned out so indistinct and bad after all that I rejected them, and as the artist had tried at least thirty times without success, I gave up the affair as hopeless.

---

11. This was a marker in cross-stitch, on thin perforated cardboard, with the words: "Here I fell asleep!"

We have sent for another French book from England; it is entitled *La Femme dans l'Inde Antique*, and is the work of a lady; it has been "couronné" by the French Academy, so it must be a well-written book.

The Prince is at present the guest of the Maharaja of Cashmere. He is having very good sport there; one day he killed six tigers with his own gun; the forest where the tigers are has been surrounded by six hundred trained elephants to cut off every kind of egress from the jungle. The Prince will arrive at Allahabad about the seventh proximo, on his way back to Bombay, which city he will leave about the 14th of March. The *Serapis* and the *Osborne* left Calcutta a few weeks ago; they are now at Bombay, waiting for the Prince. Lord Northbrook will leave Calcutta in a day or two, to meet the Prince at Allahabad and bid him farewell. The Governor of Madras, His Grace the Duke of Buckingham, is at present in Calcutta. We saw him two or three times during our evening drives. The Prince, it is said, is keeping a diary, which he means to publish on his return to England. It is to be edited by Dr. Russell, and will no doubt be very interesting reading.

Several weeks ago a man brought a large cobra to show us. He is a blacksmith by profession, but has initiated himself a little in the mysteries of snake-catching. This reptile he had caught himself only four days ago. A doctor of the neighbourhood had given him two rupees for the poison teeth, which the doctor himself extracted with a pair of pincers. The reptile was very fiery and full of life. It would not come out of the earthen vessel (in which it had been placed): at last the man had to draw it out by the tail, at which it hissed frightfully.

The visit of the Prince to Babu Juggodanundo Mukherjee's Zenana has been made into a farce and acted at the native theatre here under the title *Guzadanundo*. This was a very bad action on the part of the managers of the theatre, and Lord Northbrook has very rightly put a stop to it, and by an Ordinance has empowered the Lieutenant-Governor to suppress any play which is likely to create any disaffection against the British rule, also any play which the Lieutenant-Governor thinks immoral or unfit to be represented.

March 2nd.

Mamma had a very bad attack of her pain yesterday at half past eleven in the forenoon; she suffered a great deal yesterday and last night. Today she is much better; the acute stage of the attack is past; there is still a dull sort of pain, but I hope it will quite pass off in the course of the day. My grandfather and grandmother came to see her yesterday, and stayed all night; grandmother kept awake the whole night through, so did Papa; grandfather and I slept. I hope father will not get ill. Grandmother has now gone to the Garden-House; she will come again in the afternoon; she is an invaluable person during illness, so patient and careful.

March 3rd.

Mamma is a great deal better today. I hope she will soon be quite well and strong again. Today we received a visit from Mr. Jones of the Bengal Civil Service. We knew him very well at Cambridge; he used to come to learn Bengali from father. It seemed so funny to see "Jones, undergrad of St. John's", turned into the Anglo-Indian *burra-sahib* S. S. Jones, Esqre., B.C.S., with a large *sola* hat!

He was very glad to see us again. He is now stationed at Sasseram and came down to Calcutta yesterday; he is going away again today.

The day before yesterday my mother's *cousine* was married. She is a Hindu and so is her family, so of course we were not invited. We heard all the particulars from my grandmother, who had been invited. Hindu marriages generally take place during the night or late in the evening. There are some very pretty ceremonies to be gone through. When the bride is unveiled she meets the gaze of the bridegroom for the first time. After a good look at each other, they exchange the garlands of flowers round their necks. Then a small bouquet is given to each, which also they exchange with each other, and which are also afterwards put by in a box. Toward morning the bride's mother takes her daughter's hand, puts it into that of the bridegroom, and tells him most pathetically and with tears in her eyes, to take care of her daughter, whom she now resigns to him.

March 4th.

Today is my twentieth birthday: I am getting quite old, *n'est-ce pas? La Femme dans l'Inde Antique* arrived most opportunely this morning; I received it as my birthday present. It is a big volume and seems very interesting. I was looking it over here and there.

Are the Fishers still in Germany? Have you seen Mrs. Baker lately and is she a little better?

Jeunette and Gentille are quite well and flourishing in health. If you could see all the books I have bought about horses, and the veterinary art! I have also now got a veterinary medicine-chest. I make a tincture or an ointment myself now and then, according to the prescriptions in one of my veterinary books, and I myself doctor Jeunette and Gentille when they want it, which I am happy to say is very seldom.

Latterly there has been some rain and the days are close and sultry. I hope there will be a change for the better in the weather soon, for this hot sultry weather makes one feel very sleepy! O, for a breath of the biting, refreshing March wind! I hope to write to you again soon. I trust you have received the photographs of Baugmaree safely and in good preservation.

If you should see Mrs. Cowell again, please give my love and Mamma's and Papa's kindest regards. I am glad you like M. Boquel. Does he continue to live in the house opposite Sayle's shop?

Papa went to see the sale of Lord Northbrook's horses: among the lot there was a grey Arab saddle-horse which was very beautiful; Papa said it seemed a *little* too spirited and fiery to suit me, or else, he said, he would have bought it for me; I have been begging so much and so long for a riding-horse; I hope he will give me one, but as I have never ridden before, he is afraid. Dr. Cayley (who attends us during our serious illnesses) has such a beautiful roan Arab saddle-horse; it is only a little *too high in flesh*, otherwise it is a perfect animal. I have nothing to write about, and I am afraid you will find this letter very dull. There! I hear the carriage wheels on the gravel; grandmother is come to see Mamma, I must leave off.

March 7th.

I have been obliged to give up Sanskrit for some time. I shall begin again from today if my pundit comes, for his wife was unwell on Saturday, suffering from cholera.

Lodgers are coming tomorrow into the house lately occupied by one of my aunts, about whose sudden death I wrote to you in my last. Her son has let it to a native Christian Babu, who will occupy the premises with his family either tomorrow or the day after.

I have been lately only reading articles from the *Revue des Deux Mondes*. I shall now take up *La Femme dans l'Inde Antique*. It will be very interesting reading, as it will give me a good insight into the old Hindu legends, which I hope to be able to read in a couple of years in the original Sanskrit.

I must close my letter here, as the mail leaves today. By the by, Sir Salar Jung is going to England. The Duke of Sutherland invited him, it is said, to go and see the "Barbaric West". If he is going only as the guest of the Duke, or for political reasons, is not known, though it is generally thought that he is going for the latter. Mamma is better, but she is not able to leave her bed yet, I am sorry to say.

If you call on the Misses Hall, please give them my love, and tell them how deeply I feel and sympathize with their loss.

Give kindest regards from all to your father and mother, and my best love to yourself.

Calcutta
March 13, 1876

Many many thanks for your long and welcome letter which I have just received. What a lot of questions all at once! I am going to describe our house and answer your questions first of all. There is no conservatory at Baugmaree; the shrubs that you see through the open door on the ground floor grow on the lawn; the rooms on the ground floor are, beginning from the left-hand side, a long drawing-room with three windows, then a small antechamber, then appear the two windows of the verandah, the front door, two windows, which also belong to the verandah; the last window belongs to a small outside room, where Papa receives his *acquaintances*; the drawing-room being reserved for *friends*. I must go over it again, for I have omitted one room; after the three windows of the drawing-room and the one of the antechamber, comes that of the library, then the verandah, &c.; in front of the last room (where Papa's acquaintances are received) you see a small verandah: it is very nice sitting out there; Mamma has had it surrounded with a wire network, which has been covered with creeping plants, and which makes the place more inviting. On the second floor, beginning from the right, first, there is the window of our dining-room (the staircase is just below that window), then the next window belongs to a small room, which is generally known as the "clock-room" (because our clock is kept there), and which is furnished "à l'orientale" with cushions, &c., where we take our ease during the heat of the day; the next three windows belong to the bedroom and the last two belong to the bathroom and the closet; on the third floor, there is only one room, which is generally used as the lumber-room. On the right hand side of the house you perceive another building: this contains the pantry, kitchen, and out-offices. I have explained all that is visible in the photo, I hope satisfactorily. Now I shall say a little more of what is not visible in the photo. The rooms which appear in the photo look to the south: on the north there are similar rooms: that is, on the second floor, there is Papa's bedroom and another extra room, on the ground floor, three extra rooms, two small and the other large. You see we have quite enough room to lodge you and your father and mother if you come here! The men standing in the middle of the walk must be some of the gardeners: do you perceive Mamma's favourite cow and calf to their left? The bridge is *inside* our Garden and belongs to us; it conducts to the small island which is surrounded all round by the sheet of water (which is called a *jheel*), which is crossed by the bridge. The little island is full of mango trees which we have let out this year for a considerable sum. The building is not *on* the bridge (though it looks as if it were, on account of the bad photo), but opposite it, and is the domicile of our gardeners or *mâlees*. I must stop here, for luncheon is ready. Have I explained it all satisfactorily, dear?

Skating rinks are already on the *tapis* here; I believe they have one already at Bombay. A new zoological garden has just been started in Calcutta; it is far from being complete yet, but specimens are pouring in of all kinds of animals; the tigers, elephants, Cashmere goats, &c., &c., which the Prince has received as presents from the Rajas, were kept there, pending their removal to the *Serapis*. The zoological grounds are also to contain an aquarium. Calcutta will soon be quite a European city!

Thank you very much for what you say about calling my countrymen "natives"; the reproof is just, and I stand corrected. I shall take care and not call them natives again. It is indeed a term only used by prejudiced Anglo-Indians, and I am really ashamed to have used it.

About my age. It is not a forbidden subject at all, and if I did not answer your question it must have been from mere carelessness. I was born in 1856, so I complete my twentieth year and enter into my twenty-first this March.

I am sure your composition will receive M. Boquel's approbation, for there are very few English girls in Cambridge that know French as well as you do.

If you see Miss Rosie Fullerton again, please give her our kind regards; also to her aunt. I am sorry that she wants to leave St. Leonards, for we liked the place very well when we were there. Give my best wishes to Miss A. L. if you write to her on her birthday, please. Mr. Mittra is a Bengali; I am sure of this from his name, though I do not know anything about him. There are many Bengalis now in England; almost by every mail we see a countryman's name in the list of passengers for

England. All generally go either to compete for the Civil Service, to enter the Bar, or to be created an M.D. by the Edinburgh University. If they could only enter on new careers, say, as civil engineers, naval commanders, or military officers: I believe they are not allowed to enter the military or naval service as officers here. There are Bengali troops and soldiers, but they generally are commanded by Europeans; perhaps the Government thinks it dangerous to place a Bengali regiment under the orders of a Bengali officer.

My book is now almost ready; you will receive it by the end of April. The Prince is now on his way back to Bombay, whence he will start for England. He is now at Indore, I think. Canon Duckworth (who was tutor to Prince Leopold) is very ill; it is believed he will be unable to accompany the Prince on his way back, as he is very weak: he will follow his Royal patron in a few weeks.

Last night we had a great shower of rain, which has freshened up the trees and flowers amazingly.

As I had been ill, Jeunette and Gentille had an uninterrupted rest of three days; on the fourth day I went out; they were beautiful to see in their eagerness to start; like a horse described in a book that I was reading lately: "elles étaient terribles d'impatience"; a cart stopped their way just as they started; they reared; then, the road being cleared, went off "comme un trait".

Have you read any of Mrs. Barrett Browning's pieces? I like her poetry very much. There are some verses of hers called the *Wine of Cyprus*, addressed to H. S. Boyd, who used to teach her Greek. When I am reading Sanskrit, some of these verses occur to me *malgré moi*. The Sanskrit is as old and as grand a language as the Greek.

> *And I think of those long mornings*
> *Which my thought goes far to seek,*
> *When betwixt the folio turnings,*
> *Solemn flowed the rhythmic Greek—*

Mr. Boyd was blind and she addresses him thus, in one of the last verses of the piece above mentioned:

> *Ah, my gossip! you were older,*
> *And more learned, and a man;*
> *Yet the shadow, the enfolder*

> *Of your quiet eyelids, ran*
> *Both our spirits to one level:*
> *And I turned from hill and lea*
> *And the summer sun's green revel,*
> *To your eyes that could not see.*

If Papa laughs when I make a mistake in my Sanskrit (which he does very rarely, but which he can do much oftener, for he understands Sanskrit better than I do), I quote the above two lines:

> *Ah, my gossip! you are older,*
> *And more learned, and a man!*

Then her piece entitled "The dead Pan" is very beautiful too. Listen:

> *O twelve gods of Plato's vision,*
> *Crowned to starry wanderings,*
> *With your chariots in procession,*
> *And your silver clash of wings!*
> *Very pale ye seem to rise,*
> *Ghosts of Grecian deities,*
> *Now Pan is dead!*

> *Jove, that right hand is unloaded,*
> *Whence the thunder did prevail,*
> *While in idiocy of godhead*
> *Thou art staring the stars pale!*
> *And thine eagle blind and old,*
> *Roughs his feathers in the cold.*

> *. . . . . .*
> *Bacchus, Bacchus! on the panther*
> *He swoons, bound with his own vines;*
> *And his Maenads slowly saunter,*
> *Heads aside, among the pines,*
> *While they murmur dreamingly,*
> *"Evohe——ah——evohe——!"*

I shall be quoting the whole piece! It is founded on the well-known story relating to the death of the Lord; that while he was being crucified, some boatmen who were on the sea in their boat heard a great cry of "Pan, Pan is dead". Her other pieces *Bertha in the Lane, Catarina to Camoëns, The Swan's Nest, The Romaunt of the Page*, and others I like very much also. But I shall be quoting them, so I shall leave off the subject. Her verses entitled *A View across the Roman Campagna* are very good: in them she addresses the Pope in no very flattering terms. *A Musical Instrument* is an exquisite little piece.

I have just come in from measuring out Jeunette and Gentille's *picotin*, and from peeling and cutting in small pieces a long piece of sugar-cane for them. Horses are very fond of sugar-cane, which has the qualities of the carrot, in giving them a shining coat, &c.

Do you see a small mound in front of the house in Baugmaree? Well, it is one of Mamma's *chefs-d'œuvre* in gardening; it is composed of pebbles and earth, covered over with green grass and planted with shrubs and trees; it is supposed to be a miniature mountain. Isn't this making a mountain of a molehill?

Mamma is now quite well. It was only yesterday that she came downstairs for the first time since her illness.

The weather is extremely hot now, and the punkah has become a necessity. A large banian tree which stood on a piece of ground lately bought by a neighbour (and in front of our house) has been cut down by the new proprietor. We were all sorry when we saw the men cutting its fine large branches; it was a tree of long standing; as far as Papa can remember it has stood there. It reminded us of a French poet, Laprade's, lines on "La mort d'un chêne":

> *Quand l'homme te frappa de sa lâche cognée,*
> *O roi qu'hier le mont portait avec orgueil,*
> *Mon âme au premier coup retentit indignée,*
> *Et dans la forêt sainte il se fit un grand deuil.*

The piece is rather long but rather well written. Speaking of fine verses, I subjoin the following lines, which are extremely beautiful and which show how, with a few touches, a truly great poet can describe scenery. I came across the lines in the *Revue des Deux Mondes*: they are by M. André Theuriet (some of whose pieces you will find translated in my book) and entitled *La vigne en fleurs*. I shall copy a paragraph and the verses from the *Revue:* "La pièce était à la fois lyrique et descriptive, le poète avait essayé de rendre l'espèce de griserie produite par la fine senteur des vignes fleuries dans une tiède soirée de Juin. Il se peignait pris lui-même par cette enivrante odeur. Il remplissait son verre et buvait joyeusement aux noces fécondes des vignes et à la poésie du vin. Dans ces vers imprégnés d'un naturalisme voluptueux, on respirait l'haleine du printemps et les chauds parfums de l'automne; on entendait les rumeurs du pressoir, le bouillonnement du moût écumeux dans la cave, les rondes tumultueuses des vendangeurs, la nuit, sur les coteaux.—Puis le poète, sentant sa tête s'alourdir, laissait tomber sa coupe vide, et la pièce se terminait par cette strophe:

> *Je m'endors, et là-bas le frissonnant matin*
> *Baigne les pampres verts d'une rougeur furtive,*
> *Et toujours cette odeur amoureuse m'arrive*
> *Avec le dernier chant d'un rossignol lointain*
> *Et les premiers cris de la grive——"*

Are they not fine, these lines? I have very little news to give you, so you see I have been filling up my letter with quotations; if you get tired of them, skip over without any ceremony.

About my cough, Dr. Cayley says Europe or even the south coast of England in summer would do me a great deal of good. There is nothing serious at present, but that my lungs are very delicate, and so on. I should like to go to England very much, just to see you, dear. Then I should like to go to the South of France in the vine country, to be all day long in the fresh air, to breathe *cette odeur amoureuse* of the vine. I am sure that will set me to rights at once. There are so many things to be done before we can go, and sometimes when I am *attristée* I think it would be better to live here in my own country all my life, but this thought does not occur often.

I must finish my letter tomorrow, and send it off early, for the mail goes tomorrow. I shall stop for today, for I have got to dress and get ready for my drive; it is already 5 P.M.

March 14th.

Last night as I was thinking about you, I heard the cry of the jackals. You have never heard it, and I am sure you would be startled, if you ever come out to India, to hear it for the first time. In the suburbs especially the jackals are very numerous. In Baugmaree, how often have I been awakened by their dismal wailing in the still hours of the night.

I sometimes am unwilling to go to sleep again, for fear that I should be again awakened by their lugubrious cry. It is not so bad when they are close under your window, but when the weird *hurlement* comes from a distance, one is filled with a sense of the loneliness of the place and the stillness of the night.

Yesterday we received two more books from Hachette and Company, books which we did not send for, but which they have forwarded to us, because there was a balance in our favour in their hands. The books are a poem, *Olivier*, by François Coppée, and *Le conscrit*, a tale by Henri Conscience. I have not read them yet, so I am unable to pass any judgement on them.

Have you been to see the Misses Hall? Please give them my love when you go to see them. I have not read *Govinda Samanta*; I am glad you like it. I am sure the author, Mr. Dey, would be very much flattered if I told him what you think about his book.

I shall give here for your edification the song of welcome sung to the Prince by Bengali musicians at the entertainment given to him at Belgachia. It is from the pen of an influential and wealthy Bengali gentleman, Raja Jotendro Mohun Tagore.[12] He made it originally in Bengali, but translated it himself into English for the benefit of the European part of the audience.

> *Hail noble prince! All hail to thee!*
> *With joyous voice we welcome sing;*
> *As bursting into festive glee*
> *Bengala greets her future King.*
>
> *Tho' humble our reception be*
> *And tho' our strains may halting run,*
> *The loyal heart we bring to thee*
> *Is warmer than our Eastern sun.*

Isn't he a promising genius?

The Prince of Wales has started from Bombay for England. The Lahore paper says "that he has invited Ressaldar Anoop Singh, a well-known native officer of the 11th Bengal Lancers, one of the finest specimens of an Irregular Cavalry officer that could be found anywhere,

---

12. Afterwards Maharaja Sir Jotendro Mohun Tagore, K.C.S.I.

to accompany him in the *Serapis* to England. The Ressaldar was with the detachment under Major A. H. Prinsep, which formed H.R.H.'s escort during his tour through the Terai. We have just seen a note in which he announces the fact of his approaching departure to Europe to a European officer. He simply puts it thus: 'The Prince asked me to come to England, and of course I could not refuse.'" If this is true, it shows a high sense of obedience and discipline and loyalty in Anoop Singh, as it must be with considerable inward qualms that a Sikh made up his mind to cross the *Black Waters*, that is the seas. Anoop Singh is said to be a most handsome man, well made, with a striking appearance, and he will in all probability attract much attention as a sort of "show man" of the Indian army.

The ex-Gaekwar of Baroda, Mulhar Rao, finding time lie heavy on his hands in his prison at Nungumbakum, has devised a means to amuse himself. Twice a week an apothecary waits upon Mulhar Rao, equipped with a suitable apparatus, and to the bewilderment of the ex-Baroda chief and family conducts experiments in chemistry. The apothecary of course receives a remuneration for his performances, but whether the chief thereby receives more instruction than amusement is a moot question.

A new Photographic Exhibition has been opened here. We have not yet been to see it, but we shall go some day. The building from the outside has a very imposing and grand appearance.

Some degrees were conferred on several distinguished men yesterday at the Calcutta Senate House. Professor Monier-Williams was one of them. Papa had a card but he did not go. And now, dear, I must say good-bye. I hope to write to you a more interesting letter next time, *pour vous dédommager* of this one. Give kindest regards of Papa and Mamma to your father and mother, their love to you. Love to all and especially best love to your darling self.

Calcutta

March 24, 1876

I send along with this letter a copy of my *Sheaf gleaned in French Fields*. I have not had it bound in cloth, but I send it to you in its original paper cover, as it is easier for transmission thus than otherwise. Write and tell me which of my pieces you like best.

I am pretty well just now, but a few days ago my cough increased, and I spat some blood: it was all owing to a window being left open in my bedroom, on account of the extreme heat and closeness of the weather.

Our Governor-General, Lord Northbrook, is going away on the 7th proximo. He will be a great loss to this country, for he was beloved by the Bengalis, and he highly deserves to be so.

Some of the Prince of Wales's horses were lately sold in the Punjab by auction; I suppose they were the presents of some of the Rajas here and the Prince finding them to be rather too numerous has sold them. Lord Beresford bought a few, a pair of Walers and an Arab. The Prince has taken with him, besides his three English hunters and his own horses, some more, presents from the Maharajas and Chiefs; among them are a team of small grey Arabs, a chestnut Arab saddle-horse for the Princess, and a pair of hill ponies, to improve the breed of the Shetland ponies at home. There is rather a good story going about the papers lately, which has highly pleased the Bengalis. At some public reception or other, the Prince of Wales observed a European push a Bengali gentleman roughly from the platform. The Prince immediately sent his aide-de-camp to interfere, and was highly displeased with the European official, and the Duke of Sutherland and others expressed their displeasure at the European's conduct, who, on the other hand, seemed very much surprised at this general condemnation of his conduct, and at the interest of the Prince in favour of a "native!" You see how my countrymen are treated by Anglo-Indian *Sahibs*!

I have lately been reading *Tolla*, a novel by E. About. The book is founded upon fact; the scene is laid in Italy. M. About was accused of plagiarism, but he has defended himself by saying that founding a story on a true fact is not plagiarism, &c. It is a very nice and interesting book. *Olivier*, a poem by François Coppée, is not bad reading; there are some very fine passages, for instance, this charming little picture: the writer is supposed to be a blasé young man of the world, and here is a description of his friend's daughter, a young country girl:

> *Espiègle, j'ai bien vu tout ce que vous faisiez*
> *Ce matin dans le champ planté de cerisiers*
> *Où seule vous étiez, nu-tête, en robe blanche.*
> *Caché par le taillis, j'observais. Une branche*
> *Lourde sous les fruits mûrs vous barrait le chemin*
> *Et se trouvait à la hauteur de votre main.*
> *Or, vous avez cueilli des cerises vermeilles,*
> *Coquette, et les avez mises à vos oreilles,*

Tandis qu'un vent léger dans vos boucles jouait.
Alors, vous asseyant pour cueillir un bleuet
Dans l'herbe, et puis un autre, et puis un autre encore,
Vous les avez piqués dans vos cheveux d'aurore;
Et, les bras recourbés sur votre front fleuri,
Assise dans le vert gazon, vous avez ri,
Et vos joyeuses dents jetaient une étincelle.

Mais pendant ce temps-là, ma belle demoiselle,
Un seul témoin, qui vous gardera le secret,
Tout heureux de vous voir heureuse, comparait
Sur votre frais visage animé par les brises
Vos regards aux bleuets, vos lèvres aux cerises.

The weather is very hot now; in the middle of the day it is as hot as it must have been in the fiery furnace: except in the mornings and evenings, which are pretty cool and pleasant yet. One would like to sit the whole day under a water-pipe, or in a bathing tub! One can never appreciate cold water enough till one comes to Calcutta! Instead of saying: "O, that I had the wings of a bird!" "O, that I had the fins of a fish" would be more appropriate here.

All my uncles and cousins have been praising my book to the skies. I am afraid I shall burst with vanity some of these days, like the frog in the fable, who tried to be big as an ox.

Our Sanskrit is going on, we are making but slow progress; I hope it is sure progress also. By the by, in my *Sheaf*, you will find among the notes two Sanskrit lines, from the *Ramayana*. They are uttered by Dasaratha, King of Ajoudhay (modern Oude), when he was obliged to send his eldest son, Ram, into exile in the forest of Danaka, on account of a rash promise given to one of his wives (Ram's stepmother), to grant her her desire. She asks for Ram's banishment and the coronation of her own son, Bharata. On this the king bursts in a passion of grief. His reply to the queen is beautiful. The lines in my book mean that, "The world may live without the sun, the corn without water, but my soul will not live in my body without Ram." Would you like to pronounce the words in the Sanskrit? Then read:

Thistai,	loko	bina	shurjong,	shoshong	ba
might live	the world	without	sun,	corn	or

		sholilong	bina,			
		water	without,			

Nau	tu	Ramong	bina	dahay	thistaytu	momo
not	but	Ram	without	(in) body	shall live	my

jibitom
life.

I wonder what the papers will say of my book. Of course there will be *for* and *against*, and I have already armed myself with stoicism.

When *Jane Eyre* was first brought out, of course there were some papers which cut up the book. Thackeray, who was a friend of Miss Brontë, went to see her the day after, to observe how she read and took an attack on her book which had appeared in one of the leading daily papers.

Please write and tell me M. Boquel's address, as perhaps I shall send him a copy of my *Sheaf*.

Have you seen the Halls lately? Do Mary and Lizzie attend any of the lectures?

We do not go much into society now. The Bengali reunions are always for men. Wives and daughters and all women-kind are confined to the house, under lock and key, *à la lettre!* and Europeans are generally supercilious and look down on Bengalis. I have not been to one dinner party or any party at all since we left Europe. And then I do not know any people here, except those of our kith and kin, and some of them I do not know.

The remainder of Lord Northbrook's horses are to be sold on the 28th. I have asked Papa to go and have a look at them.

The life we lead here is so retired and quiet that I am afraid you find my letters dull.

Bishop Milman is dead; he succumbed to an acute attack of dysentery, and congestion of the liver. Bishop Gell of Madras is now in Calcutta, a guest of Lord Northbrook; he is temporarily officiating as Bishop of Calcutta, and it is said he is likely to be permanently so.

Jeunette and Gentille are well, so are all my pets.

Have you read a book by Frederika Richardson, published by Macmillan and Co. and entitled *The Iliad of the East*? It is an abstract of Valmiki's Sanskrit poem *Ramayana*. I am sure you will like it, and I can heartily recommend it to you, as it will give a good idea of the heroes and heroines of our mythology. I have no doubt that Mrs. Cowell has one, for you know that Professor Cowell is a great Sanskrit scholar and admirer of Sanskrit literature.

28th.

I hope you will excuse the shortness of my letter. It is all due to the dearth of news. Have you ever taken a young coco-nut? I daresay not. Those that we do get in England are old and over-ripe fruits, but a green coco-nut is delightful. The milk on a thirsty and sultry day is most refreshing, better than the best champagne. Water melons are coming into season now: by the by, Professor Cowell considers the water melon the best fruit in India. Mangoes are not ripe yet; the unripe mangoes we eat cooked, put into curries and sauces. Cholera has shown itself in the suburbs and in Calcutta too. I hope it will soon disappear.

I have sent two more copies of my book to Cambridge, one to Mrs. Cowell and the other to M. Boquel. I was saying to Papa that M. Girard, our French tutor at St. Leonards, would be pleasantly surprised if he were to see my book (for he dabbles in poetical translations now and then) and I should rise ten times more in his estimation. M. Boquel, on the contrary, is likely to say, that translating is good, but I would have done better if I had applied myself more to the "beautés de la grammaire française", and instead of wasting my time on light literature, had learnt "les verbes irréguliers" by heart!

I must "shut up" now. I am really ashamed of my scrawl. Give our best regards to your father and mother, and my best love to your dear self.

Calcutta
April 24, 1876

I received your nice long and interesting letter yesterday. Many thanks for the same; by the time this reaches you, you should have received my book. I should like to hear which of the pieces you like best, and also those you dislike most. Papa likes *A Souvenir of the Night of the Fourth* and *On the Barricade*, both by Victor Hugo, most; he thinks them the two *best* pieces in the volume. I agree with him. The papers have been noticing it favourably. The notices of the *Hindu Patriot* (edited by Babu Kristo Dass Pal), the *Englishman* (Mr. J. W. Furrell, editor), and the *Indian Charivari*, I like best. To the last-mentioned paper we did not send my book to be reviewed, and I am thankful to the editor (though I do not know his name) for his kindly and unexpected notice.

The article in the *Englishman* was generous and candid, pointing out some mistakes in the versifying, but altogether very favourable and sincere, with some extracts from the book, namely—*To Pépa* by Musset, and the last sonnet addressed to Papa. We wrote off to the editor in the well-known verses of the poet-laureate:

> *I forgave thee all the blame,*
> *I could not forgive the praise!*

Mr. Furrell must have been quite flattered in receiving the poetic note.

Lord Lytton, our new Governor-General, arrived the week before last and has gone away to Simla on Saturday, where he will pass the hot and rainy seasons. Lord Northbrook of course is on his way to Europe. A good many people were gathered to bid him "Farewell and God-speed" near the jetty. He shook hands with all who were present, taking care not to miss a single person in the crowd; he wore a sad yet genial expression on his countenance, and very suitable to the occasion.

On Friday we went to the Garden to meet the sister of my younger aunt. My uncle, as I have already written to you, my maternal uncle, that is, has got two wives. The eldest is not fair, *neither* very pretty (Leah in fact), so my uncle married a Rachel. My "new aunt" as we call her, though she is no longer new, for she has been married about eighteen years, though she is only twenty-six now—my "new aunt" is, on the contrary, very fair and very beautiful, and very good-natured into the bargain.

We wanted to see her elder sister, a great beauty, and so my "new aunt" brought her to our Garden to meet us; also she brought her younger sister, a little lassie of eight, already married, and oh, such a beauty! She has been photographed, and my "new aunt" gave me a copy; it is a beautiful photo and can vie with any face in an annual of beauties.

I also received a photo of my "new aunt's" father, Raja Narendra Krista, whose name I dare say you have come across among the reports of the visit of the Prince of Wales to Calcutta. He is a very nice kindly old gentleman; I have only seen him once or twice. He was a very handsome man in his youth and very "fast" too; many an English beauty of Calcutta he has led out for a quadrille in Government House "when *he* was young"; perhaps he adds like Coleridge (if he has read that poet, which I doubt very much) "Ah, woeful *when!*"

I have finished *La Femme dans l'Inde Antique*. It is very interesting, and I liked it very much. I heartily recommend it to you. You would then see how grand, how sublime, how pathetic, our legends are. The wifely devotion that an Indian wife pays to her husband, her submission to him even when he is capricious or exacting, her worship of him, "as the god of her life" as old Spenser has it. The legend of Nala and Damayanti, that of Savitri, who followed "Yama" (Pluto of the Heathen) even to the lower regions, and by her wisdom, her constancy, her love, made him give back to her her dead husband alive; the legend of Sacountala and Douchmanta; that of Queen Gandhâri, who, because her husband was blind, put a band on her own eyes, thus renouncing to enjoy a privilege which nature had denied her husband: "Lest I come to reproach my husband for his misfortune," said she. And last, but not least, the grand legend of Ram and Sita.

Mademoiselle Bader thus sums up the character of Sita: "D'ailleurs, dans quel siècle, dans quel pays, dans quelle littérature chercher un type plus admirable que celui de Sita? Quelle lyre jamais chanta plus pure et plus touchante héroïne? Quelle création analogue rencontrer chez les tragiques d'Athènes et les poëtes de Rome? Et, dans les temps modernes, depuis les héroïnes de Shakespeare jusqu'à celles de Racine, où trouver ce suave mélange d'amour, de chasteté, de grâce, noble et naïve, de dévouement passionné, de dignité, de fidélité au devoir, qui font de Sita le modèle idéal de la perfection féminine?"

You ought indeed to read the book or even *The Iliad of the East* by Frederika Richardson, to get an idea of the nobleness of my country's heroines. . .

The weather is awfully hot now, there is a very comforting and strong south wind today, but the sun is as hot and glaring as the fire of the fiery furnace must have been! I wish we could exchange our weather with yours: send us some of your cold weather and I will send you some of our hot!

Jeunette and Gentille are going on capitally well. I wish you could see them so sleek and fine, with their black manes and their slender black feet; they are dark bay in colour, not a single white hair have they; and they are—so beautiful! Sometimes I take them out to grass, myself, early in the morning; they never misbehave when with me, neither do they so with anybody. They know my voice and even my step from another's; Gentille whinnies with pleasure and Jeunette turns her soft dark eyes wistfully towards me and pricks up her delicate small ears.

I am writing to you from the roof of our house. It is nearly 5 P.M. and the sun is going down in the West. It is very cool and breezy up here. Day and May, our favourite kittens, are basking in and enjoying the last rays of the departing sun. Day has jumped up on my writing table to coax out a pat and caress from me. My inkstand is in imminent danger, as well as my letter. There! Day has jumped down to run after a crow, without spilling the ink! . . .

Papa went to see the sale of the last lot of Lord Northbrook's horses. There was a splendid Irish gelding, brown, bred by the late Lord Mayo, and his favourite riding-horse, aged eleven years. It was bought for Lord Lytton; there were also some nice Arabs, among which was the grey which Lord Northbrook used the most often to ride, and on which we saw him three or four days before his departure, when we were taking our evening drive. I like to hear Papa's descriptions of the horses, and he goes, when there are likely to be excellent ones in the auction, to please me, and also himself a little, for he is very fond of horses.

So you are quite rich! Je vous en fais mes compliments! What are you going to do with your money? I should advise you to take a passage out to India in one of the P. and O. steamers and come and see us in our Indian home, qu'en dites-vous? We should be so pleased to see you; you can be quite sure of a warm welcome and of hearty friends; "pensez-y bien, belle Marie" (the original has "marquise").

Spelling bees must be very amusing. There are funny accounts of how Mr. Lowe, M.P., was floored by the word "brazier", which he spelt with an "s" though it was clearly told him, that he was wanted to spell the word which means the person who deals in brass! and the Lord Mayor also made some funny mistakes.

Have you seen, or been at, a skating rink? It must be pleasant if there were no falls! Mistress Day is teasing me again, naughty pussy.

The Sanskrit is going on tolerably well; we are now reading the *Ramayana.*

The census of Calcutta was taken a few days ago; I asked Papa to put in my column "Authoress" as a profession, with which request he did not comply!

I had the first mangoes of the season from our Garden for breakfast just now. They were delicious. I wish I could send you one with this letter!

What beautiful cold weather you are having at present! I wish I was there!

Do tell me which of the pieces in my book your papa and your dear mother like? You see I am full of my book! *Entre nous*, I confess I am a little proud of it! Though I see its faults as well as its merits.

I am quite as rich as you are, dear! For I have got in the Savings Bank about the same sum as you have in the Cambridge Building Society. If I was not afraid of people calling me extravagant, I would spend the whole amount in buying a splendid stud of horses!

What *shall* I write about? Our cow, one of our milch cows, that is, did not give any milk for two days running. Voici pourquoi: a servant had the stupidity to introduce a large owl into the dairy; the cows got so frightened that they ran out quite wild from the shed, and it was a whole day's work catching them! and though this happened about five days ago, the cows do not on any account approach the shed, and we have been obliged to keep them in another. One of our best hens, with a pair of young turkeys which she had hatched, was run away with by a jackal, to Mamma's great sorrow and dismay! Are not these very interesting items?

The Maharaja of Pattialla died a few days ago at Simla of apoplexy. His infant son succeeds him.

I am sure you will like *Wives and Daughters*. It is a very well-written and interesting book. All the Brontës were rather inclined to the sensational in their works, but they are wonderfully interesting. *Wuthering Heights* treats of the supernatural, I have heard, for I have never read the book; I have only read *Jane Eyre* by Charlotte Brontë. Though the *moral* is not very high (for the authoress favours bigamy), the work is written with a masterly power, and shows a gift of discerning characters, which is wonderful in a woman. If you once commence the book, you will not be able to sleep unless you finish it! Have you read any of Thackeray's works? They are very good. I must stop my chatter for a while to read the paper.

My grandfather has hired a house and garden near ours, where he intends to stay with his family for three or four months. We went to see them yesterday; they will remove today, and we are to go and see them this evening in their new home. I wish you knew my grandmother; a kinder, or gentler, or more loving woman never breathed. How all her dear face lights up when we go to see her! I wish she would become a Christian. She is so much better than many who profess to be Christians, but whose conduct is anything but so. And she is so fond of me and so proud of me, is my grandmother! She thinks me the handsomest, the best, and the most accomplished girl that ever breathed! She would spoil me quite, if I lived with her a week! And she is so proud of Papa! You know that Hindu mothers-in-law generally do not talk with their sons-in-law. Isn't that funny? When Mamma was ill she came and stayed with us, keeping awake two nights running. . .

I have just been turning over a collection of Shirley Brook's poems, which have been chosen out from his contributions to *Punch* by his son. I have come on a piece which I cannot help writing out for you. It is entitled "Dagon" and is on the death of Nicholas, the Emperor of all the Russias, in 1855. It appeared in *Punch* and created a great sensation at the time. It is finely written and is full of spirit.

> *Smitten—as by lightning—smitten*
> *Down, amid his armed array;*
> *With the fiery scroll scarce written*
> *Calling myriads to the fray.*
> *There—but yesterday defying*
> *Europe's banners, linked and flying*
> *For her freedom—see him lying*
> *Earth's Colossus—earth's own clay.*
> *Let no triumph-shout be given,*
> *Knee to earth and eye to heaven!*
> *God hath judged the day.*

> *Ark of Freedom! lightly-spoken*
> *Vows to thee vain kings have said,*
> *Many an oath thy priests have broken,*
> *Many a flight thy guards have fled:*
> *But thine ancient Consecration*
> *Sealed as oft by stern libation,*
> *Lifeblood of a struggling nation,*
> *In the foeman's doom is read.*

> *Still, O Ark! the hand that gave thee*
> *Strikes, in peril's hour to save thee*
> *Here lies Dagon—dead!*

Have you read any of Bulwer Lytton s novels? The *Last of the Barons* is very interesting and well-written, in the Walter Scott style. He once attacked the Laureate in a satire in Pope's style, calling the Tennyson school, "Miss Alfred!" The Laureate answered him in verses which were anything but school-girlish and which appeared in *Punch*. Lord Lytton attacked him under the nom-de-plume of the *New Timon*, and the Laureate, after alluding to Shakespeare's *Timon of Athens* says:

> *——here comes the New,*
> *Regard him: a familiar face;*
> *I thought we knew him. What, it's you,*
> *The padded man that wears the stays;*

> *Who killed the girls and thrilled the boys*
> *With dandy pathos when you wrote;*
> *A Lion, you, that made a noise,*
> *And shook a mane* en papillotes.

> .   .   .   .

> *What profits now to understand*
> *The merits of a spotless shirt,*
> *A dapper boot—a little hand,*
> *If half the little soul is dirt?*

I quote from memory, so you must overlook mistakes if you find any.

It's dreadfully hot today, even the crows seem oppressed by the heat and keep silent, except now and then, when a very thirsty one utters a parched "caw!" The grass on the lawns has assumed a dry burnt-up appearance, which is never seen in England. In the streets, horses are often falling down, smitten by heat apoplexy. The other day we saw one: poor animal! it seemed to suffer terribly; it was unable to rise, and dashed its head against the pavement in vain efforts to do so; water, large bucketfuls, was thrown over it to relieve its pain, but to no purpose. I am afraid and never allow my Jeunette and Gentille to be driven during the middle of the day for fear of their getting sunstrokes.

Please give my love to A. L. when you write to her. I am sorry to hear that your dear father has not recovered quite from the effects of his last illness, but I hope he will with the warmer weather. I am keeping well myself; so is Papa and Mamma. My grandmother has made lots of chutnies, Indian jams, &c., which are exceedingly palatable, I can tell you, notwithstanding their extremes of being either too acid or too hot, &c. Best love to your dear self, and love and kindest regards from all to your father and mother.

Baugmaree Garden House

May 3, 1876

I am sitting down to write to you, not that I have anything new or special to say, but because I know each letter *from* me is sure to make you write an answer *to* me; and your letters are such a treat, never mind whether they seem to yourself short, dull, long or stupid, they are always very welcome things to *me*. If you could see how eagerly I tear open the envelope, after first reading my address in your dear well-known hand, and looking at all the postal marks, you would write oftener, I think.

You see that we have removed to the old Garden House. We came away from Calcutta on Monday last (today is Wednesday), it is so much more pleasant here than in the town.

Mamma got a very bad fall yesterday, but she is all right now. At 2 P.M. (you cannot imagine how hot it is at that hour), she went downstairs, notwithstanding our protests, to give some orders about her poultry house. She was sitting on the steps, when all at once she fell down—the sun and the heat were too much for her—she was so dazed after her fall, that she could not remember anything that had happened the minute before.

We thought she had received a sunstroke, and it was very like one; however, eau-de-Cologne, cold water, and an unripe mango, boiled and made into a *sherbet*, soon set her to rights. She is quite herself today; I hope this will prevent her for the future from going out of doors during the heat of the day, *malgré nous*.

I am *very* well, so is Papa. Pets also are thriving.

I make the horses go through their morning exercises myself; I generally take Jeunette, and one of the grooms takes Gentille. Jeunette trots along the long walk (see the photograph), I running by her side, both enjoying ourselves immensely. Gentille and the groom bring up the rear. Today after the trot, Jeunette's beautiful eyes fell upon the bunch of roses I had at my belt. She smelt them, took one daintily, and ate it with relish; then she took another and allowed me to keep the rest! I see them dressed and cleaned before me, except when I am inevitably prevented from being present.

One of our cows was delivered of a fine dark red calf a few days ago. Plenty of fresh milk and butter are the happy consequences.

Our Sanskrit is getting on well enough; our Pundit will from today come here to give us our lesson.

Mangoes are coming now, but those of our Garden are not fully ripe yet. Lichees are still in season, but they will soon disappear, as they are like the strawberries in England, very short-lived. I must stop here for the present, as I am going out to measure my horses' *pittance*. It is already hot now. Excuse this scrawl; the next sheet, I hope will be written more intelligibly.

I wish I could send you one of these *champa* flowers which are on the table in a glass of water. They are of a pale yellow colour, with six petals, three outside and three inside, and they have a beautiful strong fragrance which fills the whole room. The glass of water also contains one *Gunda-raj* (literally, king of fragrance). It fully justifies its name; its odour is a *little* fainter than that of the *Champa*, but very sweet. It is a snow-white flower. I wish you could see our Indian flora. Our Garden in the early morning is full of sweet sounds and fragrance. Just in front of the window, by which I am sitting, is the great Banian tree or Indian Oak, which was planted by my grandfather (paternal grandpa) before I was born, more than twenty years ago. Is it visible in the photo I have sent? I am afraid not. We have received our first basket of *Jum-rools* of the season this morning. They are a boon this hot weather and are of a whitish colour, with just a shade of very pale green, very luscious, large as a nectarine and a great thirst-quencher.

Several days ago, we paid a visit to an old friend of my father's and of my grandfather, too, Mr. Manickjee Rustomjee, a Parsi. This is the second time that I have paid a visit to any friend since our return to India! We only stayed half-an-hour, as Mr. Rustomjee himself was unfortunately out, but his son received us very cordially and introduced us to his sister; his mother also came in; she knew us while we were in Bombay in 1863. They wear the Parsi costume. Mrs. Rustomjee does not know English and spoke to me in Hindustani, and said: I was that height (indicating a certain height with her hand) when she last saw me in Bombay. Her daughter is rather handsome and very fair. She spoke

English very well. I was rather amused by her abruptly asking me if I had any children! Was not that amusing? I had to confess that I was not even married. Marriage, you must know, is a great thing with the Hindus. An unmarried girl of fifteen is never heard of in our country. If any friend of my grandmother happens to see me, the first question is, if I am married; and considerable astonishment, and perhaps a little scandal, follows the reply, for it is considered scandalous if a girl is not "wooed and married" and a' before she is eight years old! The other day one of my Grandmother's cousins was not a little taken aback on my replying to his question if I were not married, that I was now going to, since I had his permission, for it was only his permission that I had waited for! He was the more surprised, as I was looking over a picture book, like the meekest and humblest of human beings!

There is something about *me* in the paper today; Papa is reading it aloud, so goodbye for a moment.

It is now 2 P.M., and the sun is at its height; it is quite dazzling to look on the scene before me, tanks, lawns, and trees. There is nothing for us to do, but shut up all the shutters, and *se tenir coi* in the room with just one south window open, for the south wind is here always welcome.

I was lately reading Charlotte Brontë's *Life* by Mrs. Gaskell: indeed it is only today that I have finished the book. To think of those three young sisters in that old parsonage, among the lonely wild moors of Yorkshire, all three so full of talent, and yet living so solitary amid those Yorkshire wolds! The quotation in the beginning of the book from Mrs. Barrett Browning is very appropriate, at least so it seems to me:

> *Oh, my God,*
> *Thou hast knowledge, only Thou,*
> *How dreary 'tis for women to sit still*
> *On winter nights by solitary fires*
> *And hear the nations praising them far off.*

How sad their history is! How dreary for the father to see one by one all his children die, and to live on alone and infirm, in that solitary parsonage in Yorkshire! In truth there is no greater tragedy in fiction than what happens in our real, daily life.

Today Papa and I saw a large snake, about six feet in length, just below the steps of our front door; its movements were so rapid that it had disappeared in the round garden plot in front of our house (*vide* photo) before we could kill it: fortunately it was not of a very venomous kind. We caught a small wild hare in our Garden lately; we are going to let it go free this evening, as, poor young thing, it seems home-sick or rather warren-sick! When I told Uncle Girish about it, he was in raptures, a live wild hare! he is a keen sportsman, and fond of guns and fowling-pieces, &c., &c. He means to try and bag a couple of hares in our Garden some day, for Baugmaree is full of them! One of our guinea-pigs is afflicted with a *goitre*. It is very hideous and distressing to look at, the poor animal has got quite thin; it will soon die, I hope, for existence in its present state is a calamity.

Last night Papa and I, sitting out in the verandah, were expatiating on the calm beauty of the scene before us. I am but a poor hand at description, but I shall try to tell you what were then before us. The night was clear, the moon resplendent; one or two stars glimmering here and there; before us stretched the long avenue bordered with high *Casuarinas* very like the poplars of England; dim in the distance the gateway; around us the thick mango groves; the tall betel-nut trees, straight, "like arrows shot from heaven"; the coco-nut palms, with their proud waving plumes of green foliage, and all wrapt in a sweet and calm silence. Papa said the scene was as lovely as any we have seen during our sojourn in Europe. I agreed with him.

The papers are still noticing my book; the *Indian Mirror* has, it seems, noticed it. I have not seen the notice yet; I must go to town tomorrow and buy yesterday's issue.

This letter is very meagre; please excuse it; it is only to get an answer out of you, that I have penned this; I am going to prepare my Sanskrit lesson, the pundit will soon be here. Kindest regards from all to your father and mother, and best love to your dear self.

Dear! dear! what a smearing.

Baugmaree Garden House,
May 13, 1876

Your long-expected and welcome letter came this morning. Many thanks for the Easter card; it is very pretty and has pleased me very much, the "Forget-me-nots" too are very welcome and pleasant to me. They brought to my mind some French lines:

Lors que je serais mort, oh je vous en convie,
Si vous vous rappeliez une heure de ma vie,

Amis, où d'amitié j'ai oublié la loi,
Oubliez-moi.

The piece is of about eight verses; I should have copied it out for you, but unfortunately I have not got the book with me. It ends with the poet's saying that if some one of his acquaintances were to say that he (the poet)

——était un bizarre égoïste,
Un damné misanthrope, un pédagogue triste,
Pas plus qu'en son génie en quelque autre il n'eût foi,
——Oubliez-moi.

But if some other—

——se lève et dit,—Mensonges!
Il croyait au grand Dieu qu'il voyait dans ses songes,—
Et quand il était seul, il priait à genoux,
——Souvenez-vous.

But truce to quotations and poetry!

Mamma thanks you very much for the photo; you know how she will value it.

Some bits of your letter brought tears to my eyes; I do not deserve all your kind affection. Papa is so pleased to read your letters; after reading them, his invariable remark is: "Let us return to England; where in Calcutta will you get such warmhearted friends, Toru?" "Where indeed," say I. And it is four years since we last met! How swift Time passes. I was about sixteen then, "in my life's morning hour, when my bosom was young"—now I am getting quite old, twenty and some odd two months, and with such an old-fashioned face that English ladies take me for thirty! I wonder if I shall live to be thirty.

Don't fear that I shall resort to any rinks, if they come in use here. I am not very social, or rather, I am somewhat shy of a large company of ladies and gentlemen "enjoying themselves"; whenever there used to be a dance on board (on our way from and to England), I used to beat a hasty retreat into the saloon or in our cabin as soon as I saw preparations going on for it, such as removing benches, lighting lights, opening the piano, &c.

A few days ago, we went to see my Grandfather in his new garden. My uncle gave me a bouquet. Among the flowers were two I did not recognize, but as soon as I smelt them their

> .   .   .   .   *Odour, like a key,*
> *Turned noiselessly in memory's wards,*
> *To set a thought of sorrow free.*

"Why, Grandmamma," exclaimed I, "this flower used to grow in your old house at Connaghur, near your seven Hindu temples!" She was astounded. "Can you remember it all, dear?" quoth she. "Why, you could not have been more than four years old when you last came to see us at Connaghur, sixteen years ago!" I was myself surprised at the power of the fragrance of the flower. I did not even care to look at first at the flower, never recognized it even, and when I smelt it nonchalantly, the whole picturesque scene of Connaghur came upon me suddenly and vividly, like a flash of lightning: the seven temples on whose pinnacles the parrots used to build, the old half-ruined house, the vast and placid Ganges flowing smoothly by—I saw it all in a moment!

I wish you could see our date-palms. They are so beautiful now. The dates of a rich orange colour, hanging in immense clusters among the leaves, stand in striking contrast to the green plume-like leaves. If a painter were here, a "landscape painter", that is, he would revel in this world of variegated foliage. There are so many shades of green; from the light, yellowish and bright one of the tamarind tree, to the dark blue, sombre, green tint of the mango or the dusty brownish green of the sky-reaching *Casuarina*, Such a deep breath sweeps across the *Casuarinas* in the still evening. It is like the heaving of the sea, and brings St. Leonards to my memory.

The *Life of Charlotte Brontë*, by Mrs. Gaskell, induced me to read some more of Miss Brontë's works; *Shirley* is well-written and interesting; *Villette* is a failure; there is one character which is interesting, a French "professeur", M. Paul Emanuel; he sometimes reminds me of M. Boquel.

By-the-by, I suppose you received a letter, which I wrote some months ago, and which enclosed a note to Mrs. Baker; as the old lady has not yet given an answer, I am doubtful if you received it.

How vividly you recollect old times! Do you keep a diary that you even remember months and dates? I remember the first visit I paid you, after dear Aru's return to Regent House. It was in the morning, at about ten; you had a sprained ankle, and obliged to keep at home. How you fretted at not being able to take walks with me. The Fishers came in, and I came away soon, rather "contrariée" I confess it, for not being able to have a longer chat, *tête à tête*. You accompanied me to the door, notwithstanding the bad foot. I wish, I do wish, I were with you again.

About our next-door lodgers. We do not know them except by sight and hearsay, and what we do know, does not incline us to be friendly or even courteous with them. They are quiet as neighbours.

Gentille had a slight attack of heat apoplexy the other day. I was so distressed. Papa had been obliged to go out on business, during the middle of the day; I accompanied him, it was a distance of some nine or ten miles, the sun was fiery; when we came back, the poor horse was panting, with her nostrils,

> *like pits full of blood to the brim,*
> *And with circles of red for her eyesockets' rim.*

I was almost afraid she'd drop down: such a sight is very frequent in the streets in this tremendously hot weather. However Gentille was cooled, buckets of cold water were poured over her head, as well as wetted cloths applied, and she is quite well now. Jeunette bears the heat admirably.

There was a very good and favourable criticism of my book in the *Madras Standard* a few days ago, only the critic had taken me for a gentleman, and used "he" and "his" every time! I was rather amused and (shall I confess it?) perhaps a little flattered at this mistake.

The nights are dark now, but soon they will be as moonlit as they were four days ago. The moonlight nights are so beautiful and silent and peaceful in the Garden. It is a beautiful sight to see the moon rising large, serenely bright, full, behind the tall palm trees. She seems a peaceful watcher sent to watch over our lonely Garden; for Baugmaree is a little lonely and very quiet. At nights when I wake, it is so strange and beautiful to look at the moonlight on the floor of my room. Our windows have got bars, iron ones, it is safer; and how bright the shadows of the bars fall on the floor in the faint yet clear beams of the moon. It reminds me of convents of nuns. I rise very early, at half-past four A.M., I generally take my bath with the moon benignly looking in through the iron bars; at five, I am ready dressed and going out for a turn in the

Garden with my cats, or for a trot with my horses. I go to bed at half-past nine; you see I follow the sage proverb:

> *Early to bed and early to rise*
> *Makes a man healthy, wealthy, and wise.*

Punch says that, "early to bed and early to rise, is sure to give a man red eyes!"

It is dreadfully hot just at present. If you could see me now, quite wet with perspiration, you would really pity me. Oh for a cool nor'easter!

That was rather an amusing verdict, which is now going about in the papers, in the case of a sudden death, when the learned jury declared, after deliberating solemnly for a long time—"Died by the visitation of God, under very suspicious circumstances!" This reminds me of one of my uncle's stories about his father-in-law, who was a judge in the Small Cause court. At some trial or other, the witness, a Bengali (you see I wrote "native", but I have scratched it out), was asked by the opposing counsel what his profession was? "A teacher in the missionary school." "What do you teach?" (Witness). "The Bible. I read one chapter to the pupils daily." "What did you read today?" No reply. "Speak." Still the witness kept silence. (The judge, a Hindu, and who did not know a word of the Bible, encouragingly), "Answer the question." (Witness, scratching his head and dubiously), "I read today about—about Jesus plucking the fruit and giving it to his disciples!" My uncle was clerk and a Christian, the judge cast a sidelong glance at my uncle, to see if what the witness said was all right and if such an incident is really spoken of in the Bible.

I am glad that "Maddy"[13] as you term her (what *is* her name? I do not remember it, though I remember her very well indeed) is at last able to come to you. I am sure you would show her my book, I should like to know what she thinks about it; she knows English as well as French; I am not vain yet, but I am afraid I shall soon be with all the praises showered on me!

I have sent a copy of the *Sheaf gleaned in French Fields* to Mary and Lizzie Hall by this mail. While I am on the subject I must tell you that the *Madras Standard* article ended by saying: "as the taste of the pudding is in the eating of it, we append one of the pieces, a translation of Hugo's well-known satire." Then followed "Napoléon le petit". If

---

13. Mlle Verry.

you should want any of the originals, I can copy it out in my letter, to compare with the translation.

I wish you were here to see the wild monkeys. You would enjoy the sight immensely. A couple of days ago there were about fourteen of them, in front of our windows, gambolling and eating plantains; how delicately they peeled the fruit and with what relish they ate it! There were young and old ones; quite baby-monkeys there were too; the leader of the band was an immense brute almost as big as a man; such are very formidable indeed to encounter when they are irritated; they are so powerful and fearless too.

Tupsee-fish, or rather mango-fish, are come into season now. They are a very fine-flavoured sort of fish and are greatly relished by Anglo-Indians; one old gentleman's remark after tasting them (I mean the fishes not the Anglo-Indians) was, that it was worth a journey to India to taste the *tupsee*. He was an enthusiast, an *épicurien*, wasn't he?

Our Sanskrit is going on but slowly. We are now reading extracts from the Mahabharata.

Sometimes I wish I were out of Calcutta; especially this feeling comes upon me when in our town-house; Calcutta is such a horrid place, socially and morally; backbiting and scandal are in full swing. But the Garden, dear old Baugmaree, is free from every grievance, so quiet and peaceful; I asked Papa which was the place he would like to live his days out in; he answered, "Baugmaree or St. Leonards"; I quite agree with him.

As I am writing, I am taking a look now and then at *Villette*. I was just now quite amused at a description of M. Emanuel's bearing "en classe"; it is like M. Boquel.

The Prince is at last home again in merry old England; the Princess boarded the *Osborne* with her children while the vessel was in the Solent. She must have been anxious about the Prince and quite happy to see him again.

Lord Lytton is gone up to Simla. He had been suffering severely from a bilious attack, but is recovered now, I believe.

I am at a loss how to finish the two pages which are remaining. I am very glad that Cambridge has won this time; also there only remains one victory of Oxford to pay. Cambridge, I know, will pay it next year and then the two Universities will be square.

I have no idea who that Bengali gentleman may be, whom you describe as a boating man; don't you know his name?

I liked your father's "Address to a young lady" very much; it is very amusing.

Do you like the Misses Hall? We used to very much, when we were in Cambridge; they were such a nice quiet sort of girls and very handsome too; whom do you think the prettiest and whom do you like most? As for you, you are "my friend"; do you know, since you sent me your last photo, you seem to me more "like me". I mean no disparagement; before, I looked quite too old to be a friend of yours, you looked so young and girlish; now there is a kind of *fellow-look* in your face, which pleases me much.

I must close my letter now, as I have really nothing to write about. I send you a few dried leaves from the creeper from which I take my name. Mamma sends you her love, as does Papa; our kindest regards to your father and mother, and best love to your dear self.

How CAREFULLY AND NEATLY MY letter begins and with what a scribble it ends! On inspection of the leaves, I'd better not send them; they are pitiably dried—shrivelled would be the word.

Baugmaree Garden House

June 1, 1876

I received your welcome letter about five days ago, and as tomorrow is mail-day I must try and write an answer today.

I shall gladly send you copies of any of the originals of my translations that you may like to compare with them. Several of "Roland's" verses are very fairly done, though I say it myself, who should not, but I am afraid I have not been able to keep up the spirit of the original throughout. The "Wolf" is one of Uncle Girish's favourites, but Papa and myself consider it very mediocre. "The Rose and the Tomb" is, we (Papa and I) think, smooth and literal. Here is a translation of the same piece done some years ago by a Civil Servant, Mr. Hodgson:

> *With those bright tears of limpid dew,*
> *Which on thy leaves each morn I view,*
> *What dost thou, flower of beauty, do?*
> *One day demands a Tomb.*

> *The Rose replies: In stilly night,*
> *With those sweet tears of pearly white,*

> Are fed my flowers of rich delight,
> That all around perfume!

> And what awaits, demands the Rose,
> Those at the eve of life's last close,
> Who with their weight of sins and woes,
> Are cast in thine abyss?

> All pass my portals, Death replies,
> For every mortal being dies,
> But from my womb they all arise,
> Angels of love and bliss!

Which do you like best? Do not flatter me, but say frankly which you like. I shall copy the original out also, so that you may compare both the translations with it:

> La tombe dit à la rose:
> —Des pleurs dont l'aube t'arrose
> Que fais-tu, fleur des amours?
> La rose dit à la tombe:
> —Que fais-tu de ce qui tombe
> Dans ton gouffre ouvert toujours?

> La rose dit:—Tombeau sombre,
> De ces pleurs je fais dans l'ombre
> Un parfum d'ambre et de miel.
> La tombe dit:—Fleur plaintive,
> De chaque âme qui m'arrive
> Je fais un ange du ciel!

The other pieces you mention are among the first I did. Here is the Principal of the Benares College (Griffith's) rendering of the Sanskrit lines which I have quoted in my book. He has translated the whole of the *Ramayana*:

> The world may sunless stand, the grain
> May thrive without the genial rain,
> But if my Rama be not nigh,
> My spirit from its frame will fly.

Today's telegram is that the Sultan of Turkey has been dethroned and his nephew is to reign as Sultan in his place. What does this ordering of the ten ironclads to Besica Bay mean? Is England going to "fight it out" with Russia single-handed? If there is a war, the seas will become unsafe for travelling.

We shall have to leave the Garden soon. There have been several preliminary showers and the rains will soon begin. A week ago there was such a thunderstorm. It began at 6 P.M., and lasted till three the next morning. The night was pitch dark, the sky was covered by thick black clouds. It was a sight worth seeing. The trees swung their boughs to and fro with a weird moaning sound, the rain fell in torrents; suddenly a bright dazzling flash of lightning darted across the heavens in fiery zigzags, lighting up the gloom for one moment, then it became dark as ever, you could hardly see a yard before you, a loud peal of thunder followed, then other flashes and other peals. It was a tropical storm, a sort of cyclone, such as one would never dream of seeing in Europe. It was a grand sight.

So poor Mrs. Humphrey has broken her arm at the rink. I am sorry to hear this; but her husband, being one of the best surgeons in England, has, I fervently hope, set it all right long ere this. We all liked Dr. Humphrey very much; he was so attentive and kind during dear Aru's severe illness at Cambridge.

I got a letter from Mrs. Cowell along with yours. Such a nice kind letter! It seemed as if Mrs. Cowell had suddenly come before me in flesh and blood and talked with me in her warm impetuous way.

The papers are, as I said before, noticing the book more or less favourably. Nine newspapers in India have already noticed the book. I cut out the "critiques" and paste them in a book. The *Madras Standard* noticed the book very favourably and selected "Napoléon le petit" as a specimen.

The monkeys in our Garden have been exceedingly troublesome for the last few days. One, a very large one, five feet on its hind legs I should think, frightened one of our cats (May, a half-Persian) so much that the next day it gave birth prematurely to a dead kitten. Poor May was in such a plight! She ran to me and then to her little dead kitten, licked it, and then looked up at me, mewing most piteously. Luckily she has got another kitten today and has evidently forgotten the dead one. The monkey would not run away, though Papa and I both threatened it with shouts and loud clapping of hands! It sat bolt upright, grinning and showing its teeth in the most fierce manner. We were obliged to shut the door, and after a minute I saw it leap down to the ground and disappear among the trees. This morning I was in our dining-room (There! just now as I write, I hear the cry of the monkeys, a deep "Whoop! whoop! whoop!") playing with a cat. (The dining-room is the first room beginning with the right-hand side, which has a glass window, and which belongs to the second storey.) Well! I was sitting in the dining-room, when all of a sudden I heard a loud step, descending the stairs leading to the third storey. I looked up. A black face was peering over the banisters at me; I gave a startled cry of: "Hunuman!" (that is the Bengali name for monkeys), and ran to our sitting-room. My voice frightened it and it fled. A quarter of an hour after, we saw five just under our windows; some had young ones in their arms. They would not go off in spite of our threatening gestures, till at last I brought out Papa's revolver and pointed it, unloaded as it was, as though I were going to shoot them, when they all scampered off in the greatest hurry. It is, in my opinion, very heartless to kill a monkey for the mere pleasure of using one's gun: the poor animals, when wounded, look so fearfully human in their agony, and in their vain efforts to staunch the blood of their wounds.

The weather is dreadfully hot now. Here go a few verses by the late Mr. Parker, B.C.S., which seem very appropriate and which exactly describe my own present sentiments. It is entitled:

CALCUTTA STANZAS

FOR MAY

Happy the man whose hair and beard
Are glittering stiff with ice and snow,
Whose purple face with sleet is sear'd,
His nose also.

Happy the man, whose fingers five
Seem to have left him altogether,
And feet are scarcely more alive
In wintry weather.

And happier he, who, heavenly cold,
From warmth and sunshine far away,
Lives, till his freezing blood grows old,
At Hudson's Bay.

He in a beauteous basin, wrought
Of frozen quicksilver, his feet
May lave in water down to nought
Of Fahrenheit.

The whole year round too, if he pleases,
Far from the sun's atrocious beams,
He may unbaked by burning breezes
Live on ice creams.

And if for comfort, or for pride,
He wants shirt, breeches, coat or vest;
Let him but bathe, then step outside,
And, lo—he's drest,—

Drest in habiliments of ice,
More bright than those of old put on,
At royal birthdays, by the nice
Beau Skeffington.

Happy the man, again I sing,
Who thus can freeze his life away,
Far from this hot blast's blustering,
At Hudson's Bay.

Oh, that 'twere mine to be so blest,
For while my very bones are grilling,
The thoughts of such a place of rest
Are really thrilling.

Instead of jackets, I would wear
A coat of sleet, with snow lapelles,
Neatly embroidered here and there
With icicles.

Snow shoes should brace my burning feet,
And how I should enjoy a shiver,
While snow I'd drink, and snow I'd eat,
To cool my liver.

I'd tune my pipe by icy Hearne,
By frozen Coppermine I'd stroll,
And now and then, might take a turn
Towards the Pole.

But all in vain I sigh for lands,
Where happy cheeks with cold look blue,
While here, i' the shade, the mercury stands
At ninety-two.

June 2nd.

Such a large fish has been caught by our coachman today. It is a *Roheet*, and is often called the Indian salmon. The one that has been angled today weighs fully twenty-five pounds. The other day, also, another was caught by our coachman, but it was smaller than the one of today; it weighed sixteen pounds only. Every morning for breakfast I have whitebait (that is, Indian whitebait) caught fresh from the tank. Sometimes we call in a fisherman, who, with his net, once caught a big eel from one of our tanks, and a large *Bata*, a very sweet-flavoured fish, somewhat like the English bream, besides some Indian whitebait. Our *Baylay* or sand-fish is very like the English whiting; it is highly relished by my countrymen, as it is considered a very clean fish, feeding only on sand, whence its name.

The mangoes are in full season now. How I wish I could send you some from our garden! Our Baugmaree mangoes are famous for flavour and beauty. A basketful is now before me, emerald green, or vermilion red, some beautiful and radiant with all the colours of the rainbow; and oh, so delicious! The *leechies* are over now, they are very short-lived; one month, at the most, are they to be had at the shops.

Our new Bishop of Bombay is an Oxford man; I think his name is Mylne, but I forget. He was consecrated only a few days ago to the See of Bombay in St. Paul's Cathedral, and has not yet left England. By the by, this reminds me of a certain German missionary of our "connaissance", who spells "abbey" with an "e"—"ebbey"—and who, however, aspires, and even firmly hopes, to be created Bishop of Calcutta some time or other! Voilà ce que c'est que l'ambition!

One morning last week, as I was trotting Jeunette up and down the walk (she had been out of work for two days), a dog crossed our path: Jeunette leaped aside and reared. Oh! she looked so spirited and beautiful with her "front hoofs poised in air". I was a little taken by surprise by this sudden action of hers, but I was not a bit frightened, and quite as cool as ever. I continued trotting her till she quieted down. This coolness on my part raised our coachman's opinion of my presence of mind and courage a good deal.

Poontoo (the coachman) is rather afraid of horses when *out of harness;* he keeps always at a respectful distance from a horse's hind-legs! But he is a capital driver, and very careful in driving, using the whip rarely; and he once broke a horse, known to be vicious, into single harness, after it had been given over as quite unmanageable by the cleverest horse-breakers. Papa bought the animal for a song, it was so perfect in form; and by force of kindness and good management it became within a month the gentlest and the quietest horse ever seen. We sold it when we went to England, and it is still working hard under its present owner. Poontoo is a very old servant; he came into Papa's service long before I was born: I think it is twenty-six years that he has been a coachman to Papa.

The Zoological Gardens of Calcutta are now open to the public, but they are far from being complete as yet. Its menagerie at present consists of a jackal, an otter, a pair of leopards, a black bear, and a wild cat!

Five of Mamma's best hens were devoured by a wild cat a few nights ago. We did not see the animal, but by the footprints and the scratches of the claws on the ground we knew that it was a wild cat.

A young wild cat was caught several years ago; it was so fierce one could not approach it; at last one of our servants wrapt a blanket round his hand and arm and body, and so caught it. We kept it for some days in an iron cage, but it would not eat anything and moped so much that we were at last obliged to let it go free.

I am very glad to hear that you see Mary and Lizzie so often; they are such nice girls. Reginald was a great favourite of my mother's. He is such a bright intelligent-looking boy. I hope the Misses Oakes are quite well, and their mother, kind Mrs. Oakes. Please give them my kindest regards when you see them.

Is Blanche A. L.'s younger sister? Give my love to A. if she comes to see you. I have written three letters by this mail—one to your dear self, another to Mrs. Cowell, and another to M. Boquel. I enclose a small little flower; it bears my own name, *Torulota* or Creeper-Toru, and I know you would be pleased with it. Please give our kindest regards to your father and mother, and Mamma's and my own love to your mother and yourself.

12, Manicktollah Street,
Calcutta
June 26, 1876

Your nice long letter of the 22nd May I received on Saturday, that is, the day before yesterday. I could not answer it sooner as I had just recovered from a slight attack of fever and felt very weak.

Your letter is very interesting indeed. Of course the Rama of Sîta is the same whose name occurs in the Sanskrit couplet inserted among my notes. Do read *La Femme dans l'Inde Antique*, or even *The Iliad of the East*. I should so like to hear what you think of my country's legends and heroes and heroines. I am glad to hear that you are enjoying the May gaieties of Cambridge.

As for the state of demoralization of English society, I shall neither be surprised at nor afraid of it. Calcutta is a very sink of iniquity. Not only among the Hindus (in the midst of whom there are many respectable and nice people), but even among the Bengali Christians, the *moral* is so execrable. And the saddest thing is, that Hindus have a very bad idea of Christianity and only think it a cloak which some people take to commit under its cover a multitude of sins. But let me stop here; the manners of Bengali Christian Society (with a very few exceptions) are such as would sadden the merriest heart and dishearten the most hopeful.

Did I ever tell you about the Syrian gentleman on board our vessel when we were coming to India? He only spoke French, and knew English very imperfectly indeed. Well, one day, dinner was over, and the dessert had just been put on the table; he helped himself to some fruit; and as the steward in taking away his plate asked him if he would take "anything else, sir?" he answered "Nothing", but he pronounced it "Nutton". The next minute the steward (a little surprised at the request) brought him a plateful of roast mutton and potatoes! Our Syrian was a good deal taken aback; but as he saw that explanations would only make matters worse, he contented himself with muttering below his breath, in a sad desponding manner, "Est-ce là qu'on appelle 'nothing'"?

You are indignant at the way some Anglo-Indians speak of India and her inhabitants. What would you think if you read some of the Police reports which appear in the Indian daily papers? I shall tell you of a case which I read some months ago, and which impressed me then very much. I do not remember the details, but I shall tell you all that I can remember about it. Several soldiers went out for a holiday, having their guns with them. In a village they chanced to spy some peacocks, and they began shooting at them. The birds were the property of a Bengali farmer; of course he protested. He was told to "be off and be —— !" He called his neighbours. From words they came to blows; one soldier was severely beaten; the others decamped, leaving *nine* Bengalis *dead* and some seven Bengalis wounded. The case was brought before the magistrate; and what do you think his judgement was? The villagers were fined each and all; the soldiers acquitted: "natives should know how precious is the life of one British soldier in the eyes of the British Government——."

Yesterday a horse of one of our neighbours was struck with heat apoplexy. It had been taken out to exercise in the afternoon (when it was very hot), and when it came home the groom turned it into the stall without dressing or cooling the tired animal. The consequence was it rushed madly out of its stall and fell in a neighbouring tank (or pond), just behind our house. After a great deal of trouble it was got out. I saw it this morning from the roof of our house. Poor animal! It had been left lying on the damp mud, behind the owner's stable, with not a single man nigh to allay its sufferings. Isn't this cruel and inhuman? After some twelve hours it was lifted up by bamboo props (and a free use of the lash and administration of buckets of cold water into its nostrils and eyes!) and conveyed inside the stable. It is a Waler, that is, an Australian horse. I do not think that it will live. Jeunette and Gentille are well and in excellent condition. Jeunette is very fond of bread; she would follow me about anywhere in the hope of getting some. Gentille prefers sugar cane and other sweet things. They have just thrown off their winter coats and are now sleek and "satin-skinned" in their new summer ones. I wish you could see them!

Papa was telling me of some of the events of the Mutiny of 1857, the other evening. I was only a year old then. Papa and my uncles enrolled themselves as volunteers, and each bought a gun, the first they had ever handled. He remembers one evening, at some entertainment at Government House, as he was going up the broad staircase, the sort of "saisissement" he felt as he looked in at the large hall, where a small English guard was going through the evolutions, "Shoulder-arms!" &c. We had an old Sikh porter, who had formerly been a soldier. It was he who first brought us the news of the outbreak at Barrackpore. We were at that time in the Garden. When questioned about it he used to shake his grey head and say sadly, "Ah! the English have mismanaged the whole affair! If they had explained and smoothed away the matter, all would have been well. But now—they have all gone" (meaning the Indian troops), "all gone! the best, the bravest, the strongest!"

27th.

The poor horse over the way! During the night it had somehow or other got out of the stable, and is now lying in the mud, all covered with dirt, and with not even a kindly hand near to frighten away the crows which come to pick its quivering flesh! The eyes are very intelligent still. When it hears the pawing of its stable companions in their stalls it turns a wistful eye towards the stable, as if it longed to get in there. It should have been shot, and put out of this misery. It is sad to see it lift its head as if to rise; then, seeing the attempt vain, let it fall hopelessly on the ground. It was a fine animal, of a dark grey almost turning to black. Australian horses suffer very much from the heat; hundreds die of congestion and sunstrokes during the hot season of Calcutta. The stud-breds are more inured to the climate, being born and bred in India. If the horse, which is now dying, had been properly and kindly treated from the first day of its illness, it *might* have lived.

You see we have removed from the Garden to our town house. The reason is, the rains have commenced. Today it rained in the middle of the day, and so the late afternoon has turned out cool and fine. It pours continually for weeks sometimes. I was very sorry to leave the Garden; I used so to enjoy exercising Jeunette and Gentille.

We shall be going to Baugmaree again at the end of the rains, that is, in the beginning of November.

I have not read much lately. The *Revue des Deux Mondes* has been my only solace for the last week. I was reading an article on Baron Stockmar's book, by Saint-René Taillandier. A very ably-written article it is, and gives you the whole of the Stockmar memoirs in a condensed and interesting form, truly delightful.

The papers say that Lord Lytton will resign and return to England by the end of the next year. It is said that he thinks India is very unhealthy. He has been suffering from constant bilious complaints since he has gone to Simla. He liked Barrackpore pretty well when he was there, for he wrote in a telegram to Lady Lytton that he found the above-mentioned place very charming indeed, just like an English country seat.

We were so amused the other day with reading in the *Illustrated London News* that the Prince of Wales created "Bullen", "Smith," "Degember,"

"Mitter," as Companions of the Order of the Star of India. "Bullen-Smith" is one gentleman, and not two, as "Bullen", "Smith" would seem to imply, and "Degember Mitter" is ditto! By the by, we saw Babu Degember Mitter today as we were taking our morning drive at five o'clock.

The afternoons now turn out generally wet and cloudy, so I am going to take my drives in the morning instead of the evening. I got up at half-past three this morning to be ready for my drive before five. The morning was cool and fine, and I enjoyed the fresh air very much. I wish you were with me, bowling smoothly along at the rate of fourteen miles an hour, with the fresh breeze blowing in your face, and Jeunette's and Gentille's wavy black manes glancing in the sun, just visible if you lean forward to look at them. The streets were very quiet; not a soul, except the policemen, was to be seen.

Where shall you go this summer? To the Lakes again? I am sure you would enjoy a trip to the Continent, and who knows if you venture as far as Italy that you might not embark at Brindisi, and just lengthening your voyage a little come to Calcutta! Ah! dear, I long to see you again. I feel a little lonely sometimes. In England life was so much more active and free; here, on the contrary, I lead a rather solitary and sedentary life, but not in the least do I feel it dull, *au contraire*, it is a quiet peaceful sort of life.

28th.

The poor horse is dead. I am glad it is out of its misery at last, for the way it was maltreated by the wretches (I mean the grooms) was simply atrocious.

One of our relations, a second cousin of mine, is going to England very soon; I think he starts on the 11th of next month. He is a very studious lad; his parents are poor and with a large family. He studied hard and has won the Gilchrist scholarship, which provides for him for life as it were. All Gilchrist scholars have to go to England; the funds left by Dr. Gilchrist provide them with money for the passage and for expenses in England. They have to study five years in either the University of London or that of Edinburgh, and then to choose a profession for themselves. This relation is a Hindu, so is his family; there will be a sad break-up of their home circle when the boy goes away.

I am keeping house alone today. Papa has gone out and Mamma has gone to see my grandfather and grandmother. She will not return till late in the evening, and I don't expect Papa till four in the afternoon.

Our Sanskrit is going on rather slowly. It is a difficult language and it takes one a long time to master it thoroughly.

29th.

I have just returned from my morning drive. I got out of the carriage and walked a little on the Maidan; but I had to get in the barouche again, as one feels very soon warm and perspiring in this hot weather.

Papa brought yesterday some French books for me. Among them are two volumes of Sainte-Beuve's *Causeries de Lundi*. They are standard works, and I have read extracts from them in various books. I am sure I shall enjoy reading the *Causeries*; you know of course that they are principally critical essays on French prose-writers and poets, in the style of Lord Macaulay's essays.

It is very hot today, though there was a heavy shower last evening.

There was rather an interesting letter in the *Daily News* yesterday on the superstitions concerning natural history which prevail among the peasantry of Bengal. The bears are said to be born thus: the she-bear vomits clots of blood, which are subsequently hatched, shapen, and developed into perfect animals by the warmth of the mother's body. The porcupine is regarded as an animal of ill omen, and a quill stuck in the thatched roof of a hut is considered sufficient to ensure domestic discord. The common water-snake, the most harmless of all Indian ophidians, is said to be extremely venomous on certain days—Friday for instance. A curious story is attached to the green tree-snake, known in India as the *nowdanka*. It is said that after biting a person the snake ascends to the topmost branch of the loftiest tree in the neighbourhood, and there establishes a look-out and refuses to descend until he beholds the curling wreaths of smoke from the funeral pyre of his victim. Those who are acquainted with this feature in the habits of the animal proceed to light a fire in the neighbourhood the moment anybody is bitten, and with the descent of the snake abate also the baneful consequences of its bite, and the patient recovers. Another most popular belief is that the tiger is always attended by an animal, called a *phao* (but which I take to be nothing else than a superannuated jackal, whose dismal and solitary howls may often be heard in the outskirts of our own city), "a kind of nasty awkward customer who is always getting into the tiger's way and warning off his intended victims." My aunt had a maid-servant, whose sister, with three children, were bitten by a *nowdanka*. She was personally present at the funeral rites of her sister, who was quite dead, as well as two of the children bitten; but the third, a little girl, had a spark of life in her. My aunt's maid-servant asserted that she saw with her own eyes the serpent descend from a cocoanut palm. The girl survived, she said, but the mother and the two other children were too long dead to revive. The serpent, I believe, was caught, put in an earthen vessel, the opening of which was shut and sealed, and was thus committed to the bosom of the Ganges to sink or swim as it pleased the goddess of the river, Ganga. Sometimes at nights we have heard in our own Garden the weird cry of the *phao*. The howl is quite distinct from that of the jackal, and can be recognized at once. One of our servants, newly arrived from his native place, hearing the *phao*, immediately said, a little frightened, that "some tiger must be near, for there was the *phao*".

Our bishopric seems to be going a-begging. Nobody apparently will take it. The Rev. Mr. Milman, a cousin of our late Bishop, is said to have refused the offered See; so has another reverend gentleman, I forget his name. Everybody seems to be afraid of the climate of Calcutta.

Have you read Victor Hugo's grand speech in the French Assembly for the release of the French communists? I should like to read it in the original.

My little cousin, Varûna, came the other day to see us. He has got a new brother and is of course a little jealous of the "baby", with whom his Mamma is consistently occupied. Varûna is so interesting. I wish you could hear him sing "'Ock-of-Ages cleft fo' me" (Rock of Ages cleft for me), slowly and in a solemn way keeping excellent time, with his small hands clasped behind his back (great Napoleon fashion), and walking about with small quick strides.

I must stop now. Thank you again for your very interesting letter; mine seems insipid and dull beside yours, but I live so like a recluse.

Papa's and Mamma's and my own kindest regards to your father and mother, and their love to you. Best love to your dear self from me.

PS. I send you some flowers picked from our garden. Unfortunately they have lost their vivid purple colour in the process of drying.

12, Manicktollah Street,
Calcutta
(No date, probably July 1876.)

I was very glad indeed to receive your nice long letter of the 30th May. It was quite an unexpected pleasure. Dear, how good you are to treasure up my good-for-nothing letters; they do not deserve to be made so much of; yours are *very* precious to me.

As I have nothing new to write about, I shall comply with your desire and copy out fragments from the notices of my book, which have appeared in the Indian papers. The *Englishman* says: "There is evidence of rare ability, promise of great achievements, in this volume of poetry by a young Bengali lady. To expect translations made from one foreign language into another by one so young, as we understand Miss Toru Dutt to be, would be to expect a miracle. Yet, there are pieces in the work before us, which, though they must have presented considerable difficulties to the translator, are almost perfect. 'To Pepa' from Alfred de Musset, is one of these, and the concluding sonnet shows not only true poetic feeling but an artistic touch and delicacy of finish, which would do credit to a much older poetess writing in her mother tongue. Miss Dutt's metre often limps, her grammar is not always faultless, and her expressions are sometimes quaint or tame. But faults of this kind were inevitable; and it is in the highest degree creditable to her that they are not more frequent. If the translations were arranged in the order in which they were written, they would probably show a rapid progressive improvement in all these respects. The last piece in the book, a sonnet, which, from its subject, we take to be also the latest in point of time, is faultless" (then follows concluding sonnet, "A mon père"). "The other piece to which we have referred is hardly less successful, though in a totally different style." (Then follows "To Pepa".)

The *Friend of India* says: "We cannot pretend to have read the whole of this volume, but we have dipped into it here and there in leisure moments and have never seen reason to change the opinion formed from the first few snatches, that it deserves very high commendation. It contains a hundred and sixty-five translations in verse from French authors, besides a dedication and concluding sonnet. The versification is generally good, and the translations, we believe, intelligent and faithful. We might have dismissed the volume without further remark, had it been the work of an Englishwoman, as we could easily have believed it to be; but what would have been ordinary commendation, in the case of an Englishwoman, becomes very high praise, when we state that the lady who gathered this *Sheaf* is a native of this country, and that this Bengalee lady has given us a really good book of translations from French poets in highly creditable English verse. Those who have seen the *Dutt Family Album* are aware of the taste and talent for poetry that characterize the family, and we cordially commend to their attention the present volume by a young lady of that family. The lady was, we understand, educated in Europe, but that fact, though it may lessen our surprise at the excellence of her workmanship, does not detract from the very high praise that is justly due to her. We take the book as a good omen for the future of women in India. We have been told that the fair sex in India is gifted, not only with a strong love of poetry but also with a love for poetical composition, and that in some parts of the country the women are the song and ballad makers of the districts. When child marriage is abolished, and young girls are properly educated, and woman once more assumes her rightful position in India, we may expect that the influence of the sex on literature, and through literature, on the elevation and refinement of the people, will be great indeed. We trust Miss Toru Dutt's high example will not be without effect on her countrymen, and we trust the book will be widely circulated among native gentlemen, that they may see what education may do for their wives and daughters."

The *Indian Charivari* writes thus: "I should like to draw your attention to a little volume of poems called *A Sheaf gleaned in French Fields.* It is a series of translations by a Miss Toru Dutt. But for the name of the author I should not have dreamed that it was the production of a native of this country. The versions are most graceful, and show a knowledge both of English and French which would not disgrace the most polished of British-born translators. Miss Dutt seems specially to enter into the spirit of Béranger; witness her version of 'My Vocation':

> *Le bon Dieu me dit:*
> *Chante, pauvre petit.*

I recommend every one to procure a copy of this new addition to the Lays of Ind."

Mark that I did not send a copy of my book to the editor of the *Indian Charivari*, and I think it very good of him to notice the book so kindly, merely from reading about it in other Indian papers. The only little funny mistake in the notice was that "Toru" was printed with a "Z"—Zoru. Are you tired or shall I go on with a few more notices? The *Madras Standard* says: "*A Sheaf gleaned in French Fields* is a title of a volume published in Calcutta, containing translations in English of various French authors, most of whom are familiar to students of

French literature. Toru Dutt, a member of a well-known literary family in Calcutta, has furnished in this volume to English readers some of the brightest efforts of the French muse in a neat, elegant, and attractive English dress. The poets of France, whose compositions she has translated, are many, from Leconte de Lisle, a creole born in Mauritius, to that noble and eccentric genius, Victor Hugo. There are one hundred and sixty-six translations in the volume, and Toru Dutt has contrived to give the spirit and the life of the originals in a remarkably successful manner. As the proof of the pudding is in the eating thereof, we give in another column her version of Victor Hugo's famous poetic satire, 'Napoléon le petit'."

Lastly I shall take the notice of the *Bengalee* and then I shall stop. "There were learned ladies, like *Gargi, Khona*, and *Lilabati* in ancient and mediaeval India. But from the dark days of Mohammedan invasion, ignorance and seclusion became the lot of woman in this country. It is only of late that people have come to perceive the necessity of educating her; and though very little has yet been done to improve her mind, some result of the intellectual movement has already become perceptible. Some Bengali ladies have betaken themselves to the field of literature, and written poems and dramas of considerable merit in their native tongue. But Miss Toru Dutt has not only surpassed them all, but has shown a culture very rare even amongst our best-educated men. The *Sheaf gleaned in French Fields* which she has presented to us is an octavo volume of 234 pages, containing poetical pieces mostly translated from modern French writers. The extensive knowledge she displays, and the command she shows over the English tongue, appear to us simply marvellous when we learn that the accomplished authoress is yet in her teens. Miss Toru Dutt belongs to a family distinguished for its literary talents, the Dutt family of Rambagan, in this city. Her father, Babu Govin Chunder Dutt, is the editor of the *Dutt Family Album*, and she resided with him for some years in England and learned French while she was in France. Occasional quotations and references in the book under review show that she has some knowledge of German and Sanskrit. We doubt whether there is any young man of her age in this country who has learnt so much. The work of translation has been so well done that the spirit of poetry breathes through every line. While the original has been followed very closely, there is no slavish adherence to the letter at the sacrifice of the true spirit of song. The following extract will show that we have not exaggerated the beauty of the translation." (Then follows Victor Hugo's "The Ocean, an address to the people"; afterwards the notice continues:) "The authoress appears to be endowed with no mean poetical powers. We hope she will try to write original poetry in her native tongue, and following the footsteps of the greatest poet of the Dutt Family, Michael M. S. Dutt, enrich our vernacular literature with the wealth of her contributions. In a note at the end of the volume, the authoress adds, 'the pieces signed A. are by her dear and only sister Aru, who fell asleep in Jesus, on the 23rd July, 1874, at the early age of twenty years.' To show what loss our country has sustained by the premature death of this accomplished lady, we give below one of the pieces, to which her initial is attached." ("The Captive to the Swallows.")

Now, dear, I hope you have had quite enough of it. You see I have become quite a public character, like L. E. L. or Mrs. Hemans!

The M. S. Dutt mentioned in the last notice is not related to us in any way, though the critic seems to think so. I have only taken notices from some of the papers, to give you an idea of the criticisms that have been written on the *Sheaf.* Today is mail-day, but I do not expect any letter from you, as I received one by the last mail.

I am adding some more translations to the *Sheaf* and revising it, in case there should be a second edition; for Mr. Knight, the bookseller, told us the *Sheaf* was in great demand, and that he had received several orders.

Last week there was a great storm with thunder and lightning; one house was struck, two persons were killed and part of the house was destroyed.

Today there has been some rain in the early morning; then the sky cleared up, but it is looking cloudy and threatening again. The thunder peals so loudly that the houses are shaken to their foundations, and the flashes of lightning are blinding.

I am now reading articles from the *Revue des Deux Mondes*; the more I read this periodical, the more I like it. The articles are very ably written and the style is beautiful; I never tire of reading the magazine.

Aru's pet canary died the other day: I buried it under an arbour in our small back garden. Poor thing, it had been suffering from asthma for the last few days. I am sorry for it. Now there are only two left of the thirteen birds we brought from England, a canary and a goldfinch.

A skating-rink has been opened here since yesterday. I have not been to see it, nor do I think I ever shall.

I was very sorry to hear from Mr. Clifford, a Cambridge man and a friend of ours, that Mrs. Babington[14] has been suffering very much from some affection of her spine, that she is unable to get up, and that there is scarcely any hope that she will ever rise from her bed of illness. Poor lady! We used to know her very well indeed in Cambridge, and we all feel very sorry for her. By the by, how is the Orphanage that she planned and instituted getting on? There was a very interesting little inmate of this Orphanage, whom we all used to pet, little Bertie. I wonder if she is still there.

I heard from Mr. Clifford that Mr. Jones (who occupied the ground-floor rooms at Mrs. Baker's while we were at Regent House, and whom and whose family I am sure you have not forgotten), is going from Ceylon for good. Mrs. Jones has been very poorly since they have left England, and it is her delicate state of health that obliges Mr. Jones to leave his mission work and return to Europe. Their daughter, Jenny, is now with them in Ceylon.

The day before yesterday there was a very interesting letter in the papers from the Captain of the *Alabama* (I think that is the name of the steamer), which was nearly wrecked, but which, thanks to the efficiency of its captain, reached Bombay in a broken state, it is true, but with no lives lost. The Captain, George Hamlyn, we knew very well indeed. He was Captain of the *Arabia*, in which steamer we returned to Calcutta from Bombay. He is a very religious, and grave, serious man. He used to be very fond of us, especially of our brother, with whom he used often to play chess. I speak of things that happened twelve years ago. His letter is so graphic and modest, yet so terrible in its simplicity.

The ship sprang a leak, and they encountered stormy weather for two days; they gave up all hope, for the water increased in the hold, overflowed into the engine rooms, and so of course the engines became useless.

Baguette, my first favourite cat, is come to interrupt me, and divert my attention; her name is derived from *Bâg*, which means a tiger in Bengali. You know that the Bengalis say that cats are the aunts of tigers, because of the resemblance that a cat bears to a tiger.

---

14. The wife of the late Charles C. Babington, of Cambridge, Professor of Botany, who died in 1895. He was author of the *Manual of British Botany*, now in the fourth edition. His widow died in 1919.

There is a sort of serpent in India, very harmless, but which the Bengalis say suck the milk of cows from their udders, winding themselves round the animal's hind-legs in order to keep it still, for of course the cow fidgets, and gets restless. I do not know if this is true, but naturalists say that the serpents are unable to suck, by the formation of their mouths. . .

I have nothing to write about, so please, dear, excuse this scrawl. Mamma's and Papa's kindest regards to your father and mother, and their love to you. With best love to your darling self from me.

12, Manicktollah Street, Calcutta
July 15, 1876

Your very interesting and welcome letter I have just received. I was going to write to you when I received your letter, so I shall answer it at once. I do not know of any French book of rules for composition both in poetry and prose. I once lighted upon the name of a book, such as you want, in one of Hachette & Co's catalogues; if I chance to find it out again, I shall tell you the title. Here is a French translation of the "Hindu wife to her husband" from the *Dutt Family Album*, by one of my friends, le Chevalier de Châtelain. I give it, because I think you will like to read it:

> *Pour des yeux étrangers, oh! non, je ne me pare*
> *De bijoux précieux—lumineux comme un phare!*
> *Ni pour les yeux d'autrui n'entasse les splendeurs*
> *De mes longs vêtements aux si riches couleurs,*
> *Ne souhaite non plus que se soit vu mon sourire*
> *Par tout autre que toi—que toi seul que j'admire.*
>
> *Sans les plaisirs du monde, on me dit que mon sort*
> *Est triste, est archi-triste, équivaut à la mort;*
> *Comme un oiseau captif qu'à gémir condamnée*
> *De ce vaste univers je suis l'abandonnée,*
> *Et que les diamants, que l'esprit, la beauté,*
> *Enfouis à jamais, ne valent jours d'été!*
>
> *Oui, l'on me dit aussi qu'en un festin assise*
> *Être le point de mire est une chose exquise,*
> *Que de trôner suprême est le bonheur parfait,*
> *Que là seul est la vie, et son plus grand attrait!*

Que se poser enfin la plus belle des belles
Est le plaisir des Dieux n'ayant de parallèles!

Oh! loin qu'un tel avis ait accès dans mon cœur,
Je le repousse ainsi qu'on repousse une erreur!
Pour moi je la méprise, et la danse et la foule,
De ces plaisirs mondains me préserve la houle!
Comme une reine heureuse, avec simplicité,
Aux seuls miens je m'impose, avec bénignité!

Pour aller d'autres yeux guigner les étincelles,
Dans leur triste logis, à leurs foyers, ces belles
N'ont elles su goûter le charme de la paix
Et d'un chaste bonheur les séduisants attraits,
D'admirateurs nouveaux pour s'en aller en quête,
Et chercher sans vergogne en faire la conquête.

Pour toi, mon seul amour, je porte ces bijoux,
Pour toi seul, mon aimé, pour toi, mon cher époux,
Un gentil mot de toi,—de toi, cher! que tant j'aime
Est le roi des plaisirs, fait mon bonheur suprême.
A toi seul mon sourire et mon plus doux regard,
Le trop-plein de mon cœur—de mon amour le nard!

You must know that the Chevalier de Châtelain is the well-known translator of several of Shakespeare's plays, of Chaucer's *Canterbury Tales*, and many other poetical works.

The short legends at the commencement of F. Richardson's *Iliad of the East* all belong to the *Ramayana*, which epic poem contains in the original Sanskrit many such episodes, in no way relating to the chief subject of the poem.

I know the hymn you mention, I have never heard it sung in choir; the air is, as you well say, splendid, and in full choir it must be something magnificent.

Serpents generally prefer warm and sunny corners; Heber says:

Child of the sun, he loves to lie
'Mid nature's embers, parched and dry,
Where o'er some tower in ruin laid,

The peepul spreads its haunted shade,
Or round a tomb his scales to wreathe,
Fit warder in the gate of death!

Some parts of your letter have gladdened my heart so much, dear, that I read them over and over again. How good you are! By my last I told you in detail, what the papers were saying about my book. Only one notice has appeared since then. The *Calcutta Quarterly Review* says: "A collection of charmingly light and tasteful translations from French Lyrics, selected from the works of Béranger, Sainte-Beuve, Victor Hugo, and other poets. The translator is, we understand, a young Bengali lady, but she uses the English language with all the facility and grace of a skilled English writer, and we cannot but conclude that she has received much of her education in Europe. In any case, however, this book of short poems is a most interesting and pleasing one—pleasing by its intrinsic beauties, and interesting as showing the high degree of natural taste, improved by culture and refinement, that may be found amongst the daughters of the country."

I think I shall give up Sanskrit. It is *very* difficult, and the grammatical rules are legion, and so minute. We have finished the three parts of the *Riju-Pât*, and we are now going to begin *Sakuntala* by Kalidasa. Have you ever read it in any translation, and do you know the story? It is a charmingly written drama. One of my cousins is called Sakuntala after the heroine. The Bengalis are very fond of the name. *Sita* is a name which no Bengali will give to his daughter, because Sita was so unfortunate and had suffered very much. It is an unlucky name.

I have had another attack of fever a few days ago, it is only since yesterday that I have come downstairs. We went to drive this morning at 4.45 A.M. We got down on the Maidan to take a walk, but we had hardly gone a quarter of a mile when it commenced raining, so we got into our carriage again.

I feel very complimented indeed that you call your doves by my horses' names; I am glad you like the names—I am sorry to hear that the cock dove has flown away, but it has been so long in your house that I think it may return.

Jeunette and Gentille are doing exceedingly well. Gentille is the better trotter, she can do her fourteen or sixteen miles within the hour in capital style; Jeunette is good at a gallop, she would have made a splendid riding-mare; she is a grand jumper, there is nothing, I believe, that she couldn't climb or clear; once she got loose in Baugmaree, and the way she cleared the tall fences was beautiful; she never touched them even with her hoof, but leapt clean over; she must have been taught before, I think, by her trainer.

Papa has hired a piano again for me, as I was getting out of practice. This is a beautiful instrument and quite new. I shall do nothing today till I have finished this letter, for the mail leaves on Tuesday and this is Saturday.

From the first of this month, the postal arrangements have been altered a little, and the charges have been lessened; now a letter not exceeding ½ an ounce costs only six annas, formerly it was eight annas. The charges too for newspapers and parcels have been decreased.

Here is a small police case which appeared in yesterday's papers. A magistrate sent out for an afternoon airing, in charge of a boy, four or five amiable dogs, who seem to have been taught by him to snarl and bite at everything that comes in their way. During their promenade, they saw an old woman's goat, and flew at it straightway and worried it almost to death. A lad (a Bengali schoolboy, of some seventeen years), generous and brave, rescued the goat, and hit one of the dogs so, in the struggle, that it died. He was told by the dog-keeper that they were the dogs of the Magistrate-Sahib; our spirited boy said, he would go himself to the Magistrate, and tell him about the affair; so he did. Well, what do you think he received; commendation, praise, for his pluck in fighting with five dogs, for his humanity in saving a poor old woman's goat (on which she depended for her livelihood) from being worried? Nothing of the sort. He received sentence of three weeks' imprisonment with hard labour. The unjust, nay, the unlawful sentence was confirmed by the Sessions Judge. The High Court emphatically reversed it, that is true, but it was too late, for the boy had suffered the term of imprisonment awarded him already. The Magistrate, Joint Magistrate, and Sessions Judge were of course all Europeans. The papers are speaking against this crying, scandalous shame; the Magistrate and the Sessions-Judge ought to be dismissed for so monstrous a perversion of the law. Imagine the row that would have been made in England at a Magistrate sending a boy to the treadmill under such circumstances.

Calcutta has no Bishop even yet; the *Daily News* had some funny verses on the subject a few days ago by a correspondent.

"Conference of eminent divines in London."

First eminent divine loq.:

> *"Although I love all heathen souls*
> *Far more than I can utter,*
> *They can't expect me in such*
> *A climate as Calcutta."*

Second ditto:

> *"Salisbury tried it on with me;*
> *Said I, 'My lord, no butter*
> *Of course can draw me to a town*
> *Unhealthy as Calcutta.'"*

Third ditto:

> *"Well, for my part," a third was heard,*
> *Full dubiously to mutter,*
> *"I'd like the pay, but lack-a-day!*
> *Just fancy hot Calcutta."*

Fourth ditto:

> *"Well, I'll be honest and say out*
> *I'd rather have a hut, a*
> *Little hut in England, than*
> *A palace in Calcutta."*

Chorus of eminent divines:

> *"We'd all be glad to go, but then,*
> *Since life at best is but a*
> *Span, we fear to risk it by*
> *A sojourn in Calcutta."*

My maternal uncle is ill with the fever, so Mamma has gone to see him today.

I do not correspond with Miss Ada Smith; I only wrote a letter to her when I sent her my *Sheaf* which Papa had promised her, and got a nice answer in return. She is somewhat older than I am, thirty or thereabouts. She seems to like Amritsar pretty well.

Our relation who is going to England has been unavoidably delayed. He does not start till the 25th. Pity he is not going to Cambridge, as then he would have been soon acquainted with our friends there, who would have been able to help him a little.

There's Papa calling out to me to rest a *little* before the Pundit comes!

I have found out the name of the book I mentioned in the commencement of my letter: it is *Traité de versification française*; I have not seen the book myself, so I cannot give my opinion on it; the title seems to indicate the book to be such as will suit you. But I think the better plan is to do away with all "traités" and rules, except of course the very essential ones, and only read the French poets, enter into their spirit, understand and appreciate them thoroughly, see how they manage their rhymes, metres, idioms, &c. I can recommend to you several good French poets, modern or ancient, but you must not read *all* their poetry, for they are sometimes very loose and vulgar. Lamartine is always to be trusted. Victor Hugo's poems have nothing *very* bad in them, as far as I know, though there are a few rather bad ones; his recent works are better. Then there is Béranger, but you must be very particular about reading his *good* ones, for he and Musset, though both were greatly talented and full of genius, are often, sad to say, immoral. Vigny, too, is not always what his *Moïse* would seem to indicate. His *Le Cor* is splendid. Then there is a host of rising and living poets, first of whom is Theuriet, then there is Leconte de Lisle, Baudelaire, Angier, Autran, &c.

As I am writing to you it is raining, "For the rain it raineth every day" here now.

Dear, your letters are such a comfort. The 23rd July is indeed a sad anniversary for us; the 9th too of July, for my brother, Abju, fell asleep in the Lord on that date in 1865. How hard it seems sometimes, but we have our hope in Christ: what should we become without His blessed promise of the life eternal? There we shall see them again. We were reading this morning the fifteenth chapter of the 1st Corinthians. It is a beautiful chapter, isn't it?

I wish you many happy returns of your birthday, for by the time this letter reaches you, it will be the 21st August. I wish I could tell you all that passes through my mind, when I think about you and our friendship, face to face; I wish I could congratulate you on your birthday in person. But, dear Mary, though we may never meet again here below, we shall meet again in our eternal home. At times, when at night I cannot sleep, I think of you, of the pleasant intercourse we have had together, of your bright face and sunny smile, and then I long to see you again; sometimes, I think the best thing to be done is to sell off the Garden, at any cost, and go off to England. But that cannot well be accomplished. I shall write to you often, merely for the sake of writing to you, and getting your dear good letters. I feel so much better after reading them: it brings back our pleasant former life so vividly before me.

The Pundit has just gone after giving us our lesson, so I have taken up my writing again.

Do you know that hymn, beginning with the words: "Toss'd with rough winds and faint with fear?" It is a very beautiful little piece and was often sung in St. Paul's Church. The air too is very pretty. I sometimes sing it, for I am not allowed to sing often, and even when Papa does permit me, he adds that I must sing very gently, Papa is *so* careful! I tell him, he should keep me under a glass case, for I am not half so delicate as he makes me out to be, or as he is afraid that I am. He says we must go to Europe for my health's sake; and the slightest cool breeze makes him order me to wrap something about me! I told him laughingly that I would not go to England for the life he'd lead me there! what with the wraps and flannels and no going out when it should become a little cold!

The worst of Calcutta is that it is so damp. The atmosphere is sultry and yet moist and damp. I am perspiring, but I am afraid to open the window, because of the wet atmosphere.

We shall not be very sorry to lose our present Lieutenant-Governor; he is not at all an energetic sort of man. I do not know who his successor will be. The *Daily News* said today that Sir John Strachey is likely to succeed our Governor-General and Viceroy when Lord Lytton retires, which he will do by the end of next year, as his health has been suffering very much since he has come out to India.

The rink, which has been opened only a few days, attracts a great many people. I have not seen it, nor ever shall.

Do Mary and Lizzie Hall attend any of the lectures? Lizzie used to attend the German, French, and Latin lectures. Mary used to go to the two first ones, and instead of the Latin, she used to attend the lectures of Dr. Garrett on harmony.

I am now reading *Maître Gaspard Fix* by Erckmann-Chatrian. It is a well-written book enough, but not in his usual vein; it is a tale of the *coup d'état* of the late Emperor Napoleon.

We have sent for two books from Hachette & Co. by this mail, namely, an illustrated edition of Hugo's *Les Misérables* and a new work, *Son Excellence M. Eugène Rougon*, by M. Zola. The latter work treats of the flourishing days of the Second Empire; we saw a review of it in the *Pall Mall Gazette*, which interested me very much. I have been reading lately Pusey's *Commentary on the Minor Prophets*. I liked that on Hosea exceedingly.

There! Jeunette and Gentille have just finished their evening pittance. I must stop one minute to go and give them some dainties, bread or sugar-cane. They are so handsome, my horses! I wish I could show them to you! I ordered the grooms to take off their blankets, and such sleek, shining coats, such beautiful proportions, were displayed to my delighted eyes! It reminded me of a picture in one of my "Horse" books, entitled "Unclothing the beauties of the stud".

I am glad you are getting warmer weather now; I remember you never could like the cold weather, or a fall of snow.

M. Boquel has not written to me yet; I suppose he will as soon as he receives mine.

I should not like to live in that drawing-room at Regent House. The dining-room with its bay-window looking towards Parker's Piece was very comfortable and cheerful, but the drawing-room! No fire on earth could make it warm and comfortable. It was such a chilly room, I suppose because it was rather large; the piano used to be kept there and of course we were obliged to practise, but our fingers used to be quite benumbed and stiff!

The fall in the price of silver is the general topic now in Calcutta. Newspapers are full of the subject. I do not take much interest in it. A new Municipal Act has been passed which dictates that the members of the Calcutta Municipality are henceforth to be elected by the ratepayers. So elections are going on, but the general public does not seem to take great interest in the subject, as only as yet some hundred and fifty persons have applied to be qualified as electors in the eighteen wards of Calcutta.

The Zoological Gardens of Calcutta are not advancing much, as to the menagerie: a fox, an otter, a few birds, that is all.

Give Mamma's and Papa's best regards to your father and mother, and mine too, of course. Papa and Mamma send their love to you. I have nothing else to write about. But it is such a pleasure to write to you, dear, and to hear from you. Does not Maddy intend to pass a few days with you this year?

The guinea-pigs and pigeons are thriving. So are the cats. May has now got two kittens; nice playful little things they are. Dear, I must say good-bye now.

12, Manicktollah Street,
Calcutta
August 7, 1876

Your letter of the 26th June has been lying unanswered for the last week, though not unread, for I have read it over and over again. Yes, by all means write a review of my book; how can you ask my permission? you can do whatever you like with my book and with myself. I shall only be too glad to see it reviewed in some of the English papers. Cut it up savagely *s'il vous plaît*. A little rough handling will, I think, do me an immense deal of good.

I have already sent you some of the articles on the *Sheaf*. After I had posted that letter, I felt a little compunction, thinking that reviews of my book would be rather dull reading for you, though of great interest to myself. But now I am glad I sent off the letter, as you write to me in your last to give you an idea of the manner in which my book has been criticized.

One of the pieces in the *Sheaf*, "My Vocation," by Béranger, has been inserted in the "Course of English Reading" for the use of candidates for the Entrance Examination in Calcutta.

The compiler of the Selections is the Rev. Mr. Macdonald of the Free Church mission.

Mrs. Macdonald died a few days ago of typhoid fever. She once called here, and we of course returned her visit. Papa attended her funeral, by desire. There was a great concourse of mourners, about three hundred or more.

I am so glad you like the *Ramayana* and that my country's heroine has won your heart. Don't you like Laksmana? I like him immensely. Such a bold impetuous warrior he was. Is not the sad tale of Dasaratha's fault about the hermit youth, whom he killed by accident, beautiful? The description of the feelings of the king, when he discovered that he had killed a human being, instead of an animal, is vivid and thrilling, and the sorrow of the blind old father of the hermit-youth is most pathetic. I also like very much the episode about the nuptials of Ganga, "the fanciful, dripping and bright"; and the charming description of the nymph Menaka. Are not Sita's conversations with the old hermitess, Anousuya, beautiful? Her description of her own birth and of her marriage with Rama are exquisite.

We are now reading *Sakuntala* in Sanskrit. It is very difficult but very well written, and describes the calm, peaceful, and rustic life led by the ancient anchorites and devotees. If you can get hold of Sir William Jones's or Monier-Williams's translation, you will have some idea of what I am reading.

Saturday was mail-day. I have not got any letters from England by this mail. I expected one from M. Boquel, as you said in your last letter that he had received mine. I am afraid that one of my letters to you has been lost, as my impression is that I wrote to you by the same mail as to M. Boquel, and you do not mention having received any letter from me. It may be that my impression is wrong (I do hope it is), for in your last but one you acknowledged receipt of one from me.

I have not been keeping very well the last few days. I have been suffering from fever at night for the last fortnight. I feel well enough during the day. These night-fevers have weakened me a good deal. I am writing in bed, so you must excuse the bad writing. Dr. Cayley comes to see me every other day. I am now taking by his orders Dr. Churchill's newly discovered hypophosphate of lime along with my cod liver oil. It is very sweet and thick, just like honey. I hope I shall be able to get up and run about as usual in a few days.

The newspapers have been crying out against Lord Lytton for a certain official letter of his; and "thereby hangs a tale". I shall tell you the affair from the commencement: A certain Mr. F.[15] an English pleader, at Agra, one Sunday was about to drive to Church with his family. When the carriage was brought to the door, the syce (groom) failed to be in attendance, but made his appearance when sent for. For this cause, Mr. F. struck the syce with his open hand on the head and face, and pulled him by the hair, so as to cause him to fall down. Mr. F. and his family drove on to the Church, the syce got up and went into an adjoining compound, and there died almost immediately. Mr. F.

---

15. It is thought better to use initials instead of the full names.

was placed to take his trial. The medical officer, who conducted the *post mortem* examination, stated that the man had died from rupture of the spleen, which very slight violence, either from a blow or a fall, would be sufficient to cause, in consequence of the morbid enlargement of that organ. The Joint-Magistrate, Mr. L., found Mr. F. guilty of "voluntarily causing what distinctly amounts to hurt" and fined Mr. F. *thirty rupees* (£2), and let him off scot free! The High Court of the North-West Provinces did not find that the sentence was open to any objection. You see how cheap the life of an Indian is, in the eyes of an English Judge—£2! Lord Lytton immediately wrote a severe official letter on the subject. The Governor-General in Council had no doubt that the death of the groom was the direct result of the violence used towards him by Mr. F. The Governor-General found that besides his error of judgement, Mr. L. had evinced a most inadequate sense of the magnitude of the offence of which Mr. F. was found guilty. The Governor-General considered the sentence wholly insufficient and that to treat such offences with practical impunity was a very bad example and likely rather to encourage than repress them. For these reasons, the Governor-General in Council considered Mr. L.'s conduct with grave dissatisfaction; he should be so informed, and should be severely reprimanded for his great want of judgement and judicial capacity. Mr. L. should not be entrusted even temporarily with the independent charge of a district, until he had given proof of a better judgement and a more correct appreciation of the duties and responsibilities of magisterial officers for at least a year. The Governor-General could not say whether Mr. F. would have been convicted of a more serious offence, such as that of causing grievous hurt or that of culpable homicide, had he been charged with it. But this he could say, that in consequence of Mr. F.'s illegal violence his servant died, and that it was the plain duty of the Magistrate to have sent Mr. F. to trial for the more serious offence. Mr. L. had framed the indictment under Section 323 of the Indian Penal Code of "voluntarily causing hurt". That was an offence which varied infinitely in degree, from one which was little more than nominal to one which was so great that the Penal Code assigned to it the heavy punishment of imprisonment for a year, *and* a fine of Rs. 1,000. The amount of hurt and the amount of provocation were material elements in determining the sentence on such an offence. In Mr. F.'s case, while the provocation was exceedingly small, the hurt was death. The class of misconduct, out of which this crime had arisen, was believed to be dying out, but the Governor-General took this opportunity of expressing his abhorrence of the practice of European masters treating their native servants in a manner in which they would not treat men of their own race. This practice was all the more cowardly because those who were least able to retaliate injury or insult had the strongest claim upon the forbearance and protection of their employers. The Governor-General considered that the habit of resorting to blows, on every trifling provocation, should be visited by adequate legal penalties, and those who indulge in it should reflect that they may be put in jeopardy for a serious crime. Vive Lord Lytton! say I. All the papers are crying out against "such an unprecedented interference" on the part of the Viceroy. Lord Lytton in his letter says he "regrets that the Local Government (of the North West Provinces) should have made no inquiry, until directed to do so by the Government of India, into the circumstances of a case so injurious to the honour of British rule, and so damaging to the reputation of British justice in this country".

Miss Tucker, better known as A. L. O. E., who has written a great many small tracts (and who gave some time ago a prize for the best Bengali poem by an Indian girl on the subject of Jesus Christ), is at present at Amritsar. Though I do not know her personally, she must have heard about me from Miss Ada Smith and seen my book, for she wrote me a very nice letter a few days ago and sent me a small book of religious poems of her own.

What is the name of the young lady who "helped you in cutting up the buns and rolls" at your school-treat and with whom you "fell in immediately"? I cannot make out her name. Please write out the name *very distinctly* when you mention her next; I should like to know it.

Do you know I keep a *boîte à part* for your dear letters only? They are all tied up in packets, ticketed, and dated, so that I can take out any I like and read them over and over again. It seems sometimes as if you were there speaking with me. I do like your letters so much, dear; they are such a pleasure and comfort to me.

Have you read *The Newcomes*? It is one of the best of Thackeray's novels, and in my opinion stands next to *Esmond*. I have been looking over it again during my illness; I have read it through many a time.

Jeunette and Gentille are going on very well. They have had a long rest, as I have been unable to go out on account of my own illness and also that of Poontoo, our coachman, who has taken leave for a week as he is ill. Today, I am going out for a drive if I can. You should see

Jeunette trot up, with playful curvets, to the manger at the hour of her evening meal, in spite of the efforts of the groom to maintain a stately and decorous walk. Gentille is gentler, as her name implies; she is a little older than Jeunette and is always quiet and meek.

I have not been able to read much on account of my illness. I have only been reading some of Prosper Mérimée's short tales. "L'enlèvement de la redoute" is very graphic and spirited.

Among Saturday's telegrams was the news of Sir Salar Jung's return to India by the end of this month. He has stayed a very short time in Europe, hasn't he? I suppose this hasty retreat is owing to the near approach of winter.

Have you read Thackeray's funny poem on the visit of the Nepaulese ambassador, Jung Bahadoor, to England, several years ago? If you have not, do so; I am sure it will amuse you and that you will thank me for telling you about it.

August 8th.

I had no fever last night (though I perspired a good deal towards the morning) thanks to the eight grains of quinine which I took in one dose last evening.

The new drainage works, which were finished in the Bengali quarter of the town last winter, have not succeeded thoroughly. At the first heavy showers of the rainy season many of the streets gave way and went four or five feet below the level. There were several accidents, in consequence, of carriages and men going down with a plunge. We were almost afraid to drive in the narrow streets during the commencement of the rains. Now, however, all damage has been repaired and the roads are safe again. How I wish the rainy season were over! November with its cool winds and sunny days would be a real blessing. It is so delightful driving about at noon during the winter in Calcutta. The sun is then warm without being hot, and the wind is refreshing "like that of England's June".

There is a new Albert Hall opened here. Such a ruinous paltry building with small windows and broken panes! It is a shame to call it by such a high-sounding name. The new Government Telegraph Office on the contrary is a most grand and majestic mansion.

The Hon. Mr. Justice Phear, brother of the Master of Emmanuel College, is about to retire soon. He is a great advocate of female education in Bengal and is generally liked. Of course he is being overwhelmed with farewell addresses before his departure for England.

Papa has bought for me, from a bookseller *ambulant*, a beautiful edition in eight volumes of Victor Hugo's works. I shall, I am sure, find great pleasure in reading them.

As the mail goes away tomorrow, I must finish this letter today. I am afraid I must stop here, dear, for I feel a little tired. Papa's and Mamma's and my own kindest regards to your father and mother, and their love to you, and best love to your dear self, from me.

> 12, Manicktollah Street,
> Calcutta
> August 26, 1876

Your welcome letter has been lying unanswered for more than a fortnight. I do not feel strong enough yet to be able to sit up and write, so you must excuse this delay in answering you, dear. I am bettèr than I was a week ago, but not quite well; the fever at nights has abated but not quite gone.

Many thanks for the two beautiful photo scraps. Just like your kind self to send them to me. I am highly pleased with them, especially with that of the horses. Mine (my horses, I mean) are as well-conditioned as ever. They are bay with black legs, you know; the white one in the photograph resembles Jeunette a little, but Jeunette's head is finer and her eyes are more spirited.

I am translating some small Sanskrit pieces. I would have copied one or two for you, but they are too long for that. I have sent one to the *Calcutta Quarterly Review* which the editor (Mr. Lethbridge[16]) has accepted. Papa is very pleased and so am I, for the *Calcutta Review* is the best of its kind in India.

As I am too weak to be able to go downstairs, I have had my piano brought into my bedroom, for I am allowed to play a little now and then, by Dr. Cayley, to amuse myself, that is without getting tired.

Calcutta is now taken up with the Municipal elections. Papa has given his vote to the Hon. Baboo Kristo Das Pal, the editor of the *Hindu Patriot*.

Lord Lytton had a very bad fall recently from his horse, as he was riding at Simla. He went down the *khud* several feet, but luckily escaped with a few bruises. Colonel Burne, his private secretary, was present at the accident, and was terribly frightened, it is said, on seeing the

---

16. Afterwards Sir Roper Lethbridge.

Viceroy fall. He was private secretary to Lord Mayo, and was a witness of that Viceroy's murder by the convict.

How nice to have A. L. with you. You are enjoying yourself to your heart's content. Give my love to A. L. Is she as fond as ever of Byron? I like Byron's "Siege of Corinth" very much. There are some very fine and spirited lines in it, especially at the end: the description of "Alp, the Adrian renegade" who is known by "his right arm bare" in the battle fields; that of the fight within the Church:

> *Where the last and desperate few*
> *Would the failing fight renew.*

His "Verses on attaining my thirty-fifth birthday" are highly pathetic, and there is a ring of sincerity in them, very rarely to be found in Byron. "The death of the gladiator" is well known as one of the best pieces among his poems. Papa was saying the other day that he had heard that once Professor Wilson ("Christopher North") reading aloud the piece, broke down at the line:

> There were his young barbarians all at play,

and was so moved that he could not read further.

28th.

Your dear letter of the 26th July arrived yesterday. I was at first a little surprised at the writing of the address. Papa suggested that it must be a letter from M. Boquel, but I soon guessed that it was Miss A.'s hand, and your letter confirmed my suspicions. Indeed, dear, I shall write to you as often as possible when I get well again. I am very weak, you see, and am apt to get soon tired, if I exert myself ever so little. I hope you will excuse me my faults and delays in not writing to you as long as I am ill. I was thinking of you, dear, the other night. It was a Sunday night, and I could not sleep because of the fever, and I kept awake for two or three hours. I heard the clock strike one, and then I thought you were perhaps at Church, at evening service, and then I wished I could be with you and

> *Hear once more in college fanes*
> *The storms their high-built organs make,*

And thunder-music rolling shake
The prophets blazoned on the panes.

Your last letter was very nice, dear, I read it several times over.

If our Garden could be sold, we could start for England immediately. It is a pity, Papa says, that it is so difficult to sell off. Of course, it would be very nice to be able to go to England, but the Garden is so full of past recollections, that when it comes to the point (as it very nearly did two months ago) to sell it off, one feels a pang; and I was rather glad than otherwise when the intending purchaser, who had come to see the Garden, said that the place did not suit him quite.

You see I have been more than a month ill, and I have not been to church for such a long time; a short drive even tires me now. Papa and Uncle Girish say the hypophosphate of lime has done great things for me (though it is hardly a month since I began taking it), and that it will do more. I feel stronger, as I said before; and if the fever goes off completely I shall be on my legs again, and writing long letters to you.

The weather is much finer now. There is always a soft northern breeze, indicative of the near approach of our pleasant winter. The rains too have abated, though sometimes of an afternoon there are heavy showers. I hope the rains will soon be quite over, for already there has been more rain than the average. The skies are beautiful now, serene and blue, dapple with white silvery clouds. I must make this letter as long as I can, but it must go by this mail, and I hope I shall be able to write to you again next week. It will be quite a task for you to make out this scrawl, but you see I am lying in bed, and writing in that posture in a legible manner is rather a difficult thing.

I heard that Mrs. Cowell has had my book noticed in some English paper, the *Christian Gazette* or some such paper. Have you heard anything about it?

I am glad you see the Halls pretty often. Is Lizzie as shy as ever? I suppose not, for you say she sang, and I remember she was so shy before, that she never played even before Aru and myself. Does she or Mary attend any of the lectures? I suppose you do not go now to the French lectures, as you never mention them.

Shall I describe to you the bed-room in which I am now lying? As I have nothing better to write about, I had better I think. The room has four windows, two to the east, one to the south, and another to the north, and two doors looking west, so we can have plenty of fresh air, you see; it is smaller than Mrs. Baker's drawing-room, but larger than her dining-room. It is furnished very strangely, half in the English and half in the Bengali style. A large cushion or *guddee* of white linen, in the centre, furnished with smaller cushions and pillows, very tempting to a sleepy person. A few chairs, a rather small bed in a corner with *muslin* mosquito curtains, my piano at its foot. Over the piano hang our family likenesses, namely those of Papa, Mamma, and my brother, Aru and myself. A small desk at one corner, covered with sundry English, French, Bengali, and Sanskrit books; my box of veterinary medicines in the opposite corner; near the bed on a small side-table, the canary and goldfinch in a roomy cage. The window on the north commands a view of the busy street and the neighbouring houses, and below is our small front court-yard; just under the window are the wooden mangers of Jeunette and Gentille. The east windows look towards Uncle Girish's house, the south one overlooks our back-garden, and then beyond our wall there are several huts and a tank, a most dirty and unhealthy affair. The east windows are closed just now, the north and south ones are open. The sky is so blue and so peaceful. The sun is not *very* hot, a cloud is over it at this moment; the north breeze is so soft and refreshing; a very calm and quiet hour this is (2 P.M.).

I have been reading one or two of Victor Hugo's plays, *Cromwell* and *Hernani*. He is not always pure in his writings as Lamartine was, but *Cromwell* and *Hernani* are interesting; the latter, however, is not to be recommended. Papa is reading Carlyle's *French Revolution*. I told him to read it; he now reads it to me sometimes (I have read it through before); he is a very good reader, and if he had taken lessons in elocution, I am sure he would have become a second Bellew. Have you ever heard poor Bellew read? He is dead now. I heard him once while we were at St. Leonards. I never passed a pleasanter evening. He read selections from Shakespeare, Dickens, and other well-known authors; but the best was his rendering of the "Vagabond", a poem by an American author; I forget the name, but I have the piece in one of our books.

By last mail we heard that Madame de Châtelain, wife of the Chevalier de Châtelain, had died in July. Le Chevalier de Châtelain is, you must know, the translator of Chaucer and Shakespeare, and of other English and German poets. We have never seen him, but we know him very well by correspondence. He was very fond of his wife, for he says that "pendant 33 ans, et plus, elle fut *l'ange* de la maison". He is a friend and schoolfellow of Victor Hugo.

I have been obliged of course to give up my Sanskrit lessons. I shall resume them as soon as I am a little stronger.

It will be very pleasant for you to go again on a visit to old Malvern and see the dear well-known faces; I am sure you will enjoy yourself. I should have liked to be with you when you visited the Royal Academy, for though I cannot draw even a dog-kennel (that seems the easiest to me), I am very fond of paintings. Aru used to draw very well latterly.

I have been thinking and thinking to write to you about something more interesting than my own self! My letter seems full of myself! So selfish it looks, but you see I have nothing to write about, except of ourselves, as I do not go out much, especially now.

Our winter skies are so beautiful and variegated in colour, that dyers and weavers try to imitate them in the colouring of the borders of *saris*, but of course they never succeed in giving the rich, splendid, soft, and harmonious tints of the sky.

As it is past six, Papa tells me to leave off, and not tire myself, because of the slight feverishness at night. So good evening, dear, for the present, and "au revoir" till tomorrow morning.

Jeunette and Gentille are eating their evening meal under the window.

29th.

Papa and I were talking last evening about the number of my books that we have sent to our friends in England and from whom we have not received any acknowledgement. The number amounts to sixteen; the friends are of our most intimate ones, and not likely to let a letter remain unanswered. This makes us half-afraid that the letters and books have been lost, or that some of the post-office men must have tampered with the stamps, taken them, and thrown away the letters and books; for we sent three or four at a time, which amounts to ten rupees more or less, a great temptation to poor men. Such things are very common in India, more so than in England. Some years ago a postman was caught in the very act of throwing several packets of letters into the river! It was proved that he was in the habit of doing so, to save himself the trouble of going his rounds! So you see we are rather in a fix to find out where those books and letters are gone. Will you kindly ask Mary or Lizzie Hall if they have received the book and letter which I sent them in May last, and will you please write and tell me if they have or not in your next letter?

I have made a slight mistake about the pages of this letter; the reason is that I blotted a page frightfully, and was obliged to tear it off; if you follow the numbers on the corner of the pages you will find it all right. I only hope that you will be able to make out this illegible scrawl.

Today's telegram announces that the English press approves Lord Lytton's minute on the F. case; the *Indian Daily News* has a most whimpering sort of article on it this morning, trying to unsay all it had said against Lord Lytton and his minute before.

Sir Salar Jung has arrived at Bombay. He will be glad to be home again, I am sure. I must close here, dear, as I feel a little tired. I shall write again as soon as I feel a little stronger. Papa's and Mamma's and my own best regards to your father and mother, and their love to you, and best love from myself.

12, Manicktollah Street,
Calcutta
September 6, 1876

I thought of writing to you last week, but was prevented. I hope to make this letter long, for I have got plenty of time before the mail leaves.

On Monday there was such an accident in my Uncle Girish's garden. One of our neighbours had very recently bought a pair of Walers; they were a very vicious pair, at least one of the pair was in the habit of biting and kicking his grooms. Well, the day before yesterday, my uncle and I were sitting on the *perron* of his house when we heard a hubbub, and in a second we saw the cause. The pair of horses were rushing madly towards my uncle's house. His porter was on the point of shutting the gate; Mamma, from our house, called out to him to step aside, or he would be crushed. On they came, furious, the carriage was almost overturned by a garden seat, but it rose straight again, the pole was pushed between three tall betel-nut trees, and all the three were snapped in two; one fell on the haunch of one of the horses. They would have rushed on again, but the chain of the pole broke, and each turning in opposite directions they thus pulled against each other, and for one minute seemed bewildered and stood still, but trembling with excitement. The grooms gathered round and secured the animals. One of the horses had been severely injured, but it was very fortunate that no lives had been lost. We are so often walking about on my uncle's and our own grounds, that I felt very thankful that no one was run over, and that we were not walking about at the time of the accident.

Jeunette and Gentille are as well-behaved and as spirited as ever. One day when they came all harnessed, just before they were put to the carriage, I called Jeunette; at first, she looked at me rather suspiciously, and made a step or two, then stopped again, peeping at me through her blinkers, uncertain whether to come or not. I took out a piece of bread from my pocket, and she came at once. Now I have only to call and she obeys me at once, whether I have a slice of bread or not.

8th.

I could not write this letter yesterday, as I received a letter from the editor of the *Bengal Magazine*, asking me earnestly to come to his help, in the shape of an article for the October number of his Magazine. I was busy yesterday copying out three pieces of poetry from my MSS., but I am at liberty today.

I received a small book from Mrs. Cowell by the last mail. It is entitled *Oliver of the Mill* and is beautifully got up. It is written by her sister, Miss Charlesworth, author of *Ministering Children* and a great many other books. I have been reading it and I like it very much. Have you ever seen Miss Charlesworth? We used to meet her very often when she once came on a visit to her sister in Cambridge. She is such a good Christian lady. We all liked her greatly.

I received also by the last mail a letter from Mrs. Hutchinson in acknowledgement of my book and letter. So all my books, at least, are not lost. I was very much pleased when I got her letter.

Here is a little story quite true for you. The place where this happened is Lucknow. A Mohammedan kept a school. One of the pupils, a lad of twelve, absented himself for a day or two. When he came to school again, the master shut him in a dark room (where a snake had been seen some days ago, and which had not been killed) as a punishment. Presently the lad cried out that the room was very dark, and that he was frightened; the Mohammedan did not answer him even. Soon the poor boy called out that there was a snake in the room, and he begged hard to be let out. The inhuman master told him to open the door himself if he could; but the door was shut from the outside. Some minutes afterwards the child said they might as well let him out now as the snake had bitten him, but the brutal man did not even open the door to see. When the lad's father came in search of his son, he was told that the boy had been shut up, as he had been absent for two days. The father asked the schoolmaster to release him now. They both entered the room. The boy lay dead on the floor, a snake was coiled round his throat; he was bitten in three or four places, near the ankle and foot. The schoolmaster has been hanged.

I am now quite well, but I have been obliged to give up Sanskrit for the present till I am stronger. We have just come back from a drive, I enjoyed it very much. The morning was cold and sunny. I have not been reading much lately.

I have just received a letter from you, dear. Such a duck of a letter! Mr. Knight's address is:

Messrs. W. Newman and Co.
Booksellers,
Dalhousie Square, E. Calcutta, India.

Little Varûna has been ill, but is now quite well. He is so intelligent. He knows all about Moody and Sankey. Some months ago he had a book about them in his hand; I was looking at their likenesses on the cover, when he explained to me: "this is Moody, he preaches; this other one is Sankey,—he sings," and then he breaks forth into one of their well-known hymns: "F'ee f'om the law" (which means "Free from the law") or "Ho! my comwades!" (Ho! my comrades).

How you must have enjoyed seeing your school companions again! I suppose it will be some time that you will be away from Cambridge, at least four or five weeks. I shall always send my letters to Cambridge, as that will be safer.

I hope I shall be able to bring out another "Sheaf", not gleaned in French but in "Sanskrit Fields"! If I succeed, then I shall follow your advice, and send two copies to Professors Max Müller and Monier-Williams, respectively; as it is, I have only as yet gathered two ears, and my "Sanskrit Sheaf" is far from being gathered and complete.

We shall go to the Garden by the end of next month. I wish we were able to go earlier, but that is impossible on account of the recent rains. The Garden is so beautiful! I wish you could see it. And then it is so quiet and peaceful there. It is not perfect:

Ce n'est pas le séjour des dieux,

. . . . . .

Mais ce que j'aime encore mieux,
La paix que l'on y trouve est grande.

HARIHAR DAS AND TORU DUTT

I am glad you like *Pendennis*. Read *Newcomes* next. You will, I think, like it better still. All Thackeray's works are delightful. One never feels dull or tired with any of his books. *The Book of Snobs* is very amusing, and, sad to say, very truthful.

Would not the contemplated Channel tunnel be a grand thing, if it could be made successful? I remember the *trajet* from Boulogne to Folkestone. Aru and I were so dreadfully sea-sick; we remained all wrapped in our cloaks, with our faces buried against the cushions of the miserable little private cabin; the steward shook his head, I recollect, on seeing our woebegone attitude! I have heard that very few people cross the sea from France to England without feeling sea-sick.

I do not know whether Anglo-Indian officers' wives are in the habit of horse-whipping the Indian soldiers, but it is not unlikely, as I have heard of Anglo-European *ladies* (?) beating, whipping their Indian servants.

We have no real English gentlemen or ladies in India, except a very few.[17] People generally come out to India to make their fortunes, you see, and real gentlemen and ladies very rarely leave home and friends for the "yellow gold". M. About has a very true remark on French and other people of foreign countries who come to make their fortunes in Egypt; his remark is highly applicable to Europeans who come to India with the same motive.

He says: "Oh, l'étrange racaille! et faut-il que l'orient nous juge sur de pareils échantillons! Je me rappelai malgré moi qu'un jour, à Scutari, comme je me promenais seul sur la rive asiatique du Bosphore, mon attention fut attirée par un long rouleau de choses mortes, brisées, corrompues, à moitié détruites, que le flot apportait, reprenait, et abandonnait enfin. Cette épave sans forme, sans couleur, et sans nom, ne ressemble-t-elle pas un peu à l'émigration de rebuts humains qu'un courant invisible pousse à l'est de la Méditerranée?"

It is so dark and cloudy at this moment. It has been raining, though the morning was very fine and sunny, and there was not a cloud in the sky. The room (library we call it, for it is furnished with six *almyras*, or glass-shelves of books) in which I am writing has only two windows, which makes it rather dark on a cloudy day. It has four doors; two have been shut up by the two book-shelves, and two are open; one leads to our dining-room in the east, the other is the door of exit. We

---

17. Written in 1876.

are rather hard up here for rooms, there is no regular drawing-room; old Baugmaree is much more comfortable with its sunny rooms and halls. I wish you were with us at Baugmaree; would it not be pleasant going about the dear old place with you, feeding the ducks and pigeons, angling, having the cow milked before you? are you not fond of milk? ours is the best of its kind, thick as cream, and we make such rich butter from it. I am not fond of milk at all. Mamma's cows are such beauties, though they are a little fierce; they never made friends with me or Aru, though we used to try hard to get into their good graces by dint of dainty newly-grown cusha grass. And then how I would enjoy walking with you in the Garden! Come this cold season; there are no snakes out among the grass during the winter in Calcutta. Oh, if you really could come! writing about it makes me, for the moment, believe it possible, nay, very likely; but the reaction comes soon after; and I feel sad when I think of the impossibility of such a thing. I wonder shall I ever see you again. If not here on this earth, have we not the sure hope of meeting in a better and a far happier home?

I must rest a little as it is nearly 4 p.m., and Papa is calling out to me from upstairs not to tire myself.

I saw in the papers today the narrow escape of Archdeacon Emery (of Ely) and his family. I suppose you have seen it in the Cambridge local papers.

There has been a *dacoity* near our garden. (I suppose you know what that is?) I hope the *dacoits* will be well punished, for they have been caught by the police.

I think I had better stop here, dear, as I have nothing to write about. Kindest regards from Papa and Mamma to yours and their love to you. Best love from me to your dear self.

> 12, Manicktollah Street,
> Calcutta
> September 16, 1876

Your letter of the 15th August came to hand this morning. Many many thanks for it; I need not repeat how welcome it was.

A terrible accident happened last Sunday. We were taking our usual morning drive when, in a very crowded part of the street, a very infirm old man ran against our horses, and was knocked down. It seems he was running away from another carriage and ran right against our horses. We did not think he was seriously hurt at the time; he seemed only a good deal bruised; Papa had him immediately carried to the Medical College Hospital, which was not far off. The surgeon in attendance did not find the man much hurt, but the old man has since died; isn't this dreadful? The man was so infirm that he could not have been less than seventy or eighty years old. We were going at a very moderate pace, and Jeunette and Gentille behaved in the most exemplary manner, stopping the moment they were checked. The carriage wheels did not pass over the man, I believe; perhaps one of the horses' legs might have struck him. We shall know all the particulars as soon as the inquest comes off, which is to be held on the 18th instant (Monday). Our coachman is very much frightened; he has never had an accident since he has been in our service, and that is more than twenty-five years. He is a very cautious driver; if there is a carriage just before ours, he is in the habit of slacking the pace of our horses, and following in the wake of the carriage just in front; of course when the road is perfectly clear he drives on.

Papa will have to give his evidence; he has never given evidence, though he has taken many a one, when he was Deputy-Magistrate many years ago. The old man, it seems, had no relatives or near kinsmen; there is an old woman in whose house he used to lodge. She said to our coachman that the old man was subject to fits of trembling, and that on the very morning of the accident she had begged him not to go out as he might drop and die in the street. Poor old fellow! He should have kept on the pavement and not tried to cross just as so many carriages were crossing each other. I hope the affair will soon end satisfactorily, as Papa is rather anxious about the poor coachman, lest he be punished unjustly. The inquest was to have been held yesterday, and Papa went to the Coroner's office, but one of the jurymen was absent, so Papa came back. The course of law is very tardy in India and not *very* impartial. I have not been out for some days, as we think the coachman will be a little nervous till this coroner's inquest is satisfactorily over. I have covered a whole sheet with this accident, but as it is a subject which engrosses us all most at present, you must excuse me, dear.

Papa and Mamma have gone to see Uncle Girish, who is ailing a little from a slight attack of feverishness. I am going there, so good-bye for the present.

Little Varûna has not been to see us for some time. He is a very delicate child; with his intelligence, his affectionate ways, he wins every heart. He knows more about the British Pharmacopoeia than

I do! He has only once to be told the name of a medicine, and he never forgets it. He pronounces the hard names of the medicines so charmingly; "anisee vate" (aniseed water), "essence" (with an accent on the second syllable) of peppermint; "swandy" (brandy) is the funniest; then there is "nit'ic etho" (nitric ether). He will never own that the smell of any medicine is disagreeable to him; even cod-liver oil, he does not hesitate to say that he likes. Several days ago he was handling my phial of cod-liver oil; I told him to leave the bottle alone as it was sure to make his little hand smell terribly. He denied this, and wanted to smell it; so I opened the stopper, he took a long breath, his little nose shrunk up in spite of his efforts to keep a good face. "Well," I said, "how do you like it?" "Very much" was the reply, with a shrewd naughty little smile. He is very fond of the piano, and used to be very good friends with me, because I allowed him to play (?) on mine sometimes, when he came here. I wish you could see him; I am sure you would like him; are you fond of children and do they easily come to you? I am a very bad hand at making friends with children and babies; the latter I am quite afraid to take on my lap, for fear of hurting them. Aru was a better hand with children in general; they took more kindly to her sweet face and gentle manners; she used to be extremely fond of babies, but like me, although in a lesser degree, she was afraid to handle the very young ones. But with Varûna, I made friends the very day of our arrival. He was pronounced not very pretty by Mamma on the first evening, but I quite disagreed with her, and now she agrees with me that his little face is the most intelligent we have ever seen. If he sees us dassing in the street, from their house, his triumphant cry of "Uncle!" or "Toru!" as the case might be, is the most gladdening and joyous sound that can be heard. You told me to write to you about him; I hope you are not yet tired of hearing about his little winsome ways. The other day his mother forbade him to bother Papa about his gold watch. He came to our house, and the first thing he said was, "Mamma said that I am not to *ask* you for the watch, but that I may take it if you give it yourself without my asking. Now give it of yourself, I am not asking!" Wasn't this fine logic?

I must go now and dress for dinner. In India, Bengalis and some Europeans, too, take baths twice a day at least, one in the morning and one in the evening, in consequence of the heat. I know how hot the weather has been this summer in England. All the correspondents of the Indian papers complain of the dreadful heat in England this year.

I received a letter from Mary Hall[18] on Saturday afternoon. It had been directed to Baugmaree and so was a little delayed. She speaks about you and says what a good correspondent you are; indeed you are a *very good* correspondent. You know I generally receive a letter from you every fortnight, and as I got one by the mail before last, I did not expect one by this mail; it was quite an unexpected pleasure, and I was so glad to receive it; you are a faithful friend indeed; when I am asked by Uncle Girish if I have received any letters from England by the last mail, my invariable answer is, "Yes, from faithful dear Mary." Yours is indeed a rare and warm affection for me, and, dear, I feel at times such keen pleasure when I think about it. God bless you, dear, for it; and though we may not meet in this world, perhaps we may through His grace meet in that happier and far better home.

Mary Hall says they have received my book, so *all* are not lost, and it was wrong of us to think that the post-office men were to blame! What is your whole name, dear? I found that one of the very first letters you wrote to me is signed "Mary E. Rodd Martin"—so please tell me your full name in E. It is quite a shame not to know my best and only friend's name, is it not?

Have you read Thackeray's *Esmond*? I had read it long ago, before we went to England, but I read it over again a few days ago and it is very interesting. Papa thinks it is Thackeray's masterpiece, and I quite agree with him.

Miss Thackeray, whom we met at Cambridge at Trinity Lodge,[19] told us, I remember, that her father took the greatest pains with *Esmond*, more than with any others of his works, and that he, too, used to think it his best work.

There was a good deal of rain on Saturday, but today the weather is very fine.

Mamma has caught a cold; it is all owing to her having the window of her bed-room open, in spite of our remonstrances. The dews are now very heavy during the night, and, whatever poets or bards may sing in praise of them, dews are very unhealthy, and one is apt to catch a bad cold, if one stays out late in the evening without a hat. This reminds me of Pope's lines in his "Elegy on an unfortunate lady" and how they (the

---

18. Now Lady Sandys of Cambridge.
19. Dr. Thompson was then Master of Trinity College.

couplet, I mean) were parodied by Catherine Fanshawe, and applied to the then newly-opened Regent's Park. Pope wrote:

> *Here shall the spring its earliest sweets bestow,*
> *Here the first roses of the year shall blow.*

Catherine Fanshawe only altered one word of the first line and a single letter of the second, and made the couplet run thus:

> *Here shall the spring its earliest* coughs *bestow,*
> *Here the first* noses *of the year shall blow.*

I must stop here for the present, though I have very little time to finish this letter, as the mail goes on Tuesday. From the week after next the mail-day will be changed from Tuesday to Friday, on account of the monsoons on the Indian Ocean, which grow less during the cold weather.

Dr. Cayley called to see me the other day. I am quite well now. He recommended us to go to Hazareebag or Bangalore for a change; he would have recommended a sea-voyage, if he had not been told that I get sea-sick. He said we ought not to go to Europe before March, so as to have the spring before us when we land in England; as if we were going so soon or, who knows, perhaps at all! The return to England is becoming a very vague and shadowy thing; it grows fainter and dimmer every day almost. Travelling in India by rail is rather unpleasant, especially for Bengalis; there was a meeting yesterday at the Town Hall on the subject. We did not attend the meeting, but we shall see the report, I suppose, in the papers soon.

18th.

Little Varûna came to see us yesterday evening. The child was so glad to see us; he kept talking, laughing, and jumping about, in his delight. We were also very glad to see him. His joy reached its summit when I opened the piano, and played some of Sankey's hymns; he would not at first touch the piano for very joy, but I begged him to play (?) just a little before the servant came to take him away, and he touched one note, laughed out gaily, and then ran to his servant and went home quite happy. Poor child! he has got very thin on account of his recent illness; he is now taking "Pepysine wine" (Pepsine wine) he informed us, and "Hunjarian wine" (Hungarian wine), but the latter was very "hot", he said, so he does not take it any more. He constantly asked, sure of the reply, if we were not very glad to see him. He is very fond of all of us.

The afternoon has been rather cloudy today. I hope it will clear up tomorrow morning. The London correspondent of the *Indian Daily News* writes by this mail that the weather had been much cooler in England for the past week, the thermometer having gone down forty degrees. Do you find it cooler? I suppose you'll not be back in Cambridge when this letter reaches you, as you are going to stay six weeks at Guildford, and it does not take more than three weeks for a letter to go to England, via Brindisi. I must close here. Papa's and Mamma's kindest regards to yours and love to you, and with my best love to yourself.

P.S. Our coachman has been discharged; the jury found that he was not at all to blame. Papa simply related what had happened to the Coroner. The Sub-assistant Surgeon of the Medical College Hospital said that the old man was stone blind. Poor old fellow! It was very rash to venture out in a crowded street without a guide.

> 12, Manicktollah Street,
> Calcutta
> September 25, 1876

This letter will be very short, for I am going to enclose a translation from the Sanskrit, which I have contributed to the *Bengal Magazine* for October. There are, of course, one or two mistakes in the printing. The thirteenth line of the poem is too close to the foregoing one; does it not seem as if the thirteenth line, like Dhruva, whom it describes, also "longed to clamber up, and by his playmate sit". You must tell me if you like the piece. I have not received any letter from you by this mail, but I did not expect any, as I got one by the last mail but one.

I received a very nice *Recueil Choisi* from the Chevalier de Châtelain. Poor old gentleman! his wife has lately died, as I wrote to you before. Inside the book on the flyleaf he has written "A Miss Toru Dutt, de la part d'un cœur désolé" and then lower down—"A bientôt" which means, I suppose, that he will write soon. There are several translations from French into English and vice versa, of poetical pieces by himself and his late wife.

The cold weather is coming on slowly, the mornings are already cool and pleasant, and at night the dews fall heavy. You are now in the warm autumn season of dear old England.

There were few people at Church yesterday, owing to the *Durga Poojah* holidays. Every one is going from Calcutta for a change; this is the longest vacation of the year, extending to more than two months.

Varûna came to see us last evening. I made glad his heart with the present of a small "Dolly's photographic album". I at first feared that he would refuse to take it, for he has a shy sort of pride which disdains any favour; but the small album was too tempting. "Was he to take it home?" "Yes." "And not return it again?" "No, it was his property now." He was so delighted with it, showing it to everybody. Some time ago he was sharply rebuked by a not very good-tempered gentleman. The child burst into tears, and Papa and I took him away. "He is a very naughty man," said Varûna, as he walked sobbing between me and Papa. "Yes." Then in a burst of revengeful indignation, "We will charge a gun with small shot and shoot into his eyes," he cried. We could not help laughing outright at this most sanguinary proposal.

The din of music at nights from the houses of our Hindu neighbours is something awful. During the *Poojah* they have theatrical representations at their own houses, much to the annoyance of quieter neighbours like ourselves.

The Garden is much more retired and quiet during the *Poojah*. There are very few rich men's houses near Baugmaree, and these, too, are mostly visited from time to time by the owners, who very seldom like to live for a long time in such a secluded spot. The only wealthy family who do live there permanently are the Mullicks, who are our very next door neighbours. Their grounds are separated from ours by a high wall.

Mr. J. Wilson, the editor of the *Indian Daily News*, has been summoned for libel against the Chairman of the Municipality, Sir Stuart Hogg. Mr. Wilson in his paper said, that he (Mr. Wilson) had votes enough to have been a Municipal Commissioner, but that Sir Stuart had tampered with them, and so prevented his being elected. Now this is a very serious charge, and Sir Stuart has very rightly asked the magistrate to issue a summons against Mr. Wilson. The magistrate said that Sir Stuart had been libelled, and granted the summons. Sir Stuart Hogg has borne with Mr. Wilson's invectives long enough, and the editor does want a lesson. Every day he used to abuse Sir Stuart most unjustly and for nothing at all. But he has already commenced apologizing and whining in his paper for his "misapprehension".

There will be a great Durbar at Delhi during the cold season, when the Viceroy will proclaim Victoria, no more Queen, but Empress of India.

Sir Bartle Frere, the papers said on Saturday, was likely to come out as Governor of Bombay again.

So Murad V has been deposed on account of his insanity, and his brother Hamid reigns in his stead. I am afraid it will take a long time to have a permanent, just, and powerful government in Turkey.

I have not read anything lately. Since my last illness I have got to be very idle, I think. A whole month passed in laziness in bed is very bad, and apt to make one idle and good-for-nothing, even when one is strong and well again. I have got three more letters to write by this mail. I hope I shall be able to do so, as there is plenty of time before me. The mail does not leave till Friday; they have changed the mail-day from Tuesday to Friday-on account of the monsoons.

Lord Lytton had a son born to him at Simla; this is rather a new thing, as no child had been born to any of the Viceroys while they held that position. The baby-boy is to be named Victor Alexander, by the Queen's desire, who has wished to stand as one of his sponsors.

There is another skating rink opened at the Calcutta Zoological Gardens; very few ladies, the papers say, venture on the rink, but there is always a good company of gentlemen. A French company of actors is coming out to India in November, so we are going to have French plays acted.

Our relation, about whom I wrote to you, has no doubt by this time reached England long ago. As he and his family are Hindus, we are not on visiting terms. His father comes now and then to see my Uncle Girish, for they were in the same class when they were boys at school. Mamma had a slight attack of fever, but she is now, I am happy to say, quite well.

Last night we had a heavy shower. But this is the last of the rains. The days now seldom turn out rainy and soon the rains will cease altogether. The mornings are pretty cool now, but the days are warm; even now I am perspiring profusely as I write to you.

Jeunette and Gentille are going on very well.

A few days ago I lent Jeunette for the evening to one of my cousins. His coachman harnessed her to a light carriage along with one of my cousin's own horses, a heavy and rather stupid Waler, with no paces and no speed. My cousin's coachman drives rather too fast, and Jeunette went off at a rattling pace. Fortunately there was no accident. The Waler could not keep pace with Jeunette and she had to draw the carriage and the heavy Waler into the bargain! She came home rather *essoufflée*, but neighing and impatient to see Gentille.

There is not such another for speed as Jeunette, and she is as sound as a bell, never been laid up even for a day.

I was reading your last letter over again, dear. It is such a nice letter, and the first page has pleased and comforted me especially. Yes, indeed we may firmly hope to meet in that happy Jerusalem, if we may not meet here on this earth. Do you know a hymn about that new Jerusalem, beginning with the words:

> *For thee, O dear, dear country,*
> *Mine eyes their vigils keep;*
> *For very love, beholding*
> *Thy happy name, they weep.*
> *The mention of thy glory*
> *Is unction to the breast,*
> *And medicine in sickness,*
> *And love, and life, and rest.*

It must be a grand and beautiful city, indeed, that new Jerusalem:

> *With jasper glow thy bulwarks,*
> *Thy streets with emeralds blaze;*
> *The sardius and the topaz*
> *Unite in thee their rays.*

The last two chapters of the *Revelation* I read often, they are so beautiful.

I must close here, dear. Kindest regards from all to your father and mother, and love from Papa and Mamma to you, and with best love to your dear self from me.

12, Manicktollah Street,
Calcutta
October 2, 1876

Your very welcome letter arrived on Saturday. Many, many thanks for it. You must have learnt by this time through my previous letters that

I had been unable to write to you on account of illness. I am now resolved to write to you by every mail unless I am prevented by illness or anything very serious; else I shall not be able to be square with you; you are such a good correspondent! I wrote to you by the last mail and I wrote three letters besides by the same mail, so I have been very busy last week, you see.

We did not go to Church yesterday, as Gentille has been laid up for the last four days with a bad foot. She is better today, but not quite well; I am afraid I shall have to get a new horse, and sell Gentille off, as she is not a very hardy animal. Jeunette is never unwell, and she is forced to remain idle during all the time that Gentille is laid up; we must get an animal as healthy as Jeunette, as soon as the horse-sellers come down to Chitpore, which will be about the end of this month. I have not gone out for the last few days on account of Gentille's bad leg. I shall be very sorry to part with Gentille, for she is a beautiful animal, such fine proportions she has, and she carries her tail just like an Arab; we shall not part with her unless we find it absolutely necessary.

We received the two books sent for from Messrs. Hachette & Co., and I am now reading Victor Hugo's *Les Misérables*. It is very interesting, but there are some wicked parts in it (as there are in almost all French books), which would have been better left out or not written. But the book is powerfully written, and one feels the touch of a master-hand on each page. Do you know the story? Hugo, you know, is a rank democrat; he has his own opinions about human justice, and the book is mainly written to show the baseness of society and the injustice done by human laws. Jean Valjean, the hero of the tale, was first "émondeur" at Faverolles. He used to maintain his poor widow sister and her seven children with his paltry earnings. When he used to come home, tired, of evenings, after a hard day's work, and take his place at the meagre supper, his sister would take the best pieces of food from his plate and give them to her children, and he bore all things; the little ones one day stole some milk from the milkmaid's can, and he paid the milk-woman without telling about this matter to his sister, for he knew that the children would then be punished. There was "disette" at Faverolles, and one night, made desperate with the pitiful cries of the children, he went out, and breaking the pane of a window in a baker's shop, put in his hand and stole a loaf of bread. He was caught and tried for "vol avec effraction" and was condemned to five years in the galleys at Toulon. He tried to escape three or four times, and for these attempts his term of imprisonment was extended to nineteen years. Nineteen years "pour avoir cassé un carreau et pris un pain!" He was set free, but with the "passeport jaune", and, of course, the police kept a surveillance over him. On his first day of freedom, wherever he went he was turned out; the "passeport jaune" designated him as a man "très-dangereux". He had walked "douze lieues" that day, and in the evening he stopped at a village; but no one took him in, even the innkeepers turned him out with a "Va-t'en". At last as he was lying on the pavement near the Church, an old lady came out from the edifice, and learning the state of things, told him to knock at a small house, which she pointed out to him. It was the house of the bishop of the place. The bishop was a very good man, and received him and treated him as an equal, calling him "monsieur", much to the surprise of Jean Valjean. "Un forçat! vous m'appelez *monsieur!* vous ne me tutoyez pas!" But at night when the whole household was asleep, the old instinct awoke within the "forçat". He stole the silver plate of the bishop, was captured in the morning by the police, and brought to the bishop, who told the "gendarmes" that he had given the silver plate to the man, and also two silver candlesticks, which the man had evidently forgot, and he took these from the table, and gave them to the "forçat", who stood stupefied and motionless; the bishop assured the police that they had made a mistake, and they departed. Then the bishop (Monseigneur Bienvenu) said to the man, "Jean Valjean, mon frère, vous n'appartenez plus au mal mais au bien. C'est votre âme que je vous achète; je la retire aux pensées noires, et à l'esprit de perdition, et je la donne à Dieu." The story is very long; it tells how the "forçat", Jean Valjean, prospered, but was again and again tracked and hunted down by the police. His character is powerfully drawn, also that of Javer, the police "mouchard". Monseigneur Bienvenu and his sister Mademoiselle Baptistine stand out in pure clear outlines. You should read extracts, not the whole book, for as I said before it has some bad parts. The character of Gavroche, too, the Paris "gamin", is drawn to the life; nothing is new to him, anything you show him as a surprise elicits only a phlegmatic "connu"; brave he is, and would stand before the mouth of a cannon as the bravest soldier. Victor Hugo's French too is so grand. Have you read any of About's novels? He is called the Thackeray of France. You should read his *Roi des montagnes*, which book I dare say you have heard of, if not read. His *Trente et quarante* is very amusing too. I have not read the other book which we received also by the last mail, *Son Excellence M. Eugène Rougon*.

As you say, it would indeed be very nice to have readings together on our return to England. (Will that ever be?) Papa and I often read together. Before I got my cough, we used to read aloud to each other, by turns, from any French book. Papa is a great authority on poetry. Now of evenings, as we do not read much by candle-light, we repeat together pieces of poetry, English or French, or else it is a stray Sanskrit line. Do you know Victor Hugo's lines, entitled "Guitare" simply, and beginning with

> *Gastibelza, l'homme à la carabine,*
> *Chantait ainsi:*
> *Quelqu'un a-t-il connu doña Sabine?*
> *Quelqu'un d'ici?*

and the refrain is:

> *—Le vent qui vient à travers la montagne*
> *Me rendra fou!*

The song is very musical, and beautiful. We lately bought from an itinerant book-seller a *Life of Napoleon the Great*, by M. de Narvins. It is finely illustrated with coloured plates besides the wood engravings. It will be interesting reading to me, for I am a great admirer of the "bronze artillery officer", as Carlyle styles him.

October 4th.

Gentille is quite well today, but I mean to give her a rest today, and commence working her from tomorrow. Papa and I went out in a hired carriage to the city, shopping. The hackney cabs are so miserable in Calcutta, that I am always afraid of their breaking down in the way.

We bought *Ginx's Baby*, for I had heard of its marvellous popularity. Papa read it and declared it was nothing better than *Dame Europa's School*, and that it was a catch-penny.

Les Misérables is one of the most difficult French books that I have read. Victor Hugo seems to prefer hard and unusual words to words more in use; for instance, instead of saying, in describing a man, that he was getting "chauve" he would say "qu'il ébauchait une *cavitie*". However, the story is very interesting.

We shall, I hope, soon go to dear old Baugmaree. There are few showers now, and, very likely, it will be in November that we shall move out of our town house.

I do not require the piano any longer, so we desired Harold & Co. yesterday to take it away today; the men are now taking it away. The hire of a piano costs two pounds ten shillings monthly. Is it not dear? As we are going so soon to Baugmaree, I thought I had better dispense with the piano for the present.

It is not yet 8 A.M., and we have not had our breakfast; but I have taken an early cold bath; Papa would not allow me taking a bath so early as 6 A.M., if I had not proved to him that I was all the better for it and that a little "roughing it" was good for me. It is so hot, especially in this room. I think it must be on account of the bookshelves, I feel dreadfully warm with my hair all loose on my back; it must get dry before I venture to put it up, or else I shall have a splitting headache.

I do not take any interest in the war in the East;[20] it is very difficult to follow minutely all its details.

I hoped to make this letter longer, but I must stop here, as I have nothing to write about.

Papa's and Mamma's kindest regards to yours, in which I join, and best love to your dear self.

12, Manicktollah Street,
Calcutta
October 7, 1876

I have commenced this letter with the intention of fulfilling my promise of writing to you every week unless I am absolutely prevented from doing so by something or other.

I wonder when the rains will be quite over; I thought they were, but today it is pouring hard. The rain commenced last evening and has never ceased since, even for a moment. The sky is of a dull leaden colour. I hope the weather will clear up during the afternoon, though it hardly looks as if it will.

There was a terrible torpedo accident on the river on Wednesday last. There was a wreck which required to be blown up, so a torpedo boat with fifteen men on board was sent to clear up the wreck. Sergeant Harrison, the commander of the other ten Hindu sailors, most thoughtlessly

---

20. The Russo-Turkish War.

poured some melted wax round and over some of the plugs of the cask; and the immediate effect was of course the blowing up of the cask; it contained 2,000 lb. of gunpowder. Sergeant Harrison thought that the plugs were not fitted tightly enough and that the cask would leak. His remains have not been found; he was bending over the cask when it blew up. Many men who were walking in the vicinity of the river have been wounded by large pieces of iron and wood. The streets presented a horrible sight: parts of human bodies, charred and burnt, were lying about; a large piece of iron and the breast and arms of a man fell on the roof of the Calcutta Public Library.

A new disease has recently made its appearance in the suburbs of Calcutta. It is called *Kotkotea*, and many cases have been fatal. It is a sort of sharp pain which first attacks one of the feet and gradually mounts up, if not arrested, till the person dies. The remedy is to bind the foot at one of the joints tightly, just above where the pain is felt, and so arrest its progress, and then take other medicines. It is likened to the pain felt by a person bitten by a venomous snake, and its progress is very rapid. One of our maid-servants has bound pieces of string tightly over all the joints of her legs for fear of being attacked by this disease. "Prevention is better than cure." She follows this advice *rigidly*, you see!

Mr. Wilson, editor of the *Indian Daily News*, has been committed to the next Criminal Sessions of the High Court, which open on the 20th proximo. Sir Stuart Hogg is not at all to blame for having taken such a step against Mr. Wilson. For the *Indian Daily News* was sure to say something every day against Sir Stuart.

Today's telegram says that the venerable Archdeacon Johnson of Chester has accepted the Bishopric of Calcutta. I am glad of this, for the way that Calcutta was going a-begging for a bishop was too bad.

We have given our barouche to be thoroughly repaired, as it had got to be somewhat "seedy" in appearance. We shall not have it for at least two months.

We shall receive our mail letters tomorrow (Sunday). I wonder if I shall get one from you. I do not think I shall, for I received one by the last mail

Have you seen the notice of my book in the *Examiner* of the 26th August? I have just seen it, and both Papa and I liked the review exceedingly. It is rather a long notice, full two columns, and very generous and frank and a little funny too. It is the best notice that has been written on the *Sheaf*, and I thank the reviewer, whoever he may be, most heartily.

Have you seen any notice of my book in the *Standard*? I have not, and I do not think that I shall, for no one takes an English daily paper in Calcutta, though many do the weeklies. The notice in the *Examiner* is very good. If you chance to see any notice in any English paper, please let me know, or send me a copy of the notice.

I have plenty of time before me, as this is Saturday, and the mail does not go till the next Friday, 9th October. I received your welcome and very interesting letter yesterday morning. I see from it that you have not read or met with the notice of the *Sheaf* in the *Examiner*. As I have said just before, it is a most generous yet discriminating review. I also received yesterday a copy of the *Courrier de l'Europe* with a small notice of my book in it by the Chevalier de Châtelain. It is a very short notice, in which he remarks that the English is "de bon aloi" and that the translator is a very young lady of Calcutta, "qui vient d'atteindre sa vingtième année."

I have not been "photo'd" since the last likeness I gave you; I would have sent you a copy if I had been taken again. I do not think I am very much changed "since last you saw my face" (the line is, you know, "since first I saw your face"), a little more oldened perhaps; you see I have three years more than when you saw me; I am past twenty; next March I shall be twenty-one. Grandfather often deplores my not having married! His impression is that I have turned *une nonne!* In Hindu families, one is almost a grandmother at the age of twenty-four. One of my *cousines* who is a Hindu and who is only about thirty-two has already four or five grandchildren!

My horses are now getting on capitally. I took the loan of a carriage of one of my cousins, and had Jeunette and Gentille driven in it, for it would not do to keep them idle. Jeunette would get too fat; she is now in prime condition, as well as Gentille. They are so very quiet yet spirited; "Elles sont douces comme une fille, elles vont comme le vent!" In the open country, when there are no people about, I let them have a freer use of the rein; they will go fifteen miles an hour, "au grand trot", and be pulled up quite fresh.

I do so want to learn to ride, but I do not think that my wish will ever be gratified, for Mamma was afraid of allowing any of us to ride. Papa was telling me the other day about his riding-horses, which he used to have when he was young. He had once a fall from a half-caste

Arab that he had purchased two days before at an auction. He had ridden some way, when he found out that he had forgotten his whip; he came back for it, and returning for a ride, when before the stable (which he had to pass), the horse showed an inclination to enter; Papa pulled the other way, and the horse reared up suddenly; Papa fell from the saddle, and the horse, unable to keep his balance (he had reared so high), fell on Papa's ankle. He was laid up for six months, and was unable to get up from bed all that time. He had to sell off the animal; it was an incorrigible rearer, Papa used to have Burma ponies. They are a race of very small ponies, and they come from Burma, as their name implies; they are very hardy, and have a very pretty way of trotting or rather ambling, very comfortable for the rider. Their only fault is that they have almost always very hard mouths, and consequently pull a little.

Papa tells me to write to you about the notice in the *Examiner*. I have already done so; I am sorry I have not the paper with me, else I would have copied out bits from the article. If any of the daily papers here reprint the review (as very probably they may) I shall tell you more explicitly about the notice. Yesterday the weather was abominable, but today it has turned very fine, and I have taken an early bath at 6 A.M. I do not feel warm with my hair down, for it is cool today, and there is a beautiful and refreshing north breeze.

You speak about your difficulty in getting up French literature. Why, you know enough of it already, I should think. Without Papa I should never have known good poetry from bad, but he used to take such pains with us (though he never thought it was trouble at all, but was only too glad to help and assist us in our readings) when we were quite little ones. He has himself a most discriminating mind, and is an excellent judge of poetry. He commenced writing poetry before he was twelve; and, do you know, he left school at the age of fourteen and commenced business before he was seventeen? I wonder what I should have been without my father; nothing very enviable or desirable, I know; without Papa we should never have learnt to appreciate good books and good poetry.

12th.

The *Englishman* has reprinted the notice from the *Examiner*. I shall pick out some lines for your edification. It begins with: "This remarkable volume seems expressly arranged to tantalize the sympathetic reviewer.

It is roughly printed, and bound in paper, comes, too, from an obscure Indian press and by no smallest preface or introduction deigns to give us the least inkling of its genesis. . . It is obvious, then, that to have translated pieces from the best French poets, such as might come under a pupil's notice in any ordinary school anthology, into English prose, would have been a respectable feat for an Indian girl. What, then, is our surprise, to find Miss Toru Dutt translating, in every case into the measure of the original, no less than 166 poems, some of them no less intricate in form than perplexing in matter! This amazing feat she has performed with a truly brilliant success." The kind reviewer has quoted Aru's "Serenade" by Hugo, commencing with, "Still barred thy doors," &c., and says of it, that it "could hardly be improved by a practised poet of English birth; and when we reflect that it was the work of a Hindu girl of less than mature age, it may indeed command our admiration." . . . "A rare virtue of Miss Toru Dutt's translations is their absolute and unaffected exactness. An English translator will always try to smooth over an inelegance, rather than give us a true but awkward equivalent of the original. Miss Dutt is less anxious to be graceful on all occasions; she translates what she sees before her, and if it is impossible to make the version poetical, she will leave it in its unpolished state, rather than add any tropes of her own, or cut anything away from her author's text. In consequence, her book recalls the French more vividly than any similar volume we are acquainted with; and if modern French literature were entirely lost, it might not be found impossible to reconstruct a great number of poems from this Indian version." Is not this high praise? Of the notes, the review says: "The notes supply very considerable learning, combined with some odd omissions. For instance, Miss Dutt has no idea of death concluding the lives of any of her favourites. She will grieve, we are sure, to learn that neither Charles Baudelaire nor Alexander Smith are in a position to profit by the prim little advice she gives to each. We are bound also to break the news to her, of the death of her adoration, Sainte-Beuve." . . . "In short," concludes the writer, "her book, taking for granted that it really is what it seems to profess to be, a genuine Hindu product, is an important landmark in the history of the progress of culture." I wish I could have given you the whole article, but it is very long and you are already tired enough, I am sure.

I got a rather amusing packet by the post today, containing a small poem of some thirty pages. The packet was directed thus: "A Toru Dutt, poète, Bhowanipore, ou Bhowalpore, Indes Orientales." Within the book on the title-page was written: "Au Poète, Toru Dutt, hommage, Auguste Fourès, Castelnaudary, Aude, France." This leads me to think that my *Sheaf* has been favourably noticed by some French paper, most likely by the *Revue des Deux Mondes*. It seems to me that I have seen the name "Fourès" in some French book or periodical. But I was very pleased with the "hommage" though I do not know anything about the sender.

I must close here, dear, for the mail goes away tomorrow. Kindest regards from father and mother to yours, and their love to you. With best love from me to your dear self.

12, Manicktollah Street,
Calcutta
October 15, 1876

It is past seven and we have just had our dinner. As in the evenings I do not read much, and as I have nothing to do, I take up my pen to commence my weekly letter. I was busy during the whole day, what with the accounts of the washerman, the translation of a French piece, and looking for the meaning of several hard and big French architectural terms. Sometimes Victor Hugo gets rather difficult, when he goes deep into "claveaux" and "impostes", &c., &c., or in describing vessels, when he enters into the domain of "bordé" and "bordages", and "vaigrages", he is "inépuisable", but tiresome. Without Littré's dictionary, it would be hard to understand all these technical terms. His description of the battle of Waterloo is magnificent; I have never read finer chapters on the same subject. The repeated charges of the cuirassiers of Milhaud to break through the English regiment are described vividly and splendidly. The last few men of the "vieille garde", who died and refused to surrender, are finely drawn. I was reading this description last night; I was so interested, that I could not lay by the book till I had read all the chapters about Waterloo; the consequence was that I went to bed rather late. I was soon fast asleep, and was dreaming of what I had just read; I saw the repeated charges, the flash of cannons, the rearing and trampling horses, the dying men, vividly in my dreams; I was awakened by a noise, and the first instant I was under the impression that I was still on the scene of the battle, but soon I was thoroughly awake, and I smiled to myself; for the noise was the voice of Papa, speaking in his sleep, in the next room!

Papa has been lately busy with a small article. A Bengali gentleman is writing the life of Mr. Hare (who died several years ago), and he asked Papa to lend him any letters or papers of Mr. Hare that might be found amongst my grandfather's papers; for Mr. Hare and my grandfather had been great friends during their life-time. As there were none, Papa, who used often to see Mr. Hare when he was a boy at school (I mean when Papa was a boy, not Mr. Hare), wrote down some of his reminiscences and sent them to the biographer.

But I must tell you who Mr. Hare was. He was the founder of the Hare School, and one of the founders of the Hindu College. He was a great advocate for education for Bengali boys, and used to take great interest in the progress of education in India. He was a very kind man, and was very fond of all the school boys.

Our large bedroom has been divided just in the middle, so that, there being now two distinct rooms, Mamma may keep her windows wide open now at nights, without any fear of increasing my cough. We are going to have a carriage-room built in our back compound; as, at the end, it is cheaper, Papa says, than hiring one for our carriage. Jeunette and Gentille are going on very well. I had them taken out for a long drive; they are in such splendid condition, with their skins like shot-silk, or satin, shining and bright.

Have you seen an article in *Fraser's Magazine*, entitled "Taxation in India"? The writer, Babu Shoshee Chunder Dutt, is a cousin of Papa's.

I must close now for the present, as tea has been brought in.

One of my cousins, whom we had not seen for some years, and who is just married, came to see us the other day. She is just seventeen, and is now a tall young bride; when we saw her last she was a child of eight or nine. She is a Christian and so are her parents, who have a large family of children.

It was so rainy two days before, I thought we were going to have a second edition of the rainy season again; however, the weather has cleared up for the last two days. England will be getting pretty cold by this time, and by the time this letter reaches you, you will be commencing to have fires in your rooms. My uncle Girish often speaks of the sense of cosiness and comfort that one must feel when sitting beside a blazing fire, in the heart of the winter, in England, while the wind and snow beat and howl against the window-panes. He is never tired of hearing my impressions about England. The sharp, biting wind, cutting in its coldness, yet so invigorating, the beautiful soft snow, the frozen water-pools, the ways frosty and hard as iron, he is ever ready to listen about these. He means to accompany us in our next visit to England, if that does take place. We often talk about the places we shall stop at, the things we shall see and hear, the English fruits we shall eat, the English fishes and dishes we shall taste on our next visit to Europe. My uncle is a great lover of fruits, and the tales I tell him of the luscious English peaches, the large juicy grapes, the red-cheeked apples, the delicious nectarines, and the sweetly-flavoured strawberries, and the piquante flavoured cherries, almost make him determined to sail for England by the very next steamer! Varûna's little brother and Varûna himself came to see us the other day. I was afraid to take such a little baby in my arms, for I am not used to babies. Varûna was as talkative and lively as usual. He was very proud in showing off his little baby-brother, and laughed exultingly when he saw my inability to take the baby; but he was rather pleased than otherwise at this, as children are sometimes a little jealous. Varûna is so sometimes; it is rather tiresome that a new-comer should depose him, and reign in his place! I must stop now, for it is rather late.

17th.

I could not write more of my letter yesterday, as my maternal uncle and his favourite wife (whom we call amongst ourselves, Suruchee, vide the Legend of Dhruva), and their two boys, came to see us last evening. They stayed till about nine, and saw from our windows the display of fireworks at the houses of our Hindu neighbours; for yesterday and today also there is the *Kali-Poojah*, or the worship of *Kali*. One feels sometimes so sad when one looks on all these processions following a graven image, offering goats, and other sacrifices to it, and bowing themselves before it. Oh, that all India should turn to the true and loving God, who is alone able to save us and cleanse us from our sins!

Have you ever seen a picture of the idol, *Kali*? It is the most hideous thing you can imagine. She is represented as a female as black as night, with her tongue of the deepest red, thrust out of her mouth, almost half a yard long, with a chaplet of skulls round her neck; with one hand she holds a sword, the other grasps the newly-severed head of a human being by the hair. She is said to be very blood-thirsty. I dare say you know about her, for you have read Tod's *Annals of Rajasthan*, have you not?

Lord Lytton is becoming very popular among his Bengali subjects, and he deserves to be so, I think, for he has in several cases, besides the great F—— minute, shown his true and free English spirit, doing justice to the meanest deserving and wronged person.

Have you read Gladstone's late pamphlet on the Turkish War? Is it not finely written?

Our pastor of the Old Church is going away for some time, and another missionary from Manchester (I think I am right, though I am not *quite* sure if it *is* Manchester) is coming to take charge of the Old Church during Mr. Barry's absence.

I received no letters from you by this last mail, but I was not expecting one, as you wrote to me by the one just before; but I shall receive one of your dear welcome letters by the next mail. This letter will be short; as we live so retired we do not know much about the outside world of Calcutta.

The day before yesterday my uncle Girish rescued a little kitten from the hands of the children of the lodger next door. They were tormenting it fearfully, and when they had ill-used it enough they threw it out of the window. My uncle, taking his usual afternoon walk, perceived the poor little thing crouching in the middle of the road; on looking up, he saw the grinning faces of the cruel boys, and asked them if the kitten belonged to them; on an answer in the negative he took it up and brought it home. He gave it to his cat who had just had a litter of kittens, and she has taken kindly to the foundling and nurses it as one of her own kittens!

One of Mamma's most promising heifers died this morning of snake-bite at Baugmaree. The gardener came to report this sad news; he said the poor young animal foamed at the mouth a good deal before it expired.

I must close now. I am rather tired, as I daresay you see by the bad and unintelligible writing.

Kindest regards from father and mother to your parents, in which I join, and their love to you. With best love from me to your dear loving self.

12, Manicktollah Street,
Calcutta
October 24, 1876

Here at the dead of night,
By the pale candle-light,
Weary and sad I write,
Sitting alone.

Yes, I am a little sad and disappointed at not getting any letter from you by the mail this time. Are you ill? I do hope not. I feel beforehand that I shall not be able to make my letter long this time. I am not in a letter-writing humour, and I have moreover nothing new or interesting to tell you. We live such a quiet life, that one day resembles another. Do you know the song I have just quoted? It has been set to music, and the song and the air are both very beautiful and pathetic. We heard it sung by Mme Patey at several concerts in St. James's Hall, while we were in London; I have the song and the music with me here.

The weather is getting to be splendid now; I am very glad of this, for the sooner the weather gets better and more dry the sooner we shall be able to go and live at Baugmaree. Papa says that as soon as the new coach-house is ready we shall remove to Baugmaree. That will be in a week, for the building of the carriage-room is progressing rapidly. But I do not think we shall be able to go so soon.

What atrocities the Turks do commit! Have you seen the picture of the wounded Servian soldiers tied to trees and burnt to death? Is it not dreadful? Some Mohammedan gentlemen, the *Indian Daily News* says, are gone to join the Turkish troops.

Last night I was thinking about you; you came so vividly to my mind; I always liked your pretty way of saying: "Is it not?" when you used to ask me any question; I used to say curtly "Isn't it?" (you may often find this "isn't" and "doesn't" in my letters), but your "Is it not?" seemed to me so quaint and pretty. I have been racking my brains to find out anything that might interest you, but alas! all my search has been fruitless. However, I must keep my promise; if you find my letter very dull, tear it up.

We went for a long drive today; I borrowed one of my cousin's carriages. The carriage is a *Palkee-Gharry* or covered carriage. It is very light, and the horses rattled along at a tremendous pace; as soon as we leave the city and its thoroughfares behind, the coachman loosens the reins a bit and off they go. It is so funny and yet so pretty to watch the four pairs of legs trotting along, or rather skimming along the smooth plains. In the cold season the horses even seem to improve, and enjoy the bracing breeze; the sun is so hot during the summer that a horse soon gets tired and covered with perspiration, especially a Waler or Australian horse.

As soon as it gets dark I go at four in my uncle's garden to play with the cats, Day and May. Have you seen a certain picture entitled,

"My Aunt's Airing"? I saw it in some periodical or other. "My Aunt" is represented taking an airing with at least half a dozen dogs, terriers, pugs, and spaniels, as companions. Well, I resemble that "Aunt" somewhat; instead of dogs I have cats! I cannot help smiling to myself when I see around me Day and May playing about on the green sward of 13, Manicktollah Street.

My aunt is having her portrait taken in oil by a Bengali artist. Lord Northbrook spoke well of this artist's portraits, but I do not think they are very *superior*. I must stop here for tonight, for it's getting late.

26th.

We went out for a drive today; we went a good way but the sun was very hot, two o'clock in the afternoon being perhaps the hottest part of the day in Calcutta. We passed the old English cemetery. It is a dreadful-looking place, so dark and gloomy. The monuments over the graves are, I should think, a century old, and being generally made of brick by bad architects look very heavy. I should not like to lie underneath one of them. The cemetery of Ore, near St. Leonards, which we once visited, seemed to us so quiet and peaceful; indeed, our own little burial ground at Manicktollah is a much better place than this old English cemetery. A new burial ground in the European quarter of the town is now used, for the old is full. The Roman Catholic churchyard is very well kept and is very pretty.

I have made a small mosquito curtain for the canary cage; it was so pitiful to see and hear the little things flapping their wings at night, on account of the mosquito bites, that I made this curtain, and the canaries sleep the sounder for it, I think.

I am still reading *Les Misérables*. Its chief defect is that it diverges too much from the main thread of the story. At least four different tales might have been made from it. But it is very well written, in parts especially. The descriptions of the quiet life the nuns lead in their Convents is very beautiful; their abnegation is something so grand that it fills one with awe.

Have you read Théophile Gautier's well-known lines addressed to Zurburan the celebrated painter? It is a long piece, but a very fine one. It is on a celebrated picture of monks by Zurburan.

> *Moines de Zurburan, blancs chartreux qui, dans l'ombre,*
> *Glissez silencieux sur les dalles des morts,*
> *Murmurant des Pater et des Ave sans nombre,*

Quel crime expiez-vous par de si grands remords?...

Tes moines, Lesueur, près de ceux-là sont fades:
Zurburan de Séville a mieux rendu que toi
Leurs yeux plombés d'extase, et leurs têtes malades...

Comme son dur pinceau les laboure et les creuse!
Aux pleurs du repentir comme il ouvre des lits
Dans les rides sans fond de leur face terreuse!...

Deux teintes seulement, clair livide, ombre noir,
Deux poses, l'une droite, et l'autre à deux genoux,
A l'artiste ont suffi pour peindre votre histoire...

O moines! maintenant, en tapis frais et verts,
Sur les fosses, par vous à vous-mêmes creusées,
L'herbe s'étend...

Quels rêves faites-vous? quelles sont vos pensées?
Ne regrettez-vous pas d'avoir usé vos jours
Entre ces murs étroits, dans ces voûtes glacées?

Ce que vous avez fait, le feriez-vous toujours?

Are not the verses beautiful? I must drop the subject or I shall be quoting the whole piece.

I have said before, in the commencement of this letter, that it will be a very small and a very dull letter.

27th.

I have written so much today, five sheets of foolscap paper have been filled up by my scribbling. They were all French translations for the press. I am so tired that I do not think I shall be able to do more than fill this page.

I saw my aunt's picture today; it is not half finished yet, and it will be rash to pass an opinion on it in its present state.

I must shut up now. Excuse the shortness of this letter. Papa's and Mamma's kindest regards and mine too, to your father and mother, and with best love to your dear self.

12, Manicktollah Street,
Calcutta
October 31, 1876

I received your duck of a letter yesterday morning. So many many thanks for it, dear; it was such a good one; I was very much pleased with it, it brought you so vividly to my mind. And what have I to give you in exchange for such an interesting letter; nothing but a very dull one, I am afraid.

I have often thought about that poem which you asked me to write for your album. The best way that we can manage will be, I think, for me to write a piece on a nice thin sheet of paper, and then you could paste it in your album. I have just finished a translation of a French piece; it is rather long, but the original is very fine, and I think you will also like the translation. I shall send it within this letter for your album, if I am unable to fill this letter up by other items of news, which I think very probable. I shall begin this letter by copying out Arnault's "La Feuille", which you want.

De ta tige détachée,
Pauvre feuille desséchée,
Où vas-tu? Je n'en sais rien.
L'orage a frappé le chêne
Qui seul était mon soutien;
De son inconstante haleine
Le zéphyr ou l'aquilon
Depuis ce jour me promène
De la forêt à la plaine,
De la montagne au vallon.
Je vais où le vent me mène,
Où va la feuille de rose,
Et la feuille de laurier!

The carriage-room is not yet quite finished, but it will be so, I think, by the end of the week, and then we shall go to Baugmaree. I am looking forward to this removal. We are so quiet and retired down there among the trees and woods, far from the dirty, busy, scandalous Bengali quarter of the town. We do not visit any people about the neighbourhood, except uncle Girish, and we cannot take any walks about, for no lady goes out except in a carriage or in a palanquin. It is considered *infra dig.*, unladylike, immodest, to walk in the street on foot. In the dear old garden I can do anything I like, run about with my horses, feed them myself, and water them sometimes, in spite of the couple of grooms, without fear of any peering and scandalized neighbour, staring in surprise and contempt at my "strange man-like ways". Oh! how I wish you were with me! Do you know, I think I am getting to love our lonely life too much, and that I want a little shaking up, before I become quite an anchorite!

Try and come to see us this winter at Baugmaree. Do you not think you could manage it?

The Rev. Mr. B.'s sermon reminds me of rather a funny story about a German missionary. Uncle Girish was sitting one evening in the verandah of his (the missionary's) house; it was after dinner, and the missionary had taken a glass too much; soon a fire-balloon appeared in the sky, far up, red and bright; I suppose the Rev. gentleman's eyesight was slightly dimmed by his after-dinner glass, for he said to uncle in a solemn manner: "Ah! behold the signs of the last times!"

Nobody takes much interest here in the Turkish War. Some Mohammedan gentlemen have set up a relief fund for the Turks, and several others have left for Turkey to join the Turkish forces. I wrote to you about this in my last.

You must send me the number of the *Queen* in which you propose to write a notice of my *Sheaf*. Please thank your father very much for taking all that trouble and going to M——'s about my book; it was very kind of him indeed, but I think he must have been prompted by you. Did I not write to you, that we sent a copy to M—— to ask if they would undertake to publish it, and that they declined on the same ground as you write in your letter?

You have not seen the notice in the *Examiner*; I am sure of this, because you do not mention it in your letter; I have written about it in my last.

Mr. Clifford came to see us today. As visits are very rare at our house, it was quite an event! His brother, a painter (and a very good one too, for his pictures are admitted in the Royal Academy Exhibitions), is coming to India next month (November). Mr. Clifford promised to pay us a visit with his brother at Baugmaree. We were very glad to hear from him that Mr. Welland (our late pastor of the Old Church, who went home very seriously ill) was much better.

The reason why I can go through a book so fast is very plain and simple, it is simply owing to our quiet and retired mode of life; the time we would have had to give to dinner, lunch, breakfast, croquet, lawn-tennis, or picnic parties, is wholly given up to reading; and then I was always a bookworm, even when I was quite a child. No, I am not above novels; why, *Les Misérables* is a novel, but I have not read the one you mention, *Her dearest Foe*. Have you read Black's *A Princess of Thule* or *A Daughter of Heth*? They are both very readable and rather well-written novels. *Far from the Madding Crowd* is a very powerfully written novel by a Mr. Hardy. It reminds me in places of George Eliot's *Adam Bede*.

Yes, I have seen copies of the famous picture of Napoleon crossing the Alps, by David the great painter. There is a very good piece by Béranger on David's funeral. The painter's remains were not allowed to be buried in French territory, as he was a follower of Napoleon. I do not remember the original French, but there is a very spirited translation of the piece in one of our books of selections: the lines referring to the above-mentioned picture are very fine:

> *His pencil traced on the Alpine waste*
> *Of the pathless Mount Gothard,*
> *Napoleon's course on his milk-white horse;*
> *Let a grave be his reward.*

His friends, you know, are supposed to be praying that his remains might be buried in his native country. I remember seeing that very snuff-box which Napoleon gave to Lady Holland, and on which those well-known lines were written, commencing with:

> Lady! Reject the gift, 'tis tinged with gore, &c.

Are you an admirer of "le petit caporal"?

I quite understand, dear, what you mean about Miss ——. I have often been placed in similar situations, and even now I have to keep up appearances of friendship and politeness with people with whom I have no internal friendship, no free-opening of the heart. I hate to keep up this sort of acting, and I quite sympathize with you in your present embarrassing situation with regard to Miss ——. Do you know I cannot make out her Christian name yet! Is it Lennie or Louise?

Many thanks for the recommendation of Spigelia for Papa's neuralgia attacks. He is comparatively free from them at present, owing to his having lost one of the bad teeth a few days ago. He is getting quite old, isn't he? And so am I. I feel so old sometimes.

I do not know the Mr. Dutt whose marriage with a young Bengali lady of twenty years was mentioned in the *Queen.* He is a Brahmo or follower of the doctrines of Baboo Keshub Chunder Sen. By-the-by, *Sreemutty* means Miss, so it is not one of the names of the bride, as you understood it to be.

I have, on second thoughts, copied for your album a smaller piece than the one I first thought of. The piece that I send has been finished after I commenced this letter. If it suits you (I hope it will), please tell me.

I have just been to our third storey window to witness the procession of the idol, *Paresnath,* which is worshipped as a deity by the up-country Hindus. The procession was a very large one and a very grand one too. The small idol is as big as a two-year-old baby, and made of solid gold; his throne is of gold and silver studded with precious stones; his umbrellas, *chasse-mouches,* flags, &c., are all brilliant with precious stones and diamonds. His horses, four in number, one dark bay, two grey, and one white, were beautifully caparisoned with chains of pearls round their necks, and brilliant and costly aigrettes on their crests, and with saddle-cloths all chased with gold and bespangled with pearls. Oh for one of those saddlecloths and aigrettes for Jeunette! thought I; would not Jeunette and Gentille look splendid with such aigrettes and such rich saddle-cloths! The horses of *Paresnath* were rather fagged-looking animals, without any spirit or action to speak of, so it seemed quite a pity that costly things should be lavished on them.

I must close here, dear, for I have nothing more to say. Papa's and Mamma's kindest regards to yours, in which I join, and their love to you, and with best love from me to your dear self.

12, Manicktollah Street,

Calcutta

November 13, 1876

Many, many thanks for "The Gardener's Daughter"; it is beautiful. How delicately and exquisitely drawn it is! I am never tired of looking at it; it is really a most charming present and I thank you heartily for it, dear; I shall value it exceedingly. My uncle said that it was the work of a master-hand, of a genius; he is very enthusiastic. My aunt's portrait is progressing; I wonder how it will turn out. Mr. Bagchi showed us a copy that he had done some time ago of a portrait of Vandyck,—"that Flemish painter, Antonio Vandyck." It is very well done, and does Mr. Bagchi credit.

How tiresome that the *Queen* refused your notice, dear. But never mind, I never thought much of the *Queen*. It did not notice the *Dutt Family Album* very favourably.

So "le beau malheur"! as somebody from the Right said in 1851 (when the late Emperor Napoleon was President of the Republic and meditating his coup d'état), when M. Victor Hugo, making his last speech from the Tribune at the National Assembly, said that "le jour où la tribune ne sera plus libre, j'en descendrai pour n'y plus remonter".

You must have guessed by my not writing to you last week that I was unwell; I was so indeed. You know I always suffer from an increase of cough, spitting blood and congestion of the lungs, every winter since our return to India I kept pretty well last winter, but last week it all came back again. I, of course, felt too weak and ill to write. I am better now, though.

You know I sit out every afternoon in my uncle's garden. I suppose I look very contented and absorbed, reading *Les Misérables* and having my cats, Day and May, frisking about me; for Papa has made a couplet on the subject!

Que faut-il pour être heureux comme dans le pays des fables?
Une chaise, deux chats, et *Les Misérables!*

Papa makes such funny couplets on me and my doings!

We went for such a long drive today in the country, and saw such a number of cows and calves, buffaloes and buffalo calves at Chitpore. I suppose you have seen buffaloes at the Zoological Gardens. The domestic buffaloes are very useful. Their milk is very nourishing, and the butter made from it is very nice, and white as snow. But the buffaloes are very ugly, so coarse-looking, and seem like unfinished rhinoceroses. By-the-by, we saw the rhinoceros of the Seven Tanks. It is the only rhinoceros in Calcutta, I believe, and though it has been there more than ten years, it still attracts people to the Seven Tanks. The Seven Tanks is a large garden, as large as Baugmaree; it was there that the Duke of Edinburgh was entertained, I believe, when he visited India in 1869. It is well laid out and contains seven tanks (from whence its name) full of very ancient and tame fishes; these are so fearless that they take food from any one's hand, and seldom quit the bank when any visitor is nigh.

Past the Seven Tanks is a very beautiful garden, the property of the Seals, a very rich family of Calcutta. There are rather nice-looking statues (which it is not very easy to find in the other gardens of rich Bengali gentlemen; statues, there are plenty, but not good ones), and a very imposing building in it.

A few nights ago I was bitten by a scorpion; I was at that time very ill with my cough. I was fast asleep in bed, within mosquito curtains, when I was sharply awakened by a sting; I clutched with my nightgown at the place where I was bitten, and then I got out of bed to see what had stung me; I half opened the *handful* of nightgown that I still grasped with an iron grasp! And lo and behold! I saw the wriggling tail of a scorpion! Mamma got out of bed and killed it. I felt a good deal of pain, but the appliance of a caustic pencil acted like a charm.

3 P.M.

Here I am installed comfortably in my easy-chair in Uncle Girish's garden, with my "deux chats" and *Les Misérables*. But I am not going to read now, but write to you, dear. The sky is so beautifully blue and serene, it reminds one of the pure skies of the Mediterranean coast. The crows and sparrows are cawing and twittering away with all their will. I can see through the gate into the opposite garden belonging to a neighbour. There some fourteen children are playing and romping about. They are riding by turns on a meagre undersized country hack, without the least good point; it seems half sleepy and walks drowsily round and round. The day before yesterday one of the children had a fall, but he was more frightened than hurt, for he howled and wept in a way which showed that he was not seriously hurt, and the next morning I saw him again in the garden.

Have you seen a book of verses entitled *Lays of Ind* by Aliph Cheem? It is rather an amusing collection of original *vers de société*, chiefly on Indian subjects. The writer is an officer of the 18th Hussars and shows considerable talent. Papa was much amused with the book. . .

Papa is coming, I can see his tall figure through the trees, so I must stop for the present. Our coach-house is almost finished. I look forward to our going to Baugmaree, though last night Papa and I both dreamed of murders committed at, and murderers prowling about, Baugmaree and the house! Was it not a dreadful thing to dream about?

We shall have our carriage back from Messrs. Cook & Co. in three weeks; my cousin's carriage is a great deal too light for Jeunette and Gentille; it is so amusing to watch the different sorts of conveyances and horses that pass along the street, through our north window. I have come to know almost all the horses, which pass the street constantly. Very seldom is a pair equal to Jeunette and Gentille seen. Large big pairs of Walers pass now and then; there is a very nice pair of duns which is as good as my pair. And there are some such vicious ones; they kick, jib, rear, break the traces, and do all sorts of vicious tricks; but fortunately, I have only seen two of the vicious sort, and of these, one is getting somewhat more docile and manageable.

I suppose you have already commenced having fires and wearing warm clothes. I now wear a slightly warmer dress than I wore a week ago, a light gown of mohair; and on my head, when it is near evening, if I remain out at my uncle's, I put on a sort of hood; you see I am wrapped up as if it were freezing cold; I sometimes wonder what Papa will make me put on, if we do go to England, during the winter!

There was a terrible cyclone in Backergunge, a district some two hundred miles from Calcutta. A great many lives have been lost. Mr. B——, who is magistrate there, is doing his best to succour all who are in need; the papers are all full of the cyclone and Mr. B——. He came out in the same vessel with us; and his manners were rather rough and a little too supercilious. He would come and stand before us on board, with his arms akimbo, and his superior air, and say: "Wall, and how do you get on?" in the most awful drawling way. He must be a good and able man at the bottom, as he is doing so much for the sufferers from the cyclone; but we did not much like him, and his "Wall, &c." was anything but agreeable.

The *Sheaf*, after that *Examiner* notice, is much in demand. People sometimes think that Toru Dutt is a fictitious person, and that the book is the work of some European! I have heard several of my friends say this; they were asked if Toru Dutt was really a Bengali girl in flesh and blood, and then would follow questions about Toru Dutt's education, whether she mixed in society, or kept in the Zenana, &c., &c., *que sais-je!*

We are still in the dirty town, you see, but I hope we shall be able to remove to Baugmaree soon.

Do you know Francis Miles, the gentleman who has sketched "The Gardener's Daughter"? Does he paint too?

The telegrams of today make my uncle believe that England will declare war with Russia. I do not think so, and Papa is also of my opinion, but if it does happen, it would be very dreadful, would it not?

I must close here, dear. Papa's and Mamma's kindest regards to yours, and their love to you. With best love to your dear self.

12, Manicktollah Street,
Calcutta
December 1, 1876

Your two dear letters have been received. I cannot answer them now, as I am very ill. This little note is only written to bear to you my best wishes for a Merry Christmas and a Happy New Year.

I have been coughing up a great deal of blood, and am quite weak and prostrate. Papa has gone out to get a spray-producer. I am under strict orders from him and Dr. Cayley to keep very quiet and lie down, and indeed I feel so weak that I can do nothing but keep quiet and lie down. God bless you, dear.

With best love.

P.S. I hope to be able to write soon a much longer letter, and so make amends for this miserable little note.

12, Manicktollah Street,
Calcutta
December 25, 1876

I got your most welcome letter yesterday morning; was it not a nice present for me on Christmas Eve? I was so pleased with it. And, though this is Christmas Day, I must write to you.

I have four of your dear letters lying unanswered in my desk. Is it not shameful on my part, and after all my fine promises, too, of writing to you by every mail! But you know how ill I have been, dear, and even now I am not very strong. I again wish you a Merry Christmas and a Happy New Year, with many, many merry and happy returns of the same. I envy you your snowy Christmas and your cosy fires! I was always fond of snow, do you not remember? I shall answer your letters, one after one, and then write about ourselves. I shall commence with the one dated the 16th October last.

You want to know whose son little Varûna is, among the contributors to the *Dutt Family Album*. He is my Uncle Hur's, Papa's second brother's child; Uncle Hur wrote those lines commencing:

God in times of old communion held,

which you like so much.

The doctors are of opinion that we should go to England, as that would be the best thing for me, they say. But Mamma's health is also to be considered, and she keeps much better health here than she used to do in Europe. And then, as you say, it is always sad to leave home, where so many happy and sad days have been passed; and after all, India is my *patrie*. But on the other hand, Calcutta is such an unhealthy place, both morally and physically speaking, especially Rambagan (by the way, Rambagan means the garden of Rama, a misnomer decidedly, but I suppose the place was worthier its name in the "days of auld lang syne").

Dear old Baugmaree is far better; indeed, it is as good as England; in some respects, at least in my opinion, it is better. One feels more at home, and more at ease in one's own house than in a hired one, where one is generally anxious about the cracked water-jug or the loose-stoppered mustard-pot! Only Baugmaree gets so unhealthy during the rains.

As to friends and relatives, dear, I have not one friend as true as you, and you are quite mistaken to think that we should be greatly missed by them, if we leave Calcutta; except, of course, by a very, very few.

René was a king and a great patron of the Troubadours; you will find an account of him in any book of ancient French history.

Mr. Knight has forwarded a copy of the *Sheaf* to you. I hope you have received it safely.

You want to know who wrote *Vishnu Purana*. It was Vishnu Sharma (hence the name of the book). These Puranas were written such a long time ago that one cannot be very sure as to the authors of each.

I know the song of the "Erl-King" from Sir Walter Scott's translation. Yes, it is very pretty. I have Mendelssohn's "Songs without Words". They are beautiful and are each and all so characteristic.

We do not know Sir William Hill, so I cannot say if he is a nice man. I wonder what he meant by saying that he knew us; perhaps he mistook us for some other Dutts; but from your account of him I wish I had known him.

You dear old Mary! you cannot imagine how your letters are precious to me. Every time I come to read them over I long to be with you. "Oh, think you we shall ever meet again?"

I have not heard from Mary or Lizzie Hall; and I think our correspondence has ended. They are very busy, I think, with their lectures and other things.

Papa says that if Miss Richardson says that Vilmiki was not a Brahmin, she must have strong grounds for saying so, and that she must be right. Griffiths, I think, has translated the whole of the *Ramayana*, but I am not quite sure.

Dear, what do you mean by saying that writing to you by every mail might be a tax on me? No, indeed, writing to you is such a great pleasure. I am afraid I shall be unable to join the Bible and Prayer Union, though I wish it every success with all my heart. Herewith I return the card as desired.

I quite understand, dear, all you say about your not being able to write by every mail, and I am not at all disappointed, for I never expected to hear from you by *every* mail; though two of my letters for one of yours is hardly a fair exchange; and I am so often prevented by illness. I have been very ill this time. Dr. Cayley was absent, so Dr. Smith of the Medical College came to see me. As no gallic acid, which I used to take in large quantities, thirty or forty grains a day, stopped the blood-spitting, and as neither digitalis did any good, he punctured my arm and injected some ergotine through my skin, but that did not stop the bleeding.

Dr. Cayley, at my Uncle Girish's suggestion, prescribed the inhalation of tannic acid spray through an inhaler, but that did not arrest the bleeding quite, though it did some good. Dr. Cayley and Dr. Smith both recommended a change strongly.

Dr. Smith wants us to go to Davos, near the Upper Engadine, in Switzerland. He brought me several pamphlets describing the place. It is very cold there, but very dry. It has lately become the sanatorium of persons with weak chests. Have you seen a book called *Our Indian Alps*? The coloured pictures in it of the Himalayan scenery are beautiful. The book is written by a lady, and Dr. Smith kindly lent it to me. By the by, I must here tell you something about my *Sheaf*. When Dr. Smith first came to see me, he wore a very professional air, and only asked professional questions. Suddenly his eyes fell on the table, where the *Sheaf* lay in all its orange-coloured glory; a light dawned upon the doctor. "Are you the author of this book?" said he. You should have seen his redoubled interest in my health! "This *poitrinaire* is then the author of this book!" He was surprised, interested, and pleased. So you see the *Sheaf* has at least done something!

We went a few days ago to see the horses at Chitpore. We want to buy another horse, *de rechange*, you know, so as to have always a pair to drive whenever Gentille falls sick. But it is difficult to get an exact match for Jeunette. The day we went to Chitpore (Papa spells it *Cheatpore*, as persons are there *cheated* by the horsedealers), we first ordered to be brought out a mare, bay of course, which had drawn our attention a few days ago. Dunnet, the horsebreaker, was with us. The mare was a very fine strong animal, but of a more solid build than Jeunette; it would have made a fine brougham horse. Then came another; this one seemed to Dunnet to be the very horse wanted, but in my opinion it was a little too aged, being fourteen years old; but it was a nice animal. Afterwards was brought a country-bred, very pretty, but almost an inch shorter than Jeunette, and then when it was trotted out it stumbled three or four times, so it was rejected. Then a very young pair was brought out, but they were both very skittish, kicking, rearing, and playing all sorts of tricks; so they were out of the question; and the result was, we came away without buying a horse. Jeunette and Gentille are getting on very well at present; I gave them two extra loaves of bread each today, and perfect rest, because it was Christmas Day. Our barouche has not yet come home from Messrs. Cook & Co.; is it not tiresome? They have promised to send it before the 1st of January, though.

Mr. Clifford, our clergyman at the Old Mission Church, came to see us a few days ago, and we took him and his brother (who is a great painter and who has lately come here) to see our Garden. I have told you in some of my letters, I think, about Mr. A. Clifford, and that he is of St. John's, and that we used to meet him often at Mrs. Cowell's. His brother, the painter, showed me his album, photos of the pictures he has painted. They are mostly, in fact, almost all portraits of some of the nobility of England. Lady Brownlow's portrait is well executed; the Queen admires her style of beauty very much, Mr. Clifford said, but she is a little *passée*. The portraits of the Countess of Pembroke and Viscountess Castlereagh, both as regards execution and features, were exceedingly good; the latter is decidedly the more beautiful of the two, but the Countess of Pembroke has also a very fine face, with a settled sad expression. The portrait of Mary Countess of Ilchester seems to have come down from an antique canvas, and is extremely well done. Viscountess Castlereagh might stand for Sappho; she is so beautiful. There are about fifty portraits, and a good many of them were exhibited in the Royal Academy. Mr. Clifford is such a modest nice man. He was highly pleased with Baugmaree and the scenery around, looking at everything with a painter's eyes. Do you know what he admired most? It was the clear shadow of a tall coco-nut palm, reflected in our *jheel* (small lake). We passed a most pleasant afternoon at Baugmaree. Mr. Clifford is going to Delhi, where he hopes he will get a sitting from the Maharaja of Cashmere, and perhaps also from other Chiefs and Rajas. He is coming back to Calcutta in three weeks. As to my aunt's portrait, we three do not think very highly of it. When Mr. Clifford comes to see us again, we shall show him the painting, for he is sure to see all its merits and demerits at one glance. We are not capable, we think, of passing any judgement on works of art.

27th.

You have no doubt read in the English papers about the storm-wave which swept away 125,000 people in the district of Dakhin Shahabazpoor. The particulars are most terrible. Is it not dreadful?—125,000 human beings! It is more dreadful than the earthquake at Lisbon or the burying at Pompeii. One of our relatives, a civilian, has been posted there; he finds the place not very healthy, and I believe has asked for a few days' furlough.

I have not yet finished *Les Misérables*; indeed, since I have been ill, I have not read much. Have you read any of Shakespeare's plays? I daresay you have; if not, you should make haste and read some of them; you would enjoy them very much. We saw several of his plays acted while we were in London: *Hamlet, Macbeth, Richard III, Merchant of Venice, As you Like It*, and *A Midsummer Night's Dream*. The last was by far the best got-up, and it had a run of some two hundred nights; all the fairies, on the boughs of trees, sitting and dangling their small legs, looked very pretty; and Puck and Titania and Oberon, how glittering and dazzling they were in all their tinsel finery!

Dear, your friendship is so precious to me; I sometimes think I do not deserve so much from you. If you do intend coming to India, dear, some time or other, do make haste, for I long to see you.

Calcutta is almost empty now. Every one seems to have gone to the Delhi Durbar. There will be a durbar held, on a much smaller scale of course, on the Maidan here. We see the preparations going on for it, when we take our daily drive on the Course. I have made a mistake in arranging these pages; if you follow the numbers you will find them all right.

I have not seen the Arctic number of the *Graphic*, but as soon as the Christmas holidays are over, I shall get it from the Calcutta Public Library. Was not that a fine picture which appeared lately, on the first page of a number of the *Illustrated London News*, of the *Alert*, on her journey homeward bound? How she is cutting her way through storm and snow, all her rigging covered with icicles! Have you ever seen a poem on Sir John Franklin and his expedition, by an American poet. I forget the name; but the verses are very fine, and begin thus (I quote from memory):

> *"O whither go'st thou, Sir John Franklin?"*
> *Cried a whaler in Baffin Bay.*
> *"To see if between the land and the pole*
> *I may find a broad sea-way."*

Have you read any of Poe's poems? "The Raven" is the one which is sure to be met with in any selection of poetry. It is very well written, and I daresay you have read it.

The charge of defamation against Mr. Wilson, editor of the *Indian Daily News*, has been decided, and in favour of the defendant.

I do not think now that it was the *Revue des Deux Mondes* which noticed my book; for I have seen the numbers of the *Revue* up to August, and there was no mention of my book. I wonder how M. Fourés came to hear about the *Sheaf* in his far-off home at Aude. I wish something or some one would throw a little light on this mystery!

Guinea-pigs are getting so dear! Do you know we sold off two pair the last time, at the rate of six shillings for the pair; the buyer was ready to pay anything we asked. We have only three left; they have been lately dying off; which is a pity, as we should have made our fortune by the sale of guinea-pigs! Aru's canary and goldfinch are doing well.

And now, dear, I must bid good-bye for the present. Kindest regards from Papa and Mamma to yours and their love to you, and with best love from me to your dear self.

VI

Letters to Miss Martin: January 1877–July 1877

12, Manicktollah Street,
Calcutta
January 8, 1877

My dear Mary,

This is my first letter to you this year. I wonder if I shall be able to keep my promise. What a heap of letters you will have, if I am able to do so, by the end of the year!

Yesterday your letter was quite a pleasant surprise, as I did not expect one, having heard from you by the last mail. Many, many thanks for the card, it is very pretty; I showed it to Varûna, and he was delighted with it.

How jolly and gay you are of an evening! I cannot think how you can find the time to write to me such nice long letters.

If the "Cedars of Lebanon" does not quite suit you, I shall send you another piece; for I have translated a good many since the *Sheaf* was published.

As to Lamartine's knowledge of the Bible, very few French poets know more than he does; Victor Hugo is very vague indeed, when he likens himself leaving Paris and its festivities under the Empire to "le noir prophète qui fuyait Tyre". To what prophet does he allude? Sainte-Beuve, I think, was the most religious man of all the later French poets. He was a Roman Catholic at first, but he entered the Protestant Church long before his death; he was a great friend of a celebrated abbé, I forget the name; they were college-friends and had had many a controversy on religion, which terminated in Sainte-Beuve's becoming a Protestant, while the abbé:

Plus ferme en Saint Pierre y fonda son repos.

These very interesting facts I gathered from a biographical notice of Sainte-Beuve in one of the numbers of the *Revue des Deux Mondes*.

Hindus are getting more liberal in their views; there are some orthodox families who will not mix with friends or relations who have been to England, unless these make the necessary purifications ordained in the Hindu Shastras and by Pundits, consisting in bathing several stated times in the Ganges and in something else which I shall not mention, and which must be dreadfully disagreeable. But these families are becoming rarer every day. You see Hindus have to mix with Europeans here; European judges, European officials, they come in contact with them daily. Indeed, Hindus, liberal ones, will dine at a European's table without much demur, but it is done *en cachette*.

As to my Christian relations, I hardly ever see any of them except Uncle Girish and his wife, my aunt; Varûna comes now and then, when his mother lets him, and he always pleases and amuses me.

The Durbar at Delhi went off splendidly, I believe; I never read the articles written by "our special correspondent" from Delhi; the letters are dreadfully long and dull to me; what on the earth do we care to hear whether the Raja of Burdwan got a salute of twelve or thirteen guns or who got certificates of honour or silver medals! There was a durbar, on a smaller scale, held in Calcutta on the Maidan; everybody received a card of admittance. But neither Papa nor my Uncle Girish went. We heard from those who were foolish enough to go, that they sadly rued their loyalty, for they had to stand in the sun for three mortal hours, from eleven to two, without any tent or shelter over their heads, and there was nothing to see after all.

We went on Friday to Major Luard's. He has taken a great interest in the *Sheaf* and in its author! and desired to make mine and Papa's acquaintance. He sent a copy of the *Sheaf* to Trübner, the well-known publisher, and Trübner wants to get the book reviewed in one of the English papers, and so wants to know more of me and mine. Major Luard was not known to us before; he read my book and asked my cousin if Toru Dutt was a relation of his; Hem (that is my cousin's name) of course said "Yes", and that is how we came to pay a visit to him on Friday.

Have you read any of Coleridge's pieces? "Christabel" is a very fine and touching poem, and the music of the verses haunts the ear for a long time after you have read the piece. "Kubla Khan" is very beautiful too, though unfortunately it is only an unfinished poem. Coleridge used to eat opium, and one morning he fell into a dose from its effects, and in his dreams he saw the "pleasure dome" and the "caves of ice" and other beautiful things so vividly that as soon as he was awake he began to write down his impressions; the verses flowed involuntarily, without any effort and as if inspired, from his pen. He was interrupted by a visitor, who came on business to see him, and who stayed a pretty long time; after his departure, the poet returned to his piece "Kubla Khan", but to his mortification, found that he had forgotten his enchanting vision, and only after long efforts could he remember fragments of his dream.

I could not write to you by the last mail, as I did not feel strong enough, but I hope to be more regular now.

We have received several French books from Hachette & Co. They are Gramont's *Chant du Passé*, Moreau's *Le Myosotis*, a drama by Vacquerie, and another book of chosen bits of prose and poetry from writers of the nineteenth century.

Our barouche has come at last; it is beautifully done up and looks quite new; it is so comfortable driving in it, after the close palanquin carriage of my cousin.

This letter will be very short and dull, as I am not in a letter-writing mood; so please excuse its dullness.

Sir Richard Temple, our Lieutenant-Governor, has been gazetted Governor of Bombay, and Sir Ashley Eden has been created Lieutenant-Governor in his stead. Sir Bartle Frere, you have no doubt seen in the papers, has been made Governor of the Cape.

We have not yet gone to the Garden, you see. Mamma and I want to go very much, but Papa is averse to our going even now to Baugmaree; "If you should fall ill there," he says to me; and of course I cannot promise not to fall ill, can I? But I think the place is now dry enough, and that there is no fear of fever there now.

I sometimes wonder, if you ever should come here, how Calcutta and its inhabitants would impress you—favourably or otherwise. I think it would not realize all your ideas about the "city of palaces".

I have got a splitting headache today, owing to our having gone out for a drive in the middle of the day. It is now getting warmer, and the sun is almost unbearable during the afternoon: we must change the hour for going out.

Papa's and Mamma's kindest regards to yours, and their love to you. With best love from me to your dear self

Believe me, yours very affectionately,

Toru Dutt

I have commenced this letter, partly to keep my promise, and partly in anticipation of your letter, for I expect one by this mail. I have nothing to write about, but as I have neither anything to do, I have taken up my pen.

I feel very dull and low-spirited today. Perhaps it is the weather that makes me so, for it has been raining all day, without the sun showing himself even for a minute, and the sky is so dark and gloomy! There will be no going to Church tomorrow if this rain continues.

We have changed our hour for driving out, and instead of twelve, we go now at nine, just after breakfast. The morning is pleasant and cool and the air fresh and reviving without being cold, and the sun warm but not hot. I greatly enjoy the sight of the horses being broken to harness and saddle on the Maidan. As the course is generally free and without any people during the forenoons, the horse-breakers are generally doing their business during the mornings. There are daily thirty or forty horses, waiting their turn to be put in the brake; some of them are very fine and spirited animals, but the majority look seedy.

Gramont's sonnets are very fine; and Papa and I are congratulating ourselves for having had the brilliant idea of indenting all our French books from England.

Gramont's sonnets are often so full of deep thought and meaning that they remind me of Milton and Wordsworth.

I have not yet finished *Les Misérables*, but I am nearly at the end; there are only about a hundred pages more. Gavroche, the Paris *gamin*, his life, his death, are all vividly and very cleverly described. Gavroche is killed at last at a barricade during the revolution of 1832.

My Uncle, Mamma's brother, who lately went to the North-West has come back. He has brought for me a beautiful little model of the Taj Mahal at Agra. He was telling us about it, and his description reminded me strongly of "Kubla Khan's" "pleasure dome". I would like to see the Taj very much; would not you?

Lord Lytton arrived in Calcutta this afternoon; he has had a nasty wet day to cheer him, after all the beautiful weather up at Simla.

I have sent another poetical contribution to the *Calcutta Review*; it is a translation from the French of Sainte-Beuve, entitled *Les Larmes de Racine*. The original is very fine and beautiful; and Papa says the translation has also been done very well and creditably. I have done almost thirty pieces more since the publication of the *Sheaf*; a goodly number, is it not? We shall get, at least we expect to get, a volume of Theuriet's poems by the next mail, which is due on Monday, that is, the day after tomorrow.

15th.

I have been hearing an account of Dakhin Shahabaz-poor, recently visited and almost depopulated by the stormwave, from an old family servant, who had accompanied our relative, Mr. Romesh C. Dutt, to that district. Our cousin has been placed there as Joint-Magistrate. The servant, Sampad, said that on the first night of their arrival, his master told him to get down from the boat and find a suitable place, for cooking his (Sampad's) supper. He went down with a lantern, and a sight met his eyes which made him soon return to the boat: dead bodies of men and of cattle were lying about. He said that all the village was strewn with corpses and dead cattle. Bodies were seen hanging on the trees, as if in the last struggle to grasp at some branch; bodies lying clasped together, as if in the desperate last attempt for life; mothers with their babes in their arms. He said that no putrefaction had set in among the corpses, but they were dried and blackened, like "dried and salted fish", that was his expression. No Englishman would stay in the place, so our cousin was posted there. There were no dogs or jackals prowling about, not even any vultures, only now and then a raven was to be seen, with its ominous croak; all the animals had perished in the storm-wave. The tanks and reservoirs of water were almost filled with dead bodies; there are so few men alive, and so many dead, that the work of burying the bodies goes on but slowly, in spite of the efforts of Government officials and men.

8 P.M.

I received your welcome and very interesting letter this morning. Indeed, I should be very happy to see Miss L. H., if she ever comes out to India. I would ask so many things about you, and I should welcome her very heartily indeed for your dear sake. Oh, if you were coming instead of L. H.! Yesterday morning, at about nine, I heard the wheels of a carriage on the gravel; a wild, queer thought passed through my mind: "It may be Mary!" Then I thought of you and my welcoming you here, in Calcutta, in our own house, and our mutual joy at meeting again. Shall we meet here on earth again? And if so where—in England or in India?

Your account of Bishop Johnson interested me very much, as also the speech of the Rev. Mr. Jacobs. There is a Bishop's Palace in Calcutta, near Garden Reach. Mr. Jacobs has an article in the last number of the *Calcutta Review* about Bishop Milman. I have not yet seen the *Review*. In it has also appeared one of my Sanskrit translations, entitled "The Royal Ascetic and the Hind". I shall send you a copy of the poem, if the twelve copies of my piece due to me, as a contributor, are sent in before this mail leaves.

How fast you are getting on with the *Ramayana*. I would advise you to read *La Femme dans l'Inde Antique*; you will find there a great variety of tales, and almost all the standard Hindu legends and stories; I am sure you would like it. I am keeping in pretty good health now. There is a little blood-spitting off and on in the cough, but nothing to speak of; I feel much better, only I get rather out of breath getting upstairs, and of course I cannot *run* a mile, but I can *walk* one easily, I think. The doctors advise a change; I wonder if we shall go anywhere. I myself do not relish the idea of travelling about in search of health; travelling in India is no small matter; there are many comforts and conveniences in travelling about in England which are not to be had here for love or money. Dr. Cayley says England would be a very nice place for me in July or August; what would you do, if you saw me one warm sunny August morning knock at No. 11 Parker's Piece! and I wonder what I should do?

> If I should meet thee
> After long years,
> How should I greet thee!
> In silence and tears.

16th.

How provoking of Miss Yonge to refuse your notice of the *Sheaf* on account of want of space! Please send me the notice to look at, if you can, for I should very much enjoy reading it. Is it long? I do hope you have cut me up savagely! I heard from Mr. Dey the other day; you know he is the editor of the *Bengal Magazine*, in which several of the pieces in the *Sheaf* first appeared, and to which I still continue to contribute often. Mr. Dey wrote to me about Sir W. Herschel, son of the well-known astronomer, who is Commissioner at Hooghly. Sir W. Herschel spoke with warm praise to Mr. Dey of the *Sheaf*, and of my other recent contributions to the *Bengal Magazine*.

Jeunette and Gentille are getting on capitally. They are as fond of me as ever. Jeunette is very hardworking; Gentille gets tired after a journey of twelve miles, at the rate of ten or twelve miles an hour, but Jeunette can do twenty-four miles; I think Gentille is sprightly and full of fire in the beginning of a journey, but she feels the sun when it is very hot; Jeunette, on the contrary, gets more and more impetuous as she gets warm; she gets almost wild with delight when we come to drive on the Maidan; the fresh breeze and the green grass send joy and energy into their hearts, and Jeunette and Gentille trot away in the open and free Maidan. How I wish I could have you with me! If you come here, how many things I shall have to show and tell you! Uncle Girish and Auntie, Baugmaree with all its treasures, my horses, my cats, and then all the things to be seen in Calcutta!

I must not make this letter longer, as I have received copies of my piece, one of which I enclose within this letter. Please tell me what you think of it.

Papa's and Mamma's kindest regards to yours, in which I join, and their love to you, and with best love to your dear self from me.

> 12, Manicktollah Street,
> Calcutta
> January 22, 1877

How very kind of you to write to me by this mail! I received your letter of the 12th December, 1876, last week, and this week I did not expect any, of course, but I was so very happy to have it; it was very interesting. I am quite well now, dear, that is, I mean I am a *great deal better*; so please do not be anxious about me. I am very sorry I made you so anxious with my short note enclosing the Christmas card. What a lot of presents you have got!

We went yesterday afternoon to Baugmaree; at least, I went with Uncle Girish and Aunt. We had such fun gathering the Indian plum (they are called Indian plums); the Bengali name is *kool*, and they more resemble the English cherry than the plum, I think. I brought such beautiful camellias from Baugmaree for Papa; one is pale red, and the other pure white; they are in water just before me as I write. How I wish I could send them to you, as fresh and beautiful as they are now.

We went the other day to Baboo Shib Chunder Bannerjee's house. He used to teach us English when we were quite young; he has been our English teacher ever so long; we, as children, were very fond of him; and older, that affection grew, mixed with esteem. He was so gentle, and yet so firm during lessons. He is such a truly Christian man, and sympathizes so sincerely in all our joys and sorrows. Mrs. Bannerjee, too, is a very nice and amiable person. How we used to try to while away lesson time, by chatting and talking about trifles! But he never allowed us to chat long. We used, I remember, to ask, one after one, about the health of everybody employed in the Financial Department! How interested and anxious we used to get all at once about Mr. So-and-so's doings, health, and affairs! We used to read Milton with him latterly, and we read *Paradise Lost*, over and over again, so many times, that we had the first book and part of the second book by heart. He has got a large family of children. He showed some letters that he had lately received from his niece, who is in England. His niece is the wife of his brother's son, Mr. W. C. Bannerjee, who is the most rising and the most clever Bengali barrister in Calcutta. Mrs. W. C. Bannerjee and her children went to England some time ago; she has been baptized since she has been there, but her husband has not yet become a Christian. He sent his wife and children to England, to have them educated well and thoroughly.

I went with Mamma to see Grandmother, who is ill with persistent, intermittent fever; she has consequently become very thin and weak. My Grandfather hopes to be able to give her a change soon. They will probably go to Benares.

24th.

I think our Bengali language is very rich in words. Now take, for instance, the word *uncle*. Uncle in English may either mean paternal or maternal uncle, and one's father's or mother's sister's husband is alike one's uncle. Now in Bengali, Mamma's brother is *Mama* (Mamma or Mother is simply Ma or Mata), Papa's elder brother is my *Jayta*, and younger one *Kaka*, and so on, for each one we have a different appellation. Is it not nice and convenient?

We went today to see an old friend of ours, Miss Pigot, who has just returned from Europe. She went there on account of her health. She had a dreadful cough before she went, but she has now got quite rid of it, she said. She had tried many places in England and Scotland without feeling any better, and at last she went to Germany, somewhere near Wiesbaden. She got back her health there; she said she felt quite a new person, and got back all her strength again. She told us about the beautiful scenery around. She also spoke of the Bridge of Allan as a very nice and warm place; but it did not suit her.

I got a letter today from Monsieur P. Girard, acknowledging receipt of my book. He was our French teacher at St. Leonards. He used to come twice or thrice a week, to give Papa and me lessons in French; Aru, of course, did not read with us. He is very fond of poetry, and translated some two or three pieces from the *Dutt Family Album* into French verse. He speaks with warm admiration of the *Sheaf*, but says that it deserves "une étude plus sérieuse que celle que j'en ai faite; étude intéressante et profitable, que je me promets de faire pendant mes vacances".

I wonder if M. Boquel will reply to my letter. Do you ever see him now? I suppose not often, as you have given up the French lectures.

M. Girard has also opened a course of French lectures for ladies at St. Leonards.

I could not write yesterday, as I got a little feverish during the evening, and it is generally after dinner that I take up my pen to write to you.

We continue our morning drives; they are very refreshing, and I think do me great good. We saw the other day a gentleman riding a white pony; the pony had such a beautiful tail; it was hardly an inch above the ground and so thick too; the poor little animal could hardly move it, to drive away the flies.

The Viceroy held a levée yesterday, and Lady Lytton will hold a drawing-room on Friday. There was a great question amongst the women-folk concerning the order issued some time ago that all ladies going to Government House would have to wear trains. Now trains cost a great deal, especially as they are generally brought out from England; but fortunately yesterday's paper announced that trains were not absolutely necessary, and that ladies might do as they liked. There were so many letters and articles on the subject, it was quite astounding! "Much ado about nothing!" People who could not afford trains might as well have stayed away from the lordly parties at Government House. What a fuss one makes about nothing!

I send you within this letter two pieces of translation: the printed one for your amusement and the written one for your album. If "La Cavale" does not quite suit you, you must tell me, for I must then look out and send you another, more to your liking; as I promised you one in case the "Cedars" should not suit, I send you "La Cavale".

We did not get Theuriet's poetical works, as we hoped, from Messrs. Hachette & Co., by the last mail; they say it is out of print, but they will try and send us a copy, if they can get hold of one, in two or three weeks. This reminds me of the story of the farmer who, going to buy a copy of the Holy Scriptures, did not find any to suit his sight exactly, and at last asked the bookseller if one could not be "printed" for him in a week or two!

26th.

We went to see Mr. Clifford today; Mr. Barry, the Secretary of the Church Missionary Society, has returned from his tour in the North-West, and was very glad to see us. His daughter has just come to Calcutta from England. She seemed a very nice and amiable young lady. Mr. Clifford, the painter, showed us a portrait of his brother (who is the rector of the Old Church) in water-colour that he is just doing. It is not yet finished, but it is a beautiful portrait in resemblance as well as in execution. The colours are so soft and blending; there is no harshness; and it took Mr. Clifford only eight hours to do it. He was very pleased with what he saw in Delhi. He spoke of the costumes and jewels of the Indian Princes and Chiefs with great admiration, especially of the necklace of the Gaekwar of Baroda. It looked in the sun, he said, like a necklace of fire.

The Mohammedan festival, *Mohorrun*, will take place on Friday, tomorrow. There will be no driving tomorrow, for all Mohammedans will have a holiday, and all coachmen and grooms are Moslems.

I have no more news, and as the mail goes off tomorrow, I must close this letter. Papa's and Mamma's kindest regards to yours, and their love to you, and with best love to your dear self.

12, Manicktollah Street,
Calcutta
February 3, 1877

I could not write to you last week, as I had one of my bad fits of blood-spitting. I wonder if England will suit me now, for I seem to get ill during the winter here more than in any other season, and English winters are so dreadfully cold.

It has been raining awfully today, and it is very cold. Uncle Girish was asking me if it was not as cold as it is in England in November, and seeing me smile, he said: "Well then, as cold as October's last days?" He was a little surprised on my assuring him that it was cold enough to remind one of a raw April day. He longs to see Europe. I am afraid his wishes will never be realized, for he is not at all a travelling man, and has never been out of Calcutta for a day.

I expect your looked-for letter tomorrow; I am longing for it; I wonder what I should do without your dear letters; there would be such a gap in my everyday life, if I did not receive them.

5th February

No letter! It is a sad disappointment, as I expected one. I hope you are all keeping well, dear.

I received the answer to my letter from Lizzie Hall. It is a nice letter, and interested me very much; it is very rarely that I hear from them.

Do you remember the games at chess we used to have together of an evening? How I look back to those days! They seem so far off. I always used to think that you made me win the game knowingly; and I am of that opinion still, I am such a bad player. Do you know Lord Lytton's pretty little piece of poetry commencing:

> *My little love, do you remember,*
> *Ere we were grown so sadly wise,*
> *Those evenings in the bleak December,*
> *Curtained warm from the snowy weather,*
> *When you and I played chess together,*
> *Checkmated by each other's eyes.*

The above lines were recurring to me last night, while I lay in bed, thinking about you. You are such a true friend, dear, I think of you often with a thankful heart.

Lord Lytton is now staying here. He has been making himself popular by giving garden-parties, balls, levées, &c.

As we go to drive generally in the morning, we often see the review of troops which takes place on the Maidan. There are English and Indian regiments, and the different uniforms look very pretty. The sight is beautiful, with the bayonets gleaming in the rising sun, and the clear words of command ringing across the level plain, and the officers prancing about on fine spirited horses, and the men marching or kneeling down to fire a volley of musketry. But after seeing the French regiments in Paris, "les lanciers, grenadiers," &c., with their pennons and flags flying, the regiments here seem poor affairs. Have you ever seen a French company of soldiers?

The weather has been dreadful for the last week; it has been raining almost incessantly and the sky is never free from clouds. Today it rained a little in the morning, but it is pretty fair now and the sky is putting on its accustomed robe of blue, but the air is very damp, and so we could not go out, but sent Jeunette and Gentille out with the carriage for exercise, for they have been without work for two days, and they get fresh and spirited after a long spell of idleness; but they are the quietest horses living, I think, they went off so quietly and gently; there is no vice in them, no kicking or biting or jibbing.

Mr. Dey is, we hear, going to start a weekly newspaper. He wrote to Papa about it, and he says in his letter that he will have a Poet's Corner in his paper, which is to be set apart for me, and which he hopes I shall fill up every week!

Mamma's cow has got a calf, and we are enjoying fresh home-made butter every morning. Mamma has got two grown-up cows, and two heifers. The cows are very fierce and bad-tempered, but they are very pretty and rather small in size; they are so nice to look at, as they graze around the *jheel*, or go to drink water at the tank.

Papa has received a book about the use of the hypophosphates, by Dr. Churchill, the discoverer, from Longmans & Co., this mail, and he and my uncle are deep in reading it.

Dr. Watt, who is Professor at the Hooghly College, and who was a fellow-passenger with us on our return voyage, called on us the other day. He had travelled all over lower India, or rather Bengal, on foot. He was telling us about his adventures. He said he had seen real wild men of the woods; they were quite naked, and at the approach of himself and guide, ran up the trees and began chattering like so many monkeys. His guide said to him that he (Dr. Watt) was lucky in getting sight of these men of the woods, for they never came near the towns and villages, and only lived on fruits and roots. Dr. Watt said that they were not higher than three feet. They must have been a species of the monkey or ape tribe, I think; and Dr. Watt's taking them for wild men of the woods was simply because he and his Indian guide did not understand each other well. For *Bon-manoush* is the name in Bengali for the Ourang-Outang, and may also stand, when speaking of a large-sized ape; so the guide must have told Dr. Watt that they were *Bon-manoush*, meaning apes, and Dr. Watt must have understood him literally, for *Bon* means wood and *Manoush* means men!

I do not think I shall be able to make this letter long, or interesting; we are so quiet and retired here that there is nothing new to tell you about; and then the non-receipt of your fortnightly letter has made me more dull-headed than usual. I am sure you are very busy, or perhaps my letter made you anxious, and so made you wait till you had heard from me again. I am quite strong again now, so don't be anxious.

My grandfather and grandmother came to see us this afternoon. Grandmamma gave me a beautiful ivory comb which my "new" aunt (Suruchee) had brought from Delhi for me. It is a long time since I saw grandmamma, and I was very glad to see her again. It is not yet nine o'clock, and I feel so tired and sleepy that I must shut up and go to bed. So good-night, dear, and God bless you. Kindest regards to your father and mother from mine, and their love to you, and with best love to you.

> 12, Manicktollah Street,
> Calcutta
> February 12, 1877

Your welcome letter of the 10th January last came to hand on Saturday. Many thanks for the same. I have nothing new to tell you, and if you find this letter dull, I should advise you not to read it to the end. I warn you beforehand, because "forewarned is fore-armed".

Ada Smith came to see us with Mrs. Dyson. Miss Smith has taken a holiday of three weeks and come down to Calcutta for a change. She is probably on her way back to Amritsar, for she is going to start this evening. She said that it is very cold in Amritsar during the winter, and very hot during the summer. They are obliged to have fires till May, she said, in every room; there is a good deal of frost, but no snow. She lives in a bungalow along with A. L. O. E. (Miss Tucker). She is going to stay in India seven years, then take a year's holiday, to go to England.

I am quite well now; at least, much better. I have left off cod-liver oil, hurrah! Papa read in Dr. Churchill's book that giving the hypophosphates along with the oil was like yoking a railway engine with a jackass. Papa and Uncle Girish have both a very high opinion of

Dr. Churchill after this perusal of his book; and, thanks to him, I see brighter days dawning for me, days with no cod-liver oil to take (ugh!) before every meal!

I am busy now writing the notes of my later pieces of translation. These keep me occupied during the most part of the day; but I am almost at the end now, and in a couple of days more I hope to finish all.

Uncle and aunt have just been here. Mamma, I and aunt fell to talking about England and Europe. Auntie wanted to hear again of our English friends; I assured her of the warm welcome she would assuredly receive from you and your mother, dear, if ever Uncle Girish and she go to Cambridge. Then she exclaimed: "Why, all your best friends seem to be those at Cambridge, the Halls, the Cowells, the Babingtons, and now the Martins!"[1]

13th.

We went for a drive this morning. The other day we had a very long drive of about twelve miles; the day was cloudy and there was a good strong wind; Jeunette and Gentille were not at all tired, though they did the twelve miles within the hour; there were no crowds, for it was out of the town.

14th.

Grandmother and my two aunts came here yesterday. Also Varûna, the baby, and Muktamala, Varûna's younger sister. Varûna has just learnt to pronounce his *R's* properly, and is consequently very proud!

Have you read Dumas' *Impressions de Voyage*? It is a very interesting book. I have not finished *Les Misérables*: am I not dreadfully slow? I have very little time to give to reading just now, as I am so busy with adding pieces and notes to, and correcting, my *Sheaf*.

Papa's birthday was on the 28th of January; he is forty-nine years old. I gave him a book of photographs taken from the paintings of the great masters of the Georgian Era. I like Gainsborough's "Blue Boy" very much. We saw the original in the Kensington Museum. Did you go to the May Exhibition of the Royal Academy? I have been looking lately

---

1. The Girish C. Dutts travelled to England that same year, and Miss Martin and her parents had the pleasure of meeting them both in London and in Cambridge. The news of Toru's death in August reached them on their way back to India.

into some of the late numbers of the *Art Journal*; I like the *Art Journal* very much. There are such beautiful steel engravings in it.

I have so little news to give you, that I have half a mind to tear up this letter, and try to write a more interesting one next mail.

There was a slight cyclone last week; and several boats and men were lost in the river. As I cannot fill this letter up with anything, I am going to copy one of my translations from Gramont, with the original and also with a sonnet of Wordsworth, which it resembles very much.

SONNET

Sous des barreaux de fer le lion renfermé,
Le lion souverain, a l'œil triste et terrible,
Et qui, vaincu, se sent en lui-même invincible,
En stériles efforts ne s'est point consumé.

Sans vouloir s'agiter et comme accoutumé,
Il s'assied; sous son poil rentre l'ongle infaillible,
Qu'on n'affrontera pas, et sa ride inflexible
Ne dit rien des fureurs dont son cœur est armé.

Quelquefois seulement, quand l'odeur de l'orage
Vient remuer ses flancs, magnifique et sauvage
Il se dresse, et dans l'air étend sa grande voix.

Ses geôliers ont frémi, lui de nouveau s'affaisse,
Il n'a pas pour longtemps à supporter leurs lois:
Il étouffe, et la mort va finir sa détresse.

(*Translation*)

By iron bars the lion proud hemmed round,
The sovereign lion with the terrible eyes,
Vanquished, yet still invincible, defies
Not by vain efforts but a calm profound.

Idle, he sits, as wont, upon the ground,
His claws drawn in their sheath, and none descries

In his unchanging front the rage that lies
Deep in his bosom without sign or sound.

'tis sometimes only, when he snuffs the storm
Sweeping afar, he stirs and lifts his form,
Savage, magnificent. Then to hear his roar

The gaolers tremble;—but he drops anew;
Not long has he to pine on dungeon floor;
He chokes for freedom: death must soon ensue.

EAGLES (WORDSWORTH)

COMPOSED AT DUNOLLIE CASTLE IN THE BAY OF OBAN.

Dishonoured Rock and Ruin! that, by law
Tyrannic, keep the bird of Jove embarred
Like a lone criminal whose life is spared.
Vexed is he, and screams loud. The last I saw
Was on the wing; stooping, he struck with awe
Man, bird and beast; then with a consort paired,
From a bold headland, their loved aery's guard,
Flew high above Atlantic waves, to draw
Light from the fountain of the setting sun.
Such was this prisoner once; and, when his plumes
The sea-blast ruffles as the storm comes on,
Then, for a moment, he, in spirit, resumes
His rank 'mong freeborn creatures that live free,
His power, his beauty, and his majesty.

Whose do you like best, Gramont's or Wordsworth's? And is my translation a fairly literal one? I hope "La Cavale" suits you.

I see from the papers that Mr. Buloz, the editor of the *Revue des Deux Mondes*, has lately died. He was editor for a very long time. I wonder who his successor will be; Charles Mazade writes the literary notes, perhaps he will take up the editorship.

The *Indian Mirror*, edited by Keshub Chunder Sen, says that two Indian girls (I forget the names) have passed the Entrance Examination very creditably. We are in a fair way of having our

Merton Hall[2] you see, are we not? I do hope Indian girls will be in the future better educated, and obtain more freedom and liberty than they now enjoy.

I must now close, dear. Papa's and Mamma's kindest regards to yours, and their love to you, and with best love to yourself.

12, Manicktollah Street,
Calcutta
February 18, 1877

I take up my pen to write to you, not because I have anything new or particular to say, but because I feel in a letter-writing mood.

Yesterday, a Miss Featherstone called here with a letter of introduction from Mrs. Cowell. She is a friend of Miss Perry, whom we knew very well at Cambridge, and whom we liked, too, very much, and has come out as a Zenana teacher. She is very nice and amiable, and is going to Barrackpore for the first half-year, but hopes to be permanently stationed in Calcutta.

Have you read "*Up the Country*", by Miss Eden, sister of Lord Auckland? It is rather an interesting book. It consists chiefly of letters and journals addressed to her sister in England. She used to draw very well, and Papa remembers how one of his schoolfellows, a very handsome, fair Bengalee boy of seven, was sent for by Miss Eden, who wanted to sketch a likeness of him.

Little Varûna was telling us some incidents of Bible History, which he had lately heard from his mother; one was the fight of David with the lion; and it was funny to see Varûna take hold of Papa's beard and chin and show how David killed the lion. He is very fond of hearing stories, and my uncle improvises tales of ogres and tigers for him; he has such a good memory, he goes home and tells the stories next day to his mother or brother. His baby brother, Meelun, is getting rather interesting, but he is not so sharp or intelligent as Varûna; he came to me yesterday for the first time, and sat on my lap till I felt tired and gave him back to the maid-servant; he is somewhat steadier than he was a month ago, and can hold his head straight and crawl on all fours, and says "Ba-ba", which is Bengali for "Papa", and also can pronounce "ak",

---

2. The words Merton Hall refer to the early days in Cambridge of the Higher Education of Women, when Miss Clough became associated with the movement, and lived at Merton Hall before the buildings at Newnham were begun.

which means sugar-cane in Bengali; poor little fellow, he has got a bad cold just now, but he is a little better.

19th.

We went to Church yesterday. One of the hymns was "Just as I am"—an old favourite of ours; I dare say you know it. Our new bishop was duly installed in the Cathedral last Sunday; he has preached his first sermon; the subject was "Charity". I hear he has brought his sister with him.

Today we went for our drive with the intention of going to Baugmaree, but we found Manicktollah Bridge under repair, and as the other road is very round-about, we returned home.

Dr. Cayley is going to England on furlough for eight months, so I must look out for another doctor! and fall from the frying-pan into the fire!

Uncle Girish and aunt are busy preparing for a voyage to Europe! We have so often seen these preparations going on that we are rather hard of belief! and we do not think they will be able to stir out of No. 13, Manicktollah Street! Papa also is thinking seriously of going to England again; but, strange to say, I do not much relish the idea of leaving Calcutta. I am very fickle, I suppose, for it was I who regretted the most leaving England; and two years ago I was longing to return, but now the idea of it makes me down-spirited and dull. I wonder why it is so. Aunt says it is the thought of parting from Jeunette and Gentille; but it is not that, I know. However, if we do go, I shall see you again, and that is some comfort.

20th.

We did not take our usual drive today, as I want to give one day's rest to my horses.

Little Varûna came yesterday evening. He is so very interesting. He is very fond of pictures, and his favourite picture-books are Erckmann-Chatrian's *Le Conscrit* and my *Book of the Horse*.

The weather is getting warm again, and we shall soon have our hot summer weather. This morning it is very foggy, quite a London fog. It is not very cold, though, and I hope we shall be able to take our morning drive as usual, for I get a headache generally if I go out for a drive at noon, now it is so very hot; and in the evening everybody goes out for a drive, and the course and strand are so crowded, and then I feel a little tired of an evening.

I was reading an article on the rising French novelists, in the *Revue des Deux Mondes*; the principal *romanciers* are Theuriet, G. Droz, V. Cherbuliez, A. Daudet, and Flaubert and Zola. I have read a novel or two of all except Daudet and Flaubert. I must try and get hold of one or two of their works, *Mme Bovary*, or *Jack*, or *Fromont jeune et Risler aîné*, but I have not finished *Les Misérables*; it drags somewhat at the end.

We went for our usual morning drive, and have just come back. As Papa has monopolized the paper, I think I had better finish off my letter. We saw a band of prisoners, evidently just arrived from the Mofussil, guarded by soldiers, come out from the railway station; they were followed by two others, guarded by five or six soldiers; the last two are the ringleaders, I suppose, or else they are the most dangerous and desperate men of the whole band, for they had chains to their feet. This reminded me of Jean Valjean's description of the horrors of the *bagne*: "Oh! la casaque rouge, le boulet au pied, une planche pour dormir, le chaud, le froid, le travail, la chiourme, les coups de bâton, la double chaîne pour rien, le cachet pour un mot, même malade au lit, la chaîne." The men were very fierce and sullen-looking, and seemed to be up-country people. Jeunette and Gentille shied this morning at the sight of a railway engine; and we were obliged to stop them, and the grooms patted them and encouraged them till they were quiet.

It is such a fine day; all the fog has gone, and a mild air, "like that of England's June", is blowing.

Have you read any good English novel lately? I like some of Black's novels very much: *A Princess of Thule* and *A Daughter of Heth* are very interesting; and then he makes his titles very taking; his last work *Madcap Violet* has been favourably noticed by almost all the principal papers; his descriptions of scenery are always very fine. I read some parts of *Madcap Violet* from *Macmillan's Magazine*, where it first appeared, but unfortunately I never finished it. Have you read Tennyson's last dramatic work *Harold*? I think he has written himself out, and I do not care to read his later productions, though I am never tired of his earlier poems, and the "Idylls" and the "Princess" will be ever favourites with me. I like "Elaine" best. I daresay you have not read any of Miss Braddon's novels; they are very sensational, and she almost rivals Wilkie Collins in that respect. Thomas Hardy writes exceedingly well, and is sometimes as powerful with his pen as George Eliot; but his heroines have always at least three lovers, one after the other, and then they generally marry the man they loved the least! I must shut up. With best love.

12, Manicktollah Street,
Calcutta
February 26, 1877

Your welcome letter I received on Saturday morning last. It was a very interesting and *good* one. I showed the card of your Zenana Association Fund to Papa and Uncle Girish, who were both much pleased with it.

Little Varûna came here last evening in great trouble and crying tremendously. He had had a fall, which had caused a slight bruise to one of his knees, and he "was sure he would be lame—oh, quite lame". Papa told him about the fall *he* had (Papa had) some twenty-five years ago from his horse, and how he was unable to get up for six months, and now, at present, he is quite well, and does not limp a bit; but that, instead of comforting poor Varûna, increased his fears; "Oh! then I shall be quite lame!" We were in a sad dilemma, but after some time we succeeded in quieting him and allaying his fears. His mother had, it seems, given him a bit of a sermon, telling him that he had been punished by God for his naughtiness, and so forth; of course, that is not the way to comfort a child of four, though it may do very well for grown-up people. Varûna, a little comforted by our assuring words, asked if God would not make his hurt well? "Of course," said I. He went home in more cheerful spirits. When he came, he was in such a sad plight, impatient, weeping, all his face expressing terror and dismay at the idea of getting lame. He is very nervous, and gets excited very easily. His little brother is getting rather interesting. He comes to us now, and is very pretty and fair; he is teething, which makes him a little querulous sometimes.

Have you read *Daniel Deronda*, George Eliot's last novel? I was reading an abstract and review of it in one of the numbers of the *Revue des Deux Mondes*. It seems interesting, in an abstract; but in the original there is too much about Jews and their religion, and the author philosophizes in a manner which, I dare say, she herself thinks highly of, but which is very tiresome to the reader. The book would have been better if it were more condensed, for the author displays high dramatic powers in portions of it. So says the *Revue*. When M. Buloz, its editor, who died lately, was on his death-bed, it is said, he called his son (the present editor), and said to him: "François, tu prendras la direction de la *Revue des Deux Mondes*; quant à moi, je prends la direction de l'autre monde." I suppose this is a *canard*, but it is rather good.

The *Revue* sometimes gives an abstract of an English or American novel, and gives it very clearly, reducing a three-volume novel to as many leaves, and yet containing the gist and matter of the whole story. These French writers and contributors to the *Revue* are very clever men. I do not think there is any periodical, English or foreign, which is greater in literary merit than the *Revue des Deux Mondes*. Its contributors are mostly members of the "Académie" or of the "Institut". Saint-René Taillandier is writing a very long clever notice of Baron Stockmar's book.

It is getting hot now, and we have begun to wear our summer clothes and take our drives earlier, at eight or half an hour later. One of my cats presented me with a litter of four kittens; just imagine my horror! I am fond of cats and kittens, but this is too much, four all at once! I must look out for their settlement. For I always give away my extra kittens, when they are big enough, to kind people, such as our gardener, our milkman, our cook, and so on.

I am feeling somewhat weaker. Perhaps it is the hot weather, for it is not downright weakness, but a sort of lassitude which makes me more inclined for the couch than the chair. I am only taking the hypophosphate of lime now, which is very sweet and nice to the taste; I am glad to get rid of the cod-liver oil; it used to interfere with my appetite.

As we were taking our drive this morning, we saw a poor horse, with its mouth bleeding from the effects of a bad bit; it was being broken into harness; it will have lost all the fine sensibility of its mouth by the time it is thoroughly broken in. Then there was another pair of fresh horses, which was nearly coming in contact with ours; however, we escaped; there is one black mare so very beautiful; we see it almost daily. I like to look at a handsome good horse; I could stand hours contemplating it; there is nothing more beautiful, more noble, than a fine horse, be it Arab, or English, Australian, stud-bred, or of any other country and kind.

Papa is trying to sell off Baugmaree; that is, he is not *trying* but he desires to sell it off, in case we should go to England. Uncle Girish is busy making his usual preparations. I wonder if he will really be able to go to Europe this time; if we go, I think he will go, although he has never been out of Calcutta, but if we do not, then I very much doubt if he will be able to start all alone with aunt. But as I do not think we shall, I had better let this subject alone.

27th.

I dreamed of you last night. I thought that we had gone to England, just for one day, and that I, with Mamma's permission, had set out to see you. I saw Parker's Piece vividly, and as I was near your house, I saw you looking out from the drawing-room window, and you did not seem to recognize me. I rang the bell, and you came down yourself to open the door, with some excuse about the housemaid's being busy downstairs—and as you were speaking, all at once you recognized me and a joyous exclamation burst from you. Then you took me upstairs to your mother and then we all fell a-talking, and you said I was not changed much, and that I had not become at all thin, only I looked taller, you said, with longer hands and arms; and then I proposed to write something in your album, as it was the last opportunity I was ever likely to have, and you brought your album and I opened it, took a pen, and commenced one of my later sonnets from Gramont; just as I had written half a line, "In thy strong teeth——" I awoke. Was it not a nice dream? I shall send you the sonnet in my next. I wonder if you ever see me in your dreams; I often dream of you; this dream was so vivid and like reality.

How are your doves getting on? Have you recaptured the one which flew away? I like to hear of the Halls and Cowells; you say the latter have removed to Scrope Terrace; the name seems familiar to me, and yet I do not exactly remember the locality; it is so long since we were in Cambridge. We were all very sorry to hear of Admiral Davis's death; of course he was very old; but he used to look so hale and hearty that one would have thought he would have lived at least ten or twelve years more. He used to walk with us sometimes, and he was always so good-humoured and full of spirits. He had a beautiful dog, a Newfoundland, which followed him everywhere, even to Church, I think; the dog used to remind us of our dog, "Dogsa", which was a great favourite of Aru's in Calcutta. Have you heard anything of Mrs. Babington? I hope she is better. I suppose you hear from the Fishers now and then; are they still in Germany? Yes, indeed, A. L. does seem to be having a gay time of it.

Today it is very hot and soon it will be dreadfully so. I am very sorry to hear about Mrs. Burton's illness, though I do not know her; does she live near you? and is she obliged to keep her bed?

Have you seen Mrs. Baker lately? I must close here, dear. God bless and keep you. Papa's and Mamma's kindest regards to yours, in which I join, and their love to you, and with best love from me to yourself.

12, Manicktollah Street,
Calcutta
March 5, 1877

Yesterday was my birthday, and Papa gave me a beautiful edition of Sainte-Beuve's *Femmes célèbres*, with magnificent steel engravings. Mamma gave me a pretty phial of scent, with a nice little case, representing a small carriage drawn by a pair of goats.

The great news of the week is—I have finished *Les Misérables*! I am so glad! I have already been reading some of the lives of Sainte-Beuve's *Femmes célèbres*, and I found them very interesting.

We went on Thursday last to see Mr. Clifford's pictures of Lord and Lady Lytton and their three children. They were beautiful, and done in water-colours. Lady Lytton is very handsome. She is taken in evening dress with a yellow rose on her bosom, a necklace of pearls, and with earrings. Lord Lytton looked a little sunburnt and thin. He has been in very indifferent health since he has been in India. The group of the three children we liked best: the eldest girl looks about twelve or fourteen, and is very beautiful; the expression of her calm face and downcast eyes was very thoughtful. The next, a girl of about nine or ten, seems more *espiègle*, and has darker eyes and hair than her elder sister; the third and last is about four, and is the prettiest little fairy imaginable, with flaxen hair and large blue eyes. One very rarely sees such well-executed pictures in India. Mr. Clifford went away the same evening and started for England via Bombay.

Babu Keshub Chunder Sen made a speech in the Town Hall today amid an enthusiastic and numerous audience, among whom were present Lord and Lady Lytton.

The weather is already dreadfully hot, and we are only in March; what will it be in May?

We take our early drives as usual. I wish you could see my horses. Jeunette has the finer head, set on a neck and shoulders perfect in form; indeed, I sometimes think it is a great pity that she should have been broken into harness, she would have made a grand saddle-nag; she has such excellent sloping shoulders; Gentille's hind-quarters are perhaps better than Jeunette's, and her tail is much better set on—

Gentille has the Arab blood in her hind-quarters, and Jeunette in her forequarters; they are in beautiful condition, sleek, and up to any amount of work.

Everybody seems to be going away from Calcutta; Dr. Cayley is going in April; Dr. Smith is going too; the Rev. Mr. Macdonald is gone, Mr. Clifford is gone, all the Missionaries and their families seem to be going, and last, we too perhaps. If we go to England first, and stay in London or Hastings, or anywhere else, you must come and be the first to welcome us; you will come, will you not?

When I commenced this letter, I thought I could make it very long and interesting, but alas! I find I was mistaken. Attribute the dullness and shortness of this epistle to ill-health and consequently downcast spirits; for I have been suffering from fever for the last three or four nights, and it was only yesternight that I did not feel feverish; and then the cough has been very troublesome, and Dr. Cayley put on a blister which prevented my sleeping comfortably on the right side. Now have I not excused myself enough? Papa has been created a Justice of the Peace, and an Honorary Magistrate of the town of Calcutta. He never asked for the above honours, but, as I told him, modest virtue and merit are sure to be recognized at last!

If we go this time, it is most likely Uncle Girish and Aunt will accompany us. They are only afraid of the climate, but I tell them they would be all the better for the change.

On Wednesday, Dr. W. W. Hunter[3] is coming to see us. Mr. Lethbridge wrote to me to say that Dr. Hunter had read my book in England and admired it very much, and wished to have the honour of making my acquaintance and also that of my family. Just fancy! "My family," why, I am getting quite an important personage! Dr. Hunter, you must know, has written a great number of books, *Orissa, Life of Lord Mayo*, &c., and is a very literary man.

I send the promised sonnet.

With kindest regards to all from all and with best love to yourself.

12, Manicktollah Street,
Calcutta
March 9, 1877

I begin this letter in anticipation of yours which I expect on Monday.

---

3. Afterwards Sir W. W. Hunter.

Dr. Hunter[4] came to see us on Wednesday. Papa had arranged with him beforehand that we would take him up from the "Ward's Establishment" at Manicktollah where he had some business on that day with Rajendra Lal Mitter, the Bengali antiquarian. We took Dr. Hunter first to Baugmaree. He spoke in very high terms of praise about the *Sheaf*. He had brought a copy with him to show me what pieces or lines he liked exceedingly, and to ask me how I did this piece or that, for that rhythm seemed very difficult, and this piece was rather obscure, and so on, *cela ne tarissait pas*. His copy of the *Sheaf* was underlined and underscored. He is very courteous and made much of me and my abilities. Indeed, I felt quite ashamed, for after all it is only a book of translations, and Dr. Hunter himself has written such a great number of books.

He said that Colonel Malleson and Mrs. Trevor Grant desired very much to have the pleasure of making our acquaintance, and he asked if I had any objection; of course not. He praised Jeunette and Gentille too. "That is a fine pair of stud-breds", said he; and Papa said that was the greatest compliment he could pay me. On that he redoubled his praises. He asked me which was my favourite, and I said "Jeunette", and he said, "Yes, she had a magnificent chest", and he had had a pair of stud-breds, just like mine, fifteen years ago. The horses were a little impatient and inclined to be frisky, for they had done no work on the previous day, and Dr. Hunter remarked, "They were gay little horses." Then we came to our Calcutta house, for he wanted very much to see my French books. He compared some of the translations with the originals. When he went away, he told me, and repeated it to Papa, that he should be very pleased if there should be any service which he could render us, and he asked me to write to him at the India Office in London whenever I had need of his help or literary advice; and he said he would remember us and the pleasant day he passed with us, always. We were all very much pleased with him.

10th.

We went yesterday morning, Papa and I, to the City Press, to have some of my later translations printed. The office of the Press was not opened, and Papa had to talk through the locked glass doors to a sleepy bearer, who directed us to the private house of the printer, Mr. Smith,

---

4. Afterwards Sir W. W. Hunter.

just behind the office. We went, and on the staircase found one of the compositors putting on his coat; Papa told him what we wanted, and at that moment the head printer, Mr. Smith, came out, and when he learnt that I was Miss Toru Dutt, he was all politeness, and would insist on my coming into his drawing-room and listening to a boy of his who played very well on the piano, and who was not more than ten years old. Mr. Smith reminded me very strongly of our Italian courier, Salvageot; he was very talkative and active, and seemed a good and kind father. He showed me his youngest children—twins. The little boy who played appeared to me very talented. I wondered, as I listened to him, what his future would be; this little genius, sitting and playing on the broken old piano, all his soul in his eyes, and his little thin hands running over the keys, seemed like a Mozart in embryo.

Mr. Anundo Mohun Bose came to see us yesterday. He was at Cambridge, and we used to meet him there often. He is a Wrangler and a barrister. He wanted me to visit his school for adult Hindu girls. The girls are not generally of orthodox Hindu parents, but rather of Brahmo's or followers of Keshub Chunder Sen's religion. He was sorry to hear that *probably* we should be going to Europe, for he thought I would be of great help and use in the education of my countrywomen.

I send you my last contribution to the *Bengal Magazine*. The original runs very smoothly. I hope you will like the translation.

We must change the hour for driving out, for even eight in the morning is not cool enough; I think we shall go out in the evening from tomorrow.

There is to be a consecration of Bishops in the Cathedral tomorrow. Dr. Hunter asked if we should like to go, as he would have great pleasure in providing tickets for us, but I declined. We are not able to go to Church every day, and the Consecration ceremony would take a long time, and I would perhaps get tired, and then, there is sure to be a large concourse of people, and it is troublesome to fight one's way through a crowd, at least I think so now; formerly I rather liked it, just to show how well I could take care of myself in a crowd!

12th.

Your welcome letter has arrived. What a long and interesting one it is. Many thanks for your kind wishes, and also for the woollen shawl; so good of you, dear, to have taken the trouble of making it for me. I need not say how I will value it; I will wear it often and think of the loving and loved donor. Papa will go to the P. and O. Office to bring it as soon as it comes in.

I received a letter from Mlle Clarisse Bader this morning in answer to my request to translate her *La Femme dans l'Inde Antique*. It is a very nice and warm letter, giving her authorization with all her heart. She is very pleased with my book which I sent her, and showed it to M. Garcin de Tassy, the well-known Orientalist. She says she showed him my letter too, and he was "si émerveillé de votre généreux courage, qu'il prit votre adresse pour vous envoyer, aujourd'hui même, l'un de ses ouvrages." She spoke of Aru too, saying that: "le Seigneur a rappelé auprès de lui l'âme qui avait si fidèlement interprété le chant de *la jeune captive*." She says: "la sympathie d'une enfant de l'Inde" is very precious to her, and that, when the Archbishop of Orléans asked her: "chez quelles femmes j'avais trouvé le plus de beauté morale, je répondais: Si j'en excepte les femmes bibliques, c'est chez les Indiennes que j'ai trouvé le plus de pureté et de dévouement." I must close here, dear. God bless you. With best love.

12, Manicktollah Street,
Calcutta
March 22, 1877

What a beautiful shawl! Many, many thanks for it. So kind of you, dear, to have made it for me. It is delightfully soft and warm, and will be of great use to me. I was sitting in my uncle's garden when it arrived, and everybody was eager to have a look at it, and I took it out triumphantly and put it immediately over my shoulders, all the time thinking of the dear kind fingers that had worked it. Perhaps I shall be unable to finish this letter today, but I shall do my best to finish it, for if it does not go off by the afternoon, it will be too late for this mail. We have been very busy during the last week, and yesterday I felt unwell and feverish; these two things combined prevented me commencing this letter.

Do you know what we have been doing during the last week? Packing! Making preparations for a second voyage to Europe! Does it not seem strange and improbable? It may be that after all we shall be unable to start for Europe; but the idea of going to England again, which had become very shadowy and vague, is taking new hold of Papa's and Mamma's minds, and that which was a dream before us is becoming real. Do not be too hopeful, though, for going to Europe again with broken health and spirits is no small matter and requires a great deal of thought. May God guide us to choose the right path! If we are able to go this year we shall have to start very soon, before the Bay of Bengal becomes rough, that is, before the end of April. Perhaps we shall go by one of the French mail steamers, as that will save us a sea-voyage of forty days, and keep us confined on board for only thirty days; in that case we shall land at Marseilles and then go to Paris, where Papa wants to consult Dr. Churchill about me, and where we have made a few friends by correspondence, Mademoiselle Bader being one of them.

Have you read Lord Lytton's *Fables in Song*? There are some very good pieces in it, but the best is "Only a Shaving"; "The Near" and "The Far" are also well written.

I feel rather weak today in consequence of yesterday's fever; so please excuse this scrawl. I shall have to sell off Jeunette and Gentille, which is a great pity. I have made up the description I shall give them in the auction list: "A pair of bay stud-bred mares, warranted quiet in double harness, splendid trotters, exceedingly fast and stylish, the property of Miss Toru Dutt proceeding to Europe." That will do, I think, won't it? It will be better, if we do go, to go by the Messageries Maritimes. The cabins contain only two berths, and the steamer, which starts on the 10th of April, has Dr. Cayley among the passengers, which is a great allurement. The only drawback is that we should have to change at Galle, for the French steamers do not go straight from Calcutta to Marseilles, and the sea near Galle is almost always very rough. The P. and O. steamers go from Calcutta straight to Southampton, but their steamers rarely contain more than two or three reserved cabins; that is cabins with two berths only; and one has to pay extra for a reserved cabin; and as to going in the same cabin with two strange Anglo-Indian ladies, that is very uncomfortable. Anglo-Indian ladies are very supercilious and fond *de faire la grande dame*. And then via Southampton it takes forty days and via Marseilles, thirty days; and that is of great importance to me, for I dread sea-sickness and I suffer from it horribly. Continue to write to me, for we may not go after all, and your letters will be sent back to my address in Europe, if we leave India, by our agent here.

Dr. Hunter gave me the abridged edition of M. Littré's dictionary by Beaujean. It is very small and contains, besides the meaning of words, biographies of celebrated persons, geographical and historical information, mythological terms. It will be of great use to me, as it is so very handy, and Papa is perhaps more pleased than I am, for he always used to grumble when he saw me lifting the heavy volumes of Littré. This letter is dreadfully short, but I cannot help it. The idea of making such a long voyage, as we perhaps are going to make, renders the mind very unsettled, and disinclines one to write anything. I shall therefore close my letter.

Very kind regards from Papa and Mamma to yours, in which I join, and their love to you, and with best love to yourself.

It is sad to think of leaving home again and wandering in foreign lands, "sans feu ni lieu."

(No letters were received by Miss Martin between March 2nd and June 18th.)

12, Manicktollah Street,
Calcutta
June 18, 1877

I am still very ill—fever every day. I send you something for your birthday by packet post. All your letters have come to hand; I shall answer them when I get well. My heart is constantly with you, dear. Papa's and Mamma's kindest regards to all, their love to you; I have written this letter myself. With best love, dear.

12, Manicktollah Street,
Calcutta
July 17, 1877

I am so sorry, dear, to have made you anxious by my long silence. But indeed I have been very, very ill, but under God's blessing I am better now, though still unwell and weak; you will guess how ill I have been, when I tell you that I have to be taken downstairs in a chair when I go out for a drive. The fever has not left me quite; but it is not so intense as it was before, and I am strong enough to walk from one end of my room to the other. My hair has been cut off short, and Dr. Charles says I may be mistaken for a boy! Do you know, dear, three blisters were applied under my right collar bone all within a fortnight; they were so very, very painful, I felt quite mad with the pain; one has hardly healed up yet. Dr. Charles is very kind and attentive, sending me dishes made at his own house, for I have lost my appetite. He has lent me a wire bed, which is very comfortable. Dear, you will excuse the shortness of this letter; those you have written have been a source of great pleasure and comfort to me. God bless you, dear, for all the good you have done me. I only write this to reassure you. I am better, and in a fair way to get well; so don't be anxious any longer. I wish you many, many happy returns of your birthday; this will reach you by the beginning of August.

With best love.

PS. Your notice of my book pleased me very much. There is a notice of the *Sheaf* in the *Revue des Deux Mondes* for February 1877.

> 12, Manicktollah Street,
> Calcutta
> July 30, 1877

I am so sorry to have given you so much anxiety; indeed I *could* not write, dear; I am still confined to my bed and the fever and weakness continue. Thank you very much, dear, for all your kind letters, but most of all for your friendship. How very kind of you to write to my aunt in London; she is very much pleased with your letter.

I am very sorry to hear all you say about—. Poor girl! I do hope she will amend her ways for the future.

Your letters are a great comfort, dear. I feel sometimes very tired and weary and lonely, and this illness has made me suffer very much.

May God help us to bear our crosses patiently. Do you know a certain hymn of Dr. Newman's in which are the following lines? (I have the hymn in a book, but I can only remember two verses of it just now.)

> *I would not miss one sigh or tear,*
> *Heart-pang or throbbing brow.*
> *Sweet was the chastisement severe,*
> *And sweet their memory now.*

> *Yes, let the fragrant scars abide,*
> *Love-tokens in thy stead,*
> *Faint shadows of the spear-pierced side,*
> *And thorn-encircled head.*

I received a very nice letter from Miss Arabella Shore by the last mail. She once came to see us in Cambridge in company with Miss Clough. Of course I had forgotten her quite. She says in her letter that she had written it in 1876, after reading the notice of the *Sheaf* in the *Examiner*, and had addressed it to me at Bhowanipore (it must be lost, for I never received it); this copy of it she sends per favour of Mr. Knight (of the firm of Messrs. Newman & Co., Calcutta), who has also, she says, promised to procure her a copy of the *Sheaf*, for she has none. Her letter is very kind; and she says she is most touched with what I say about dear Aru. She also had a sister, she says, who died at nineteen of consumption. She is a relation of Lord Teignmouth. She praises the *Sheaf* greatly in her letter. I must stop here, dear, God bless you.

(This was the fifty-third and last letter from India received by Miss Martin after the return of Toru to India between the dates of December 1873 and July 30, 1877.)

VII

The Character of Toru Dutt as revealed in her Letters

This fragile blossom of song" is the beautiful, descriptive phrase which Edmund Gosse applies to Toru, and it is a phrase which one involuntarily calls to mind after reading her letters. A fragile blossom she was, a rose-bud half-unfurled, filling the little world of her Indian home with fragrance.

It may be still an open question how far our public education mars or enhances the beauty of real, feminine nature; but that *real* education enhances, rather than spoils, can be seen in the letters of Toru. She is throughout a woman-child, pure, sweet, modest, and essentially lovable, with a real Indian's love of home and country.

The woman-child! The two aspects run right through the letters. The child—full of Stevenson's "Happy Thought":

> *The world is so full of a number of things,*
> *I am sure we should all be as happy as kings!*

the woman—as Wordsworth pictures her:

> *A being breathing thoughtful breath,*
> *A traveller between life and death.*

It is as a happy child we see her getting up very early in the morning, "so as to be able to pat and caress the horses;" running gaily along at their side when they are being exercised; brimming over with delight when they learn to come at her call, or take a fancy daintily to eat the roses at her belt, playfully bestowing fine French names on them and on the favourite cat.

It is a child's tender heart that demands a mosquito-curtain for the poor little canaries, and is at rest when they, like herself, are safe from their bloodthirsty tormentors. Eagerly as a child, too, does she go every day to her uncle's garden to play with "Day" and "May", the cats.

In her actual childhood, at night, just before

Each little Indian sleepy head
Is being kissed and put to bed,

she turns to her mother with the eternal cry of the child: "Mother, tell me a story." Then she listens, eyes wide with wonder, or wet with tears, to the old stories from the *Ramayana*, thrilling like the strings of the Aeolian harp in the wind to every call of beauty and pathos. A tender-hearted little maid, indeed, merging imperceptibly into the woman! a woman still of tender heart, seeing eye, and listening ear, but a woman made thoughtful by seeing "into the life of things".

She moves in a circle where the beauty of the home-life is apparent to all, where even that greatest barrier of all—differing faiths—fails to spoil the tender affection between Toru and her Hindu grandmother.

So it is always when Toru writes of her relations; she reveals the spirit of love, which was the life of that little circle.

The supreme love in her own case seems to have been that which she bore her father, whose unwearying, thoughtful care of her is referred to again and again. His eyes seem to have followed her movements the livelong day, and it is he who orders wraps for her at the slightest cold breeze, and tells her when it is time for the busy pen to rest awhile, till she laughingly protests at times that he had better keep her in a glass case. Her father, however, did much more than look after her physical well-being. It was from him that she learned to plant her childish footsteps in the right road to literary art.

It is obvious, then, that an education begun on such sound lines should continue, as all true education does, throughout the whole of Toru's brief life. Father and daughter continued their studies together— in French, English, and Sanskrit. Only when it got to a suggestion that they should proceed with Algebra and Geometry did the daughter confess her dislike of mathematics by declaring herself "too thick-headed" for them!

Their fondness for, and acquaintance with French literature is attested by the constant references to their reading. Toru was, in fact, in a position to act as counsellor and guide to her English friend, Miss Martin, in that matter.

There are constant records of the arrival of books containing the latest French literature; a *Life of Napoleon*, sold by an itinerant bookseller, is a source of great delight, and attests Toru's admiration for that great general.

We have already referred to the fact that even the household pets were given French names, but it appears also that Toru's absorption in her books or play was the subject of many a French couplet by her father. With all her love of French literature, she was, nevertheless, not blind to its faults, and she exercised the same fine discriminating taste in this, as in all her reading. This was by no means confined to French. Mrs. Browning, the Brontës, Byron, Thackeray, Coleridge, Tennyson, Carlyle—there are references to them all, which show an intimate acquaintance with their works, as with the works of many other English authors. "I was always a bookworm," Toru says of herself, and her verdict is true. If a complete list were made of all the books mentioned as read even in this one correspondence only, covering a period of about four years (1873–7), its variety and completeness for so young a girl would astonish all who reflect on it. Moreover, when health begins to fail, and she is compelled to desist from study, she has a mind so well stocked with treasures that she can accompany her father in "repeating pieces of poetry, English or French, or else it is a stray Sanskrit line". A girl in her teens!

No less keen than her interest in contemporary literature is her interest in contemporary events, both at home and abroad. She has her own opinion on the Lieutenant-Governor's fitness for his post, on careers for Indians, on sanitation, on Victor Hugo's speech for the liberation of the French communists, on the Government of Turkey, Art, the Civil Service Examination, on the education of Indian girls.

There are criticisms of society, as in the controversy over the wearing of ladies' trains at the parties at Government House, on which she writes:

"People who could not afford trains might as well have stayed away from the lordly parties at Government House. What a fuss we make about nothing!"

Or again:

"What on earth do we care to hear whether the Raja of Burdwan got a salute of twelve or thirteen guns, or who got certificates of honour or silver medals?"

There are stern criticisms of Bengali Christian Society, the manners of which, she says, "would sadden the merriest heart, and dishearten the most hopeful." The incident of the fine of thirty rupees being imposed upon the English lawyer who violently assaulted his Syce and caused his death, and the sequel to the case, are related with a moderation that makes the indictment all the nore forcible and convincing. Her remarks on judicial matters are equally penetrating. Still more startling is the comment:

"We have no real English gentlemen or ladies in India, except a very few."

Nothing can escape the searching of those keen young eyes. Nevertheless, gifted as Toru was, with a fine power of discerning the true and the false in those around her, and in life generally, she was never bigoted, nor anything but modest in her own demeanour, and in her estimate of herself.

Her account of her interview with Sir William Hunter is characteristic:

"Dr. Hunter wished to make my acquaintance and also that of my family. Just fancy! 'My family!' Why, I am getting quite an important personage!"

When the visit had taken place, she wrote:

"Dr. Hunter made much of me and my abilities. Indeed, I felt quite ashamed, for, after all, it is only a book of translations, and Dr. Hunter himself has written such a great number of books."

It was in this modest way that she always spoke of her achievements.

So full of eager interest in all that goes on around her is the young authoress, so full of life, and joy in life, that it is with something of a shock we read such a sentence as the following:

"I wonder if I shall live to be thirty?"

Or again:

"I feel sometimes very tired and weary and lonely, and this illness has made me suffer very much."

Her life was full of pain latterly, but as soon as any respite came, the old humour was flashing out again, as when, in the hot weather, she parodies the Psalmist's wish for the wings of a dove: "Oh that I had the fins of a fish!"

Yet suffering could not have been easy to one as full of life and energy as was Toru, and perhaps it was after all a merciful thing that death ended her pain so swiftly.

With all her love of English and French literature, first and last her love is reserved for the great literature of her country's past.

Many times she begs her friend to become acquainted with translations of the *Ramayana*; for

> "You would then see how grand, how sublime, how pathetic, our legends are. The wifely devotion that an Indian wife pays to her husband; her submission to him even when he is capricious or exacting, her worship of him 'as her god'."

In this love of, and pride in, her country's great inheritance, she was Indian to the core. It was from this love that began her correspondence with Mademoiselle Bader, and it is to the latter that we owe, perhaps, the best possible summary of Toru's character as revealed in her letters. We quote it again:

> "Her letters revealed a frankness, sensibility, and charming goodness and simplicity, which endeared her to me, and showed me the native qualities of the Hindu woman developed and transformed by the Christian civilization of Europe."

True Indian as she is, yet the West, too, is proud to have a claim to her.

VIII

A Sheaf gleaned in French Fields and *A Scene from Contemporary History*

From the study of the great English poets Toru turned with eager zeal to the works of their French compeers of the nineteenth century. She did more than merely peruse their poetry; she translated specimens of their work into English: nor did she confine herself in this task to the verses of poets of outstanding fame and genius; she included in her survey the productions of poets and poetesses of inferior rank, and entitled her collection *A Sheaf gleaned in French Fields*. This book of hers contains nearly two hundred poems, the work of seventy or eighty different authors, and it possesses the melancholy interest of being the only book which she published in her lifetime. Her sister Aru was associated with her in this undertaking, but her share in the work was very small and was limited to eight poems. It is a matter of some surprise that Toru did not select for her first venture of this kind some of the literary treasures of her own land, such as those to which she did justice later in her *Ancient Ballads and Legends of Hindustan*. Perhaps she preferred to try her prentice hand on a foreign literature before she sought to render a maturer service to that of her native country. She started her translations while in England, and after her return to India she contributed them regularly to the *Bengal Magazine* from March 1874 to March 1877. The late Rev. Lal Behari Dey was the Editor, and he reserved a space in his pages for her and called it the "Poets" Corner'. Her final contribution to this magazine was the translation of Barbier's "La Cavale", which was found among her MSS., and sent by her father.

Her book was first published in 1876, without any preface, by the Saptahik Sambad Press, Bhowanipore, and was dedicated to Mrs. Govin Chunder Dutt. It bore as its motto the following lines from Schiller:

> *Ich bringe Blumen mit und Früchte,*
> *Gereift auf einer andern Flur,*

In einem andern Sonnenlichte,
In einerglücklichern Natur.[5]

Her translations were accompanied by detailed notes, dealing chiefly with the characteristics of the poets whom she has enshrined in her volume, but giving also particulars of the lives of many and, in some cases, parallel passages from English literature. The notes are helpful and interesting, and are a striking evidence of the wide range of Toru's reading. The last note of all refers to her sister's collaboration and premature death, and adds—"Had she lived, this book with her help might have been better, and the writer might perhaps have had less reason to be ashamed of it, and less occasion to ask for the reader's indulgence. Alas!

Of all sad words of tongue or pen,
The saddest are these, 'It might have been.'"

The book did not at first attract the attention which was subsequently paid to it. In India the translations were for a time accredited to some Anglo-Indian author who was supposed to be veiling his individuality under an Oriental pseudonym. No one could believe that they were the work of a Bengali young lady of eighteen. This is no wonder, for her work astonishes the English reader even now. In France and in England their appreciation was handicapped by the homely style of the volume in which they appeared. "The modest book, badly printed on poor paper, by a small native press, was in no way calculated to attract the English reader of verse, who expects to find his poetical gems enshrined in caskets matching, if not exceeding, them in excellence."[6] Fortunately, however, the work came into the hands of scholars and writers like André Theuriet in France and Mr. Edmund Gosse in England. The former wrote a eulogy of it in the *Revue des Deux Mondes* and the latter announced its discovery in the *Examiner* of August 1876. Mr. Gosse had previously had the melancholy satisfaction of sounding the only

---

5. *I bring some flowers and fruits,*
   Gathered on another soil,
   In another sunlight,
   In a happier clime.
6. Maud Diver's *The Englishwoman in India.*

note of welcome which reached the dying poetess from England. He now wrote:

"It was while Professor W. Minto was Editor of *The Examiner*, that one day in August, 1876, in the very heart of the dead season for books, I happened to be in the office of that newspaper, and was upbraiding the whole body of publishers for issuing no books worth reviewing. At that moment the postman brought in a thin and sallow packet with a wonderful Indian postmark on it, and containing a most unattractive orange pamphlet of verse, printed at Bhowanipore, and entitled *A Sheaf gleaned in French Fields* by Toru Dutt. This shabby little book of some two hundred pages, without preface or introduction, seemed especially destined by its particular providence to find its way hastily into the waste-paper basket. I remember that Mr. Minto thrust it into my unwilling hands, and said, 'There! see whether you can't make something of that.' A hopeless volume it seemed, with its queer type. . . But when at last I took it out of my pocket, what was my surprise and almost rapture to open at such verse as this:

> *Still barred thy doors! the far East glows,*
> *The morning wind blows fresh and free.*
> *Should not the hour that wakes the rose*
> *Awaken also thee?*
>
> *All look for thee, Love, Light, and Song,*
> *Light, in the sky deep red above,*
> *Song, in the lark of pinions strong,*
> *And in my heart, true Love.*
>
> *Apart we miss our nature's goal,*
> *Why strive to cheat our destinies?*
> *Was not my love made for thy soul?*
> *Thy beauty for mine eyes?*
>
> *No longer sleep,*
> *Oh, listen now!*
> *I wait and weep,*
> *But where art thou?"*

"When poetry is as good as this it does not much matter whether Rouveyre prints it upon Whatman paper, or whether it steals to light in blurred type from some press in Bhowanipore."

In May 1878 a second edition was issued by the same press containing a frontispiece portrait of the two sisters and a touching biographical notice by their father. This edition was soon exhausted. A copy of it was sent to the Viceroy and was appreciatively acknowledged.

The third edition of the book is the most tasteful. This was published by Messrs. Kegan Paul & Co. in London, in 1880, and its cover is ornamented with the picture of a sheaf. Two of the translations which it contains were also printed separately by Sir Roper Lethbridge in *The Indian Magazine and Review*. If we may judge from his article on "The Poetry of Toru Dutt" he appears to have overlooked the fact of their previous publication in England in book form. Sir Roper was also under the impression that Toru had resided for a while at Wiesbaden, whereas she never visited Germany.

A copy of *The Sheaf* presented to the Chevalier de Châtelain, the translator of Shakespeare into French, with an autograph inscription by Toru, is preserved in the British Museum Library.

So much for the outer history of the book. Its inner wealth now awaits our consideration. The special field of literature from which Toru principally gleaned her harvest was that which may be broadly characterized as the Romantic School of French Poetry. The Romantic movement corresponded in the realm of literary art to the Revolution in the sphere of politics. It was the assertion of freedom for the imagination and also of the rights of individuality. The seventeenth and eighteenth centuries had witnessed in connexion with poetry a process of restriction to certain forms of verse and to arbitrary rules. The seventeenth century was the period of Classicism—of servitude to the models of Greece and Rome. The eighteenth century emphasized reason. The Romantic School sought to give free play to feeling and to the imaginative faculty. It introduced changes too as regards language and metre. Simple, direct, and vivid words replaced high-sounding periphrases. The Romantic School proper was born towards the close of the first quarter of the nineteenth century, and has as its chief poet Victor Hugo, as its chief critic Sainte-Beuve, and in its ranks included Gautier, Gérard de Nerval, Borel, Deschamps, and others. From this initial group later groups originated. The next generation produced the poets Théodore de

Banville, Leconte de Lisle, Baudelaire, Soulary, and Bouilhet, while in the succeeding epoch the leading poets were Sully Prudhomme, Coppée, and Verlaine. Theuriet too started as a poet, but diverged to novel-writing.

Toru's book does more, however, than reproduce for English-speaking readers specimens of the poetry of the above-named authors of the Romantic School and also of the subsequent *Parnasse*. She starts earlier in that century, with poets of the transition period like Chénier, Courier, Béranger, and Lamartine. She goes back even farther, and gives glimpses of the work of Parny and de Florian of the eighteenth century, of Scarron and P. Corneille of the seventeenth, and of du Bartas and du Bellay of the sixteenth century. These form but a brief introduction to the main theme of her book. Nor has she overlooked the work of writers who stood somewhat apart from the Romantic School, e.g. de Vigny, de Musset, Barbier, Brizeux, Moreau, Dupont, V. de Laprade, Mme Ackermann, and Mme Valmore. She even includes five poems of Heine, on the ground that, though he was born in Germany, yet he lived in France and his tastes and predilections were peculiarly French. In fact, her work forms an admirable help for a student anxious to get a general idea of French poetry in the nineteenth century as well as to note the kind of verse that characterized the Romantic School. Victor Hugo occupies the place of greatest eminence in this period, and a like position has been accorded to him in this book. No less than thirty of his poems have been reproduced by Toru, and these are chiefly taken from two of his later works, viz. *Les Châtiments* and *L'Année terrible*. In these translations we find expressed the variety and vigour of his metre and the splendour and sonority of his diction. They set forth also his many-sidedness—his epic grandeur of style, his power of description, his lyrical skill, his humanitarian feeling, and his deep patriotism. The next two poets in place of importance in this volume are F. de Gramont (seventeen pieces) and J. Soulary (thirteen pieces). Soulary was probably chosen because of the exquisite sonnets which he wrote, among the best in the language, and Toru seems to have been rather partial to the translation of sonnets. Fifteen out of the seventeen translated poems of the Comte de Gramont belong to that class of literature, and this appears to be the reason for allotting so much space to this writer, whose name is not so well known as those of many others. Sainte-Beuve and Gautier are each represented by five or six translations, Barbier, Leconte de Lisle, and Mme Valmore by four poems each, while the work of the other chief poets is limited to two or three specimens each. Evidently, Toru was not writing with any idea of her book becoming a standard anthology of the French poets of the century; otherwise she would have regulated the space devoted to each individual more in accord with the position assigned to him by literary criticism. Lamartine, for instance, occupies a rank not much inferior to Victor Hugo's. The authoress herself in her notes speaks in high terms of him—"In fancy, in imagination, in brilliancy, in grandeur, in style,—in all that makes a poet—excepting purity—he must yield to Victor Hugo. In purity he yields to none. His mind is essentially religious. . . There is much in Victor Hugo—far greater poet though he be—which it would not be wise to put into the hands of young people whose principles have not been sufficiently formed; but Lamartine may be placed indiscriminately in the hands of all." She had a high opinion too of Laprade—higher than that of some other critics—and has written of him—"In truth, Laprade is one of the great poets of France, and may take rank with the greatest names of the time. . . Laprade and Lamartine are the only great modern poets of France whose works are essentially and eminently pure and religious, and it is remarkable that they both are deeply indebted for the tone of their minds to their mothers, women of prayer, large-minded and self-denying." Yet versions of but two of Lamartine's poems are given, and only one of Laprade's. Again, de Vigny and de Musset are poets deserving fuller space from a literary point of view. It is difficult for the average reader to discern clearly the principles that guided Toru in her choice of poems, or to decide whether indeed she was actuated by any definite principles. Probably different motives actuated her. One poem may have attracted her by its general style and facility for translation; another by the sentiments which it expressed. The "Sextine" of F. de Gramont was evidently selected because of the peculiarity of its metre, since Toru calls attention to the fact that it is something new in English versification, and acknowledges that the thought it seeks to set forth remains rather obscure. Not a few poems—chiefly Hugo's—are patriotic, and others deal with varied subjects—doves and butterflies and swallows, homely joys and simple scenes, kindness and bravery, child life and ideal manhood. Mlle Bader thinks that it was the authoress's Indian birth and upbringing which caused the poetry of the nineteenth century to appeal to her more than the poems of the Classical School. She found in the Romantic School that which her countrymen have always loved, viz.—the lifelike and dramatic reproduction of the sentiments of the heart, as well as wealth of imagery and warmth of colour. The subjects, however, which seem to have attracted her most were pathetic ones—

those that spoke of separation and loneliness, exile and captivity, illusion and disappointment, loss and bereavement, declining seasons and premature death. Here, as in other work of hers, her innate susceptibility to the pathos of life has manifested itself. But though the separate stalks that make up her *Sheaf* may seem at times to have been gathered at random, the *Sheaf* as a whole reflects very fairly the varied efforts of the French poets of last century. We see in her pages the secret of Béranger's popularity with the masses and the plaintiveness that helps to make the lyrics of Mme Valmore so attractive. We get a glimpse of de Musset's unrequited love and acquaintance with philosophic thought, as well as of the ties that bound Brizeux to Brittany. The two poems that bear de Vigny's name represent himself as well as his work. He was the thinker among the poets of his time and stood to some extent apart, and his picture of Moses climbing Pisgah's height is the personification of the burden of loneliness that often has to be borne by genius. Barbier's admiration for Italy and its artists, Gautier's proclivity for unusual words, not infrequently associated with the Orient, de Nerval's idealism and admiration for the past, de Lisle's recourse to foreign climes or literature for his subjects, and Dupont's sympathy with rural toilers—all these are reflected, and much more. Names of poets not so familiar out of France are thus brought before the English-reading public.

Mr. Gosse tells us, "the *Sheaf gleaned in French Fields* is certainly the most imperfect of Toru's writings, but it is not the least interesting. It is a wonderful mixture of strength and weakness, of genius over-riding great obstacles and of talent succumbing to ignorance and inexperience. That it should have been performed at all is so extraordinary that we forget to be surprised at its inequality. The English verse is sometimes exquisite; at other times the rules of our prosody are absolutely ignored, and it is obvious that the Hindu poetess was chanting to herself a music that is discord in an English ear. The notes are no less curious, and to a stranger no less bewildering. Nothing could be more naïve than the writer's ignorance at some points, or more startling than her learning at others. On the whole, the attainment of the book was simply astounding. It consisted of a selection of translations from nearly one hundred French poets, chosen by the poetess herself on a principle of her own which gradually dawned upon the careful reader. She eschewed the Classicist writers as though they had never existed. For her, André Chénier was the next name in chronological order after du Bartas. Occasionally she showed a profundity of research that would have done no discredit to Mr. Saintsbury or 'Le doux Assellineau'. She was ready to pronounce an opinion on Napol le Pyrénéen or to detect a plagiarism in Baudelaire. But she thought that Alexander Smith was still alive, and she was curiously vague about the career of Sainte-Beuve. This inequality of equipment was a thing inevitable in her isolation, and hardly worth recording, except to show how laborious her mind was, and how quick to make the best of small resources."

Such is the judgement of an able and learned critic and hence worthy of consideration; yet to the ordinary reader it is the strength of the work and not its weaknesses, and the genius of the writer and not her limitations, which are most evident on perusal and are most deeply impressed upon the memory. Toru's command of English is wonderful, and it is difficult to realize that the book is not the work of an English writer. It is not surprising that Mlle Bader should have remarked—"This Indian girl, so fond of our European civilization, instead of increasing the number of Indian poetesses of whom we have heard through the writings of M. de Tassy, has taken her rank and place among the writers of England." One is astonished at the wealth and variety of the vocabulary and at the many instances of real poetic expression. It is true that there are limping lines, and a phrase like "Epidaurus" fatal oracle' (p. 24) strikes the ear as harsh and prosaic, but such defects are exceptional. She reproduces for the most part the actual metre of her originals (or a metre as closely allied as possible), and such diversity of metre as the book displays only serves to emphasize her own talent and skill. Her translations are fairly close as a rule, though not uniformly so. In some of her versions, the ideas rather than the actual expressions of the French poem are reiterated or elaborated, and occasionally one meets with slight deviations or omissions. *Napoléon le Petit* is a good specimen of her work. Though largely a free translation, it reproduces the swing and the sarcasm of Hugo's verse, and her substitution of "Tom Thumb" for "Le Petit" is a happy and ingenious rendering. The subjoined examples will enable readers to judge for themselves the merits of the book.

Here is a verse from Béranger's "The Memories of the People" which illustrates both her faults and her merits:

> *In the hut men shall talk of his glory,*
> *With pride, not unmingled with tears;*

And the roof shall not ring with a story
But that grand one, for fifty long years.

There villagers in evenings cold,
Shall haply beg some gossip old,
By stories of a former day,
To while the livelong hours away.

"Some say that he has done us wrong,
But the people love him yet;
Mother, sing of him a song;
We love him, though his sun be set."

Of like calibre is the version of Hugo's *To Those who Sleep*, of which we give a stanza:

Sweep away the tyrant, and his bandits accurst!
God, God is with you, let Baal's priests do their worst!
God is King over all.
Before Him who is strong? Lo! He lifts up His hand,
And the tigers fly howling through deserts of sand,
And the sea-serpents crawl,
Obedient and meek! He breathes on idols of gold
In their temples of marble, gigantic and old,
And like Dagon they fall!

In the last stanza there is a change of simile from the original, but the general idea is not thereby weakened. The following two verses from Gautier's *What the Swallows Say* are an example of a different style of poem, yet Toru's rendering of them is very felicitous:

Says a fifth, "Old age, you see,
Weighs me down, I scarce can fly;
Malta's terraced rock for me!
Azure wave and azure sky!"

And the sixth, "In Cairo fair,
On a lofty minaret,

Mud head-quarters lined with hair
Make me winter quite forget."

Amongst other poems worth quoting—did space permit—are the versions of A. de Vigny's *Moses* and *The Death of the Wolf*. As a specimen of her work that is marred by weaknesses in prosody, Soulary's *The Two Processions* may be instanced:

Two processions met on consecrated sod,
One was sad,—it followed the bier of a child;
A woman was there, whose sobs bursting wild
Attested a heart crushed under the rod;
The other was gay,—a mother who trod
Triumphant, friends, and a babe undefiled
(Who sucked at her breast, prattled nonsense, and smiled)
To be sealed with the seal that marks us of God.
The service done, the gatherings crossed each other,
And then prayer's mighty work was seen achieved,
The women barely glanced at one another,
But oh! the change in both the glad and the grieved!
One wept by the bier,—it was the joyful young mother,
And one smiled at the babe,—it was the mother bereaved.

Though that sonnet may not show Toru Dutt's best work, it is marked nevertheless with the stamp of her genius.

One other quotation may fitly close this reference to this work of hers. She has not reproduced the metre, and here and there she has amplified the thought, of Parny's *On the Death of a Young Girl*, but the poem might almost have been written as her obituary notice:

Though childhood's days were past and gone,
More innocent no child could be;
Though grace in every feature shone,
Her maiden heart was fancy free.

A few more months, or haply days,
And Love would blossom—so we thought;
As lifts in April's genial rays
The rose its clusters richly wrought.

> *But God had destined otherwise,*
> *And so she gently fell asleep,*
> *A creature of the starry skies,*
> *Too lovely for the earth to keep.*

> *She died in earliest womanhood;*
> *Thus dies, and leaves behind no trace,*
> *A bird's song in a lonely wood—*
> *Thus melts a sweet smile from a face.*

The last stanza at any rate could not apply to Toru. If she had left behind her no other work save this volume of translations, she would have left behind her something that will not soon die away.

This chapter would be incomplete without a further brief reference to Aru's work. Her few translations, so limited in quantity, yet in quality deserve a place by her sister's productions. She appears to have kept perhaps more closely to the original than Toru often did, though she has left scarcely sufficient work behind her to warrant a very decided opinion on that point. A couple of examples of her work will enable readers to compare it with the extracts from Toru's work given above. Here is Aru's rendering of the first verse of Béranger's *The Captive to the Swallows*:

> *A soldier captive by the Maure,*
> *Who bent beneath his heavy chain,*
> *Welcomed the swallows from afar,—*
> *"O birds! I see you once again,*
> *Foes of the winter, high ye wheel,*
> *Hope follows in your track e'en here;*
> *From well-loved France ye come, reveal*
> *All that ye know of my country dear."*

Her version of Chénier's *The Young Captive* shows her not much less gifted than her sister. Two verses are a type of the whole poem:

> *The budding shoot ripens unharmed by the scythe,*
> *Without fear of the press, on vine-branches lithe,*
> *Through spring-tide the green clusters bloom.*
> *Is't strange, then, that I in my life's morning hour,*

Though troubles like clouds on the dark present lower,
Half-frighted shrink back from my doom?

Let the stern-hearted stoic run boldly on death!
I—I weep and I hope; to the north wind's chill breath
I bend,—then erect is my form!
If days there are bitter, there are days also sweet,
Enjoyment unmixed where on earth may we meet?
What ocean has never a storm?

A Scene from Contemporary History

Toru Dutt's unique linguistic abilities are evidenced by two other translations which she made from French into English. These were published in the *Bengal Magazine* (June and July 1875), each under the title of *A Scene from Contemporary History*. These translations deal with speeches delivered in the French Legislative Assembly at different periods by Victor Hugo and M. Thiers, together with a specimen of the poetry of the former.

The first translation is part of the speech delivered by Victor Hugo on July 17, 1851.[7] It belongs to that stormy period of French history connected with the Second Revolution following the abdication of the throne by Louis-Philippe in 1848. A republican form of government was re-established, but this collapsed before the end of 1852. Louis Napoleon Bonaparte, nephew of the great Napoleon, had been chosen in 1848 to act as President of the Legislative Assembly for a term of four years. At the beginning of 1851, however, it became evident that there was a strong tide of feeling setting in for the re-establishment of the monarchy, and the question which agitated the minds of politicians was the best means of effecting that change. Could it be accomplished by introducing a suitable legislative measure, or by having recourse to force? If the former, then a modification of the existing constitution was needful, rescinding the special clause (article 45) which prohibited the re-election of the President at the end of his four years of office. This was the focus of discussion in the summer of 1851. The revision of this clause had been proposed in the Assembly by Louis Napoleon himself in the furtherance of his own interests. Victor Hugo was an

---

7. See vol. i, pp. 357–75, *Actes et Paroles*, 1875.

ardent republican and strongly deprecated any reversion to government under an emperor. He felt that the Republic was already too much in the hands of Louis and of a clique of self-interested politicians, and consequently the rescinding of that clause would perpetuate present misgovernment by making Louis Napoleon virtually king. He did not regard Louis Napoleon as personally capable of sustaining the weight and responsibilities of Empire and of enabling France to take her proper place in Europe and to exert her legitimate influence upon European politics. Consequently, Victor Hugo vehemently opposed any alteration in that particular clause of the constitution, and the portion of his speech translated by Toru shows alike the boldness and eloquence of the speaker as well as the intense feeling which then pervaded both political parties, viz. the republican supporters of Victor Hugo, seated on the left, and the advocates of the change, on the right. The opposition of the republican party was strong enough to defeat the proposal, and Louis Napoleon had subsequently to have recourse to force and fraud in order to gain his ends.

The poem of which Toru Dutt has given a version was one in which Victor Hugo expressed his estimate of the character and achievements of Louis Napoleon Bonaparte and contrasted him with his great predecessor. The *chanson* is published in the volume of poetry entitled *Les Châtiments*.

The remaining prose translation deals with a later period of French history, but resembles it in this respect, as it describes another stormy scene in the French Senate. The date is July 15, 1870, when for more than two years the possibility of a Franco-Prussian war had threatened Europe. Bismarck had seen that the candidature of Leopold of Hohenzollern for the throne of Spain would be extremely displeasing to the French nation, and accordingly at the beginning of this month he caused the announcement of this candidature to be publicly made. On receipt of the news, the French Government sent a protest which was couched indeed in arrogant terms, but the King of Prussia had already yielded to their demands and had enjoined the renunciation of the candidature. The members of the extreme party in the Government, however, were not satisfied with this. They wanted either to humiliate the King of Prussia or to conquer him. Accordingly on the evening of July 14, relying upon information which promised the assistance of Austria and the South German States, they decided to propose the declaration of war. The following day the Legislative Assembly, without requiring further information, supported them, Thiers, Gambetta, and eight others alone opposing this momentous step. Thiers felt that, as the King of Prussia had conceded France's request, there was not sufficient reason for involving the country in a sanguinary strife. He spoke amid interruptions similar to those which Victor Hugo had encountered twenty years previously, but the opposition which Thiers led was not as effective as Victor Hugo's in 1851, when he opposed the change in the constitution. The translator has given us practically the whole of the speech, and the original may be seen in the official report of the debate published on July 16 of that year.

Toru's translations afford us vivid reproductions of both these historic debates, and they afford evidence that she had passed beyond the slavish stage of literal translation. In several passages she aptly expressed with freedom of language the thought of the speaker. She fails, however, to do this uniformly, and here and there she does not appear to have grasped fully the idea expressed in the original. Some of her renderings are not as happy or suitable as they might be, and there are a few instances of mistakes both in translating the French and in writing the corresponding English idiom. But these are, for the most part, flaws that can only be discerned by a careful and close comparison of the English version with the actual words of the orators, and the second prose translation is freer from them than the former. Despite them all, the translations, taken as a whole, quite suffice to depict the two scenes in the French Assembly and to enable the reader to gain a realistic idea of the nature of the discussions and of the oratorical powers of the speakers.

The poetic rendering of Hugo's comparison between the two Napoleons is well deserving of praise. The translation is, however, very free and far from literal, individual stanzas frequently expressing a different thought from Victor Hugo's. The last stanza approximates in idea more closely to the French than do the others, and a reproduction of it side by side with the original will serve to show both Toru's linguistic ability and her poetic power.

Quand il tomba, tachant le monde,	*Dark, dark archangel—but he fell,*
L'immense mer	*Earth felt the sound,*
Ouvrit à sa chute profonde	*And ocean opened by a spell*
Le gouffre amer;	*Its gulf profound.*

Il y plongea, sinistre archange,
Et s'engloutit—
Toi, tu te noyeras dans la fange,
Petit, petit!

Down headlong—but his
name through time
Shall overcome—
Thou too shalt drown, but
drown in slime,
Tom Thumb, Tom Thumb!

IX

Last Days

In a family where that dread disease, consumption, had already carried off a sister, it was but natural that the father should watch his remaining daughter with keenly observant eyes. Shortly after the publication of Toru's first book, his anxiety was quickened by signs of ill-health, though at times there seemed to be marked improvement. This was a characteristic deception of the disease, which, before long, too clearly showed its firm hold upon its second victim. When Toru's own doom was evident to her, with the heroism common to great souls in face of death, she set herself the more determinedly to make her mark in literature. By the end of March she was too ill to write, but she still read, and took an eager interest in all the latest books from Europe, and in the doings of the Paris "Société Asiatique".

We have seen that she attempted a translation of Mademoiselle Bader's book, but her illness increased so seriously that Dr. Thomas Edmonston Charles was obliged to be in constant attendance.

Great is our admiration for a man like Robert Louis Stevenson, whose life was one long, heroic fight with disease. Great should be our tribute to Toru, alert to the end, who died with her books strewn around her.

Writing to Miss Martin on August 13, 1877, Mr. Dutt says:

> "Toru has received all your letters up to the last which bears date the 10th of July. They have been a source of great comfort to her during her long and painful illness. I am very much obliged to you for these letters, because they cheer up Toru wonderfully when she is desponding most, and she looks forward to their arrival with intense eagerness. Pray continue to write to her, though she may be unable to send you replies yet for some time. I am sorry to say as yet she is no better. The fever for the last two or three days has been stronger than before and she is dreadfully weak, incapable even of walking from one room to another. Of course in her present state, the doctor does not recommend a sea voyage, though it would be the best thing for her the moment

she is strong enough to bear the fatigue of it. I leave a little space on purpose, in case Toru should like to add just a line for you."

In a weak and trembling hand, Toru wrote as follows:

"My own darling Mary, accept my fondest love, Toru Dutt."

Further details of her last days are supplied by Mlle Bader, who writes:

"One day she gave me the hope of seeing her in Paris, where she wanted to consult the best physicians, but it was in vain that the poor father who had already lost two of his children tried to snatch the last of his daughters from the hand of death. Her illness increased rapidly, and her state was such that it would not permit her removal to Europe. On the 30th of July, full of the delusions frequent in complaints of the chest, she hoped to the last and wrote to me in a weak hand: 'I have been very ill, dear Mademoiselle, but God has granted the prayer of my parents, and I am slowly improving. I hope I shall be able to write to you at length before long.' But she wrote to me no more, and she could have repeated to me the sweet line she had once written in a letter—that melancholy and bitter-sweet line—

Adieu then, my friend, whom I ne'er have beheld."

. . . . . .

Mlle Bader said: "I wrote to Toru to congratulate her on her sudden recovery, also I asked her to convey my congratulations to her parents. I enclosed a flower that belonged to a bouquet placed in front of my statue of Notre-Dame des Victoires. It was a *rhodanthe*, a pretty pink and silvered plant that never dies. Alas! when I sent this souvenir to my friend she had been dead a few days, and with what bitterness her parents would read my congratulations on her recovery! And my flower, intended to be the symbol of an everlasting and living friendship, became a flower for a grave!"

The end came suddenly in the evening of 30th August, 1877, at her father's house at 12, Manicktollah Street, at the age of twenty-one and a half, when the tender and eager spirit of Toru passed to eternal rest, "firmly relying on her Saviour Jesus Christ, and in perfect peace." She was buried in the C. M. S. Cemetery in the Upper Circular Road, Calcutta, by the side of her beloved brother and sister, and on her tombstone appears the following inscription:

Toru Dutt

Youngest Daughter Of
Govin Chunder Dutt,

Born 4 March, 1856,

Died 30th August, 1877.

Be thou faithful unto death and I
will give thee a crown of life.
Rev. ii. 10.

In conveying the sad news of his bereavement to Miss Martin, Mr. Dutt wrote, on August 31, 1877:

> "Your letter to Toru's address was delivered to me this morning. Toru has passed from the earth. She left us last night at 8 P.M., and her end was perfect peace. She loved you very much. I have no doubt, loves you still. I shall send you hereafter one or two trifles to keep as reminiscences, but do not find myself able to write just at present. The Lord bless you for all you have been to my beloved child. Kindest regards to your parents from self and Mrs. Dutt, and believe me ever to remain,—Your most sincere friend,
>
> Govin Chunder Dutt

To Mlle Bader he wrote:

> "She has left us for the land where parting and sorrow are unknown. Her faith in her Redeemer was unbounded, and her spirit enjoyed a perfect peace—the peace beyond all understanding. 'It is the physical pain of the blister that makes me cry,' said she once to the doctor; 'but my spirit is in peace. I know in Whom I trust.' There was never a sweeter child, and she was my last one.

My wife and I are left alone in our old age, in a house empty and desolate, where once were heard the voices of our three beloved children. But we are not forsaken: The Consoler is with us, and a time will come when we shall meet in the presence of our Lord, not to be parted again."

In not unnatural wonder, he asked:

"Why should these three young lives, so full of hope and work, be cut short, while I, old and almost infirm, linger on? I think I can dimly see that there is a fitness, a preparation required for the life beyond, which they had, and I have not. One day I shall see it all clearly. Blessed be the Lord. His will be done."

Further reminiscences occur in Mr. Dutt's acknowledgement of sympathetic letters from Miss Martin and her father:

November 26, 1877

"I received your very kind letter of the 3rd October and its enclosure, the letter from your father, some days ago. Yes, you are right, Toru was ready, and ready for a long time to meet the Blessed Saviour. You know she left us on the 30th August at 8 in the evening. Her end here was very peaceful and happy, and her mother and myself will never, never forget the expression that was on her face when all was over. Such a glory there was on it. She reckoned you as her first and best friend, and was rarely so happy as when she got a letter from you. When it was decided by the doctor that we should go to England, she purchased some *tussore* dresses for you to take with her and give them to you when you met each other. That meeting, the Lord has willed it—is never more to be on earth. But I thought it right to send you these dresses purchased expressly for you, and also her Cashmere shawl, to be kept as a remembrance of her. I could write to you much more about our darling, but I have to enclose a letter to your father. . ."

That Toru's loss was no easier to bear as the months went by is shown by other letters written to Miss Martin in 1878:

"I cannot tell you how precious to me are all your reminiscences of Toru, and the short quotations you give me from her letters to you. She always considered you her first friend, as dear to her as a sister, and she wrote to you more unreservedly and openly than she ever did to anyone else, I believe. I am become so grey now that I almost doubt if you would recognize me at first sight. Mrs. Dutt and I find it very difficult to drag on our chain, now that the sunshine of our house has gone. But the Lord will send me and her both rest and deliverance in His own good time. You are always in our hearts and in our prayers. . ."

". . . I am always very glad to hear from you. Sometimes for days and days, my heart seems brass or iron, and I almost envy my wife her softer woman's nature, but a perusal of one of your letters always brings the mist into my eyes, and I find much relief. . . Toru's MS. French novel has been received by Mlle Bader, and she thus writes of it in her latest letter to me from Paris: 'It is extraordinary that a young Indian girl should have so admirably mastered our language. Our dear Toru put into her dramatic and touching story the same grace, candour and pathos, which were the sources of her poetic inspiration. . .' Toru's horses Jeunette and Gentille still continue to be our pets. We give them work just enough to keep them in health; and Mrs. Dutt is never tired of caressing them, as well as Toru's favourite cat, 'Bag' or 'Tiger', which, poor thing! sleeps in my wife's bed. It used to answer Toru's call like a dog, and it was piteous to see how it pined for days and days after she left us. . ."

In another letter he writes:

". . . Yes, I am myself surprised at the amount of affection which dear Toru had inspired in people who had never seen her, and had known her only by her books. You say, 'it must be a great comfort to you and Mrs. Dutt to see the affection for Toru which the perusal of her books brings.' Mrs. Trevor Grant, a lady whom I have never seen and whom Toru had never seen, writes: 'There really must have been something unusually lovable and attractive about her, for most of those who have read her books seem to have retained a personal affection for her.' Mrs. Trevor Grant wrote that charming notice in the *Englishman* newspaper, which I sent you some time ago. Then again, M. Victor de Laprade—the eminent French poet— writes to Mlle Bader: 'The attachment of the young Hindu lady for our dear France has made me love her warmly. She was a poet, and her heart had high aspirations and was generous like yours.' Did I send you the short but very beautiful notice of 'Le Journal de Mlle D'Arvers' in the *Revue de France* for February 15, 1879? . . ."

From now on, Mr. Dutt's chief comfort lay in seeing to the editing of his daughter's works, both French and English, and in knowing how much they were appreciated. Writing again to Miss Martin on January 12, 1881, he says:

". . . I am glad you like the new edition of the *Sheaf*. Mlle Bader writes to the same effect, Mrs. Trevor Grant and also Professor Cowell. The latter wrote: 'We have received the copy of the *Sheaf*, the new edition. It is beautifully got-up; and the picture at the beginning wonderfully recalls them. It is certainly an astounding book. What a mind of poetic insight and power Toru had. I fear her very intensity of nature overwrought the tenement of clay'. It was the sword of fine temper wearing away the sheath. Still one cannot but feel that a keen bright insight, like hers, intensely enjoyed her intellectual life, though it was so short on earth. I dare say you remember Ben Jonson's lines in Palgrave's *Golden Treasury*, about the short-lived lily being "The flower of light"'.[8] With the testimony of such dear friends, I am fain to be content, for, do you know, I have not yet received a single copy of the new edition myself!"

Some short time after her death, the *Calcutta Review* published eight sonnets from one of her favourite poets, Gramont. The last of these sonnets, the chief thought of which is the moral victory of the

---

8. Sir T. Herbert Warren, the President of Magdalen College, Oxford, in his recollections of Professor Cowell writes thus: "Professor Cowell was also, I remember, much interested in the Indian poetess Toru Dutt, and he lent me some papers about both Padre Long and Miss Dutt."

See p. 434 of the *Life and Letters of E. B. Cowell*, by George Cowell, F.R.C.S.

Christian over physical weakness, may well be taken as typical of the authoress's own experience. In paying a tribute to her genius, a writer in that magazine remarked:

> "She wrote in English with all the delicacies and good taste of a highly educated Englishwoman."

Other publications, both in England and in India, joined in the general chorus of praise. The President of the Paris "Société Asiatique"—a society in which Toru Dutt had been deeply interested— Monsieur Garcin de Tassy, wrote his appreciation as follows:

> "On the 30th of August, there died in Calcutta, Toru Dutt, a young Hindu girl scarcely twenty years old, a little prodigy who knew, not only Sanskrit, her sacred tongue, but also English and French, which she could read and speak perfectly, which is not altogether astonishing since she had been brought up in Europe. But what is more remarkable, she had published English poems, bearing the stamp of genius, at a time of life when girls are still in school."

To quote Mlle Bader once more:

> "If the remembrance of her own life belongs to her parents, the fame due to her works belongs to the literary world. England and India claim her glory, and I like to believe that France also will keep ever green the memory of the young foreign girl who, when our country was humiliated, wished to belong to her in language as well as in heart."

M. James Darmesteter said:

> "To us French people, she is doubly dear, for her own personal value, and for the love she professed for France. She has a right to a mention in the history of our literature, since she has herself inscribed her name in it, and she must remain in our memory as a fragile and sweet figure impersonating the Hindu genius such as it might have been under the wing of French Government."

We close with a final testimony in the words of Mr. Edmund Gosse:

"It is difficult to exaggerate when we try to estimate what we have lost in the premature death of Toru Dutt. Literature has no honours which need have been beyond the grasp of a girl who at the age of twenty-one, and in languages separated from her own by so deep a chasm, had produced so much of lasting worth. And her courage and fortitude were worthy of her intelligence."

After Toru's death some lines signed "R. K. M." appeared in the *Statesman* on February 17, 1879. The writer represents England, France, and India in turn claiming Toru as her own. Death intervenes, and the respective voices are silent. The composition is faulty and full of mixed metaphors, but the sentiment is beautiful, and for the rest, our readers must decide for themselves.

> *This song-bird with its music right royal,*
> *Though it come from far over the sea,*
> *Is mine own, for its heart true and loyal*
> *And its feelings were moulded by me.*
> *I nursed it,—cries England,—and I claim it;*
> *I fed it; it has drunk at my breast;*
> *It loves me; and sure no one can blame it;*
> *'Tis my bird, and with me it shall rest.*

> *Nay, sister; it is mine; by this token*
> *That it loves me the best, for I know*
> *When my bright sword at Sedan was broken*
> *It sickened and sank under the blow.*
> *It has throbbed,—answers France,—at my story,*
> *Its eye flames at the name Eighty-nine;*
> *It has warbled the songs of my glory;*
> *'Tis my bird,—yes, it surely is mine.*

> *It was born in my womb;—shall another*
> *Then my brightest and best take away?*
> *Can ye give it the fond love of a mother?*
> *If ye cannot, with me it shall stay.*

Oh aye cherish your song-birds, ye nations,
England thy Brontës and France thy George Sands!
Leave me but mine, in my desolations,
Only her own, India asks at your hands.

Truce to vain strife! 'Tis all out of season,
I carry our song-bird back to its nest,
Question me not;—'twere highest of treason,
This is God's will, and that Will is the best.
Back to its home,—and smiling, the Reaper
Bearing the song-bird, for burden, upsprings!
A long trail of light—then a darkness deeper,
And a silence that followed the rush of his wings.

HARIHAR DAS AND TORU DUTT

X

BIANCA, OR THE YOUNG SPANISH MAIDEN, AND LE JOURNAL DE MADEMOISELLE D'ARVERS

At the time of Toru's death, her title to fame rested on *A Sheaf gleaned in French Fields*, the only book of hers which had as yet been published. This received, however, so warm a reception that her father examined her papers with a view to publishing whatever might prove to be of literary interest among them. A selection of English translations of the Sonnets of the Comte de Gramont, and an unfinished romance, also in English, entitled *Bianca, or The Young Spanish Maiden*, formed part of the harvest thus reaped. The most remarkable discovery, however, was that of a complete French novel, *Le Journal de Mademoiselle d'Arvers*.

Bianca is a romance consisting of eight chapters, which was eventually published, not in the form of a book, but in the columns of the *Bengal Magazine* (January–April, 1878), with a short foot-note (see p. 319) appended to it by her father. There is a tender and pathetic interest attaching to this tale. It is full of promise and yet incomplete, and so in harmony with the life-story of its authoress. One wonders too if the portrait given of Bianca may not reflect to some extent Toru's own feelings.

Bianca Garcia is the younger and only surviving daughter of a Spanish gentleman, who has settled in an English village. Her elder sister, Inez, has just died, and the narrative opens with an account of the burial on a dreary day in February.

Bianca and her father are the sole mourners. On her return home she cannot help contrasting her sheltered warm surroundings with the cold damp ground in which her sister's dead form is lying, and out of very sympathy goes to sit in the garden, oblivious of the weather, until Martha, the old Scotch servant, finds her and calls her in; that evening the attention which she pays to her father helps her to forget for a while the intensity of her own grief. Her place in the household had been one of special esteem rather than of special affection. Her father had been wont to consult her, but had lavished the treasure of his love on Inez. Here is the description which the authoress has given of her heroine:—

"She was not beautiful; of the middle height; her slight figure was very graceful; her face was not quite oval; her forehead was low; her lips were full, sensitive and mobile; her colour was dark; have you ever seen an Italian peasant girl? When she blushed or was excited, the colour mounted warm and deep to her pale olive cheek; she was beautiful then; her dark brown eyes—'just like Keeper's' (the dog's), her father would say, smiling,—were large and full; in fact this pair of eyes and her long black curls were her only points of beauty."

Next morning her father was taken ill, and a week of patient nursing followed for her.

More than a year passes, and she is sought in marriage by Mr. Ingram, her dead sister's fiancé, who nevertheless has not ceased to love Inez. She seeks to comfort him while telling him plainly that she can give him nothing more than sisterly affection. They meet a common acquaintance, Margaret Moore, the daughter of the widowed Lady Moore, who lives in the chief house of the village. Margaret urges Bianca to visit Moore Hall, and so next day she goes. Mr. Garcia had been reluctant to consent to this visit until he heard that the grown-up son of the house, young Lord Moore, would be away in London that day. He had no wish that his daughter should be accused of "husband-hunting". However, Bianca was already deeply in love with this young man.

We are introduced to the Moore household—the aristocratic and frigid mother; the gracious daughter; the "Benjamin" of the family, little Willie; and, at length, to Lord Moore himself in all the force and vigour of his manhood. Bianca was a great favourite of Willie's, who was charmed to have her play with him. The elder son returns home unexpectedly, and his mother is vexed because he finds Bianca there. He escorts her to her home later on, and returning comes to the determination to seek her as his wife. Just at that juncture his mother enters his room with a suggestion of another lady as his bride, and when she finds that he has no inclination whatever in that quarter, she begins to speak disparagingly of Bianca. But without avail. Lord Moore vows that he can marry no one else but her.

Matters soon reach a crisis. He and Willie call at her home, and he stays on chatting with her in the garden after his little brother has left. When he takes his departure, he is so carried away by his feelings that he kisses her. Bianca feels it her duty to tell her father, who is angry to hear of the incident, and while they are talking a letter is brought in, containing Lord Moore's definite offer of marriage. Mr. Garcia is unwilling to grant his consent and, to please her father, Bianca agrees to decline the proposal; and when her lover arrives at the house that same evening to learn his fate, she goes to her room. The young man's grief is so intense and genuine that the father relents and sends for Bianca. The strain of having had to relinquish her lover, as she thinks, has been too great for her, and she is seized with illness and delirium. Lord Moore hastily returns home to ride for the doctor, and his perturbation is noticed by his family. Another character in the story now begins to come into prominence, viz. Mr. Owen, a cousin of the Moores and also distantly related through his wife to the Garcias. He is a fascinating but unscrupulous man whose real character is apparently known only to the Garcias. Lord Moore's distress over his beloved's illness meets with scant sympathy from his mother. However, after some weeks of utter prostration Bianca recovers, and she and Lord Moore plight their troth. Mr. Owen supports Lady Moore in her disapproval of the match, and himself meets with so cold a reception from Bianca, later on, at a chance interview at Moore House, that her lover is surprised. The next chapter tells of the parting between the lovers on the eve of Lord Moore's departure for the Crimean War, and here the story breaks off.

This romance is but a fragment—and apparently an unrevised fragment—and therefore it cannot be appraised as though it were a completed work. Had it been finished, inconsistencies which now exist would have been noted and corrected (e.g., Lord Moore would not be called "Colin" in the earlier chapters and "Henry" in the later ones, nor would the rainy weather of the opening scene so quickly turn to snow, nor would Lady Moore remain apparently in ignorance of the actual engagement of her son). Some of the incidents of the story also are rather too abrupt to be consistent with reality (e.g., Bianca's sudden delirium and her quick recovery without such a period of convalescence as follows upon prolonged weakness are hardly in accord with ordinary experience). Mrs. Cranly's departure from the home is overlooked. The story, as it is, reminds one of a piece of unfinished embroidery with loose threads still left hanging which need to be worked in. The attempt to reproduce the lisping language of a child is not always successful, nor is it likely that a girl betrothed to a nobleman would, after the establishment of such a relationship of intimacy, continue to address him as "My Lord". These are, however, minor and remediable blemishes. Though the plot is not a very complex one, yet the story attracts and retains the reader's interest. The flow of language, the facility of expression, the frequent touches of realism, and the acquaintance with English life are remarkable when one remembers that the authoress was writing in a language and of a land that were alike foreign to her. The story reflects her talents, attainments, and character, her poetic imagination and powers of description, her intimate acquaintance with English and French literature, and, above all, her deeply religious nature. Had the tale been carried to its proper conclusion and its defects remedied, it would have been healthier in tone and better written than much of the popular literature of the present day.[1]

Le Journal de Mademoiselle d'Arvers

Originally this was to have been produced in collaboration—Toru's sister, Aru, supplying the illustrations; but it is doubtful if the latter saw any portion of the work completed before she died, and Toru was left to draw solely from her own vivid imagination.

A manuscript copy of the novel was sent by Mr. Dutt to Mlle Clarisse Bader, the French lady with whom Toru had corresponded, and she has recorded its receipt as follows:

"It was not without deep emotion that I received the copy of the MS. entirely written out by her old father. 'My hand is not steady, and I have to copy slowly,' he wrote, but nothing in the beautiful and energetic writing betrays the trembling hand. The father has gathered strength to accomplish this bitter-sweet task from the illusion which it creates. 'While I am writing,' he stated, 'I feel as though I were speaking with her.'"

---

1. "The gentle hand that had traced the story thus far—the hand of Miss Toru Dutt—left off here. Was it illness that made the pen drop from the weary fingers? I do not know. I think not. The sketch was a first attempt probably, and abandoned. I am inclined to think so, because the novel left in the French language is very much superior indeed to this fragment and is complete. Other fragments there are, both in prose and verse, but mostly rough-hewn and unpolished.—G. C. D."

The book was dedicated to His Excellency Lord Lytton, Viceroy and Governor-General of India, with "témoignage de profonde reconnaissance", and the title-page bears the following inscription:

> O dying voice of human praise!
> The crude ambitions of my youth!
> I long to pour immortal lays,
> Great paeans of perennial truth!
> A larger wish! a loftier aim! . . .
> And what are laurel leaves and fame?

It was published by a Paris firm, Didier, in 1879, among the "Librairie Académique", with a preface by Mademoiselle Bader, containing some account of the authoress's life and works. It had been begun, apparently, during the visit to Europe, but nothing is known as to the time of its completion.

Le Journal de Mademoiselle d'Arvers is an attempt to reproduce scenes from the life of French society in the sixties of last century, and is peculiarly interesting because of the astonishing revelation it gives of the mind and accomplishments of its writer. James Darmesteter, the renowned French scholar, describes it as the work of "a young Hindu girl of nineteen, who had learnt French for a very few years, and had resided in France for a few months only. It is an extraordinary feat, without precedent. The *Vathek* of Beckford can alone be compared to it, though such comparison is hardly fair, because, to a gentleman of the eighteenth century, the French language was, so to speak, a second 'mother-tongue'."

Darmesteter is not exaggerating when he refers to this book as being "an extraordinary feat". In a criticism of it which appeared in a Dutch paper in 1879 we read that "nothing in the book betrays the fact that the writer is a 'foreigner'". The ordinary foreigner who possesses but an average knowledge of the French tongue is surprised, as he peruses it, to find how copious is the vocabulary and how facile and idiomatic the mode of expression. What few inaccuracies or infelicities occur are such as only a Frenchman or one who had been long a resident in France would be likely to note. We question if, in the whole of the history of literature, another such example can be found of a foreign language being so completely mastered in so short a time that the production of an entire book in that tongue was possible, and that too in the finished style which this book displays. Toru Dutt was certainly a linguistic prodigy. At the age of nineteen she had mastered three languages and she wrote fluently in two. Nor is it only in connexion with the easy and graceful way in which she wrote this book that her genius is manifested. She has imparted to it a French "atmosphere", not only in matters social but also in matters religious. She has written it from the standpoint of a devout Roman Catholic. It is true that Mlle Bader, who saw the book through the press, feels that there are evidences in it of Oriental customs and modes of thought, which stamp it, so to speak, with the hall-mark of the authoress's own personality. *Le Journal de Mademoiselle d'Arvers*, in spite of the thoroughly French form and inspiration, "reminds us of exotic flowers transplanted in our country, which, though they may be acclimatized, keep the very scent of their native soil". We feel, however, that only a very acute critic would detect such traces, and that the general public would agree rather with the enthusiastic tribute of the poetess, Madame de Saffray: "This one surpasses all the prodigies. She is a Frenchwoman in this book, and a Frenchwoman like ourselves: she thinks, she writes, like one of us."

A brief outline of the story will be helpful for the better estimate of the merits of the work. The book purports to consist of extracts from the diary of a French maiden, which range over a period of about a year and a half, a period beginning with her leaving the convent school, where she had been educated, and ending with her premature death within the first year of her married life. The account of her illness and death is inserted as an epilogue to the diary. The beginning of the journal—to quote again from Mlle Bader—is "the pretty prattle of a young girl who has known no sorrow and whose heart is filled with pure and simple joys". Marguerite d'Arvers is the only child of her parents—a retired general and his wife who are living in Brittany, and she returns home in time to celebrate her fifteenth birthday. At her birthday party she meets friends whom she had known in her childhood's days: Madame Goserelle, with her daughter, and the widowed Countess of Plonarven, with her two sons, Dunois and Gaston. Three days later a young officer, Louis Lefèvre, comes on a visit to her home. He is the orphan son of old friends of Marguerite's parents. A glimpse is given of the way in which Marguerite fills up her days: in walks with her father, in tending her domestic pets, and in visiting the poor and aged in the neighbouring village. She obtains a place for one of the village girls, Jeannette, as lady's maid to the Countess, and, later on, goes herself to visit at the château, where the Countess gives her a warm welcome. She there meets her hostess's brother, Colonel Desclée. Another trip which she takes is to Paris, to stay with her great-aunt Geneviève. Marguerite's parents would fain see her united to Louis, but when he solicits her, she refuses him. She has fallen in love with Count Dunois, and the Countess one day at the château discovers the fact and rejoices. Dunois and Gaston, however, are both secretly enamoured of Jeannette, and in a fit of madness the Count kills his brother. Only on recovering sanity does he become aware of his crime and also of Marguerite's love, and then he has to confess his infatuation for his mother's maid. He is condemned to penal servitude, but in another fit of insanity takes his own life, and the Countess loses her reason in consequence. Marguerite has a very severe illness, but, when convalescent, she feels that it is her duty to marry Louis and so please her parents. Both at the wedding ceremony and subsequently she has a premonition of her early death. However, she is resigned, feeling that God knows best what is best for man's good. The sisterly affection she had at the outset for Louis develops into a deep love, and the end of the story is taken up with an account of her happy days of married life at Nice, her return home and death there, leaving a little son.

Such is an epitome of the story. Simple though it is, it nevertheless elicits and sustains the reader's interest in a way that many a novel with a more elaborate plot and a more crowded array of characters fails to do. It is told very skilfully. When first the two possible claimants for Marguerite's hand appear on the scene, we cannot tell which will be the favoured one, and, later on, when Louis has been refused, and there appears no obstacle in the way of Marguerite's becoming the future Countess, stray hints are thrown out that all is not right with Dunois, yet at the same time the exact nature of the trouble is so carefully concealed that the tragic *dénouement* is one which startles and surprises the reader. Perhaps in no part of the book is the writer's genius more evident than in the description of the scene after the murder. The awfulness of the tragedy is brought home fully, but without gruesomeness. There are no ghastly details, no sordid or vulgar incidents, such as too often characterize accounts of such events. This episode in the story is one of the most brilliant pieces of writing in the whole book. The novel, though written in French, is very different from the ordinary "French novel", as that expression is frequently used in modern parlance. Literature of this latter kind, with its predilection for low intrigue, would have devoted much space to details of Dunois's trial and to the love-affair which occasioned the crime. There is nothing of this nature in Toru's work. A high-toned spirit pervades the whole. The particulars of the trial are not mentioned—simply the verdict. The love displayed by the brothers for the servant-maid may have been ill-placed, but there is no suggestion that it was anything but honourable.

Though the simple nature of the narrative does not on the whole afford much opportunity for forcible writing, yet we meet with passages that exhibit a highly developed imaginative faculty and poetic thought. Just two specimens must suffice. The madman's dream of his brother lying dead, with eyes staring at him, while from the motionless lips there issued the hoarse cry of "Cain", is a brilliant conception. The following, too, is a passage which contains a beautiful and original idea:

> "J'ai aperçu un moineau qui y étanchait sa soif. Chaque fois qu'il buvait, il levait la tête vers les cieux comme pour remercier son Créateur."

There are many artistic settings and quaint "conceits" scattered through the book, and some of the descriptions of scenery are specially fine and picturesque. Toru was evidently keenly susceptible to the varied beauties of nature, sea and sky, woodland and meadows, the changing seasons and the solemn grandeur of night. Here is one of her "word pictures":

> "J'ai laissé ma fenêtre ouverte; les brillantes étoiles me regardent, et la lune argentine entrecoupe de clair et d'ombre ma petite chambre. Tout se tait; pas un bruit, pas le moindre souffle de l'air. La lune me faisait penser à la sœur Véronique de mon couvent, elle aussi est chaste et belle et pâle, comme l'astre de la nuit; loin du bruit du monde, dans la sainte enceinte du couvent elle mène une calme et pieuse vie."

There are not a few such passages in the book, simple in their wording and not marred by any exuberance of verbiage or thought.

Toru is happy too in her portrayal of personalities. Though there are not very many characters, the majority are clearly and distinctly drawn. Louis Lefèvre is a splendid type of a gallant soldier, a noble-minded gentleman, and a devoted lover and husband. Count Dunois is not perhaps so perfectly sketched, yet he so comports himself in prosperity that he elicits the sympathy of the reader when the dread calamity overtakes him. Mlle Goserelle is evidently intended to serve as a foil to the heroine. Her vivacity, frivolity, and gaiety, her witty and lively remarks, her attachment to the pleasures of life, are in utter contrast to the sobriety of mind, the unselfish devotion and unworldliness exhibited by Marguerite. She is the butterfly of the story—attractive and beautiful but without qualities of solidity, and was possibly suggested by one of the types of French girlhood that the authoress had met. Two other characters, though in the background, are nevertheless carefully worked out, viz. the aristocratic and elderly aunt, a relic from a previous generation and yet keenly interested in the young life around her, and Thérèse, the old and devoted domestic who had been in the service of the family for so many years. The character of Marguerite herself, however, is hardly as perfect or natural as some of the subsidiary characters are. She represents a noble ideal of girlhood, and no one can read her story without being both attracted by her and stimulated to more unselfish living, but she is hardly drawn from life like the others. In portraying her, the authoress has in all probability portrayed to a very large extent her own self and her own ideals of life; but Toru was an exceptional and not an average girl. Marguerite, we feel, is too old for her age. She manifests the experience of womanhood while yet in her teens. Her saving the life of the child in its convulsive fit and her influence in the homes of the poor are scarcely true to actual experience. So too her deep-seated faith in Providence, her unfailing religiousness of spirit, and her calm resignation are such as we associate, not with girlhood, but with the after years when, through longer and more varied acquaintance with life and its commingled lights and shadows, the soul has been brought into closer touch with reality.

It must not be forgotten that the book is written in the form of a diary. When it is viewed from this standpoint, some criticisms which naturally arise in the reader's mind lose much of their force. For instance, in an ordinary story, Marguerite's self-centredness and her constant expression of personal feelings, as well as her frequent reference to her charity to the poor, would be out of place and a distinct defect, but they are not incongruous if found within the pages of what purports to be a private journal. There is, too, a sense of incompleteness associated with the account of Jeannette. As the cause—though, apparently, the irresponsible cause—of the tragedy of the two brothers and of the consequent wreck of Marguerite's hopes, she is of some importance in the story. Yet very little is said about her, and no details are given of her subsequent history. The interest which is aroused in the reader's mind concerning her is left unsatisfied. Many a writer would have utilized the episode to tell us much—even too much—about her; Toru went to the other extreme. The book would have been better also if the lengthy conversations and remarks about the expected birth of the child had been considerably condensed. But the beauties of the book far outweigh its defects. For its pathos and poetic touches, for its simplicity, lit up by flashes of imaginative genius, and for its high-souled sentiments, it is well worth perusal.

The subjoined tributes show the nature of the reception accorded to the book in France. M. James Darmesteter included an appreciation of it in his *Essays on English Literature*, inserting it next to his critiques of Shakespeare's *Macbeth* and Shelley's Poetry. He wrote:

> "The crowning quality of this child's work, and the most striking feature, is one that would hardly be expected from a child and a Hindu—it is its moderation, its sobriety of details. There are no developments, but only indications, of facts—a masterful quality generally unknown in India, and one which betokens really great minds."

"It is a simple and touching narrative," wrote M. Adrien Desprez, "in which the writer has poured forth all the treasures of a young and loving soul. Nothing can be simpler than this idyll, and yet nothing can be more fresh; nothing can be more chaste, and yet nothing more full of passion. It is a soul that we find here, a sympathetic soul which appeals to us like a sister."

M. Garcin de Tassy, the eminent Orientalist, also paid a tribute to the genius of the young Indian girl, and deplored her loss on account of the literary hopes which her writings had raised.

England also joined in the chorus of praise, as is shown by the following extract from the *Saturday Review* of August 23, 1879:

> "There is every reason to believe that in intellectual power Toru Dutt was one of the most remarkable women that ever lived. Had George Sand or George Eliot died at the age of twenty-one, they would certainly not have left behind them any proof

of application or of originality superior to those bequeathed to us by Toru Dutt; and we discover little of merely ephemeral precocity in the attainments of this singular girl."

It is indeed a book which is a marvel, merely when considered from a linguistic point of view. It gives promise of further work, more brilliant and beautiful still. Had Toru's life been spared, who knows but that she might have devoted her unique abilities and her poetic powers to the task of giving the world a similar picture of Indian maidenhood, or of telling of the beauties, secrets, and wonders of her own motherland and her own people?

No one can read this story without feeling that in it much of the inner life of Toru is consciously or unconsciously revealed. It cannot be regarded as an autobiography in the strict sense of the term. The outward incidents of the heroine's life do not harmonize with the authoress's own career, and yet the feelings and sentiments must have undoubtedly reflected Toru's own. Mlle Bader felt this resemblance very strongly, and has directed attention to it in the *Introduction* which she wrote to the book. And so the story supplies a portrait of its writer. We see in it her deeply devout and religious mind, her sensitiveness of spirit and her unselfish readiness for service and sacrifice. We see in it a heart that was more susceptible to the shadows than to the sunshine of life, and that had premonitions of a premature decease. And when we reach the final page and read there the description of Marguerite's passing away, we wonder if Toru was hoping that it would typify her own:

"Dieu nous ait en sa garde," soupira-t-elle. "Il était son habitude depuis l'enfance de faire cette prière juste avant de s'endormir. Elle ferma les yeux; ses lèvres s'entr'ouvrirent, et son âme pure s'envola par là vers le sein de son Dieu, et Marguerite s'endormit du sommeil de la mort."

XI

ANCIENT BALLADS AND
LEGENDS OF HINDUSTAN

"The Soul of India" is a familiar phrase in modern times, and it stands for a soul which is above all else intensely religious. In India we see today, as perhaps nowhere else save among the simpler peoples of Catholic Europe, a piety which is entirely devoid of self-consciousness. The Mohammedan turns aside from his work in the crowded bazaar to perform his devotions, utterly oblivious of the stranger's curious eyes. The devout Hindu performs his rites and lays his offerings at a wayside shrine, or prostrates himself, measuring his length in the dust in fulfilment of a vow, also perfectly indifferent to the public eye. Such acts are commonplace in India and are innocent of even a suggestion of parade. It is not surprising, therefore, that piety in some form or other should be the theme of the *Ancient Ballads and Legends of Hindustan*, and that in them the religious note should sound strongly.

It is to her mother's influence that we owe these beautiful little *Ancient Ballads and Legends of Hindustan*, the leading characteristic of which is "a Vedic solemnity and simplicity of temper". This is their charm, and it is interesting to speculate where her unique gifts would have led her, if she had had the same opportunities for cultivating and expressing her powers as Dr. Rabindranath Tagore.

These poems, according to Mr. Edmund Gosse,[1] "will be ultimately found to constitute Toru's chief legacy to posterity". They are the result of about a year's study of Sanskrit. Toru's first experiments were translations into English of two stories taken from the *Vishnu Purana*—the sacred book containing an account of the god Vishnu. The first, "The Legend of Dhruva," from the *Dhruvapakhyanam*, was published in the *Bengal Magazine* of October 1876. The second, "The Royal Ascetic and the Hind" from *Bharatopakhyanam*, in the *Calcutta Review* of January 1877. Toru's studies in Sanskrit extended to the *Mahabharata* and the *Ramayana*—the *Iliad* and *Odyssey* of Indian literature, and she seems to have been fired with the idea of presenting some of the

---

1. See "Introductory Memoir" to the edition published by Kegan Paul & Co. in 1882.

grand stories of her Indian heritage in order to gain the appreciation and sympathy of English readers. In this way the *Ancient Ballads and Legends of Hindustan* were conceived and partly worked out. A series of nine were apparently contemplated, but only seven were found, the gaps being supplied by the reprinting of "The Royal Ascetic and the Hind" and "The Legend of Dhruva".

The volume was published in London in 1882, with an introductory memoir by Mr. Edmund Gosse. The quotation from Sir Philip Sidney's *Apologie for English Poetry*, inscribed on the fly-leaf of the little book, is peculiarly appropriate, embodying, as it does, a sentiment which is the outcome of the sensitiveness of the true poetic temperament to the spell of the noble past.

"I never heard the old song of Percie and Douglas, that I found not my heart moved, more than with a trumpet: and yet it is sung but by some blinde crowder, with no rougher voice than rude style."

"'WHEN I HEAR MY MOTHER chant, in the evening, the old lays of our country, I almost always weep,' wrote Toru. So do these 'tears of a poet', which a poet alone can shed, tears of Sidney hearing the blind man sing 'Chevy Chase', tears of Musset listening to the old romance sung by the street singers, link together poetic souls of all ages and races, and not least touching among them all are those of the Indian child-poetess".[2]

The chief value of this book consists in the fact that Toru had at last found her true poetic sphere. "The genius of man dives deep into the dreams of childhood: children's stories form the real basis of any heart-inspired poetry," wrote a French critic;[3] and ballads are in essence the child-literature of the past.

In relating ancient ballads or legends, a poet should be objective in his treatment: standing aloof as much as possible, not obtruding his own personality, and chiefly intent on representing as faithfully as possible something of the spirit of the past. A certain amount of modernization may be necessary, in order to be intelligible; but, if he should fail to give the reader sympathetic insight into the spirit of ancient literature, the poet has written in vain.

The ballad form in English, with its slight archaisms and its haunting refrain, is of great use in this direction, and, possibly, if Toru had lived,

2. From *Essais de Littérature anglaise,* by M. Darmesteter.
3. Ibid.

she would have found it a much more suitable representative of the splendid and stately tone of the Sanskrit original than the easy and monotonous blank verse of these her first attempts. That she was feeling her way to it seems plain from the fact that she used the octosyllabic measure for her later poems.

Neither in "The Legend of Dhruva" nor in "The Royal Ascetic and the Hind" was there much scope for originality, and their chief interest must ever lie in the fact that they mark the beginning of a new phase in the development of Toru's genius, namely, her desire to give expression to her intense love of her own land and its traditions.

It is with unfeigned wonder and admiration that we turn from these experiments to the noble poem of "Savitri", recreated and clothed in fresh beauty by Toru from an episode related in the *Mahabharata*.

Savitri is a tender and beautiful picture of the ideal Indian wife. She lives only in and for her husband—an ideal, apparently, not differing greatly from Puritan Milton's idea of the relations between man and wife in the beginning of things:

> He for God only—she for God in him.

In the purifying fires of her devotion to Satyavan, Savitri seems to grow utterly selfless, and in this reminds us strongly of her great Greek sister-heroine, Alcestis, who also offers gladly to die in her husband's stead. She gives up without a pang her happiness in his love and in her home to go out alone into that sunless land of the shades, the melancholy Elysium of the Greeks, which held in it nothing of attraction for a people with so keen a zest for life as they. It takes the mighty hero Hercules himself to rescue the noble wife from the grasp of Death at the entrance to the underworld. The Indian conception is subtler and finer than this. Satyavan is released from the power of Death by the unconquerable, wholly human love and steadfastness of his wife, and by that alone. Human love triumphs over humanity's greatest foe. Nay, more—Savitri looks unafraid into the very face of the King of Terrors, and finds it good!

"I wonder if in an Indian poet's work, a passer-by would turn round to see Savitri once more," speculates M. Darmesteter. However this may be, in these pages she is, perhaps, the most attractive personality. Were there a pageant of the heroes and heroines of the *Ancient Ballads and Legends of Hindustan*, we think the eyes of the spectators would be riveted to the end on that pure, lovely figure, and would then turn away with that look of awe which steals into men's eyes after looking on a figure of true beauty and heroism.

There is something almost classical in the calm dignity of Savitri's speeches, as when she addresses Death:

> *I know that in this transient world*
> *All is delusion,—nothing true;*
> *I know its shows are mists unfurled*
> *To please and vanish. To renew*
> *Its bubble joys, be magic-bound*
> *In* Maya's *network frail and fair,*
> *Is not my aim! The gladsome sound*
> *Of husband, brother, friend, is air*
> *To such as know that all must die,*
> *And that at last the time must come,*
> *When eye shall speak no more to eye,*
> *And Love cry,—Lo, this is my sum.*

There is a Virgilian touch where Death talks of bearing Satyavan's soul across "the doleful lake", and a faint echo of Spenser and the land of Faerie in the line:

> Was it a dream from elfland blown?

So far as the versification goes, Toru's advance in technique in this poem, as compared with its predecessors, is little short of marvellous.

From "Savitri", we pass to "Lakshman", and we are this time confronted with the portrait of the ideal brother, a splendid picture of chivalry and self-control. The Lakshman of the *Ramayana* cannot refrain, in response to Sita's wild and slanderous upbraidings, from the cynical remark: "Women are by nature crooked, fickle, sowers of strife." The Lakshman of Toru's ballad, however, gives utterance to no such unchivalrous utterance, but remains through all the tempest of Sita's scorn what Chaucer would have called "a veray parfit gentil knight". Although her words have pierced him to the quick, he lets fall no single word of reproach, and his last thought as he turns to leave her is of securing her safety, to the best of his ability. Nowhere, we think, outside Indian thought, could we get so perfect a picture of brotherly loyalty, or so vivid an insight into the strength of the bonds that bind the members of an Indian family, the one to the other.

The poem forms an interesting departure from its predecessors, in that it is not narrative, but conversational, with a touch of the epic spirit, a dramatic dialogue. In such a poem there is small scope for the usual embellishments of metaphor, simile, &c., but there is a danger of lapsing into the merely prosaic. The tone is dignified, rising sometimes to the heroic, as in the following stanza, with its hint of impending tragedy:

> *He said, and straight his weapons took,*
> *His bow and arrows pointed keen,*
> *Kind—nay, indulgent,—was his look,*
> *No trace of anger there was seen,*
> *Only a sorrow dark, that seemed*
> *To deepen his resolve to dare*
> *All dangers. Hoarse the vulture screamed,*
> *As out he strode with dauntless air.*

The gradual working out of Sita's passion forms the most interesting feature of the poem. In the opening verses, we have conveyed to us a vivid impression of Sita's anxiety on Rama's behalf, and excited appeals to Lakshman. The latter's fine vindication of his brother's courage, and his absolute faith in his unconquerableness, serve merely to set Sita at bay. The implied reproach for her lack of faith, containing, as it does, a germ of truth, causes her to turn and rend one who meant only to comfort. We can see her drawing herself up to her full height, with flashing eyes, using the truly feminine weapon of bitter sarcasm, the weapon of one proved to be wrong, but not willing to own it. She flings at him the conjecture:

> *One brother takes*
> *His kingdom,—one would take his wife!*
> *A fair proportion!*

Then, again, posing as an injured martyr, and believing herself to be one, she declares:

> *If fire can burn, or water drown,*
> *I follow him.* . . . .

I did not know thy mind before,
I know thee now,—and have no fear.

This ballad contains a not unskilful attempt at psychological delineation of character, simple and experimental, but still showing a phase of Toru's genius with which we might otherwise have been unacquainted.

"Jogadhya Uma" is a poem unique in this collection for its dreamy, mystic beauty, and gains rather than loses from the fact that its theme is drawn not from any of the great epics or *puranas* of Sanskrit, but from folklore. It is a well-known legend of the people, and was told originally to Toru by an old family nurse, Suchee, a staunch Hindu, "of whom all the children were very fond."

Mystic and dreamy, indeed, the poem is, akin to that of Tennyson's story of the brand Excalibur, "clothed in white samite, mystic, wonderful". It is yet not so dreamy but that, after reading it, there wander through the fields of our imagination two very human and altogether lovable characters: the one, an old priest whose fine face is aglow with reverent, expectant faith; the other, a homely, rather stupid-looking pedlar, whose features, too, are irradiated with an almost child-like wonder. Both are standing on the edge of a lotus-covered tank, looking wistfully for a sign.

We think no other story is more admirably suited to Toru's simplicity of touch. There is throughout the poem a delicate, old-world and Indian flavour. It resembles the illuminations of exquisite workmanship found in certain rare old Eastern manuscripts, wherein every detail stands out clearly, as well as the purity of every colour.

The poem is like a succession of miniatures: the red line of the road to Khirogram (the music of the name suggesting beauty), the meadows where the outlines of the cattle standing "magic bound", knee-deep in grass, loom through the mists which the rising sun is just tinting with rainbow hues. In the foreground is the cheery figure of the pedlar, basket on head, while dotted here and there on the road behind are other figures, intent on their avocations.

Then follows the pretty scene at the lotus-covered tank; the pedlar eagerly displaying his wares, the beautiful maiden framed against the marble archway, with one lovely arm uplifted to watch the sunlight sparkling on the colours in the bracelet on her wrist. From this we pass to a village scene, the sunlit temple in the midst, and at the open door a very human priest, of gay laugh and generous hand. He is standing unusually thoughtful now, with a vermilion-streaked box in his hand, while the pedlar watches wonderingly from the shadow. Lastly, we see the priest standing with bent head amid the noonday hush of nature by the marble ghat, and a world of longing is in his face as he waits for a sign of the goddess's presence.

Beautiful as it is, the poem suffers, with the other ballads, from its medium of expression, though, perhaps, in some slighter degree. The octosyllabic rhymed stanza lends itself to prosiness. In the interview with the goddess, the pedlar is made to exclaim like a schoolgirl:

Oh what a nice and lovely fit!

The use of the word "Manse" for the priest's house is rather naïve, and one feels that the village scene is English rather than Indian. This, however, is the chief flaw in what is undoubtedly a gem of art among the *Ballads of Hindustan*.

"In her own vernacular," says Mr. Frazer,[4] "the poem would have been sung to music so weird and soothing, the words would have been attuned to feelings so deep and sincere, that, although she had parted from her ancient faith and become a Christian, it would have been a poem destined to live in the religious poetry of Hinduism, and take a place among the songs of the people." For our part, we are glad that Toru "let it stand among her rhymes" in English, and thus gave Western readers a sympathetic insight into the simple piety of our ancient Indian folklore.

"Buttoo", in spite of the rather strange collection of trees in the wood which forms the background for the hero of the poem, is another wonderful picture of Indian life and thought, and Indian in its very essence. It is an illustration of the marvellous reverence in which an Indian *chela* (disciple) holds his master. The West would do well to learn something from the East in this, and it would be difficult to find a parallel for the act related in this poem—an act of supremest obedience even to the point of absolute self-renunciation and self-maiming on the part of a pupil towards a master who had but made him a jest and a laughing-stock before others.

---

4. Mr. R. W. Frazer, *Literary History of India*, 1898.

Not the least noteworthy feature of the poem in connexion with the development of Toru's genius is the growth of conciseness, as in the moment of Buttoo's sacrifice—where it would have been easy to succumb to the temptation to linger, and draw out sentiment:

> *Glanced the sharp knife one moment high,*
> *The severed thumb was on the sod.*

"Sindhu", a story from the *Ramayana*, again essentially Indian in spirit, is a picture of filial piety, for Sindhu is an ideal son in his cheerful service of his querulous, exacting old parents. It contains, too, an illustration of the essentially Indian doctrine of "Karma"—a man's deeds, whether voluntarily or involuntarily evil, will pursue him inevitably to a righteous retribution. The king shot Sindhu unwittingly, as Sindhu himself acknowledged, but Sindhu's death was in reality the expiation of a boyish sin when he shot a dove, and the king expiated the crime of shooting the boy by death, heart-broken after the banishment of his own beloved son.

Judging from the style, which is distinctly inferior to that of the other poems, we should place it as an early attempt with "The Legend of Dhruva" and "The Royal Ascetic and the Hind". The metre chosen (the rhymed quatrain, 8.6.8.6.), is one that can most easily degenerate into doggerel, and the poem as a whole suffers badly from this fault.

"Prehlad," from the *Mahabharata*, is the description of a boy's fearless devotion to the gods, in face of bitter opposition and ruthless cruelty at the hands of his tyrant father. It contains, too, a good picture of the Eastern tyrant, fearless in his blasphemy, as his son was in his piety. Eastern, too, is the *dénouement* wherein the tyrant is miraculously struck dead by the direct intervention of the gods, and his son proclaimed king in his stead.

We think the poem would have finished more fittingly at the picture of Prehlad, the new-crowned king, bowing his head reverently on the throne amidst the plaudits of the people; leaving out the apostrophe to tyrants in general: but this may be just a matter for individual taste.

It is interesting too to note the vaguer touch in dealing with the supernatural, as shown in the description of the "sable warrior":

> *Colossal,—such strange shapes arise*
> *In clouds, when autumn rules the lands!*

"Sita", the last poem of the series, is a dream-picture conjured up by "three happy children in a darkened room" who are listening to the sad story of Sita as it falls from their mother's lips in song. They see a dense forest where the sunlight scarcely penetrates. In the midst is a clearing around which gigantic creepers festoon the trees with flowers. White swans are gliding on a quiet lake, whilst the peacock rises "whirring from the brake", and the wild deer bound through the glades. The gold of the forest com glints in the distance, where the blue smoke rises from the altars near the dwelling of the "poet anchorite".

Artistically, the poem, short as it is, is among the best of the ballads. Simple and vivid in style, it is skilfully touched with a delicate pathos by the closing lines:

> *When shall those children by their mother's side*
> *Gather, ah me! as erst at eventide?*

Seven miscellaneous poems complete the volume of ballads, and all of these are in a sense autobiographical. These poems were discovered amongst Toru's papers after her death. The first, "Near Hastings," records, with Toru's characteristic clearness and simplicity of style, an incident in her life in England. She and her sister, the latter still suffering, were resting on the beach near Hastings, when a lady noticed them in passing. She stopped and entered into friendly conversation with them, and, before going, gave Aru some beautiful roses, and thereby won Toru's undying gratitude; for years afterwards she sang:

> *Her memory will not depart,*
> *Though grief my years should shade,*
> *Still bloom her roses in my heart!*
> *And they shall never fade!*

"France 1870", in a metre strangely irregular as regards accent, is a little poem which reveals Toru's love and admiration for France, which she hails as "Head of the human column", whilst for "Levite England" she reserves scorn. There is much of passionate feeling in the poem, and when the ear accustoms itself to the strangeness, there is a certain charm about the great irregularity of the rhythm, in which no two verses are alike.

"The Tree of Life" is perhaps the best example we have of the mysticism which lay deep in Toru's nature. The poem is an account of those daylight visions which come to mortals but rarely. Biographically, it is of interest as the last poem written by her. The opening line is vividly suggestive:

> *Broad daylight, with a sense of weariness!*

It describes how, as the invalid lay with her father's hand in hers, in that intimate, voiceless communion which the two knew and loved so well,

> *Suddenly, there shone*
> *A strange light, and the scene as sudden changed.*

In the midst of an illimitable plain stretched out before her eyes, the visionary saw

> *A tree with spreading branches and with leaves*
> *Of divers kinds,—dead silver and live gold.*

Beside the tree stood an angel, who plucked some of the leaves and bound them round the poetess's brow, till its wild throbbing ceased. So wonderful was their effect, that she pleaded for some to be bound round her father's brow also.

> *One leaf the Angel took, and therewith touched*
> *His forehead, and then gently whispered "Nay!"*

After Toru had gazed awhile, wondering and spell-bound at the love and tenderness in the angel's beautiful face, she opened her eyes upon the world again, to find the vision gone, and her father still sitting patiently beside her, with her hand held fast in his.[5]

The next poem, "On the Fly-Leaf of Erckmann-Chatrian's novel entitled *Madame Thérèse*," records the impression made upon Toru by an incident recorded in the novel, when the French lines were wavering

---

5. With reference to this poem, Mr. Dutt copied as follows from his memorandum book for Miss Martin—it is dated as far back as April 16, 1877—"Yester evening when the candles were lighted, Toru told me, in very low whispers and with some agitation, a dream or vision which she had had the day previous about 9 or 10 A.M. She was not asleep at all, but quite awake. I know now why she asked me the evening before, where the text was, 'And I will give thee a crown of life.' . . ."

before the Prussian onslaught, and the falling standard was snatched by a woman, and a charge led by her and a drummer-boy. It is marked by the same fervour as was "France 1870", and by an even greater irregularity of rhythm. It would be difficult, for instance, to determine the metre of the following line:

Va-nu-pieds! when rose high your Marseillaise.

It is rather an excess of partiality, too, that can rhyme "pont" with "confront"!

The next two poems, "Baugmaree" and "The Lotus", are interesting, apart from their matter, as being the only poems (that we know of) written by Toru in sonnet form. Their success makes us regret that she did not use the form more frequently.

"Baugmaree" is a description of the family's loved Indian garden, girt round with its "sea of foliage" of varying shades, with its vivid splashes of colour where the Seemuls lean above the pools:

Red,—red, and startling like a trumpet's sound.

The last half of the sonnet is so fine that we must quote it:

> *But nothing can be lovelier than the ranges*
> *Of bamboos to the eastward, when the moon*
> *Looks through their gaps, and the white lotus changes*
> *Into a cup of silver. One might swoon*
> *Drunken with beauty then, or gaze and gaze*
> *On a primeval Eden, in amaze.*

"The Lotus" is in a daintier, more trifling vein, and professes to give the origin of "the queenliest flower that blows". To end the strife as to whether the lily or rose were queen, Psyche at last went to Flora and asked for a flower that should be "delicious as the rose, and stately as the lily in her pride". The result was the lotus, rose-red and lily-white.

"Our Casuarina Tree" ends the little volume. It opens with a description of the giant tree, festooned with the crimson flowers of a great creeper which winds round and round it "like a huge python". By day and by night it is a centre of busy life and sweet bird-song. It is the finest object on which the poetess's eyes rest as she flings wide her window at dawn, and sometimes in the early light

> *A grey baboon sits statue-like alone*
> *Watching the sunrise.*

The shadow of the tree thrown across the tank makes the white water-lilies there look "like snow enmassed". Yet, grand and beautiful as is the tree, it is dear chiefly for the memories that cluster round it—memories of a time when happy children played under its shade. The thought brings out an intense yearning towards the playmates lost:

> *O sweet companions, loved with love intense,*
> *For your sakes shall the tree be ever dear!*

To the poetess's imagination, the tree in sympathy sounds a dirge "Like the sea breaking on a shingle-beach". That "eerie speech", she thinks, may haply reach the unknown land and strike a chord of memory there. Such a wail had always this power over her own mind. Even when heard by the seashore in France or Italy, it had always sent thought winging its way homeward bringing remembrance of the Tree as seen and loved in childhood.

The last verse of the poem, with its note of Romanticism, hints at a desire for immortality of verse, and ends with the beautiful line:

> *May Love defend thee from oblivion's curse.*

The eleven-lined stanza in which the poem is written is a new and very successful experiment.

For its rich imagery, the music of its verses, and the tenderness and pathos with which it is instinct, we would place this poem second to none in the volume.

XII

SUPPLEMENTARY REVIEW

By Mr. E. J. Thompson

I f in fulfilment of a promise I now write a few words of summary and conclusion, it is not in the hope of adding anything essential to the story that has been told in Mr. Das's sympathetic pages. The materials for judgement are before the reader, and he is in a position to appreciate this extraordinary girl.

The fact of her achievement may be quite simply stated. So far as actual performance goes, Toru Dutt's English fame rests on two books, neither of any great size, and one published posthumously. Each of these, judged by any fair standard, represents, in differing ways, a really astonishing measure of actual, undeniable success. But, further, both are affecting by the number of indications they contain of possibilities of development, often in directions where the poet's real achievement was slight. There are outcroppings of veins that were never, during her brief day of work, touched to any considerable extent. It is the knowledge of this that compels diffidence and hesitation in criticism of her verse. It is easy to feel that, in the work done, she never escaped from the influence of her favourite English poets, such writers as Mrs. Browning, whose work did not furnish satisfactory prosodic models. The metres used by Toru Dutt are nearly always of the simplest, and her use of them is marred by much crudity. Yet against this must be set the many signs of haste and lack of opportunity to finish. The punctuation of the *Ballads*, for example, is chaotic. She heard, as Lowell surmises that Keats did, a voice urging "What thou doest, do quickly"; and, especially after her sister's death, she plunged into work with energy and restlessness. Yet, even amid the many marks of immaturity and haste, there are signs that she would have escaped before long from many of her prosodic limitations. "Our Casuarina Tree," surely the most remarkable poem ever written in English by a foreigner, shows her already possessed of mastery over the more elaborate and architectural forms of verse. In any case, there is enough to show that experience and practice would have brought release from the cramping and elementary forms that she used;

which is perhaps what Mr. Gosse means when he says that "mellow sweetness" was all that Toru Dutt lacked to perfect her as an English poet, and "of no other Oriental who has ever lived can the same be said".

But, with regard to shortcomings far more serious, there is evidence again that a few more years would have brought emancipation. Her work, as it stands, is not deeply-rooted. It is usual to say that the *Ballads* are that portion of her work which has most chance of some sort of permanence for its own sake. This, I am convinced, is an error. I am not blind to their scattered beauties, the noble picture of Savitri in her strife with Death, the touches of Indian scenery which spread a kind of woodland shade over *Buttoo*; nor can the most casual reader fail to feel the presence of power, careless and diffused, yet binding the whole into unity. But the facts remain, of carelessness, and, what is more serious, lack of sympathy in the author. She stands outside her themes and does not enter deeply into them. Nor can I consider those themes as of anything like first-class value. Some have a rustic charm which strikes the mind pleasantly enough, but not deeply; others had been handled ages before Toru took them up, by writers whose minds were primitive, as hers emphatically was not, and in sympathy, as hers again was not. Of far higher poetic value, and deserving of much more attention than they have received, are the half-dozen intensely personal poems which follow the *Ballads*. I have spoken of "Our Casuarina Tree". One of the stanzas drops into conventionality, and uses adjectives and thought that are secondhand and otiose. But the poem's strength is independent of this; and its blending of pathos and dignity of spirit, its stretching out of ghostly arms to those other haunted trees of Wordsworth's in "Borrowdale", the conclusion—so recalling the last work of another poet, far inferior in genius but dying equally young, Kirke White, in the touching dose of his *Christiad*— all this forms a whole of remarkable strength and beauty, and should achieve her hope of placing the tree of her childhood's memories among those immortalized by

Mighty poets in their misery dead.

"Near Hastings" is a lyric which brings a lump to the throat, and should convince the most careless and supercilious of the grace and wisdom, the political expediency even, of receiving with kindness these strangers with whom destiny has so strongly linked us and who so often find our manners, like our northern climate, cold. The poems have touches of a boldness and imaginative vigour which have not appeared before in Toru's work. Nothing, for instance, could be finer or more vivid than the line on the *simuls* in blossom, in the Baugmaree sonnet:

Red,—red, and startling like a trumpet's sound.

Her poems on France and French affairs misread the political situation. Her love for France was passionate, a second patriotism; but no one today is likely to quarrel with her enthusiasm for the generous nation that has so long and so signally served civilization. Her letters show how the Franco-Prussian War stirred her sympathies; no Frenchwoman could have felt more poignantly for her bleeding country. It is interesting to compare Toru's verses on the war with those written by a contemporary poetess, Christina Rossetti:

She sitteth still who used to dance.

But the verses grip most of all for the vehement soul that they reveal, a soul which has had few fellows throughout time. Toru Dutt remains one of the most astonishing women that ever lived, a woman whose place is with Sappho and Emily Brontë, fiery and unconquerable of soul as they; and few statements, one feels, can more triumphantly sustain fair examination than this. The remarkable verses in which she chronicles the dream that foreran death go to strengthen this same conviction of power and fire. These verses, intensely personal all, and by that intensity breaking from convention and fetters, show her feeling her way to freer rhythms, and even handling blank verse— of which no Englishwoman has given a satisfactory example—in a way that promised ultimate mastery, or at least a very great degree of strength and adequacy. These poems are sufficient to place Toru Dutt in the small class of women who have written English verse that can stand.

The Sheaf is remarkable after other fashion. Merely to have translated so much and so well from one alien tongue into another must be a feat hardly paralleled; and the book contains much work that is individual and beautiful. In this connexion, it is of interest to note that some of the very best work is Aru's; in particular, the lines quoted by Mr. Gosse as exemplifying Toru's early mastery of English verse, and since then in constant quotation for the same purpose, have the initial A. (Aru) against them:

> *Still barred thy gates! The far East glows,*
> *The morning wind wakes fresh and free!*
> *Should not the hour that wakes the rose*
> *Awaken also thee?*

> *All look for thee, Love, Light, and Song,*
> *Light in the sky deep-red above,*
> *Song, in the lark of pinions strong,*
> *And in my heart true Love.*

But the *Notes* are astonishing beyond anything in the text. It seems impossible that an Indian girl, at such an age, should have had such a knowledge of French literature. And in the *Notes*, while never merely foolish even when boldest, she deals with French masters as one assessing the work of equals, and it seems hard to tell which to admire more—the range of reading, or the independence and masculinity of criticism. These Indian girls—though the gentle Aru, one knows, had far the smaller share in these surprising *Notes*—knew their own minds, and could express those minds with precision and a strength that compels respectful attention. I remember speaking to Dr. Brajendranath Seal of these *Notes* and the way they found me; and he told me they had made the same impression on him when he first read them. If for the *Notes* alone, *The Sheaf* merits republication.

Toru's letters, now first presented to the world by Mr. Das, are valuable for the way they enable us to see the home-life out of which her life and work sprang. It is impossible to read them without feeling how beautiful and noble that home-life was, with its encyclopaedic interests, its playfulness amid knowledge, its affection. The father, bereaved of such comrades and children in quick succession, yet keeping a scholar's gentleness and a saint's resignation through all sorrow; father and child, though Death came not as a visitant only but as inmate and constant shadow over all events, preserving their love of "the things that are more excellent", of books and pets, their care for dependants, and clinging the closer to each other as everything in their perishing world grew dim but love—these form a picture no feeling reader will be slow to take or quick to forget. Her excellent friends, her kind relatives,

Baguette the cat, the horses, the servants, all combine to form a family-circle little like the kind of family the West has learned to look for in the East. The publication of these letters, as of everything relating to Toru Dutt, is nothing less than an Imperial service, and must awaken to closer fellowship and understanding all that is best in the races so closely linked and now so often estranged. And the whole of Toru's life and work rested upon a character patient and uncomplaining, Christian in faith and fortitude. If for a time her circumstances were such as to leave her, in a sense, between two worlds, neither truly hers—so that the *Ballads*, to refer back for example, have no deep roots in the Indian sentiment from which they profess to spring—yet her mind was too independent and too truly indigenous for this to have continued long. There is abundant proof that this girl, so amazingly and richly at home in two alien literatures, was growing into her own nation and its thought, and would have shown us Christian thought and feeling, not as something alien but as truly belonging to Him in Whom there is neither Jew nor Gentile, bond nor free, English nor Bengali. What Michael Dutt was too shallow to have done, our other Christian poet would have accomplished, and in a measure actually did accomplish.

And after all, the essential thing to be said about Toru Dutt can only be said when we remember her, not solely in herself, amazing (it seems impossible to avoid this adjective in connexion with her) in her combination of intellect and knowledge and character, but in the race she represented. Indian women in legend have long been familiar to the West; and all would concede that such figures as Sita and Savitri cannot be unrelated to the race whose imagination produced them, but must have had their types in real life. And it will be remembered what a line of heroines the Rajput nation has produced till, almost within living memory, in Krishna Kumari the old-world stories of Jephtha's daughter and of Iphigeneia gained a deeper pathos with that figure of a child-martyr dying in the sunset of a noble race. But the nations of India's plains, each in its way endowed with gifts for that larger India, have seen too little of the unrealized power of their womanhood.

The story of these gifted and heroic sisters, whose brief lives found fulfilment in the liberty which Christ has brought, was the first dawn, in the Bengali Renaissance, of the day which has brought to light such possibility and such achievement as the names of Kamini Sen and Sarojini Naidu represent. It is natural to think of Sarojini Naidu, when Toru Dutt comes to mind. It is undeniable that Mrs. Naidu has a metrical accomplishment and a skill in words far beyond anything which her predecessor's hasty effort attained. But in strength and greatness of intellect, the comparison is all to Toru's advantage. And all these, both the two whose fame rests on their work in English and those who have used their own rich vernacular, sprang from the narrow circle of families emancipated from old social wrong, chiefly by Christian and Brahmo influence. If the scanty plot can bear, in so brief a space of years, so promising a harvest, what an enrichment of their nation would come, if the same possibilities of development came to the whole of Bengali womanhood? To one who loves the Bengali people and believes in their future, it seems hardly credible that so much should have been said, and so much from year to year should continue to be said, yet so little should be done. Whatever reasons may have existed for the introduction of the *purda* system, those reasons have long ceased to be operative; and with a freer life for the mothers of the people, not only would the misery of seclusion through the intolerable heats of summer pass from them, but the nation would gain a healthier, stronger manhood. Every one who has had experience of schools and colleges must have felt that in no country is teaching accompanied by so many cruel disappointments, and in no country is there so much sickness and physical feebleness as in Bengal. Part of this weakness must be inherited; and in a country where natural conditions are of themselves so hard, the generations, as they come to birth, should be given every possible chance of success in the battle which is to be so unequal in any case. But this is one side only; and woman's suffering outweighs man's. Much has been spoken against child-marriage, little has been done. Maidenhood, at the years when it should naturally be most delightful and winning, ceases to be maidenhood. Had Toru been a Hindu, the burdens of premature wifehood, probably of premature motherhood, would have made her story impossible. As regards its girls, the Bengali people loses at least five years of childhood, and the loss is one for which nothing can offer any shadow of compensation. I remember, when I made this comment to Bengal's greatest living poet, his reply: "I quite agree with you, and it is the saddest thing in our lives." Again, much has been said against the monstrous dowry-system, which renders self-respect an impossibility for the women whose worth is weighed against the rank and attainments of the men who take them, which makes education an affair of the market-place; but little has been done. When Snehalata, heart-broken at the ruin which her marriage was bringing on her family, burnt herself to death,

Bengal was stirred, and meetings beyond count were held, and students beyond count vowed that in their case, at least, the thing should not be. Rarely can there have ever been such a display of profound emotion in any land, never can there have been so little result. All things continued as they were. One would think that never among any people can there have been so distressing an episode; and nothing more depressing for those of us who have loved this people and defended them through all evil report. Here we are left without an answer when our friends are defamed, and can only assent in humiliation and despair. And first of all the many things that must be done and sought, this elementary justice must be rendered, and woman be free to expand and find herself; and Toru Dutt, in her greatness of soul and her greatness of mind, will no more be a solitary and astounding phenomenon, but the first-born star in a heaven of many lights.

Appendix

I

Translation Of The Correspondence Between Mlle Bader And Toru

Mlle Clarisse Bader, Paris, to Miss Toru Dutt, Calcutta.

February 16, 1877

Dear Mademoiselle,

Is it really a descendant of my dear Indian heroines who wishes to translate the work dedicated to the ancient Aryans of the Gangetic Peninsula? Such a desire, and coming from such a source, touches me so deeply that it must be granted. Translate therefore *Woman in Ancient India*; with all my heart do I authorize you to do it and with fullest sympathy do I wish you every success in your enterprise. Last evening I showed your letter and your charming collection of poems to an illustrious authority on India, M. Garcin de Tassy, Member of the Institute, of whose reputation you must be aware. He is a friend of your learned neighbour, Rajendra Lal Mitter.[1] M. Garcin de Tassy[2] was so struck with your wonderful courage in writing, that he took your address in order to send you one of his books at once.

You are a Christian, dear Mademoiselle; your book tells me so. Indeed the part that you are playing makes us bless once again the divine religion which has enabled an Indian to develop and to manifest the *individual* character which Brahmanism too often fetters in women. As a writer of the history of woman, it is charming to be emulated by you; and as a Frenchwoman, the elegant translations from my countrymen's poetry touch me as much, and I must thank you for them. Your beautiful book tells me that you also had a sister, who shared in your poetic tastes. The Saviour has recalled to Himself the soul who had

---

1. Dr. Rajendra Lal Mitter, C.I.E., the famous Indian antiquarian.
2. M. Garcin de Tassy followed with the keenest interest the progress of education amongst Indian women and paid his tribute of deserved homage to Miss Mary Carpenter who has helped to accelerate it. M. Garcin de Tassy was an Oriental scholar and also a lecturer at the school of Oriental languages, Paris.

so faithfully interpreted the song of "The Young Captive", and who, on arriving at the supreme moment, did not repeat:

> *The world has delights, the Muses have songs:*
> *I wish not to perish too soon.*

When your translation of *Woman in Ancient India* is published in India, I should be very grateful if you would send me two copies. Also, it would please me very much to have your photograph, in case you possess one. Let me tell you again, before closing, how precious to me is the sympathy of a child of India. Since the happy hours passed in the company of your ancestors, I have traced the history of woman amongst the Hebrews, Greeks, and Romans. Four volumes have thus succeeded to *Woman in Ancient India*... and only a short time ago, when my second father, the great Bishop of Orleans, was asking me amongst which women had I found most moral beauty, my answer was: "If I except the women of the Bible, it is amongst the Indians that I found the greatest purity and devotion."—Believe, dear mademoiselle, in my cordial sympathy,

CLARISSE BADER

C/o my father, retired superior officer of the Legion of Honour, attached to the office of the Minister of War, rue de Babylone, 62, Paris.

PS. I understand that your English translation is to be published in India. The intervention of my publisher would only be necessary in case it were printed in England. But, as he has himself told me, there is no difficulty about your translation appearing in such a distant country as India.

Miss Toru Dutt, Calcutta, to Mlle Clarisse Bader, Paris.

Calcutta, March 18, 1877

DEAR MADEMOISELLE,

I thank you very sincerely for kindly allowing me to translate *La Femme dans l'Inde Antique*, and also for your kind sympathetic letter, which gave the greatest pleasure.

I am so sorry not to have been able to begin the translation yet. I am not very strong, and an obstinate cough contracted two years ago does not leave me. However, I hope soon to begin the work.

I cannot say, dear mademoiselle, how much your affection—for you love them; your book and your letter show it plainly—for my countrywomen and my country touches me; and I am proud to be able to say that the heroines of our grand epics are worthy of all honour and love. Can there be a more touching and lovable heroine than Sita? I do not think so. When I hear my mother chant, in the evening, the old lays of our country, I almost always weep. The plaint of Sita, when, banished for the second time, she wanders alone in the vast forest, despair and horror filling her soul, is so pathetic that I believe there is no one who could hear it without shedding tears. I send you herewith two short translations from that beautiful ancient language, the Sanskrit. Unfortunately, I have been obliged to stop all my Sanskrit translations for the last six months. My health does not permit me to continue them. I send you also the portrait of myself and my sister. The latter is represented sitting down. She was so sweet and so good! The photograph was taken four years ago, when I was seventeen, and she barely nineteen. I should also be very grateful to you, Mademoiselle, if you would kindly send me your own photograph. I shall keep it as one of my most valued treasures.

I must stop here, not wishing to trespass upon your time any more. Like M. Lefèvre-Deumier, I would say:

Adieu then, my friend, whom I ne'er have beheld,

for, dear mademoiselle, I count you amongst the best of my friends, though we have not met.

Please accept, Mademoiselle, the fresh assurance of my friendship.

Toru Dutt

C/o her father, Mr. Govin C. Dutt, Honorary Magistrate
and Justice of the Peace, Calcutta.

PS. I have kept back this letter till now, hoping to have received the book kindly promised by M. Garcin de Tassy, but it has not come, and the mail leaves tomorrow. Perhaps I may soon have the pleasure of clasping your hand, as we hope to leave India next month. My father has absolutely decided upon going to Europe. He says that in France and England there are more learned doctors than in Calcutta; and also our doctors advise a change of climate, which they say will do me more good than all the drugs of a pharmacy. This change in our plans obliges me to ask you not to write till you have heard again from me.

Miss Toru Dutt, Calcutta, to Mlle Clarisse Bader, Paris.

Calcutta,
April 13, 1877

My dear Mademoiselle,

Please write to me at the address given you in my last letter. I have been ill in bed for the last fortnight. A letter from you with your portrait will do me good. All our plans are changed. We shall not be able to go to Europe in April. Man proposes and God disposes. Please convey my thanks to M. Garcin de Tassy for his review. It is very interesting. I will write to him when I am stronger.

Assuring you again of my devotion and very sincere love,

Toru Dutt

Mlle Clarisse Bader, Paris, to Miss Toru Dutt, Calcutta.

May 11, 1877

Dear Mademoiselle and gracious Friend,

What a cruel disappointment your last letter has brought me! I was greatly looking forward to your arrival, and to be able to tell you in person of the warm fellow-feeling which not only your very remarkable works but also your letters inspire in me, revealing, as they do, a refined and charming soul, and your portrait, also, so full of life and expression. I pray God that He may soon cure you, and please believe that in this prayer there is some selfishness, because your plans about travelling depend on your recovery. You are still young, and youth has such powerful resources, especially when assisted by the fine constitution revealed in your charming portrait! Do you know, dear Mademoiselle, that your photograph and letters are winning the hearts of my own friends, beginning with my father and mother? My family and friends are sharing with me the great desire to see you, and today, alas! their disappointment and mine are deeply felt! If it had been possible for me to have had my photograph taken at once, I would have made another effort on your behalf to have had done what has never really succeeded. Photographers are in despair over the mobility of my features. My portraits get continually more and more ugly, and were I inclined to coquetry, I should never give them away, especially to those who do not know me. But I am not so, and I therefore enclose two photographs, dating as far back as 1872. They were taken only a few months after enduring the terrible patriotic trials of the two sieges of Paris, and my features were still bearing the traces of cruel emotions. These photographs were taken in the country by an amateur, an officer of high rank and one of our friends. My father is with me in one of these, and he also aged wonderfully during that time.

If I am taken again, and if it is successful, you shall have another copy. I will do my best to keep as motionless as possible.

It touches me very much to have the likeness of your regretted sister, who shared your learned and poetical tastes. I thank you with all my heart for sending me this sweet family remembrance. When I see M. Garcin de Tassy, he shall have the message you have trusted me with.

This is written in the little oratory which is also my study and where I pray the good God to send you health and strength. This prayer is confided to the Holy Virgin.

Believe, dear Mademoiselle, that you have in France a friend who could be happy to clasp your hand.—Always yours,

CLARISSE BADER

Miss Toru Dutt, Calcutta, to Mlle Clarisse Bader, Paris.

July 30, 1877

DEAR AND AFFECTIONATE FRIEND,

It is now four months that I have been suffering from fever. This has prevented me from writing and expressing to you sooner the great pleasure given me by your letter and photographs. That nice and sympathetic letter arrived when I was suffering very much, and it did me more good than all the doctor's remedies. Dear Mademoiselle, pray excuse very kindly the shortness of this letter. I am not yet quite well, and I cannot go from my room to the next one without fatigue. I have been very ill, dear friend, but the good God has granted the prayers of my parents and I am gradually recovering. I hope to write at greater length before long.—Always yours,

TORU DUTT

Mlle Clarisse Bader, Paris, to Miss Toru Dutt, Calcutta.

September 11, 1877

DEAR AND CHARMING INDIAN FRIEND,

I missed the last mail to Brindisi, and regret this involuntary delay all the more, because your kind and affectionate letter tells me that you have been ill, and that you were still convalescent at the moment of writing. What! can your illness have lessened in any degree the virility of the nature revealed in your portrait? Are those beautiful eyes, full of fire, languishing? Ah! but that can only be just a passing phase. You are now quite restored, are you not? When the Exhibition is opened, you will come to our sweet French country, and the warm breezes will do you good after your hot climate.

Friends wait for you with eager hope. My parents and I—we all love you much—without having ever seen you; but your letters and your writings have revealed to us the goodness of your heart, the candour of your soul. Do then come, dear friend, to seal by your presence the affection already acquired.

An overwhelming amount of work prevents me from prolonging this letter, written, besides, under extreme nervous fatigue. I still feel the effects of an indisposition, which is certainly not serious, but which has shaken my strong health. This indisposition has been caused by overwork, as I have recently undertaken to continue defending the great cause of religion, which unhappily is always being attacked in my dear country, but which, thanks be to God, always finds defenders amongst us.

What does it matter if, in the struggles where our only weapons are faith and charity, we feel sometimes the effect of fatigue, and physical suffering! These are the wounds of battle, and these wounds are precious. Tell your worthy parents how much we congratulate them on your return to health. My father and mother were particularly touched by the simple and touching phrase which ended your letter: "I have been very ill, but the good God has granted the prayers of my parents, and I am gradually getting better." And I also, dear and interesting friend, I ask the Saviour to keep you in the good health which no doubt He has already given you, and in making this prayer, I warmly embrace you.

CLARISSE BADER

PS. I enclose a little flower of my country. It is my favourite one and it is called *rhodanthe*. This pretty flower always appears to smile, even when withered. I think that is in itself a true emblem of affection. The flower that I am sending you comes from my little private chapel. May it bring you a sweet benediction from the Saviour, as well as my faithful remembrance!

II

IT MAY INTEREST OUR READERS to learn that in December of 1907 Miss Elizabeth S. Colton, an American lady, came to visit India, and wrote a letter to one of Toru Dutt's surviving relatives expressing her desire to see the Baugmaree Garden-House. The letter will speak for itself as to how Toru Dutt's name is revered and loved even by the people of that far-off country.

31, Free School Street, Calcutta
December 28, 1907

MY DEAR SIR,

For years I have regarded Calcutta as a place sacred to the memory of the gifted Toru Dutt, and I have come to see if possible the home where she lived and left to a sorrowing world so few but precious hints of her great genius.

I should like to see the Garden-House where, as Mr. Edmund Gosse expresses it, she plunged into the mysterious depths of Sanskrit literature.

I am to be in Calcutta for a very short time, and would be grateful for an interview.—I beg to remain, Very truly yours,

ELIZABETH S. COLTON

III

THE FOLLOWING RECOLLECTIONS OF TORU Dutt were sent by the Right Rev. Bishop Clifford, formerly of Lucknow:

The Vicarage, Stoke Bishop, near Bristol
October 30, 1915

DEAR MR. HARIHAR DAS,

I am much interested to hear that you contemplate bringing out a Life of Miss Toru Dutt. I hope when it appears I shall have the privilege of seeing it.

It is nearly forty years since I knew her, and details do not remain clear after the interval of time, but I have tried in the enclosed paper to put down some slight accounts of what I remember. She was of course a shy young girl and did not disclose herself much to a young English clergyman of twenty-seven. But such as they are, here are my recollections of her and her parents. I wish I could tell you more. I shall always look back to my acquaintance with the G. C. Dutt family with the greatest interest.—With kind regards, Yours very sincerely,

A. Clifford
Bishop

I first made the acquaintance of Mr. and Mrs. Govin Chunder Dutt at the hospitable house of Professor Cowell at Cambridge in (I think) 1870. They were staying in Cambridge mainly for the sake of the education of their two daughters, who were attending lectures for women. Professor and Mrs. Cowell had become intimate with the Dutt family at the time the Professor was on the staff of the Presidency College, Calcutta.

I went out to India in 1874, and lived at Calcutta for four years. I was at the time Curate at the Old Mission Church, at which the Dutt family were regular attendants. I soon renewed acquaintance with them.

Miss Aru Dutt had died four months before my arrival. I saw the family frequently, and always enjoyed my intercourse with them. Mr. Govin Dutt was an extremely cultured man, of ample means, devoting himself to literary and philanthropic pursuits. He was a remarkable linguist, equally familiar with the tongues of the East and the West. I do not think Mrs. Dutt spoke any language except Bengali, but no doubt she understood English to some extent.

The family lived in a small Square, with a garden in the middle of it, in the northern quarter of Calcutta. I think all the houses on at least three sides of the square belonged to, and were inhabited by, different members of the Dutt clan, all of whom were gentlemen of high social standing and culture, and all, I think, converts to the Christian Faith. Mr. Govin Dutt had also a house in a large mango-orchard outside Calcutta, where he and his wife and daughter loved to retire from time to time for quietude and refreshment.

I nearly always saw Miss Toru when I visited the house; but though I was struck with her interesting face, wonderful eyes, great masses of flowing black hair, and look of originality and power, I was not at all aware at the time of her extraordinary talents. She was naturally shy of the young English visitor, and did not enter into conversation beyond a few conventional words of courtesy. I could see, however, how she was the darling and treasure of her parents—the only one now left out of the three who had but a short time before been the light of the household. Toru was her father's constant companion and his willing pupil, sharing with him those deep studies in European and Indian literature in which he delighted. The two elder children of the family had both been smitten with tuberculosis at the critical age when childhood passes into young manhood or womanhood, and one can imagine the intense distress of the parents when symptoms of the same terrible disease appeared in Toru. But the trial was borne by Mr. and Mrs. Dutt with the most admirable Christian fortitude; and no less so by Toru herself. I visited her several times during her illness, which was not a very long one, and always found both her and her parents calm and brave. On more than one occasion I gave the family (just the three) the Holy Sacrament of Christ. Toru usually lay on a mattress on the floor propped up with white pillows. I never saw in her the slightest sign of fear of death, though her memory of her brother's and sister's fate must have told her plainly what was in store for her. She met what was coming with something more than resignation—with Christian hope, and almost, one may say, with the courage of welcome. It was not till after she had passed away that the world became aware in some degree of what it had lost in Toru Dutt—the strangely brilliant talent, the great purity of soul, the keen delicacy of perception, the extraordinary facility of poetic expression in at least three languages.

I left Calcutta in 1878, but returned to it in 1880, when I found myself a rather close neighbour to Mr. and Mrs. Dutt, from whose constant kindness I received much pleasure. Mr. Dutt did not survive Toru very long. Of Mrs. Dutt I saw a good deal more after her husband's decease; and I learned to realize that if Toru inherited her rich intellectual gifts from her father's side of the family, she must have received the moral beauty and sweetness of her character largely from her mother. Mrs. Govin Chunder Dutt was a true saint of God. Never shall I forget her triumphant, overcoming faith at the time of her husband's death. She was lifted far above resignation into a truly noble and inspiring joy of spirit. Nor did that faith and courage fail her when her own end drew nigh. Her pain (it was cancer she died of) must have been something which one hardly cares to think of. But she never faltered or allowed herself a murmur. Her face, I am told, shone with radiant peace in the midst of her worst agonies. I have often since spoken of her as the most shining example I ever met of the triumph of the spirit over the flesh, and the exemplification of the great Christian saying, "Death is swallowed up in Victory."

A. CLIFFORD
Bishop

October 30, 1915

IV

THE FOLLOWING IS A LIST of Journals in which Toru Dutt's *A Sheaf gleaned in French Fields* and *Le Journal de Mlle D'Arvers* were reviewed:

Saturday Review (London), 23rd August, 1879. *Le Portefeuille* (Amsterdam), 25th October, 1879. *La Gazette de France* (Paris), 28th January, 1879. *La Gazette des Femmes* (Paris), 10th February, 1879. *The Englishman* (Calcutta), 19th April, 1876, and 21st March, 1879. *The Statesman* (Calcutta), 26th October, 1877, 15th July, 1878, and 31st March, 1879. *The Examiner* (London), 26th August, 1876, and 15th June, 1878. *The Journal of the Woman's Education Union* (London), 15th October, 1878. *Le Pays* (Paris), 25th February, 1879. *Revue de France* (Paris), 15th February, 1879. *The Sunday Mirror* (Calcutta), 31st August, 1879. The *Revue des Deux Mondes* (Paris), 1st February, 1877, and 1st April, 1878. *Trübner's Literary Record* (London) for 1877. *Revue Bibliographique Universelle* (Paris), July, 1879. *Calcutta Review*, July, 1876, and October 1877. *Bengal Magazine*, May 1876, and August 1877. *Indian Female Evangelist* (London), April 1877. *Daily Review* (Edinburgh), 11th August, 1876. *La Langue et la Littérature Hindoustanies en 1877* (Revue Annuelle par M. Garcin de Tassy) (Paris). *Le Courrier de l'Europe* (London), 9th September, 1876. *Sunday Indian Mirror* (Calcutta), 29th June, 1879. *Hindu Patriot* (Calcutta), 3rd April and 4th September, 1876. *Indian Charivari* (Calcutta), 14th April, 1876. *Friend of India* (Calcutta), 22nd April, 1876. *Madras Standard*, 26th April, 1876. *The Bengalee* (Calcutta), 27th May, 1876. *Graphic* (London),

1st February, 1879. *Obola Bandhob* (Calcutta), No. 3, *Journal des Demoiselles* (Paris), p. 145. *Bombay Educational Record*, November 1877. *Indian Daily News* (Calcutta), 8th April, 1876. *Le Parlement* (Paris), Jan. 24, 1881.

A Note About the Authors

Harihar Das was a biographer from Sidhipasa, India.

Toru Dutt (1856–1877) was a Bengali poet and translator. Born in Calcutta to a prominent family of Bengali Christians, Dutt was educated from a young age and became a devoted student of English literature. Taught by her father and a private tutor, she learned French, Sanskrit, and English in addition to her native Bengali. At thirteen, she left India with her family to travel through Europe, visiting France, England, Italy, and Germany over the next several years. In 1872, she attended a series of lectures for women at the University of Cambridge alongside her sister Aru, which further sparked her interest in academia and literature. In 1873, the family returned to Calcutta, where Dutt struggled to readjust to Indian culture. She wrote two novels in English and French before publishing *A Sheaf Gleaned in French Fields* (1876), a collection of French poems translated into English. Its critical and commercial success came tragically late, however, as Dutt died of consumption in 1877 at the age of 21. She has since been recognized as the first Indian writer to publish a novel in French, the first Indian woman to publish an English novel, and a pioneering figure in Anglo-Indian literature whose mastery of several languages at such a young age remains remarkably uncommon. *Ancient Ballads and Legends of Hindustan* (1882), a collection of Sanskrit poems translated into English, was her final, posthumously published work.

A Note from the Publisher

Spanning many genres, from non-fiction essays to literature classics to children's books and lyric poetry, Mint Edition books showcase the master works of our time in a modern new package. The text is freshly typeset, is clean and easy to read, and features a new note about the author in each volume. Many books also include exclusive new introductory material. Every book boasts a striking new cover, which makes it as appropriate for collecting as it is for gift giving. Mint Edition books are only printed when a reader orders them, so natural resources are not wasted. We're proud that our books are never manufactured in excess and exist only in the exact quantity they need to be read and enjoyed.

bookfinity™

Discover more of your favorite classics with Bookfinity™.

- Track your reading with custom book lists.
- Get great book recommendations for your personalized Reader Type.
- Add reviews for your favorite books.
- AND MUCH MORE!

Visit **bookfinity.com** and take the fun Reader Type quiz to get started.

Enjoy our classic and modern companion pairings!

Classic & Modern

Printed in the USA
CPSIA information can be obtained
at www.ICGtesting.com
JSHW022208140824
68134JS00018B/922